PRAISE FOR *HOW WE MIGHT LIVE*

'Jane is fortunate in her biographer'   ***The Times***

'Well researched and extensive'   ***BBC History***

'Fascinating'   ***The Field***

'[Fagence Cooper] traces the Morrises' shared and separate lives with clarity and judicious assessment'   ***History Today***

'Fagence Cooper succeeds, against the odds, in restoring some reality to our view of Jane Morris, giving a proper sense of a woman with striking gifts and talents identifiably her own'   ***Literary Review***

'Delightful, accessible and insightful'   ***Church Times***

Dr Suzanne Fagence Cooper is an art historian working on 19th and 20th century British art. She was a curator and Research Fellow at the V&A Museum for twelve years and is currently Honorary Visiting Fellow at the University of York. She recently curated a major exhibition on John Ruskin and J. M. W. Turner. She is the author of *To See Clearly: Why Ruskin Matters*, *Effie Gray* and *Pre-Raphaelite Art in the Victoria and Albert Museum*. She is a trustee of the Burne-Jones catalogue raisonné, and has worked as a consultant for TV and film projects. She is also an invited lecturer for the Arts Society and Cunard.

HOW WE MIGHT LIVE

At Home with Jane and William Morris

SUZANNE FAGENCE COOPER

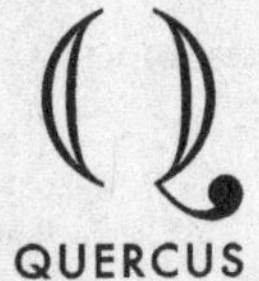

First published in Great Britain in 2022 by Quercus Editions Ltd
This paperback published in 2023 by

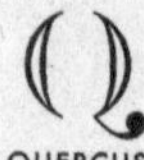

QUERCUS

Quercus Editions Ltd
Carmelite House
50 Victoria Embankment
London EC4Y 0DZ

An Hachette UK company

The authorized representative in the EEA is Hachette Ireland,
8 Castlecourt Centre, Dublin 15, D15 XTP3, Ireland (email: info@hbgi.ie)

A CIP catalogue record for this book is available
from the British Library

PB ISBN 978 1 52940 950 5
Ebook ISBN 978 1 52940 949 9

Picture credits, by chapter:
1, 5, 7, 11 © Victoria and Albert Museum, London; 2 © National Portrait Gallery;
3 © Samuel Lasner Collection, University of Delaware; 4 © National Gallery of Ireland;
6 © National Portrait Gallery; 8, Notes © The Trustees of the British Museum;
10 © William Morris Gallery, Walthamstow; 12 © British Library; 13 © William Morris Society, London;
14 © de Morgan Collection

10 9 8 7 6 5

Typeset by CC Book Production
Printed and bound in Great Britain by Clays Ltd, Elcograf S.p.A.

Papers used by Quercus are from well-managed forests and other responsible sources.

For our girls

Contents

Preface

How We Might Live

'A sanded floor and white-washed walls, and the green trees and flowering meads and living waters outside'[1]

William Morris valued the simplicity of life. With his wife Jane, he hoped to create a home where children and guests could flow easily from restful rooms to a fruitful garden. As he told a friend, 'the house that would please me would be some great room, where one talked to one's friends in one corner, and ate in another, and slept in another, and worked in another'.[2] A home, for William, was a creative and sociable space, like the handsome gathering halls described in his late questing novels.

After their marriage in 1859, William and Jane worked together to craft their delightful domestic spaces. They welcomed friends and fellow artists, encouraged them to talk and dream and rest. The tale of 'Morris & Company' began in the early 1860s with conversations around their dining table. Many of the famous wallpapers and textiles were collaborative efforts, begun in Jane and William's garden, or by their fireside. But all too often, Jane herself has been written out of the stories that flourished as the family filled their homes with beautiful things and imaginative people. Jane's life was just as radical and inventive as William's. She was skilled, opinionated and capable of extraordinary personal transformations.

And yet we see, just days after his death, that Jane was pushed to one side. In descriptions of William's funeral, she was overlooked or effaced. One mourner remembered her clearly, wrapped in a great cloak, standing beside her husband's grave. However, when we turn to the official account by William's first biographer, we are presented with a very different image: 'at the head of the grave, Sir Edward Burne-Jones, the closest and the first friend of all, stood and saw a great part of his life lowered into earth'.[3] It is as if Jane herself is merely a ghostly figure, barely visible, not worth mentioning. In this version of events, William's home life and his long, complicated marriage seem less important than his male comradeship, his art and poetry.

Why should this matter? What can we learn if we bring Jane back into focus, travelling alongside William as a pioneer in the art of living well, living differently? We begin to see the networks of women around Jane, as they work together. We can watch them developing partnerships, sharing their experiences and skills. We hear familiar accounts of artists, their studios and designs, from the viewpoint of the women who were always there, busy, aware. They are no longer simply labelled as wives or models, but become visible as individuals. This change in perspective helps us to understand the radical nature of the Morris household. It was a home where conventional distinctions – between work and play, the leisured and servant classes, public and private spaces, men and women – could be reimagined. And Jane was not just a passive observer of William's experiments in homemaking. She was thoughtful and engaged. Even as a very young woman, she embraced her opportunities to be hospitable, as she kept open house for painters and poets. In later life, Jane was admired as an 'enchanting head of a household. Whether she carved the mutton or cut the hair of the family', their home was 'tuned all the time with that delicious laugh which one never forgets'.[4]

For a century it has been almost impossible to hear Jane's own voice and laughter. We know her face very well from paintings and photographs. But her words have been scattered, until now. It is thanks to the exceptional work of Jan Marsh and Frank C. Sharp that we can read Jane's correspondence and begin to reconstruct her distinctive way of looking at the world. In 2012, they published *The Collected Letters of Jane Morris* after more than a decade of research. Jane emerges from her writings, no longer the silent figure of the Pre-Raphaelite portraits, but someone hopeful and industrious, a woman who forged long-lasting friendships. She was intellectually curious and unexpectedly funny.

As we read Jane's letters, we hear the affection within her circle, the shared memories and jokes. In particular, we notice that William is often called by his pet-name 'Topsy', and Jane is mostly 'Janey'. It is how they usually signed themselves. This raises a question: how should we refer to them now? The diminutives bring them closer, but seem informal, even patronising. William, in his professional guise, was known as simply 'Morris'. But that leaves Jane. Most people, beyond their close friends, would have known her as Mrs Morris. However, before she was William's wife, she was Jane Burden, daughter of a stable-hand and a laundress, living in a down-at-heel quarter of Oxford. So, for the present, they shall be Jane and William, on equal terms.

Through their writings, and the things they made and shared, we can follow the path of their lives. We begin at the green edges of London, in William's childhood home, and move through the cobbled streets of Oxford, then out to a peaceful backwater of the Thames at Kelmscott Manor. At every stage, Jane and William tried to create wholehearted, practical refuges from the strife and wearisomeness of modern life. For both of them, the garden was an essential part of home, and they made beautiful outdoor havens wherever they lived. Each spring was an adventure. Jane wrote from Italy, later in life:

'They tell me that flowers are coming up in the garden, and blossom on fruit trees.'[5] That would sweeten her homecoming. This sense of possibility, of new growth, of fruitfulness was woven through all their schemes for their life together.

Their gardens were also productive. Jane and William could find shade beneath a mulberry tree, or tell their friends about the ripening strawberries. Their first house in Kent was set in the middle of an orchard. In old age, Jane liked to send visitors on their way with a jar of her homemade quince jelly. She and William relished family feasts. Even in the earliest days at Red House, their friends – Philip Webb, Edward and Georgiana Burne-Jones, Lizzie Siddall and Gabriel Rossetti, Emma and Ford Madox Brown – met for weekends of chatter and decorating. Happy in his new home, William would load the dresser with armfuls of wine bottles. Jane planned picnics and suppers, and made sure there were beds for all. (The young poet Swinburne was only small and could sleep on the sofa.)

We can even look over Jane's shoulder to read her recipe notebook. At Kelmscott Manor, Jane and then her daughter May wrote out dozens of family favourites. On one sheet, there is a tried-and-tested method for orange marmalade; on another, the careful instructions for a gingerbread cake. They reflect the practical pleasures of running an orderly household. As William wrote, 'The true secret of happiness lies in taking a genuine interest in all the details of daily life.'[6]

*

Running alongside the cheerful domesticity, we find another important thread: after her marriage, Jane's house always doubled as a showroom for William's business. The family never entirely escaped the realities of buying and selling. Jane and her daughters, her sister and her friends were all part of the team working from home to produce textiles for sale in William's shop. There were looms and kilns and apprentices in her back yard. This intimate relationship between work and family life helped to shape William's revolutionary response to the divisions he saw in Victorian society. Jane had grown up in poverty, and knew the daily struggles at first hand. When William became an employer and craftsman himself, he felt compelled to speak out, to use his privileged position to agitate for change.

In his lecture of 1885, 'How we live & How we might live', William outlined his hopes for better livelihoods for all. He acknowledged the iniquities of a capitalist, commercially driven society. He also recognised his own responsibilities as a factory owner. He insisted that it was possible to reconfigure the way we live; everyone should have access to healthcare and education, time to explore their talents, opportunities to travel and work overseas. He believed that truly labour-saving machines could transform our working lives. And that fresh air, books and time spent in nature were essential to a decent life. He worried about wastefulness and 'shoddy wares'. Above all, he hoped that 'the material surroundings of my life should be pleasant, generous and beautiful'.[7]

This change began in their own home. It was a microcosm of the deeper social adjustments that Jane and William were both seeking. The Morris family worked through their own troubles, but did so with remarkable generosity. William and Jane's marriage was tested by infidelity, and the chronic illness of their daughter Jenny. There were times of sadness and dislocation. Still, these sufferings were resolved kindly. In their London home, poets and political firebrands often sat side-by-side at supper. We can hear the fierce discussions, the explosive tempers. And yet, under Jane's roof, there was always space for careful, quiet designing, for embroidery and calligraphy.

William himself was constantly trying out new ideas, writing, drawing, weaving, talking. Sometimes it was hard for Jane to keep pace with him when he was ablaze with enthusiasm about a new project. It was then that all her resourcefulness, all her patience was most keenly valued by her family and friends. But it can be hard for us to keep her quiet presence in view. Jane's experience is all too easily obscured by the bolder, more energetic career of her husband. There are many gaps in her life-story. We know very little, for example, about her upbringing in a cramped corner of Oxford, and what she might have been, had she not agreed to model for William's friends. We can only sketch out, in the broadest terms, her life before she was seventeen.

This is in stark contrast to the rich seams of information we have about William and all his doings. We can trace his movements as a boy, look into his student rooms and reconstruct his bachelor lodgings. All these early places are carefully recorded. His friends knew, even before he married, that William was extraordinary, that he was worth watching. Burne-Jones tried to take stock of William's life, after a friendship lasting forty years. He summed up the exhilaration of being close to such a man:

> When I first knew Morris nothing would content him but being a monk, and then he must be an architect, but when I came to London and began to paint, he threw it all up and must paint too, and then he must give it up and make poems, and then he must give it up and make window hangings and pretty things, and when he had achieved that he must be poet again, and then he must learn dyeing and lived in a vat and learned weaving and knew all about looms, and then made more books and learned tapestry, and then wanted to smash everything up and begin the world anew, and now it is printing he cares for and to make wonderful rich-looking books: and all things he does splendidly: and if he lives the printing will have an end, and he will do, I don't know what, but every minute will be alive.[8]

For now, we will go back to William's beginnings. We can meet him in his childhood home, in the days before he dreamed of dyeing and printing or had ever seen a girl like Jane.

Chapter 1

Epping Forest, 1834–1852

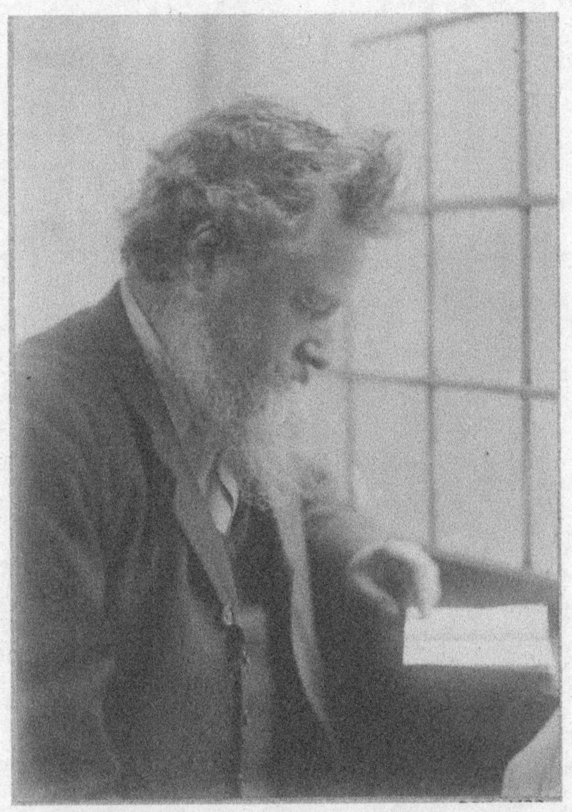

William Morris reading, photograph by Emery Walker, 1884, V&A Museum

The boy was sitting on the window seat, looking out across the wide lawn towards the moat. Books and papers were scattered beside him. This was a delightful, in-between place to write and think – perched on the half-landing, lit by the tall arched window. But he was concentrating on the greens and blues beyond the glass, the bright leaves and summer clouds reflected in the quiet water. It was May 1852, and young William Morris was supposed to be preparing for his Oxford University entrance exam. The sound of his brothers splashing across to their little wooded island interrupted his studies and drew him outside. He picked up a satchel and fishing rod as he hurried out of the garden door. Then he strode off across the parkland towards the river.

The Morris family had moved to Water House in Walthamstow after the sudden death of William's father in 1847. It was a sturdy, symmetrical gentleman's residence on the north-east edge of London, built of yellowish brick and stucco around 1750. For William, the kitchen gardens, tangled woodland and meadows behind the house more than made up for its dull façade. And he was only a mile away from open countryside and the River Lea. The Essex marshlands were not grand or picturesque, but William loved them for their low-key beauty, and their melancholy. Walking along the riverbank, he felt 'a strange balance between joy and sadness'. This was the perfect landscape for a thoughtful young man, especially one who felt torn between his longing for history and storytelling, and his yearning to watch 'the little brook, every ripple of its waters over the brown stones, every line of the broad-leaved water flowers'. In one of his own tales, he remembered how he knelt on the bank, and 'gathered a knot of lush marsh-marigolds . . . my wet hand and flowers marking the dust' on the road home.[1] These small pleasures of the English countryside – the winding streams, the wildflowers, the overhanging willows – formed the backdrop to William's imaginative world. They resurfaced in his pattern-making and the borders of his books, and they found their way into his poems. Later, they became signs of homecoming for his questing heroes. Whether he was drawing or writing, or dreaming of his next fishing expedition, William was acutely aware of the natural beauties close at hand.

*

Water House is the only one of William Morris's childhood homes that still stands. It is now a museum dedicated to his life and legacy. The long garden with its moated island is preserved as a public park, but the open spaces around have been lost under the inexorable suburban sprawl. Although he later became a strong campaigner to protect threatened buildings, William showed no interest in saving his birthplace, Elm House, or Woodford Hall, the mansion where he spent most of his boyhood. His family moved there in 1840, when he was six years old. He valued these houses for their associations, for the books he read, the games he played outdoors, the rhythms of the seasons in the garden, the feasts held on Twelfth Night, and the security he enjoyed 'when I was a little chap'.[2] But he did not value the buildings themselves. They were conventional, uninspiring, prosperous, rather like his parents.

William was born on 24 March 1834, and was the eldest surviving son of William Morris and Emma (née Shelton). His two older sisters,

Emma and Henrietta, loomed large in his boyhood memories. Then, after a gap of three years, came his four younger brothers, Stanley, Rendall, Arthur and Edgar, and two more sisters, Isabella, and lastly Alice who lived until 1942. When he was small, William seems to have kept himself apart from the rough and tumble of the other boys, preferring to stay close to the big girls and their governess. He claimed that he learnt to read when he was little more than a toddler, and to have worked his way through Walter Scott's novels by the time he was seven. This may sound outrageous, but many children of his generation grew up listening to Scott read aloud. William also seems to have been more than usually sheltered by his mother, who feared that his health was delicate. Emma Morris had lost her first-born son Charles when he was four days old. So she made a fuss of William, encouraging his bookishness, and feeding him up with calf's-foot jelly and beef tea.[3] In later life, he was susceptible to debilitating gout and rheumatic fever, long periods of ill-health that seemed at odds with William's vigorous physicality and wildness. But he was never quite as robust as his friends liked to believe.

William's earliest years were spent in a largely female household, cared for by his mother, his sisters, nurses and maids. His father barely figured in William's recollections of his childhood. After his death, William pushed hard against the shadow of his father and all he stood for. William chose to live his own life differently, both as a businessman and as a parent. But it was his father's success in the City that enabled William to enjoy the parkland and waterways, the piles of books and the unhurried adventures of his boyhood. It was also thanks to his father that William first saw Canterbury Cathedral. He later said it felt as if the gates of heaven had been opened to him.[4] After the small-scale churches of the Essex marshes, Canterbury was a revelation. William carried his love of the Gothic – its multi-layered, soaring, colourful, transformative visions – to the end of his days. This was a gift from father to son.

William Morris Senior also made sure that his son would live the comfortable life of a gentleman. His family had no money worries: the bills would be paid, the servants would be on hand, their home would be roomy and warm. Young William needn't earn his living by getting his hands dirty, or by becoming entangled in trade. His father's excellent investments would support them all. In due course, his son might become a clergyman, or perhaps follow him into the banking business.

This was the contradiction at the heart of young William's life, the founding fact that underpinned all his later choices. The Morris family were rich. William could take risks, knowing he had a safety net. He could spend money on pictures and holidays, he could marry a girl without a dowry, he could commission his own house, to his own taste, and furnish it with new and lovely things. All this was possible because he had money. And the source of that money was about as far removed as could be, from the riverbanks of his home or the sublime vaulted spaces of Canterbury. William's father had made his fortune in mining. His wealth was tainted. It was tarnished by the darkness, the pollution, the hot, cramped working conditions of the men who blasted and dug for copper in the West Country.

William Morris Senior was a financial middle-man, a bill broker who raised funds for new ventures. In the early 1840s, he and his brothers invested in new mines on the Duke of Bedford's land in the Tamar valley. Their shares in Devon Great Consols rose swiftly in value. One of the mines was named Wheal Emma after William's mother. This was a very successful speculation, one that had implications for the whole family. The Morrises could afford to live in magnificent style. They moved from the restrained gentility of Elm House to the grandeur of Woodford Hall.

Here William and his little brothers could explore their own fifty-acre park, hang around the pigsties and stables, hunt for eggs, pluck peaches from the espaliered fruit trees. And there were 'large blue plums which grew on the wall beyond the sweet-herb patch'.[5] His boyhood world was generous, filled with delights, spacious and safe. As William later described it, he was brought up first by his nurses, and then by the 'grooms and gardeners'.[6] His parents seemed very much in the background. His memories of those days were stored in scent and touch. They were out-of-doors experiences, at dusk, or on the edges of the household. He tended a little garden of his own, turning over the soil. He embedded his hands-on experience deeper into his consciousness by learning the names and shapes of plants, spending hours poring over the illustrations in a copy of John Gerard's *Herball* (published 1597). The simplified drawings of flowers and leaves made a lasting impression on him.

Many years later, William recalled how, 'To this day, when I smell a may-tree I think of going to bed by daylight'.[7] The gardens were full of hiding places and messy corners. They were a refuge, a space to learn about how things flourished or decayed. This is where his imagination could grow too – not in the drawing room, but in the orchards and shrubberies and vegetable plots. In one striking passage, written in his unpublished *Novel on Blue Paper*, William vividly described a troubled young man escaping from an unhappy house, into the kitchen garden. 'In after days,' he wrote, 'he could never smell the mixed scent of the tool-house, with its bast mats and earthy roots and herbs, in a hot summer evening', without reliving the emotions, 'every word spoken and gesture made, coming up clear into his memory'. The young man in the story grabs a garden fork, and heads for the 'melon-ground where the worm-populated old dung-heaps were'.[8] This is William's characteristic voice. He mingles the very ordinary – the rough textures and smells of a garden shed – with unsettling, almost hallucinatory images. Moving among the currant bushes, under a 'low moon, yellowing through the windless summer night', the figure in the garden 'startled the blackbirds out of their roosts in the thick leaves'. He was happier outdoors, looking at the 'light that the just lit-up house threw over the dewy lawn'.[9] We can almost see William savouring the night-time sounds and scents, and reluctant to step back into the busy house.

Many memories of his boyhood are framed in this way. They are glimpses of something mysterious, wild or tantalising in the world beyond his mother's reach. William came to recognise that there was skill in being able to 'manage a house . . . and to do it so that all the house-mates about her look pleased and are grateful to her'.[10] It must have been his mother who maintained domestic order at Woodford Hall. It was a complex, almost pre-modern establishment, nearly self-sufficient. Meat, butter, eggs, nuts, fruit and vegetables were all produced on the estate. Emma Morris oversaw the many indoor and outdoor staff; she took responsibility for the home brewing and baking. She organised the Masque of St George as the culmination of their Christmas festivities, and ensured that her growing children were given their mid-morning snack of small beer, cheese and cake. William remembered the cake especially. It was 'nicer than anything of the kind he had ever tasted since'.[11] And yet, the most vibrant recollections of his childhood were the moments of escape, into the woods, out along the river.

William's parents gave him a suit of armour and a small Shetland pony. These gifts seem almost too good to be true – like the magical helmet or shield offered by goddesses in a myth, guiding the hero towards his destiny. The image of little William dressed as a knight, trotting into the ancient forest, comes wonderfully close to the opening lines of a fairy tale. And yet, this is how he spent his early years; clattering around like a miniature Galahad, and exploring the ancient untamed woodland beyond the estate. William's garden backed on to Epping Forest. Here the young boy could think himself back into an older world, where the pull of the city was no longer felt. Here was birdsong, deep shade and soft mossy green. To a child the forest seemed vast, stretching over eight miles from its southern tip near the back gate of Woodford Hall to the northern outposts, beyond Theydon Bois and Bell Common.

Epping Forest was a remnant of an almost-forgotten way of life. It was both eerie and productive. The great trees – hornbeams and beeches – seemed strangely misshapen. But these odd forms were created by centuries of pollarding. Their branches had been lopped off for timber, leaving them gnarled and knobbly. The wood was harvested, as part of a cycle of cutting and regrowth that had persisted for generations. William was one of the last to see the forest in its medieval form, as a useful space, a sustainably managed resource. By the 1870s, the trees were 'protected' from pollarding by the City of London Corporation who had stewardship of the land. But this protection also meant that Epping was saved from the onslaught of speculative building. This was William's heartland. Looking back, many years later, he wrote about the forest of his boyhood: 'In those days, it had no more foes than the gravel stealer and the rolling fence maker and was always interesting and always beautiful.'[12]

William was under no illusion that Epping was a pristine landscape. As unenclosed common land, it was valued by the less well-off. The forest was a source of firewood, a place to raise pigs perhaps, and also a welcome respite for Londoners from the City or the East End. As one writer from the early 1850s explained, the forests of Epping and Hainault were 'the lungs of Whitechapel and Spitalfields'. Throughout the summer, they were invaded by 'joyous holiday-makers' who had saved a penny a week for their outing. They roamed the woodlands, and picnicked. They arranged 'friendly foot-races and jumping-matches, and leap-frogging and blackberrying, and foot-balling' and dancing.[13] At times, parts of the forest became a playground, noisy and littered and trampled. But the day-trippers only scuffed the surface. William had learnt to navigate the strange depths of the 'noble trees' and 'endless sinuous avenues'.[14] It was 'the biggest hornbeam wood in these islands, and I suppose in the world' and he knew it 'yard by yard from Wanstead to the Theydons, and from Hale End to the Fairlop Oak'.[15]

There were mysteries hidden beneath the trees. On his pony, William travelled miles in an afternoon. He could climb the ramparts of the great earthwork of Ambresbury Banks. This Iron Age hillfort was evidence of an even deeper history, a clearing created before the woods took hold. In places the banks were over two metres high, encircling an eleven-acre enclosure. Here, close at hand, William could run over and through a pre-Roman structure. He could see the grand scale of the site, maybe ask questions about who built it, and how they lived. In local legend, Ambresbury was where Boudicca made her last stand. William was gathering ideas about alternative communities. The tribes of the North country, their homesteads, their resilience, lived long in his imagination. They came to the fore again nearly fifty years later, when he wrote *The House of the Wolfings* and his fantasy novels. To William, it seemed that the smoke of their hearth-fires had never entirely drifted away.

If he turned his pony's head towards Chingford instead, young William reached another site that kindled his love of old places. In one of his lectures, he remembered visiting 'the Greate Standinge', a hunting lodge built for Henry VIII in 1542. It was a relic of the days when only the monarch had the right to hunt the deer that lived in the forest and pastures of Epping. The ailing king still relished the excitement of the chase but could no longer ride himself. So he watched from this grandstand as his courtiers and hounds pursued the harts and hinds. His daughter, Queen Elizabeth, also enjoyed the swift, bloody sport. She ordered the building to be made more weather-tight. For William, there was something wonderful about the strange little structure, alone on the edge of the forest. The views from its upper windows were vast. Like the queen, he could look out across the open ground and the treetops.

But it was the atmosphere inside that upper room that mattered more. This was one of the resonant spaces of his childhood. He carried it with him almost like a talisman – a sensory impression of how a room should feel or smell, how the light should fall, how the floorboards should sound, and above all, how it should be dressed with textiles. He was still thinking about it in 1882, when he wrote, 'how well I remember as a boy my first acquaintance with a room hung with faded greenery at Queen Elizabeth's Lodge . . . (I wonder what has become of it now), and the impression of romance that it made upon me.' William's desire to use tapestries or textile hangings 'to turn our chamber walls into . . . a summer garden' sprang from these moments of quiet looking and slow breathing, in the royal lodge at Chingford Hatch.[16]

*

William's peaceful childhood wanderings were interrupted. At nine years old, he was sent to school. His first formal lessons were at the Misses Arundale's Academy for Young Gentlemen. Still, he was able to ride home on his pony at the end of the day. A couple of years later, however, he was made to board, even though his preparatory school was only a mile or two from home. His parents probably believed they were doing their best for him, sending him away to become a young gentleman. William saw it differently; they 'did as all right people do, shook off the responsibility of my education as soon as they could; handing me over . . . to a boy farm'.[17] He did not even come home for weekends. On Sundays, William could see his family across the aisle in church but was not allowed to speak to them. This was a harsh, unhappy change. And all his energy, his perceptiveness counted for nothing, when he could not spell correctly. He was forced to stand on a chair in front of the other boys, in his stockinged feet, as a punishment for his spelling mistakes. As he later said, the main thing he learnt at school was 'rebellion'.

The upheavals worsened. In early September 1847, William's father died unexpectedly.[18] He was only fifty. William was fourteen. He was already separated by his schooling from the stability of home. And, to make matters harder, his father's death was bound up with a crisis in his banking business. Barely a week after William Morris Senior died, his firm appeared to be on the verge of collapse, and suspended trading. It is not clear how these events were linked – did worries about the impending failure trigger his unexpected death? Or did the business need his guiding hand to stay afloat? Whatever the circumstances, the loss of his father's income, as a managing partner, and his capital – with liabilities of over £2 million to be resolved – came as a heavy blow to young William and his family. Now only the investments in their mining shares were safe. Emma Morris and her nine children, and her large household at Woodford Hall, were entirely reliant on their interest in the Devon copper mines.

William's ability to grieve, to understand the decisions that were being made at home, to weather the turbulence – these were all undermined because he was sent away. He felt disconnected from his mother and sisters. In later years, he described that time in brisk, unemotional terms: 'My father died in 1847 a few months before I went to Marlborough.' His family were still, as he put it, 'left very well off'.[19] But Marlborough College was no haven for a thoughtful, fidgety boy. It was a 'new and rough school', opened only five years earlier.[20] The classes were chaotic and overfull, and often ill disciplined, despite the regular thrashings of boys with the cane or the birch. There was no privacy.

William boarded in A-house, a newly built block, laid out like a prison, 'a three-storey iron structure with a great well in the centre, rising to the skylight, the only source of daylight'.[21] It was an ideal place to torture small boys, by dangling them over the banisters. William did not often talk about his years there. He simply said, 'I had a hardish time of it, as chaps who have brains and feelings generally do at school'.[22] He was an odd boy: 'he mooned and talked to himself', and worked obsessively with his hands, making fishing nets.[23]

He was saved by his appetite for reading and storytelling, and for his willingness to explore the landscape outside the grounds. In school hours, William immersed himself in history and ancient languages. And he escaped whenever he could. He spent half-holidays rambling across the Wiltshire downs, finding paths through the forest of Savernake, searching for wildflowers and snail shells on Silbury Hill. As he explained later, the school was 'in a very beautiful country, thickly scattered over with prehistoric monuments, and I set myself eagerly to studying these and everything else that had any history in it, and so perhaps learned a good deal'.[24]

His three years at Marlborough were not wasted. It was here, as a very young man, that he saw the rich possibilities of multi-layered knowledge. This became his characteristic way of doing things – a combination of erudition and practical skills that was transformational in his later endeavours. Here William began drawing together his book-learning and his hands-on understanding of the countryside and buildings. In April 1849, for example, he saw the stone circles at Avebury for the first time. He was perplexed by the layout of the ancient structures, and wanted to decode the 'Druidical circle and Roman entrenchment which encircle the town'. He tried to find out more about the strange stones in the school library that evening. The very next day, he went back to Avebury 'and then I was able to understand how they had been fixed'.[25] He wanted to get to grips with the practicalities of making the place, as well as its complex meanings, as a ritual site, a gathering space for thousands of years.

On this expedition, his focus was constantly moving from the land to the man-made, and back to the land again. William was already able to 'read' the details of a Gothic church with a trained eye. He could see how the building had changed over time – noting that it 'had four little spires on it of the decorated order', while inside the porch was 'a beautiful Norman doorway loaded with mouldings'. 'The chancel', by contrast, 'was new and paved with tessellated pavement'.[26]

His description is precise, acknowledging the particular beauty of each phase.

After fixing Avebury church in his mind, William moved on to the next wonder, 'a water meadow up to our knees in water'. Again, he was keen to understand how the meadows were made. He told his sister Emma that 'You must fancy a field cut through with an infinity of small streams say about four feet wide each . . . the grass being very long you cannot see the water till you are in the water and floundering in it'.[27] He wanted her to see the irrigation system – its purpose, the way it could be turned on and off. But his letter also conveyed the sensation, the fun, of stumbling through a maze of wet grass. Only a handful of William's letters survive from his school days. They show his mind hard at work, collecting and piecing together shards of information, about the past and the present, about buildings and growing things, birds' eggs, silkworms. He wanted to share with his sister the joyous sound of boys singing the anthem in chapel at Easter. He was sad that he had not been allowed home for the Easter holidays. And here another tone creeps in. Going home 'was not to be, and it is no good either to you or to me to say any *horrid stale arguments* about being obliged to go to school for of course we know all about that'.[28] William was sent away because he was a boy. Emma could stay at home because she was a girl. This was the hardest lesson. Evidently, they had both tried to change their mother's mind, urged her to let her eldest son live within the family. But their mother had not relented. William felt cut adrift from his family.

William's letter showed his need for home comforts – 'some cheese perhaps', and he hoped Sarah the cook might 'make me a good large cake, and I should like some biscuits, and will you also send me some paper and postage stamps', so that he could write to his sisters.[29] But home was no longer the house he had grown up in. Since his father's death, William's mother could no longer afford the expense of a mansion with fifty acres, with all the essential indoor and outdoor staff to keep the household running. She had moved the family out of

Woodford Hall while William was away at school. The letter he sent Emma, after he heard about the change, is troubling. He no longer knew where home was: 'You have not exactly described the situation of the house . . . I can't understand which one you mean.' Was it Mrs Clarke's old house? Or the one next to it where William used to see 'a whole legion of greyhounds Scotch, English and Italian, do you know the one I mean'. He knew it was 'least of all our old house'.[30] There is a sense of him scrabbling about in his mind for a place to latch on to, some house that might be called home.

Despite his insecurity, William still longed to be back with his sisters and brothers. He was counting the days left of term: 'It is only 7 weeks to the Holidays, there I go again! Just like me! Always harping on the Holidays. I am sure you must think me a great fool to be always thinking about home always, but I really can't help it I don't think it is my fault for there are such a lot of things I want to do and say and see.'[31] He was weary and unable to express himself, to be himself. He would be confined in school for another two long winter months. William could not hide his homesickness. He was always thinking about home. Always.

*

William's time at Marlborough came to an abrupt end just before Christmas 1851. After years of inadequate teaching and harsh discipline, some of the boys staged a violent revolt against the staff. They stockpiled firecrackers and bags of gunpowder. The headmaster's study was ransacked and his birch whips destroyed. Gangs of boys marched out of college: 'tramp, tramp, tramp . . . eight abreast we doubled along the road heading into town, and woe to any obnoxious person whom we met'.[32] The teachers flogged the ringleaders. But the insurrection continued.

William carried his memory of these desperate days with him, far into manhood. Many years later, writing about a great fire at

Cottons' Wharf on the Thames in 1861, he said simply, 'I always did hate fireworks'.[33] And the violence he witnessed was not just between the students and teachers. It was also boys against boys, and rich against poor, as some pupils targeted local working-class people. William himself had learnt how to fight – or at least to resist – the school bullies. He developed his own idiosyncratic way to channel the hurt when he was teased for his tales of fairies and knights: 'he would rush roaring – but only half angry – with his head down and his arms whirling wildly, at his tormentors'.[34] This headlong rushing protected him, keeping the other boys at arm's length. But the vicious beatings and aggressive gangs, the burning books and terrified younger boys – this student rebellion was rage on an institutional, impersonal scale.

At Marlborough, William experienced the realities of revolution and reprisal: brutality, class conflict, fear and, running through it, the thrill of collective action, the possibility of changing the order of things. When he wrote about revolution in his later socialist works, he had some inkling of how it felt. He had seen the good and the ugly faces of uprising. In his utopian novel *News From Nowhere*, William imagined life on the far side of a social and political revolution. A visitor asks, 'Did the change . . . come peacefully?' and was it accomplished by 'actual fighting with weapons? . . . or the strikes and lock-outs and starvation of which we have heard?' The answer is 'Both, both'.[35] But William does not dwell on the details of how the change happened. It came down to individual responsibility and courage. As Fiona MacCarthy explained, 'he was repelled by the movement of the mob'.[36] At school he had seen that each boy could choose how to act, who to defy, who to support. Destructive violence only led to more violence. For Morris, the reason for revolution was to live more boldly, more imaginatively.

*

After the revolution, William was able to settle into a peaceful, thoughtful period at home. This was his new home, at Water House in Walthamstow. The moated island in the back garden made up for the loss of Woodford Hall. And perched on the window seat, William could read, dream, plan another fishing expedition. It was a respite. He spent whole days with his books. He began to prepare for the next stage of his education as a gentleman. He hoped to study at Oxford, and to become a clergyman. His letters from Marlborough revealed that William had been deeply impressed by the High Church Anglican services in the school chapel – especially the choral singing, and the solace of regular ritual. As he said, 'I thought it very beautiful'.[37] This was the reason for his choice of profession. William was never overtly pious or evangelical in his faith. For him, the priesthood seemed a natural place to pursue his love of storytelling and rich history, through sermons and the care of ancient buildings. As a priest, he could keep the world slightly at arm's length.

The mid-1840s had been a time of turmoil for the Church of England. Many congregations were divided over the idea of reviving pre-Reformation customs. Some churchmen wanted to reintroduce rich ceremonial vestments, candles, flowers, incense, altar frontals and stained glass, all celebrating 'the beauty of Holiness'. William and many of his generation were moved by the intense commitment of this movement within the church. The focus on art and poetry appealed to them as a way to rekindle faith. This resurgence of Anglo-Catholic churchmanship was known as the Oxford Movement, because so many of the leading clerics were preaching and teaching at the University. So it seemed the natural choice for William.

In the spring of 1852, he was coached by a local tutor, Frederick Guy, in preparation for his entrance exam. He spent some weeks boarding with Guy, and other weeks at home. William knew that his time with his family was limited. His favourite sister, Emma, had married a curate and moved to Kent. He too would be going away again soon. The window seat was only a temporary resting place. In June he took his examination, and won a place at Exeter College, Oxford. And in January 1853, after an autumn of waiting, biding his time, William left home to begin his studies. The city, as he approached it, seemed 'a vision of grey-roofed houses, and a long winding street and the sound of many bells'.[38] It became his second home.

Chapter 2

Oxford, 1853–1856

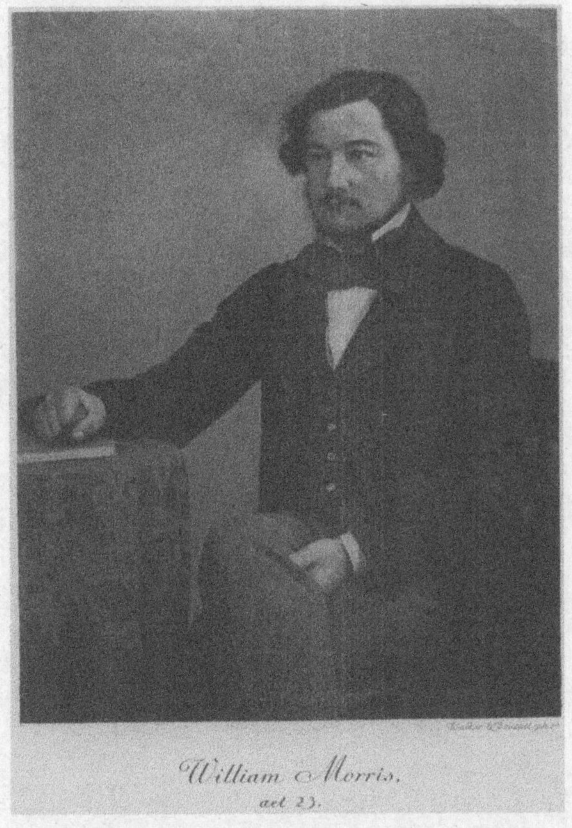

William Morris, aged 23, photograph by Walker & Boutall,
National Portrait Gallery

There is a hushed space in the centre of Oxford. Beneath the stone vaults of New College cloister, ancient sculptures of kings and saints crumble and loom in darkened corners. Sunlight slants through the arches, catching the traceries that were being carved when Chaucer was writing his *Canterbury Tales*. Past and future feel different here. There is a sense of overlapping realities, as if we could reach back to find the answer to modern problems. The noise of the living town is muffled. Squabbles and shouts from the Turf Tavern, just over the wall, are barely heard. The cramped cottages of Bath Place and St Helen's Passage, tucked behind the college, seem worlds apart from this cocooned space of green lawn and golden stone. While a working-class girl like Jane Burden cleans and stitches and earns her keep in Holywell Street, a few yards away, William Morris can retreat to this sheltered spot.

William discovered his calling in Oxford, pacing around these cloisters with his friends – the medieval arcade became one of their 'sacred places'. He hammered out his beliefs here, and on long walks through the cobbled streets, and across the meadows to Godstow Priory. He discussed ways to challenge the complacency of middle-class, Middle England, a complacency embodied by his father and mother. He would enlist in a 'Crusade and Holy Warfare against the age'.[1]

We catch a glimpse of the mood of the time in a Pre-Raphaelite portrait of an earnest young clergyman, standing in the shade of New College cloisters. Frowning slightly, his eyes are fixed on something just over our shoulder. Posed rather stiffly in his white surplice, he holds an old Bible, and seems to be pausing before he begins his work in the wide world.

This clean-shaven, dark-haired young man is not William Morris. But he is the sort of man that William hoped to become when he started his studies in Oxford. The portrait of John David Jenkins, a newly ordained curate, was painted by William Holman Hunt in the summer of 1852, while William Morris was taking his entrance exams. Like Jenkins, William intended to be part of a new generation of priests, working alongside 'his glorious little company of martyrs'.[2] He would use his faith, his reading, his energy to open hearts to the beauty of holiness. And all the while, Jane and her sister Bessie could see only a life of service ahead. They would spend their days fetching and carrying for students like William – as the unobtrusive housekeepers who made it possible for the men to read and talk, to weave their grand plans.

*

During his time at Oxford, William was constantly moving rooms, rarely settling in one space for more than a few terms. Everything around him was also in a state of flux. His chosen college, Exeter, was being rebuilt throughout the 1850s – old rooms torn down, a new faux-Gothic chapel erected in the Front Quad. William was assailed by noise, dust, a sense of impermanence, a fear that the medieval wonders of the city were disappearing before his eyes. The college was bursting out beyond its fourteenth-century boundaries. It had to build new accommodation because there were simply not enough rooms for all the new undergraduates. William could not take up his place in the autumn of 1852 because Exeter was full. And even when he did begin his degree in January 1853, the problem had not been resolved. William was constantly shifting his books and papers from one place to another. He was expected to work in a study in town during the day, but sleep in college every night: his bed was squeezed into the small third room of a senior student's set. It was all very unsatisfactory, grudging and inconvenient.

The older colleges like Exeter and New had been established to house undergraduates and Fellows, following the model of the great monasteries. The young men would come together every day for meals in the refectory or hall, and services in the chapel. They would have their own set of rooms – a study and bedroom – where they could work on their Latin and Greek, in preparation for taking Holy Orders. College servants, known as scouts, would bring hot water for washing, sweep out and lay the fires, clear away slops. It was an exclusively masculine environment. Fellows could not marry, and students had to stay in college overnight. Within the college walls, the young men were able to focus on their reading and lectures. They were in seclusion, shielded from the realities of day-to-day life. Outside, on Broad Street, were pubs like the 'Dog and Partridge', the 'North Star' and the 'White Horse'. There was a small iron foundry, and rows of shops: grocers and tea dealers, milliners and bootmakers, confectioners and tobacconists, an eco-system of making, selling and buying.[3] But inside, the undergraduates could steep themselves in theological debate, poetry and ancient languages.

William went up to Oxford at a moment of change, when the quasi-monastic structures were being dismantled. The University was modernising, growing, adapting to the new age of steam trains and Darwin. When William arrived, 'the common street architecture was still largely that of the fifteenth century' and 'on all sides, except where it touched the railway, the city came to an end abruptly . . . and you came suddenly upon meadows'.[4] Yet, by the end of the 1850s, the look and feel of Oxford had altered significantly. This was especially true for the area around Exeter on Broad Street. The architect George Gilbert Scott was hard at work, fashioning a new library and a new frontage for the college. In the process, William's old rooms were demolished – a tidy version of the Gothic, replacing the original higgledy-piggledy medieval buildings.

William Morris had finally moved into college in Michaelmas term 1853. His rooms were tucked between the Rector's Lodgings and the old stables, in a collection of buildings known as Hell Quad. Little had changed there since a plan of Exeter was drawn by David Loggan in 1675. Loggan's print showed this corner of the college, with its jumble of windows and attics, tiny staircases and high walls. The entrance to the quadrangle was through an archway known as Purgatory. This led into a garden – 'a little open space with trees'.[5] William's rooms looked out over the tops of 'the tumbly old buildings, gable-roofed and pebble-dashed'.[6]

William had spent his childhood in the crisp symmetry of Georgian houses. His school was a modern monstrosity, designed for surveillance. For a young man who had grown up with the romance of the Waverley novels, who had fallen under the spell of the tangles of Epping Forest, these rooms were a wonder. At last, here, in Hell Quad, he was able to enjoy the organic disorder of a medieval building. His rooms encouraged exploration, privacy, informality. One of his friends described the delightful strangeness of their lodgings: 'Little dark passages led from the staircase to the sitting rooms.' There were 'a couple of steps to go down, a pace or two, and then three steps to go up: your face was banged by the door.' And then 'inside the room, a couple of steps up to a seat in the window, and a couple of steps down into the bedroom'.[7] (This was all very quaint, but the ups and downs must have been tiresome for the scout, carrying trays or hot water cans.)

William Morris had rooms on the same staircase as his great friend Edward Burne-Jones. They had met during their entrance exams in the summer of 1852 and their close partnership persisted for over forty years. In their first weeks at Oxford, they went on 'angry walks together in the afternoons and sat together in the evenings reading'. Burne-Jones recalled his friend's 'vehemence'.[8] He described William as 'slight in figure in those days; his hair was dark brown and very thick, his nose straight, by his eyes hazel-coloured, his mouth exceedingly delicate and beautiful'. In later years, William's mouth and eyes were often hidden by his mass of hair and beard – which grew so vigorously that his undergraduate friends christened him 'Topsy'.[9]

Together William and Ned Burne-Jones explored their new surroundings, taking advantage of their independence from home. 'Oxford is a glorious place,' Burne-Jones announced, 'Godlike! At night I have walked round the colleges under the full moon, and thought it would be heaven to live and die here.'[10] They made jokes about ordering twelve dozen bottles of Madeira, three dozen of claret, and two dozen more of champagne. But this was far beyond the means of William's new friend. Unlike Morris, Burne-Jones was not wealthy. His father was an unsuccessful picture-frame dealer from Birmingham; his mother died when he was born, and he was an only child. Burne-Jones's upbringing was smaller in scale, more pinched in every way. His boyhood was hemmed in by the insistent noise, commerce and squalor of an industrial city.

Burne-Jones was saved by his schooling. He had moved into the Classics class at King Edward's School, and was able to set his sights on Oxford and ordination. Several of his school-fellows were already up at Oxford, studying at Pembroke College. He and Morris began to gravitate towards this group of friends: William Fulford, Charles Faulkner, Richard Watson Dixon. At the time, Exeter College 'was not a reading college . . . the vast majority of its members were only pass men, who lived healthy outdoor lives, especially on the river'.[11] Burne-Jones and William Morris, by contrast, were excited by books, by the possibilities of poetry and philosophy, Tennyson, Keats, Newman, Carlyle. They began to spend their spare time together in Pembroke. William's first biographer described how he started to fit into the group:

> At first, Morris was regarded by the Pembroke men simply as a very pleasant boy . . . who was fond of talking, which he did in a husky shout, and fond of going down the river with Faulkner, who was a good boating man. He was also extremely fond of singlestick, and a good fencer . . . His fire and impetuosity, great bodily strength and high temper were soon manifested: and were sometimes astonishing.[12]

Very quickly, they began to recognise the rigour and the wisdom beneath his physicality. One of his new friends summed up his unusual attraction: 'How Morris seems to know things, doesn't he?' Another agreed: 'How decisive he was: how accurate . . . what an extraordinary power of observation lay at the base of many of his casual or incidental remarks.'[13]

William had been a rather solitary boy at school, and his relationship with his younger brothers always seemed semi-detached. Here in Oxford, he made his first close male friends. The comradeship he enjoyed with Burne-Jones and the other thoughtful boys from Birmingham set the tone for many of his later alliances, in life and in art. The bond was based on shared literary enthusiasms, unencumbered by worries about women. They were steeped in a desire for a revived Christian faith, woven together with medieval ideals of beauty and virtue. Burne-Jones soon was telling friends that 'I have set my heart on our founding a Brotherhood. Learn Sir Galahad by heart. He is to be patron of our Order. I have enlisted *one* in the project up here, heart and soul.'[14] That *one* was William.

We only have Burne-Jones's word to vouch for the intensity of the affection between these young men. William's letters from these earliest years in Oxford have not survived. So we see him from the outside, from the point of view of his new friends, as they discovered his character and strengths. Burne-Jones was always closest to him. Perhaps his description of Morris reveals more about Burne-Jones's own romantic nature, but it still captures the impression that young William made on his intimate circle. He was: 'One of the cleverest fellows I know . . . full of enthusiasms for things holy and beautiful and true . . . he has tinged my whole being with the beauty of his own, and I know not a single gift for which I owe such gratitude to Heaven as his friendship.'

Burne-Jones went on, though, to draw attention again to William's 'boisterous mad outbursts and freaks', his uncontrolled body breaking the spell.[15] There was always this ingrained tension between the energy of William's actions – his 'habit of beating his own head', his violence when fencing at singlestick, even his prodigious bouncing hair – and his reflective inner life.[16]

Throughout their first terms at Oxford, William and Ned were wrestling with disappointment. The University was no longer seething with radical religious debates. Only a few years earlier, it seemed that John Henry Newman was stirring up ferocious and hopeful changes within the Church of England. But the heat had gone out of the Oxford Movement since Newman himself had become a Roman Catholic in 1845. For Burne-Jones and Morris, it felt like they had missed their moment. Ned explained how Newman had been central to his purpose in coming to Oxford: 'In an age of sofas, he taught me to be indifferent to comfort; and in an age of materialism he taught me to venture all on the unseen.'[17] These young men used his words as a springboard, to find their own ways of changing the world.

*

How did William and his friends rebel against this 'age of sofas'? Perhaps we can start by trying to see into their own rooms. Their college sets were their first personal domestic space, where they could arrange the furniture to their liking, decorate the walls. Most rooms were sparsely furnished, with the bare minimum – a bed, a table, a desk, a wash-stand with ewer and basin. But students quickly put their own stamp on the space. Older undergraduates would sell on their extra furniture to freshmen. We know that students bought additional pieces second-hand in town: 'an armchair, a bookcase and a writing table, all undeniable bargains, and all capable of being put into good working order after a little judicious exercise of the hinges, drawer-handles, and other component parts'.[18] Many of the objects in the room were scuffed and haphazard, witnesses to the generations of young men who had lived with them and passed them on. There might have been 'faded green window-curtains, and . . . [an] old Kidderminster carpet that had been charred and burnt into holes with the fag-ends of cigars'.[19] Standing out bright and neat against these well-handled things were the furnishings brought from home. No doubt William's sisters and mother crafted cushions and slippers for him, provided him with tablecloths, bedlinen and new towels, all carefully stitched with laundry marks. We can imagine him, like the fictional undergraduate Mr Verdant Green, who also went up to Oxford in 1853, being overwhelmed with affectionate hand-made gifts. Green was sent on his way to Brazenface College with numerous articles,

> useful as well as ornamental. There was a purse from Helen . . . a triumph of art in the way of bead decoration . . . a pair of braces from Mary, worked with an ecclesiastical pattern of a severe character . . ., a watch-pocket from Fanny, to hang over Verdant's night-capped head . . . And there was a pair of woollen comforters knit by Miss Virginia's own fair hands.[20]

Whether soft, feminine objects like these were displayed in William's rooms, or tucked out of sight when he arrived, we do not know. There are few details of how he decorated his set in Hell Quad. It seems probable, given Burne-Jones's description, that his bedroom was 'inconveniently small', and like Verdant Green, he bumped his elbows against the wall as he shaved in the morning. However, his main sitting room almost certainly had a good-sized dining table where William would be served breakfast by his scout, and a little pantry for his glasses and crockery, and packets of tea and sugar, with shelves for wine bottles, pies and cheeses, if he chose to entertain in the evenings.

Many of the undergraduates at Exeter were known as 'sporting' men. They filled their rooms with the paraphernalia of hunting, fishing and dogs. We get a lively sense of this style of decoration from Verdant Green's description of his friend Mr Larkyns's room. There he found a fox's head above the mirror, and 'a huge pair of antlers over the door'. Larkyns used the antlers as a handy shelf for his 'collection of sticks, whips, and spurs'. Then there were the 'fishing rods, tandem-whips, cricket bats . . . piled up in odd corners; and single-sticks, boxing-gloves and foils gracefully arranged upon the walls'. Letters, invitations, bills and trademen's cards were tucked into the mirror frame.

Larkyns reinforced his position in the 'fast' set by displaying a selection of pipes and cigar boxes, and by his taste in pictures. He also evidently had an eye for the ladies. Alongside gilt-framed engravings of Landseer's dogs and horses, he had chosen some 'Byron beauties . . . and some extremely *au naturel* pets of the ballet' – that is, semi-nude dancing girls.[21] This was a young man who was more interested in drinking 'punch, egg-flip, sherry-cobblers' and other tipples, than in excelling at his studies. William and Ned Burne-Jones spent most of their evenings in Pembroke College, to avoid such people.

William's taste, as far as we know, was much more austere. No doubt he too had singlesticks for fencing, and fishing-rods in the corner of his room. But mostly there were books – Shakespeare and Charles Kingsley, Charlotte M. Yonge's *The Heir of Redclyffe*, and John Ruskin's *Modern Painters*. He would 'often read Ruskin aloud'. William's friends were struck by his 'mighty singing voice' as he 'chanted rather than read those weltering oceans of eloquence'.[22] Morris was trying to get to grips with the reality of the Middle Ages, the evidence of the architecture around him, to see if it matched Ruskin's descriptions. So scattered on his desk, and on the window seat, and beside the books were copies of the architect's magazine *The Builder*, and his own sketches. At that time, William 'was constantly drawing windows, arches, and gables in his books; and even in his letters of the time, where the pen has paused, there comes a half unconscious scribble of floriated ornament'.[23] He was noting down the vocabulary of Gothic design, becoming familiar with its traceries and crockets.

This fascination with the Gothic carried through into the pictures on his walls. Instead of the fashionable prints favoured by the 'sporting' men, William pinned up his brass-rubbings. These were the images of medieval grave-markers, which he found during his expeditions to churches in Essex and Oxfordshire. Long-dead priests, knights and their ladies stared down at William as he worked. They watched over his friends as they sat in the firelight after dinner, talking and joking. His collection grew until his 'rooms were full of rubbings'.[24] And as he began to travel in the University vacations, his understanding of medieval art was enriched; he saw the altarpieces of Van Eyck and Memling for the first time in the summer of 1854, and visited the Musée Cluny and the Louvre. He brought home photographs of Dürer's engravings. These were stuck up in his college rooms too, alongside the English brasses. He kept his eyes open for original impressions of Dürer's work, and spotted one – his *Vision of St Hubert*, c.1501 – a few years later, 'and very nearly bought it but couldn't afford it'. It was six guineas, and William reluctantly decided the photographs were good enough. But he still yearned for the original engraving: 'O my word! So very, very gorgeous.'[25]

William Morris visited northern France in 1854 with his older sister Henrietta. She was his companion when he first saw the great cathedrals of Amiens and Rouen and Chartres, places that resonated with the writings of Ruskin. But this holiday was overshadowed in his memory by the Long Vacation of 1855. That was the moment when William was able to explore these Gothic shrines with his friends. It was also the summer when all the reading and talking at Oxford began to crystallise into something more distinct, a decision about his future as a priest.

*

During his second year at Oxford, William's thoughts were turning away from the Church and towards the possibilities of painting and architecture. He had become more aware of a new literary and artistic movement that was beginning to flourish in London. Through Ruskin's published lectures and the Royal Academy exhibitions, he heard the names of the Pre-Raphaelite Brotherhood. Dante Gabriel Rossetti, John Everett Millais and William Holman Hunt: these poets and painters were tackling medieval and modern subjects with a radical clear-sightedness. William Morris and Ned Burne-Jones began to seek them out in exhibitions. They even started to approach private collectors. They visited the home of Benjamin Windus in Tottenham: he showed them 'a picture by [Ford] Madox Brown, called "The Last of England"', and some small works by Millais. Back in Oxford, in the summer term of 1855, they 'got permission to look at the Pre-Raphaelite pictures in the house of Thomas Combe'. Combe had bought paintings by Holman Hunt, including his 'portrait of some surpliced friend . . . with part of the Cloisters of New College for a background':[26] this was the picture of John David Jenkins, looking rather shy after his ordination. They were able to enjoy these small works, displayed at home. Their visits were unhurried. They could take in the details of Millais's brushstrokes, or Holman Hunt's networks of symbolic details. William saw the possibilities of art in a domestic setting, away from the push and shove of the big public exhibitions. The work that struck him most strongly was a small watercolour that would have been utterly lost in a less intimate space. For William and Burne-Jones, it was a thing of 'greatest wonder and delight'.[27] The little picture of *Dante painting an angel on the anniversary of the death of Beatrice*, by Rossetti, reinforced their belief that modern art and medieval literature could be intertwined to create something beautiful and direct. They had already read Rossetti's poem 'The Blessed Damozel', which dwelt on a similar subject, describing lovers separated by death. William had seen a copy of *The Germ*, the short-lived Pre-Raphaelite magazine in which this had been printed. And it had encouraged him to persist in his own writing.

William had begun crafting poems a few months before. Burne-Jones recalled how 'one morning, after breakfast, [Morris] brought me in the first poem he ever made. After that, no week went by without some poem.'[28] He shared them in an unembarrassed way with his friends at Pembroke. They remembered hearing his earliest work: a poem, now lost, called 'The Willow and the Red Cliff'. William burnt it with many of his other verses after he went down from the University. He did not like to revisit his manuscripts. He relished the way the words seemed to come without hesitation. After his friends praised his originality, his immediacy, William apparently remarked, 'Well, if this is poetry, it is very easy to write.'[29] His subjects were tinged with melancholy, with Gothic details and an eye for colour. There is a fragment of an early unpublished verse that he sent to a friend in the Easter vacation. It ends: 'Very blue the sky above/ Very sweet the faint clouds move,/ Yet I cannot think of love.'

As he explained in this letter, 'I have begun a good many other things, I don't know if I shall ever finish them.'[30] He went on to describe how he was missing after-dinner conversations with Burne-Jones and the Pembroke men. He felt stuck between two very different worlds: Exeter College and Water House in Walthamstow. Home was too quiet, without the stimulation of new books or urgent theological discussions. His mother and sisters did not understand the way his mind was working. They were too focused on the day-to-day running of the house. 'I have no one to talk to,' he complained, 'except to ask for things to eat and drink and clothe myself.'[31] He sat up late into the night, while the rest of the house was asleep, to write and think, watching from his favourite spot on the half-landing, until he 'saw the dawn break through the window in our hall'.[32]

William longed to go travelling again. He and Burne-Jones made a few day trips, visiting Cambridge and Ely, but Morris wanted to show his friend the glories of the Gothic in France. They planned a 'walking tour . . . for cheapness' sake' in July 1855 with William Fulford, one of their own Brotherhood at Pembroke. This would be his first independent expedition, very different from the sedate tour he had taken with his sister. None of his family would be standing at his shoulder this time. William needed to take into account, as Burne-Jones explained, that 'economy [was] necessary for me and conceded by him, who never said whether he had, or had not, money'.[33] William's letters showed that he kept a close eye on their expenses; they found 'very good rooms' in Abbeville for six francs, and a full day's travelling from Dreux to Louviers and on to Rouen for nine shillings each. They had intended to walk from church to church, but this proved impossible. On their first Saturday, they trudged seventeen miles to Beauvais, and the following Wednesday, they covered twenty-five miles on foot. But William in particular was suffering. His boots rubbed his feet so much that he had to buy a pair of carpet slippers. These disintegrated by the end of the week. It is not surprising that they were footsore. William calculated that they had visited 'nine Cathedrals, and let me see, how many non-Cathedral Churches; I must count them on my fingers; there, I think I have missed some but I have made out 24 all splendid churches.'[34]

William was awed and excited by the riches he encountered day by day. He and his friends were 'in a state of ecstasy' as each building seemed better than the last: the 'Big Church' of Abbeville, which rose like a 'mountain of wrought stone';[35] 'glorious Rouen'[36] where they heard Vespers sung; 'the beautiful statues, and the stained glass, and the great, cliff-like buttresses' of Chartres;[37] and the interior of Louviers, 'so solemn it looked and calm after the fierce flamboyant of the outside'.[38] Their experience of spires and carved stone was overlaid, in some places, with colour and music. They were delighted by the stained glass and the ritual of song and movement.

For Burne-Jones, the Sunday service at Beauvais Cathedral felt like 'the first day of creation'. 'I remember it all', he told a friend nearly forty years later: 'the processions – and the trombones – and the ancient singing – more beautiful than anything I ever heard . . . And the great organ that made the air tremble – and the greater organ that pealed out suddenly, and I thought the Day of Judgement had come.'[39]

The sensory revelations of this journey did not begin and end with the Gothic churches. William and Ned found constant delight in the countryside in between. Burne-Jones, looking back, recalled 'how alive I was, and how young – and a blue dragon-fly stood still in the air so long that I could have painted him'.[40] For William, the landscape left a lasting impression. The green fields of Normandy were conjured up, again and again, in his poetry and scene-setting, and in the undulations of his textile designs. They felt almost like the backdrop to dreams. The countryside beyond Louviers, he said, was 'nearly all grass land and the trees, O! the trees! It was all like the country in a beautiful poem, in a beautiful Romance.'[41] William loved the way the meadow flowers grew thick among the corn: 'the hedgeless fields of grain' seemed 'the most beautiful fields I ever saw yet . . . purple thistles, and blue corn-flowers, and red poppies, growing together with the corn round the roots of the fruit trees, in their shadows, and sweeping up to the brows of the long low hills till they reached the sky'.[42]

Although William was eager to feast his eyes on meadows and churches, his friends were also keen to see Paris – they had never been to the Louvre, or the Opera. After a bit of a tussle, William agreed, and they 'worked hard at sight-seeing for sixteen hours'.[43] There were things worth looking at, after all. There was the moment in the Louvre when 'Morris made Edward shut his eyes and so led him up to [Fra] Angelico's picture of "The Coronation of the Virgin" before he allowed him to look, and then he was transported with delight'.[44] This vast altarpiece, filled with a vision of heaven, all blue and red and gold, had become a touchstone for other young British artists, including Rossetti and Holman Hunt. It had offered possibilities of a new visual language for the Pre-Raphaelites in 1848, and seemed just as vivid, just as potent to William and his friends.

Fra Angelico took their breath away. But perhaps the most significant paintings they saw in Paris were the British exhibits at the 1855 Exposition Universelle. The friends spent half a day looking at the seven Pre-Raphaelite pictures on display in the Beaux Arts department: 'three by Hunt including "The Light of the World", three by Millais and one by Collins'.[45] Other visitors drifted past these works without paying much attention. Only Millais's *The Order of Release* made people stop and look. For William and Burne-Jones, however, the works were remarkable. For here was a vibrant and radical group of British artists on display in the heart of Paris. The Pre-Raphaelites had challenged the traditions of the Royal Academy at home. Now they were making their mark, in Ruskin's words, as a 'new and noble school' that could rival the modernity of French art.[46]

William and his friends had arrived in Oxford too late for Newman's sermons. The fire seemed to have dwindled in the Church. All their enthusiasm, their plans to be part of a transformative priesthood had been undermined by the 'languid and indifferent' atmosphere of the University.[47] Now in France, as they walked and wondered, and looked with fresh eyes on modern art and medieval architecture, a different future seemed possible. As Burne-Jones explained, 'Slowly, and almost insensibly . . . without ever talking about it, I think we were both settling in our minds that the clerical life was not for us, and art was growing more and more dominant daily.'[48]

The crisis came as they were turning towards home. The young men had spent the past weeks standing in the shadow of medieval masons. They had begun to understand how Gothic architects had created sacred spaces from the natural forms of bending trees and unfurling leaves. And they had seen the first shoots of regeneration in contemporary British art. Now they had reached the port of Le Havre, on their way to see Bayeux and Caen, the last of the great churches on their list. Walking along the quayside as night fell, they watched the fishing boats leave their moorings and glide out towards the deeper water. Here William and Ned made their decision. In Burne-Jones's words, 'We resolved definitely that we would begin a life of art . . . he should be an architect and I a painter . . . and after that night's talk we never hesitated more.'[49] This was the crossing point. They stepped away from the Church, and towards a new vocation.

These were fine sentiments. But what did it mean in practice? They would have to explain their decision to their tutors, their friends, their parents. William made a mess of telling his mother. He felt the need to apologise, a little while later, for 'speaking somewhat roughly . . . speaking indeed far off from my heart because of my awkwardness.'[50] He knew that his sister Henrietta was also disappointed. They feared that he would become 'an idle, objectless man'. William tried to reassure his family that his Oxford years were not wasted; he had gained there 'the love of friends faithful and true . . . this love was something priceless, and not [to] be bought again anywhere'. He was obliged to return to his college in October 1855, for his last term of studies. But he intended, as he told his mother, to make himself useful: he would still strive, as he put it, for 'the bettering of the World'. The first step was to find an architect who would take him on as a pupil.

*

In January 1856, William began his apprenticeship with George Edmund Street, who had recently been appointed the Oxford diocesan architect. His offices were in Beaumont Street so William was able to carry on living close to his friends. He had taken a pass degree before Christmas, but he did not yet have to face the upheaval of leaving the city. His lodgings overlooked Martyrs' Memorial, a few yards from Street's office. And so William set to work, measuring churches, meticulously copying plans, trying to learn the trade. His drawings were overseen by Philip Webb, the son of an Oxfordshire doctor, who had grown up in the city centre. His relationship with Oxford – its buildings, its cobbled lanes – was even more intense than William's. Webb asked a friend, many years later, if he had seen 'a little and wonderstruck boy in Oxford trotting along the pavements of the streets there, [for] it might have been the ghost of my youth'.[51] Webb was significantly older than William; he was born in 1821. And yet, they developed a great friendship. 'Morris understands me,' Webb said, 'and . . . it has been a great corrective to rub shoulders with [his] hearty love-of-lifedness'.[52] It was a close partnership that lasted to William's death and beyond. Webb designed his friend's tombstone.

This lifelong alliance with Webb was one of William's compensations for stepping aside from his ordained path. The other was his chance to learn from an outstanding architect. G. E. Street loved the Gothic as much as William did, and worked towards a modern, practical reinterpretation of medieval forms. Although at this point in his career Street was preoccupied with church buildings, he also had a clear vision for domestic architecture – inside and out. Street's writings and lectures in the early 1850s anticipated many of William's later ideas. He outlined the best ways to integrate the 'Pointed style' into contemporary house-building, and demonstrated how medieval approaches to decoration could make nineteenth-century homes more beautiful. One of his essays, published in 1853 in *The Ecclesiologist*, shows how much there was for William to learn from his short period as Street's pupil. At times, it almost seems to be a blueprint for his later work. Street even pointed to what would become one of Morris's favourite sources, the manuscript of *Roman de la Rose* in the British Museum, to suggest details that could be accommodated in new houses. And there was one passage that seemed particularly prescient:

> In the middle ages the furniture of the domestic apartments of the household was as a rule as warm and elegant as our own ever is. No one, I think, can have examined ancient illuminated manuscripts to any extent without being struck with this. Walls hung with rich and curiously coloured hangings, in tissues, stuffs or leather, – or partially panelled in dark wood, partially painted in gay devices, – windows carefully finished and warmly defended by hanging curtains, carpets of rich and sometimes eastern looking patterns, chairs, bookcases, tables, vessels for drinking, vases and the like.[53]

Street urged his readers to seek out wall-hangings and drinking vessels, carpets and curtains, that responded imaginatively to the Middle Ages. In his own practice, Street collected early medieval textiles so that he could study their weave and stitching, and create a revitalised tradition of church embroidery.

As his earliest biographer wrote, for William 'The word architecture bore an immense, and one might almost say a transcendental, meaning ... it was the tangible expression of all the order, the comeliness, the sweetness ... which sustain man's world and make human life what it is. To him the House Beautiful represented the visible form of life itself.'[54]

All this was part of William's training. His sense of purpose had been shaken when he abandoned his hopes of becoming a priest. Street convinced William that there was useful work to be done, that he could make the world more orderly, comely and sweet.

Chapter 3

Red Lion Square, 1856–1859

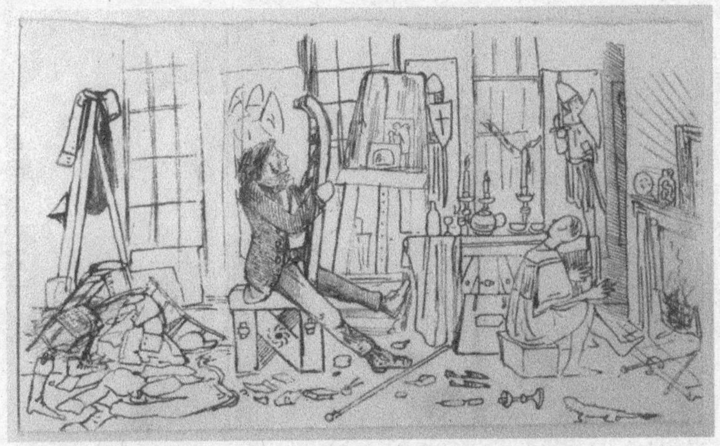

Edward Burne-Jones, *Self-portrait in the Red Lion Square studio*, University of Delaware Library, Samuel Lasner collection, c.1857

Leaving Oxford and moving to London; this was the great upheaval of 1856. For Ned Burne-Jones, it was 'the year in which I think it never rained nor clouded, but was blue summer from Christmas to Christmas, and London streets glittered, and it was always morning, and the air sweet and full of bells'.[1]

William Morris, his companion in this adventure, was more unsettled. He had given up his training for the priesthood, and now struggled to find a foothold. In his early twenties, he lived in a succession of rented rooms, mostly with friends. We read of him rushing to catch trains at the end of the working week, and trying to squeeze his art studies around his work as an architect. He was often ill-tempered. There were cross words with his mother, 'stubborn and angry' encounters,[2] clay models smashed and squashed because he could not get them right. Writing poetry, drawing, carving, travelling constantly between projects in London and Oxford: it was a time of impermanence, of constantly shifting horizons.

It is hard to keep track of William during these toings and froings. Very few of his letters survive, and many of his early drawings were abandoned, unfinished. There are two tentative self-portraits, made at this time. He looks keenly into the mirror, his pencil poised. We see the fluff of his new beard and small moustache, and the curly ends of his hair. But the results are unconvincing, out of proportion, flattened and lifeless. It is in his writings that we get a better sense of the things that mattered to him, and his anxieties. He describes the uncanny feeling of being out of place, as he worked on a tale late into the night: 'I ground at it . . . from nine o'clock till half past four a.m., when the lamp went out, and I had to creep upstairs to bed through the great dark house like a thief.'[3]

William was writing reviews and medieval fantasy tales for *The Oxford and Cambridge Magazine*. This was a joint enterprise with University friends, bringing together poems, essays and new short fiction. The first issue came out in January 1856. William was the original editor, but he soon passed this job on to his friend Fulford. Even so he contributed at least eight tales, five poems, an article on Amiens Cathedral and a review of Robert Browning's latest verse. This was the first time that the 'grinds' he had read aloud to his friends would reach a wider audience. They reveal his fascination with the chivalric world of Thomas Malory, and the dramatic effects of violence, bold colour and otherworldly romance. His distinctive reworking of the Gothic becomes visible in these writings. The story of 'The Hollow Land' is especially odd, and perhaps helps us to understand William's uncertainties as he sought a life beyond the Church.

The tale is told in disrupted, dreamlike episodes, flashing from bright mossy streams to a foggy no-man's-land without explanation. The story turns on the vengeful killing of a queen on Christmas morning, and these brutal passages are punctuated by carol-singing:

> Queen Mary's crown was gold,
> King Joseph's crown was red,
> But Jesus's crown was diamond
> That lit up all the bed
> *Mariae Virginis*

> Ships sail through the Heaven
> With red banners dress'd.
> Carrying the planets seven
> To see the white breast
> *Mariae Virginis*[4]

Here and in many other images, William seems ill at ease with the forms of traditional Christianity. He shows us an abbot, wearing armour beneath his vestments, who marches from the altar into the sunlight, at the head of his warrior-monks. It is as if William is grappling with his own faith, or lack of it, and failing to find an alternative way to look at the world; in the words of one of Florian's knights, 'how would you feel inclined to fight if you thought that everything about you was mere glamour; this earth here, the rocks, the sun, the sky?'[5] In this tale, everything is unstable. There is no clarity in the distinctions between good and evil, heaven and hell, even death and life. Fellowship between brothers is broken. The very earth slides away beneath their feet. Florian's brother leaps to his destruction. Florian also falls, but awakens in the hauntingly beautiful 'Hollow Land', and there is a young woman waiting for him.

We never know why he cannot stay in this quiet green place. A few pages later, Florian finds himself suddenly older, on 'a horrible grey November day . . . the fog-smell all about, the fog creeping into our very bones'.[6] There is a sense of physical revulsion as he touches the rusted helmet that 'pressed on my brow and pained me', only to discover that 'I laid my hand on a lump of slimy earth with worms coiled up in it . . . the rust had eaten it into holes, and I gripped my own hair as well as the rotting steel, the sharp edge of which cut into my fingers'. He has been unearthed, scrabbling out of the ground, nearly naked, dressed only in a robe that 'draggled so (wretched, slimy, textureless thing!) in the brown mud'[7] – this is a grotesque resurrection.

Despite these disquieting images of decay and loss, the blood and mud, we also discover positive signs of William's new life emerging. There is the potential redemptive power of a woman's love, in the figure of Margaret. Her appearance is eerie, not quite human, with skin 'like ivory for smoothness' and golden hair. She is dressed in white, with 'long spikes of light scarlet [going] down from the throat, lost here and there in the shadows [and] the folds'.[8] Later, he encounters his old enemy, Red Harald, named for the 'great scarlet cloth' he wore over his armour.[9] They are reconciled through the process of painting murals in the wreck of a castle, in 'yellow and red! Gold and blood', the colours of Hell. There is a nightmarish moment when Florian, kneeling over the wounded body of Harald, 'painted his face thus, with stripes of yellow and red, crossing each other at right angles; and in each of the squares so made I put a spot of black, after the manner of the painted letters in the prayer-books'.[10]

This is a precise, transgressive action, paintbrush against pale skin. Painting itself becomes a weapon, sometimes to impose order in chaos, sometimes to settle scores. Florian's training as an artist is imagined as a series of skirmishes, but 'at last [he] learned it through very much pain and grief'. Gradually, he finds peace, creating 'purple pictures and green ones . . . and always we painted God's judgements', until he could 'sit in the sunset and watch them with the golden light changing them'. And so he is able to rediscover the joys of the Hollow Land, letting himself 'down most carefully by the jutting rocks and bushes and strange trailing flowers'.[11]

As he worked through the plot, with all its hallucinatory jolts, William Morris seems to have been smoothing his own path. He was mapping, in fits and starts, the process of transformation from troubled priest to designer, from monkish student to hopeful lover. And running through the text is the feeling for material things: the notched blade of a sword or the solemn movement of a bell. Above all, he is aware of textiles – banners and robes, white albs and rags, 'surcoats, half purple and half scarlet, strewn with golden stars'.[12]

The opening scene shows William's sensitivity to the fabric of the Middle Ages, responding to intricate possibilities of colour, status, manufacture, all woven into a richly symbolic object. The Queen's crown snags the canopy held above her head and 'she caught at the brocade with her left hand and pulled it away furiously, so that the warp and woof were twisted out of their places, and many gold threads were left dangling about the crown.'[13]

The processional cloth of honour is mutilated. The peaceful life of the House of Lilies starts to unravel. And yet, in telling the tale, William can begin to resolve his own loss of direction. He discovers a delight in the look and feel of textiles and pictures, in suppleness and patterns, in the different ways of making and decorating. He brings into focus the hard task of becoming an artist. 'The Hollow Land' helps us to understand William's experience of being out of time, beyond faith.

*

When we compare this early story with William's later poems and prose romances, there is one distinct element missing. In his more mature writings, he lingers over the details of everyday life – the furnishing of bedrooms, the dining tables – adding depth to his fantasy settings. 'The Hollow Land' is more one dimensional. He skirts around the homely, and concentrates instead on battle scenes and unnatural encounters. But increasingly, he knew that this separation of real and imagined was not the way forward. William began to bring his visions of the past unexpectedly into the present. He insisted that 'Anyone who wants beauty to be produced at the present day . . . must always be crying out "Look back! Look back!"'[14] He tried to express this new vocation in a letter to his friend Crom Price, written in July 1856. He still sounded unsure of exactly how to proceed – 'I see that things are in a muddle' – but he went on: 'My work is the embodiment of dreams in one form or another.'[15]

This became William's *raison d'être*. He wanted to transform airy visions into something practical, something tangible. It was not enough to write poetry, or wallow in the world of Malory or Chaucer. He believed it was necessary to bring back the best of these vanishing beauties, to re-engage with them now. William collapsed the distinctions between the medieval and the modern. Good workmanship persisted. He acknowledged that 'my chances are slender; I am glad that I am compelled to try anyhow.' At least he would not be alone in his endeavour: 'Ned and I are going to live together. I go to London early in August.'[16]

G. E. Street was moving his architectural practice from Oxford to offices near Marble Arch. So William left his lodgings opposite the Ashmolean Museum, and rented a set of dingy furnished rooms in Upper Gordon Square, Bloomsbury. He worked alongside Philip Webb during the day – tiresome measuring and copying – and then went to a life drawing class in the evening with Ned. Their little apartment was, according to Burne-Jones, 'the quaintest room in all London, hung with brasses of old knights and drawings of Albert Dürer.'[17] Already they were imposing their own taste on the shabby Georgian interiors. William could have afforded something smarter, but he was very aware of Ned's limited finances. Instead of spending money on rent, he began to buy pictures.

William bought his first significant painting when he was still living in Oxford. He had spotted *April Love* by Arthur Hughes when he visited the Royal Academy exhibition in May 1856. It was a contemporary romantic scene, exhibited with verses from Tennyson's 'The Miller's Daughter': 'Love is made a vague regret'. The picture was filled with luminous colour and keenly observed nature. We can imagine William's delight in the glowing fabric of the girl's skirt, the details of ivy leaves and rose petals, the rich greens and bluey-purples bouncing off each other. William was 'brooding about it' so much that he asked Ned to do him 'a great favour, viz. go and nobble that picture called "April Love" as soon as possible lest anybody else should buy it'.[18]

John Ruskin was one of the painting's most fervent admirers, describing it as 'Exquisite in every way; lovely in colour, most subtle in the quivering expression of the lips, and sweetness of the tender face';[19] he had not been able to persuade his own father to acquire it. William, on the other hand, had money of his own now. He was eager to support emerging artists and make his mark within the Pre-Raphaelite circle. Arthur Hughes remembered the surprise of Ned arriving early on Monday morning with a cheque. Hughes could not quite believe that a young man, still effectively a student, would be so eager to buy his painting. But as William explained to his friend Crom Price, 'love and work, these two things only' were all that mattered at the moment.[20]

*

From late summer 1856 William was established in his London rooms, and became more involved with Ned's new friends. Chief among them was Gabriel Rossetti. To the end of his life, Ned would look at his own drawings and wonder 'what Gabriel would have thought of it, "whether he would approve it and be pleased with it, or whether he'd say it was rubbish"'.[21] William did not follow Ned so far in his hero-worship of Rossetti. But he was certainly moved by Gabriel's insistence that he should 'have no shame of my own ideas'. The younger men would leave Rossetti's presence 'cheerful and solemn' and 'carrying with them the banner of Art and Revolt'.[22]

Rossetti's response to William was less starry-eyed. Morris appeared as a potential client, as well as an acolyte. 'You know he is a millionaire and buys pictures,' Gabriel enthusiastically told the poet William Allingham.[23] In August, he introduced William to Ford Madox Brown, who noted in his diary that 'Rossetti brought his ardent admirer Morris of Oxford who bought my little hay field for

40 gns.'[24] This was a substantial sum; William had recently offered Fulford an annual salary of £100 to edit *The Oxford and Cambridge Magazine*, and many working men would be earning little more than £2 a week. So William's arrival in London – when Gabriel and his friends always seemed short of 'tin' – was fortuitous.

Within a year, William had bought five of Gabriel's watercolours: *The Blue Closet*, *The Tune of Seven Towers*, *The Death of Breuze sans Pitié*, *The Chapel before the Lists* and *The Damsel of the Sanct Grael*.[25] These pictures glimmered on the walls of William's lodgings, creating pools of visual richness in the corners of the gloomy sitting room. They were strange works, reflecting William and Gabriel's shared imaginary worlds. The young men had become fascinated with the beauty and discomfort of Malory's *Le Morte Darthur*. The watercolours were steeped in the same Gothic atmosphere. They were filled to the brim with reds, greens and golds, the colours illuminating fifteenth-century manuscripts. Gabriel showed the claustrophobic dalliances of knights and ladies, their slight bodies weighed down by embroidered robes and head-coverings. There is a melancholy intensity in many of the designs, as the figures are held fast within their tight frames. Several of these subjects became 'double works of art', when William responded by composing verses echoing the troubled mood and late-medieval scene-setting.

These poems elaborate the themes in Gabriel's pictures, dwelling on the enigmatic actions of beautiful women and their lovers. William intercuts the narrative of his poems with snatches of chanted refrains, like old carols: 'Listen! said fair Yoland of the flowers,/ This is the Tune of Seven Towers'.[26] The queens and ladies in 'The Blue Closet' are trapped in their palace, singing for a lost knight on a 'wild Christmas-eve'. Their memories of love are sensual but disturbing. One remembers how her beloved 'sprinkled the dusty snow over my head./ He watch'd the snow melting, it ran through my hair,/ Ran over my shoulders, white shoulders and bare.'

This is a chilling image, where death seems close at hand. All the while, 'the sea-salt oozes through/ The chinks of the tiles of the Closet Blue.'[27] William does not try to explain why Gabriel's women are so weary. He accepts the mood of the pictures and embellishes it.

Both painter and poet are concerned about the decorative details in their imagined rooms. William describes a 'gold and blue casket' in which one lady 'keeps all my tears'. She wonders: 'Did they strangle him as he lay there,/ With the long scarlet scarf I used to wear?'[28] As we saw in 'The Hollow Land', William concentrates on textiles. Another lady looks for 'my coif and my kirtle, with pearls arow'.[29] These objects add colour and movement to the verse, as well as a delight in archaism – the naming of these things lifts the reader out of the present.

We see William attempting to create strikingly modern writing by reworking old forms and vocabulary. He shows the precision and flexibility of the Gothic, envisioning a world before the bravura of the High Renaissance swept over the arts. William's poems were the first Pre-Raphaelite verses to be published. They were experimental. They were also poorly reviewed by the critics. However, they showed that it was possible to translate Ruskin's belief in the power of the Gothic from architecture into other art forms. Ruskin had written that 'The Nature of Gothic' allowed it to 'shrink into a turret, expand into a hall, coil into a staircase, or spring into a spire, with undegraded grace and unexhausted energy'.[30] William was now applying this energy from the Middle Ages – defined by Ruskin as savage, changeful, naturalistic, redundant, grotesque, rigid – to his poetry. And he was already hoping to make the Gothic live again in other radical design projects. He wanted to bring the vitality and brightness of the old ways into his new home.

*

In the autumn of 1856, William and Ned moved for the first time into unfurnished rooms, at 17 Red Lion Square. This was a chance to choose their own tables and chairs, beds and bookshelves. They could start from scratch, to create their own, 'small (very small) Palace of Art'.[31] These 'Red Lion Square days' were remembered with fondness by all their friends, 'days wonderful to hear tell of, days filled with Homeric laughter, strenuous work and the hundred fantastic experiments in furniture-making and decorating'.[32]

Ned described the chaos of moving in, all the 'books, boxes, boots, bedding, baskets, coats, pictures, armour, hats, easels – tumble and rumble and jumble'.[33] This sense of an unpredictable bachelor lifestyle, where easels and suits of armour sat happily among the everyday things, persisted even when the young friends had established themselves.

They had a big bright living room, overlooking Red Lion Square. The windows had been enlarged to let in more light, making it ideal for an artist's studio. Then there were two bedrooms behind. Burne-Jones took the larger one, with William squeezing himself into the box room. Rossetti spitefully described William as 'rather doing the magnificent there' – but in truth, Morris often over-compensated for his relative wealth, offering Ned the lion's share.[34] It was Gabriel who suggested that they should take this apartment. He had lived there in 1851, sharing the studio with another young painter, Walter Howell Deverell. (Deverell was the artist who had first met Elizabeth Siddall, and introduced her to Gabriel and his other friends. He died tragically young in 1854, from kidney disease.)

Rossetti was delighted to find that the rooms still bore the marks of his tenancy – with a scribbled pencil note left 'on the wall of a bedroom . . . "so pale and watery had been all the subsequent inmates, not a trace of whom remained."'[35] William and Ned, on the other hand, swiftly began to impose their own style on the studio. Rossetti told a friend that William was having 'some intensely mediaeval furniture' made, with 'tables and chairs like incubi and succubi'.[36] Several of them seem to have been lifted from Gabriel's own watercolours: unwieldy objects like the heavy throne, with built-in psaltery and bell, for example, from his 'The Tune of Seven Towers'. Ned was excited: 'When we have painted designs of knights and ladies upon them, they will be perfect marvels.'[37]

A local cabinetmaker, Henry Price, was asked to make these pieces, based on William's drawings and enthusiastic descriptions. He said that the 'tables and High backed chairs' were 'like what I have seen in Abyes and Cathedrals'. He remembered one in particular, 'A large Oak Table on tressel with a Iron stretcher twisted and partly burnished.'[38] It is noticeable that the carpenter could only compare these designs with massive ecclesiastical examples. And recent experiments in creating Gothic interiors, like Pugin's Palace of Westminster, were also institutional and designed to sit within a grander setting. Barely any original examples on a domestic scale had survived from the Middle Ages. William and his cabinetmaker were working from illuminated manuscripts, and scraps of information. Just few years later, the South Kensington Museum would house a useful collection of medieval furniture – carved chests, caskets and some tables. But the acquisition and display of these works was still in its infancy. (There is a substantial catalogue of early examples written in 1874 by John Hungerford Pollen.) In 1856, William had to rely on his own limited research, and the playful suggestions of his friends. The results were unsophisticated but bold.

Most of his designs were over-large for the modest studio. In later life, William advised his customers that 'good citizen's furniture' should be 'solid and well made in workmanship, and in design should have nothing about it that is not easily defensible, no monstrosities or extravagances'.[39] But as a young man, he was carried away by the possibilities of creating furniture from scratch and commissioned several 'monstrosities'.

The most extraordinary piece ordered by William was the settle. 'I think the measurements had perhaps been given a little wrongly, and that it was bigger than he ever meant,' Ned recalled. On the day it was delivered, the carpenter struggled to get it into the apartment: 'All the passages and the staircase were choked with vast blocks of timber and there was a scene.'[40] Ned reckoned that it took up at least one-third of the studio. But Rossetti thought it was a laugh, so all was well. The seat was big enough to double as a camp-bed for friends who could not make it home.

As Ned had imagined, the cupboard doors above the settle and the backs of the massive chairs proved irresistible. He and Gabriel set to work with their brushes. They turned to Dante and to William's own poems for inspiration. The throne-like chairs were decorated with fairy-tale figures, Guendolen with cascading hair, and Sir Galahad.[41] The chairs themselves were very upright and uncomfortable, with their chunky, revealed construction. They were not designed for lounging or long conversations. Their main purpose seems to have been to create a sense of radical experimentation, a space for more painted decoration. William was pushing back against the fashionable daintiness of the Rococo revival, and the horsehair upholstery of his childhood home.

There is a delightful self-portrait by Ned Burne-Jones showing how this new furniture dominated the room. He sits astride one of the massive chairs, oblivious to the chaos of the studio around him. This is an extraordinary document. It is of course a caricature, an exaggerated view of the bohemian life of the artist. But even so, it gives us an idea of the lodgings at Red Lion Square.

We see the tall brass-rubbings, with their images of armoured knights, pinned on the walls between the windows. Pushed off to one side is a heavy round table, partly laid with a crumpled cloth and a couple of candlesticks. There is also a teapot with two cups. And a wine bottle with two small glasses. This is a sociable, multi-functional space, where friends are made welcome, if they can find anywhere to sit. As well as Ned, with his side-whiskers and unlaced boots, there is another figure, smaller and apparently wearing a smock. He is perched on a box by the fire. His identity is unclear. It may be a large artist's dummy, posed with its foot on the fender. The odd twist of the head and wooden gestures make this likely. Ned and William each have their own easel. A jacket is thrown carelessly over one of them, and we can see a few small paintings on the other. There are more pictures stacked against the wall. And then, Ned shows us the clutter all over the floor. With deft strokes of his pen, he outlines the knives, portfolio, inkwell, maul-stick and books at his feet. The mess builds behind him into a glorious tangle: trousers, hat, toppled spindly chairs, boots are gathered in a heap and ignored, because the young men have more important things to do. Ned is busy admiring the new chair. It is all that concerns him, for now.

There is something gleeful in this visual catalogue of their bachelor existence. The deliberate mess, the oddity of the lay-figure, even the small creature scuttling across the floor, all show a cheeky disregard for conventional home life. It is almost childish, knowingly naughty. William and Ned were not interested in homemaking, but in performing their new roles as artists and 'men about town'. They did not have their own kitchen or running water, and relied on their housekeeper, Mary Nicholson, to provide the basics. She cooked their meals and took out their laundry. 'Red Lion' Mary became part of the myth-making of these years. She was remembered fondly, almost as a comrade in their adventures. Mary was not too particular about the state of the rooms and, as Ned put it, 'people more experienced than I in housekeeping said she was very untidy'.⁴² Her cooking could be unpredictable. Mary's staple dish was rabbit – a cheap and bony meal – but she also served up inedible eggs, and William was once so enraged by a Christmas pudding that he threw it down the stairs after her.

Despite these outbursts and muddles, 'Red Lion' Mary could be relied upon when the young men had guests. She was the person who made it all possible, preparing the late suppers and the prodigious breakfasts: 'Let us have quarts of hot coffee, pyramids of toast and multitudinous quantities of milk'.[43] She was willing to bring in extra mattresses and make up beds on the floor, and carry the hot water cans upstairs in the morning. They were very fortunate that her 'rough and ready hospitality was seconded by her unfailing good temper'.[44]

Rossetti flirted with her and put her in one of his pictures. She seemed to feel a little sorry for Ned, and would willingly run errands for him, hopping in a cab to collect costumes from Little Holland House, or writing notes to his Oxford friends. But her relationship with William was more complicated. Mary later said she 'seemed so necessary to him at all times' that she felt she was 'his man Friday'.[45] They worked together on his latest enthusiasm – textiles. Mary was already an accomplished seamstress, making costumes for their compositions. So William taught her to stitch 'his designs for hangings'.[46] It is likely that William had learnt about church embroidery in Street's office, and wanted to try out new ideas for his own rooms. He monopolised her time, checking up on her progress. He was in such a 'fever to see how they looked' that he 'often made her bring her embroidery frame into the studio so that she might work under his direction'.[47] She felt the force of his irritability, too. And responded by giving him 'the worst bed and the coldest water'.[48]

'Red Lion' Mary's conversations with Ned give us a useful insight into William's character. He was a good-looking young man but had no ease or charm with girls. This coolness continued throughout his life. Eventually it created a miserable emptiness in his marriage. William's writings from this time showed the strength of his desire. He created extraordinary, physical images of yearning: 'When both our mouths went wandering in one way/ And aching sorely met among the leaves;/ Our hands being left behind strained far away'.[49] Yet these romances were always tainted with violence or mishap, and they could not translate into everyday living. It was more than shyness.

As 'Red Lion' Mary put it, 'I shouldn't think Mr Morris knows much about women, sir . . . I should think he was such a bear with them.'[50]

From William's point of view, it seems that he found it difficult to live in such intimacy with a servant who, as Ned said, 'read all our books . . . read all our letters'.[51] At Oxford, he would have kept his scout or his housekeeper at arm's length. As a boy, there was a clear separation between family and staff: the servants kept to their quarters, restricted in their dress and conversation. Here the boundaries were blurred. 'Red Lion' Mary was a useful person, but William did not really know what to make of her. Still, he was pleased to find someone to help him with his embroidery experiments.

Mary was wise beyond her years, and open-hearted. There are tales of her kindness to women whose 'goodness was in abeyance'. Mary did not flinch when Ned brought home a terrified teenager he had found, presumably on one of his late-night strolls with Gabriel. He had met the 'poor miserable girl of 17' at two o'clock in the morning, 'scarce any clothes and starving, *in spite of prostitution*'. Mary, Ned and his friends clubbed together to find funds and clothes, so that she could go back to her family.[52] This brief scene was recorded in a few sentences by Georgie Burne-Jones (née Macdonald), who became engaged to Ned in 1856. It gives us a glimpse of the harsh world beyond the colourful, sociable artists' studio. The chivalric ideals the men had embraced in Oxford seemed paper-thin in the wintry light of London's streets. Class and gender relationships were far more complex than William and his friends had been led to believe by Malory, Keats, Dante, Tennyson or even Rossetti.

William was ill at ease with intelligent, independent 'Red Lion' Mary because she did not fit into a familiar female role. Unlike other working-class women in his circle – Emma Madox Brown, Elizabeth Siddall, or soon enough, Jane Burden and Fanny Cornforth – Mary was not entangled in a love affair with any of the artists. All the young men agreed that she was plain. And because she was no 'Stunner', she was unsuitable as a model for their medieval ladies. Mary was too short even to pose for figures. Ned recalled that she offered to stand on a stool, if it would help. She joined in their jokes, up to a point, helping Gabriel out of scrapes and teasing William. Even so, she would always be excluded from the essential part of their lives. She could bring in bottles and pies, clear away plates, empty slops, stitch, listen and laugh. But 'Red Lion' Mary would never be an artist or a model.

*

Painting was everything. Even William had given up his position in Street's office to devote his life to art. He had inevitably upset his mother again, not just by his change of career, but in the way he announced his decision. He broke it to her when he was at home in Essex, along with Ned. John William Mackail, Burne-Jones's son-in-law, heard that the news 'came as a severe shock' to Mrs Morris. William had spoken with 'characteristic vehemence'. He told her with 'nervous suddenness' that he was abandoning architecture – a secure profession – for the uncertainty of a painter's career.[53]

Mrs Morris blamed Ned, though in truth, it was mostly Gabriel's doing. William had been thinking about making the change while he was still living in Oxford. But he was spurred on by Gabriel. 'Rossetti says I ought to paint,' William reported to his friend Crom Price; 'he says I shall be able . . . I don't hope much, I must say, yet I will try my best.'[54] A few months later, Gabriel was describing the progress made by his two young friends. 'Both are men of real genius,' he said. 'Jones's designs are models of finish and imaginative detail, unequalled by anything unless, perhaps, Dürer's finest works: and Morris, though without practice as yet, has no less power, I fancy.'[55] For William, it was a struggle, but he insisted, 'I want to imitate Gabriel as much as I can.'[56] In the early days of their friendship, William believed Gabriel's refrain that 'if any man has any poetry in him, he should paint, for it has all been said and written.'[57]

The other great influence on William at this point was John Ruskin. The art critic and watercolourist was taking an interest in the young artists in Gabriel's orbit. He had been sent a copy of *The Oxford and Cambridge Magazine* when it was first published in January 1856. Burne-Jones could hardly believe it when Ruskin wrote back immediately, praising the poems and reviews: 'I'm not Ted any longer,' he wrote ecstatically to Crom Price, 'I'm a correspondent with RUSKIN, and my future title is "the man who wrote to Ruskin and got an answer by return".'[58]

It was Ruskin who gave meaning to William's instinctive love for the medieval. William had read Ruskin's essay 'On the Nature of Gothic' (1853). Forty years later, William described this piece as 'one of the few necessary and inevitable utterances of the century'. He went on: 'To some of us, when we first read it . . . it seemed to point out a new road on which the world should travel.'[59] Ruskin's care for materials, his affection for ancient buildings, spoke to William. He showed that art was always about more than pleasing the eye. It demanded critical thinking and even a willingness to challenge the fundamental structures of society.

Ruskin argued that classical, symmetrical art was dehumanising. He imagined the workers as slaves to the machine: 'All the energy of their spirits must be given to make cogs and compasses of themselves.'[60] He was not just writing about fifteenth-century Venice, but also about his own day, as he denounced the factory system as brutalising and soulless. Ruskin, thundering like a preacher, urged his readers to demand products that were the 'results of healthy and ennobling labour'.[61] Ruskin's framework for radical change was still deeply paternalistic – thinking in terms of 'them and us' – and at this stage, imaginative rather than practical. But it was a start.

These arguments, together with Ruskin's insistence on the need to study natural forms – 'the wandering of the tendril, and the budding of the flower . . . the interlacing of branches'[62] – stayed with William.

When he met Ruskin, he was still trying to find his own way of working towards 'the embodiment of dreams'. Ruskin helped these dreams to take shape, to weave together beauty, nature, fellowship and, perhaps, new conditions of labour. As William said later, 'It was through him that I learned to give form to my discontent.'[63] These readings and conversations coincided with William's first-hand experience of industrialised Manchester. His visit to the Art Treasures Exhibition in Manchester in the summer of 1857 opened his eyes. Not only did he find a substantial display of new work by Millais, Madox Brown and other Pre-Raphaelite painters, but as he travelled by train through the outskirts of the city, he saw the desperate environment in which thousands of people lived and worked. This was on a different scale to the manufacturing districts of Birmingham, which he knew from his visits to Ned's home. William had not yet read the damning descriptions of *The Condition of the Working Class in England*, written by Friedrich Engels in 1845, with its detailed concern for the livelihoods of men, women and vulnerable children in Manchester. Still, he was beginning to focus on the systems that created this squalor and made people, as Ruskin put it, into 'mere segments of men, broken into small fragments and crumbs of life'[64] through the division of labour.

Talking through the problems of work and art with Ruskin became, for a while, one of the highlights of William's week. He would drop in to Red Lion Square every Thursday on his way to the Working Men's College. William and Ned were delighted that Ruskin took notice of their efforts. Ruskin was often socially awkward, but was happiest when teaching or enthusing, so he was able to relax into this role with 'his dear boys'. Ned thought he was, in real life, 'better than his books, which are the best books in the world'.[65]

This male sociability, the opportunity to talk and drink and draw together, spilled over from William and Ned's time in Oxford. It was fundamental to their self-creation. The shared poems, read aloud by lamplight, and late-night grand schemes were at the heart of their plans for what they could be, what they could make. Apart from the regular drawing classes, their time was their own. William could try his hand at wood-engraving, or stone-carving, or clay-modelling. He had nailed his formal white tie to the wall in loops, so he could hang his tools up. He hated wearing 'togs' or evening dress, and this seemed a far better use of it. William would rather enjoy the informal company of Gabriel Rossetti, Ford Madox Brown and Arthur Hughes, the sculptor Thomas Woolner, or Robert Browning, 'the greatest poet alive'.[66]

They had daily access to a radical artistic community. In Rossetti's rooms, William met Holman Hunt, 'the greatest genius that is on earth alive', according to Ned. He seemed 'such a splendour of a man, with a great wiry golden beard, and faithful violet eyes'. This glorious vision was undermined by Rossetti's irreverence and easy physicality: Gabriel sat beside his old friend 'and played with this golden beard, passing his paint-brush through it'. Gabriel held court all evening, while Ned and William listened and tried to draw.[67]

*

It was inevitably Gabriel who started the young artists on their next adventure, encouraging them to join his 'Jovial Campaign' in Oxford. He had concocted a plan to create a series of Arthurian murals, and expected his young friends to work alongside him. It was a collaborative project, like the painted chairs or the literary magazine, that relied on good fellowship and common artistic goals. Again, it was an attempt to reignite the spirit of Brotherhood that Rossetti lacked, since he and Millais drifted apart. In 1853, Gabriel had written mournfully that 'the whole of the Round Table is dissolved'.[68] Now he hoped it could be reassembled, with a new group of young men. They would spend the summer decorating the walls of the new Debating Chamber in the Oxford Union, working and joking together. In the evenings they could go out to the theatre, or for rambles along the river, or pile into their lodgings for dinner and poetry.

Barely a year after he had left Oxford, William was back. He and Ned took rooms with Gabriel on the High. It was the only time that all three lived together. Sadly, we know very few details of their household arrangements – one account refers to dinner being served by 'the lodgings' slavey',[69] a very young maid-of-all-work – but we can imagine the messiness and larks, interspersed with intense conversation. 'Those wonderful seething days' were remembered in after-years as a creative hubbub of talking and painting.[70] William later decided that the whole project had been 'extremely ludicrous in many ways' and sadly 'too piecemeal and unorganised . . . to be a real success'.[71] But at the time, their wall-paintings appeared as 'sweet, bright and pure as a cloud in the sunrise' and 'so brilliant as to make the walls look like the margin of an illuminated manuscript'.[72]

They only took temporary lodgings for the Long Vacation, thinking that they would be finished before the undergraduates returned. They stayed opposite Queen's College, in an old building with a vegetable garden in the courtyard: it was all demolished, twenty years after, to make way for the Examination Schools. They spent their days on the scaffolding inside the brand-new Gothic Revival hall at the Union, and their nights comfortably in each other's company. Valentine Prinsep remembered a dinner with the three friends late that summer. The son of Thoby and Sarah Prinsep, Val had grown up at Little Holland House, and was invited to join in the camaraderie by Gabriel, who thought he had the makings of a painter. Val Prinsep was welcomed to their Oxford rooms by Rossetti 'in a plum-coloured frock-coat'. William, wearing spectacles, barely looked up from his book. Ned 'darted forward, the shy face lit up' and greeted him warmly. Prinsep wrote: 'When dinner was over, Rossetti, humming to himself as was his wont, rose from the table, and proceeded to curl himself up on the sofa.' Then he suggested that William read some of his poems, because 'they are devilish good.'

'Very well, old chap', growled Morris . . . he began to read in a sing-song chant . . . I can still recall the scene: Rossetti on the sofa with large melancholy eyes fixed on Morris, the poet at the table reading and ever fidgeting with his watch chain, and Burne-Jones working at a pen-and-ink drawing . . . I returned to the Mitre with my brain in a whirl.[73]

Standing in the Oxford Union today, it is hard to recapture the brilliancy of those summer days of 1857. The red-brick building is now the Library, hushed and dimly lit. The paintings are barely visible as you enter the vaulted space. To see them a little better, visitors must go on a small quest: first find the stairs, tucked away behind the bookcases, and then step out on a narrow gallery high above the desks, holding tight to a delicate ironwork handrail. The scenes are above your head, painted directly on whitewashed brick, tucked awkwardly between the cusped windows. Try not to lean back too far to see the details of sunflowers and queens. These are the remnants of a bold scheme. They still 'glimmer like faded ghosts on the walls'.[74]

Gabriel and his friends had no experience of mural decoration, and the walls were damp. They had planned to create a fresco cycle, like Giotto's friezes in the Arena Chapel, Padua. (Giotto's work had recently been revealed to a new audience by Ruskin.) But instead of the life of the Virgin, or the Gospel stories, Rossetti turned to his friends' sacred text, Malory's *Morte Darthur*. He wanted to paint Launcelot's dream, with Guenevere standing between the knight and the San Grael. Ned chose the encounter between Merlin and the witch Nimue, a subject that preoccupied him for the rest of his life. And William decided to draw an episode from the sad tale of Tristram and Iseult. That still left another seven sections to complete: Val Prinsep took one, Arthur Hughes another, and John Roddam Spencer Stanhope agreed to tackle a third. John Hungerford Pollen also became involved in the project. In the early 1850s, before he converted to Roman Catholicism, he was a Fellow at Merton College, and had painted angels and saints on the ceiling and walls of the college chapel. Thanks to his success with this scheme, Gabriel announced that Pollen was 'the only man who had yet done good mural painting in England'.[75] But despite Pollen's help, the experimental Union paintings soon showed signs of fading, their colours flaking off or absorbed back into the bricks.

All that remained were the bright stories of the artists at work and play. William crashing around, his head stuck in the helmet from a suit of armour made by a local blacksmith, 'dancing with rage and roaring inside'.[76] The corks of soda water bottles flying through the air. Bear fights. Val Prinsep, the tall teenager with 'hair like finest wire', grabbing Ned, and carrying him 'under one arm up a ladder to the gallery where they painted'.[77] The anecdotes, carefully recalled and collected, are all very physical, very masculine.

One of the most telling tales was recorded by the young undergraduate Algernon Charles Swinburne. He had become enchanted by Gabriel and William's poetry, and often joined the artists when they worked late in the Union. He remembered a 'great talk' when he and Ned described their idea of Heaven as 'a rose-garden full of Stunners'. They insisted on the necessity of 'kisses in Paradise'. Their irreverence shocked 'two respectable members of the University' who 'literally fled from the room', leaving the boys in a 'mutual ecstasy of delight'.[78] William and Ned had travelled a long way from the earnest theological discussions of their student days. Then they had dreamed of a future in semi-monastic seclusion. Now, they could not imagine an afterlife without beautiful young women, desired and desiring, even in Heaven.

However, their paintings of ladies and queens, their procession of Stunners around the walls of the Union, were dreamlike figures, barely known in the flesh. William, of course, had grown up with sisters, but he and Ned had little experience as lovers. Ned was now engaged to Georgiana Macdonald, although she was still only sixteen, and came from a strict Methodist upbringing. Their relationship, in these early days, was built on youthful yearning, wishful thinking and a love of Dante's writing. It does not seem to have been a passionate courtship. She appeared in many of Ned's pictures as a small, calm figure, with large grey eyes and hair neatly brushed back from her face. She was not the model for the towering sorceress, Nimue, in Ned's mural. Nimue was a seductive fantasy, a figure of dread and excitement, not to be encountered by Ned in real life. At least, not yet.

Ned's witch was a commanding figure, drawn with conviction. William, on the other hand, was struggling with his Iseult. He had not thrived in the life drawing classes in London. And now, according to his new friend Prinsep, his Arthurian princess looked like 'an ogress'. William's inability to paint a convincing Stunner seemed to be part and parcel of his failure to charm women. The other young men working with him at the Union made fun of his 'forceful and energetic manner'.[79] He seemed very unsophisticated compared to Gabriel, or even the more worldly Val Prinsep. They encouraged him to visit an inn in Godstow, telling him that the publican's daughter would make a good model. They had presumably spotted her on an evening ramble across Port Meadow. William returned empty-handed. And found a teasing notice above his bedroom door: 'Poor Topsy has gone to make a sketch of Miss Lipscombe/ But he can't draw the head, and don't know where the hips come'.[80]

Yet again, he had fallen short in his dealings with young women. To make matters worse, his friends laughed at his appearance: he was an 'unnaturally and unnecessarily curly being', he was 'grown fat – stout – corpulent'.[81] His dreams of finding a lover – someone who would stand in for Iseult, or long for him, like one of the hauntingly beautiful ladies of his poetry – seemed more hopeless as the days passed and summer faded into autumn.

Gabriel was much more successful in approaching potential models. He was always on the look-out for girls with marvellous hair, or a stately neck. They could be found in the most unexpected places – a pub or a hat shop, or simply walking along the street. In Gabriel's mural, the sleek auburn-haired angels were modelled on his beloved, the poet and artist Elizabeth Siddall who, so the story goes, was working in a milliner's before she joined the Pre-Raphaelite circle.

Gabriel's figure of Guenevere looked very different. She was long-limbed and slender like Lizzie. But her features were bolder, her nose and chin more strongly defined. And her hair was extraordinary – very dark, with thick waves restrained into a rippling texture. Gabriel had spotted her in the audience at the theatre. He liked her unfashionable beauty, the heavy eyebrows and full mouth. Guenevere's real name was Jane Burden. She was seventeen.

Chapter 4

Oxford, 1857–1859

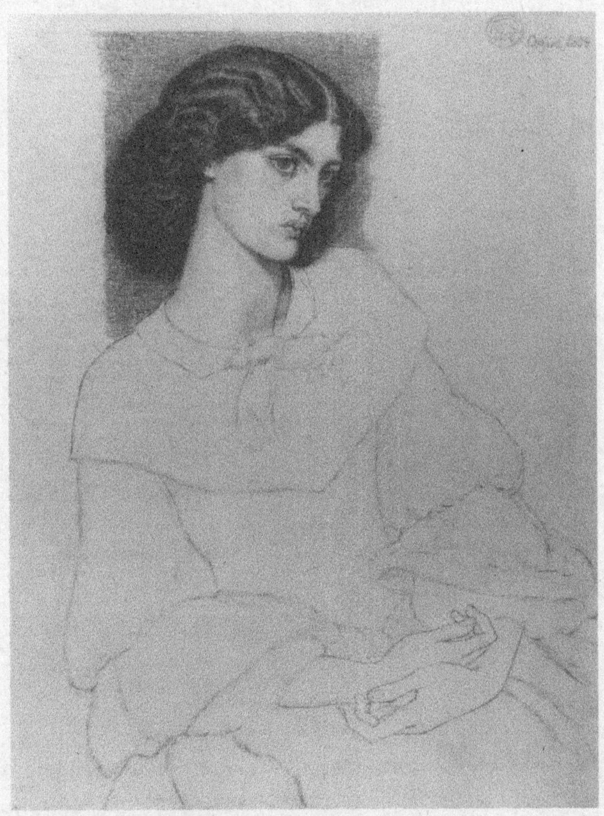

Dante Gabriel Rossetti, *Portrait of Jane Burden, age 18*, 1858,
National Gallery of Ireland

Jane and Bessie emerged on Oriel Street, glad to escape the press of people in the crowded theatre.[1] It was a warm night, with the evening light just fading as they adjusted their bonnets and smoothed their skirts. They had felt cramped and unsettled inside: the young men sitting below them had been unusually persistent. They were making comments about the girls' appearance, offering them little paper packets of nuts, trying to get the sisters to talk. This was the price the girls had to pay for enjoying a night out together. Jane and Bessie were used to fending off pestering undergraduates and loud-mouthed fellows in the street. They did not rise to the provocation, but kept their eyes down and their mouths shut. It was not Jane's fault that she attracted attention: she was so tall, with such a mass of hair. She looked remarkable, outlandish even, as she walked past the Radcliffe Camera, sharing a joke with her younger sister. She was visible, whether she liked it or not.

Bessie nudged her. Two of those young men from the theatre were following the girls, trying to catch up. They were insistent, wanting to talk to Jane, spinning some tale about being artists and asking her to model for them. They would not take no for an answer. They followed Jane and Bessie around the corner by the pub and into

Holywell Street. The girls stopped. They could see the narrow entrance to Brooks' Yard a little further down. Almost home. The young men kept saying that they were professional artists, working in the Debating Hall of the Union. Jane listened, reluctantly, and quietly agreed to sit for them. She had no intention of turning up at their lodgings tomorrow. But it was the only way to get them to leave her and her sister alone. They did not seem quite like gentlemen. The older one looked rather louche in his plum velvet coat and whiskers, and the other, thin and pale, trailed a little in his wake. Jane was relieved when they nodded goodbye and strolled off towards Longwall Street. She and Bessie ducked into the unlit passage and let themselves into their cottage.

*

Was Jane flattered by the approach of the two London artists? On that first encounter, it seems unlikely. As a working-class girl, aged only seventeen, she was aware of the fine line between respectability and disgrace, the precarious position she occupied. She and Bessie enjoyed the freedom to go to into the crush of the theatre unchaperoned, and to walk home together. They had more independence than wealthier young women, as they navigated their way around the city. But this left them open to the nuisance of men who stared too hard, stood too close. They overheard the rowdy conversations of their older brother, William, and his friends. Oxford, like any city, had its streetwalkers and kept women. Jane would have been wary of the girls who were gossiped about, who were 'fast'. There were neighbours who had tarnished their reputations, who could no longer get good references for work. Jane would not risk her own prospects by visiting these young men in their rented rooms. What would they expect her to do?

Jane and her parents had seen pictures in the illustrated newspapers, showing the great galleries of the Art Treasures Exhibition that opened in Manchester that May. They looked like enormous glasshouses, filled with long rows of naked statues facing each other. Ladies and gentlemen were admiring the carved marble flesh. Many of the finest paintings, according to the newspaper critics, showed semi-draped women cavorting, weeping, dying, admiring themselves in mirrors. Closer to home, Jane had caught glimpses of startled nudes and 'artistic studies' displayed in the windows of booksellers catering for the University men. Modelling meant undressing for money. Jane could not possibly consider doing that. Her upbringing was poor. She was not sheltered from the realities of making a living, but her family were managing; there was enough money for the girls to buy cheap theatre tickets from time to time. Jane, Bessie and their brother had all been to school, at least until they turned twelve. They were respectable enough, with her father and William having regular work.

Jane must have been working herself in the summer of 1857, but we can only guess at her job – as a college servant, a shop girl, or a laundress. There is very little we do know for certain about her early life. It only comes into focus after that night when she was proposi-tioned by the artists. We can try, perhaps, to build up a picture of her world from scraps of information she dropped later, or from what we can discover about her background: where she lived, the sights and sounds of the city, the events happening around her.

*

What do we know for sure? Jane was born on 19 October 1839 in St Helen's Passage, a tiny cut-through between Holywell Street and New College Lane. She was baptised in the little church of St Peter-in-the-East in the blank days between Christmas and New Year 1840, more than a year after her birth. Maybe she was a sickly child (although parents often hastened christenings, in case the baby died). Maybe her family were not bothered about church attendance. Certainly, as an adult, Jane was not conventionally religious. Unlike Georgie Burne-Jones, for example, faith was never the bedrock of her character. Her education was rather scrappy, too. Schooling for all young children was not compulsory until the 1870, so Jane probably learnt to read and count in a school set up by a local charity or church.[2]

Her own mother, born Ann Maizey, was illiterate. She could not write her own name when she married Robert Burden in 1833. It seems that there was no one to teach her in Alvescot, the little Oxfordshire village where she grew up. Like many young agricultural workers, she had left the land and come into town looking for work. She wanted a life that was less exposed, less hand-to-mouth.

Ann's son-in-law William Morris came to idealise the seasonal, rooted way of living that was destroyed by industry and urbanisation. But he overlooked the ignorance, the cold, the damp, the harsh grind that Ann Maizey and her generation had wanted to escape. How keenly did Jane feel this dissonance between her family's familiarity with rural poverty, and her husband's nostalgia for a pre-industrial idyll?

The gap between Jane's experience, and that of her mother, later became almost insurmountable. Jane, through her marriage, was surrounded by writers. She became steeped in the literary worlds of romance and legend. And then she was exposed to the fiery political tracts of radical thinkers. This was a way of living, creating, interacting that was unthinkable for her parents. It is perhaps Jane's greatest achievement that she was born into a home where her mother could barely read or write, and yet she transcended these limitations magnificently. Jane grew into a woman who could converse with poets, who learnt to read Dante in Italian, and taught her own bright daughters.

Georgie Burne-Jones, in her retelling of Jane's story, wondered why she had not met William or his friends 'during the time he was at College'. Jane was, after all, a beauty 'of so rare and distinguished a type' that it seemed strange that their paths had not crossed sooner.[3] Georgie of course knew the answer. But she glossed over the great social gulf between the Burdens and William's undergraduate set. Exeter College was a five-minute walk away from Jane's home. They could have passed each other on Broad Street or outside the Bodleian Library many times. However, their everyday lives were very different. For one thing, Jane was five years younger than William; she was only sixteen when William finished his studies. It is also worth remembering that during his time at Exeter College, he was writing, not drawing. He did not need flesh-and-blood models for his imagined heroines. William's circle then gravitated towards a different part of the city. They spent much of their time with friends in Pembroke College, to the south of Carfax, the crossroads at the very centre of town, or they walked west across Port Meadow to the river.

Jane moved through other quarters of the city, seeing it from her own angle. She and her family had changed lodgings several times in her short life, but always within the same limited area. Her home now was wedged in Brooks' Yard behind 65 Holywell Street. For a few years, they had lived on the other side of the road in King's Head Passage, down a tight entry beside a pub. When she was little, their home had been in Brazier's Yard, in a row of buildings backing onto 23 Holywell Street. Her childhood was unsettled, punctuated by these moves. They never shifted more than a hundred yards or so. And they always lived in the crowded courtyards hidden behind the elegant Georgian façades of Holywell Street.[4]

A short walk to the north brought Jane to open ground. Beyond Wadham College were meadows and grazing land for sheep and cattle, but these were gradually enclosed and landscaped, to become the University Parks in the early 1850s. From the other end of the street, she could reach Holywell church and the watermill, and then open fields. She sometimes walked across Magdalen Bridge to the woods beyond the Iffley Road, and came home with handfuls of violets.[5] As a girl, these were her breathing spaces, away from the cottage, where she was hemmed in on all sides.

Why did they live in such tucked-away places? The Burdens were poor, and it is likely that their lodgings were connected to her father's job. Many of their neighbours in St Helen's Passage were college servants, or their dependants – a porter from Brasenose College lived there, next to a laundress and a gardener's widow. In the houses around them were carpenters, seamstresses and college cooks. When they moved up the road, they lived among charwomen, manglewomen and labourers. Jane's father was listed on his marriage certificate and in the 1861 census as an ostler or groom. He may have worked in the livery stables at Number 7 or Number 14 Holywell Street. We can still see the great wooden gates that once opened onto the busy yards, where Burden and the other men prepared the horses for their exercise. Or he could have been employed in the stables attached to New College. Perhaps if William Morris and his friends had been keen on hunting, and kept horses in town, they might have seen Jane sooner. As it was, she went unremarked, as she stopped by the stables to bring her father his dinner. The barns and coach houses at New College were cleared in the 1870s to make way for the expansion of the college accommodation. The whole area around Jane's home was transformed then, with much of the medieval layout swept away. The stables had been built in the ancient moat, known locally as The Slype, beneath the city wall. An Ordnance Survey map of 1876 shows how the old buildings curved round the bastion, and clung to the medieval stonework. Between the stables and Holywell Street was a stonemason's yard and large domestic gardens, filled with fruit trees. All these were lost too, as New College extended beyond the wall, creating a new range of Gothic Revival buildings and an imposing gateway and lodge. But in Jane's childhood, her family lived and worked in a jumble of seventeenth- and eighteenth-century houses and cottages, interspersed with pubs like the King's Head and the Golden Ball (also demolished in the 1870s). Only the King's Arms and the Turf Tavern survived.

Sitting in the tiny beer garden of the Turf today, it is still possible to get a sense of the cheek-by-jowl environment in which Jane grew up. Like the college stables, the pub was built in the old moat, close against the city wall. The houses lean in, limiting the light. St Helen's Passage twists and kinks. There is little privacy. In the 1840 and '50s, the pale roughcast on the walls was blackened by smoke from the cooking ranges. Jane's mother is said to have worked as a laundress, but it is hard to imagine that she could have washed and dried linen at home – the soot and smells were inescapable. The family shared a water supply and a privy. (Some houses in this lane did not have indoor bathrooms fitted until the early 1970s.)[6]

Wet washing, noise from the pubs and workshops, dogs, children, hens, and not a breath of air: this was the scene outside Jane's front door. It was the same from St Helen's Passage to Brazier's Yard. Brooks' Yard was owned by a dairyman. So, in 1857 Jane could have woken to the clatter of metal churns and milk carts, and the smell of cows and curdling cream. Inside the cottage was no better. She would have shared a room, and probably a bed, with her sister. Space was tight. The rooms were dark. It was a struggle to keep clean, to tame her wild hair, to find money for a shawl or dress fabric. Home was stifling, especially in high summer. There were outbreaks of cholera in the Long Vacations in the early 1830s and again in 1849 and 1854. Dr Acland's map of Oxford, showing the locations of the cholera outbreaks, indicated that most cases were on the other side of the city, in the parishes of St Ebbe's and St Thomas. These were labelled as 'districts still undrained' with 'parts of the river still contaminated by sewers'.[7] However, there were several reported deaths in Holywell Street and New College Lane.

Anxieties about disease and the safety of drinking water were heightened again in 1857, when the *Illustrated London News* printed illustrations of magnified drops of water. These pictures made visible dozens of microscopic creatures, with tentacles and whiskers, that lived in streams and ponds. This was more evidence of the 'very offensive and unwholesome state' of urban waterways.[8] For Jane and her family, these worries were hard to ignore. Ill-health and early death had come close to home.

Jane had watched her big sister Mary Anne die of tuberculosis in 1849. Mary Anne was only fourteen when she succumbed to 'consumption'.[9] There was nothing that Ann Burden could do, as her young daughter began to lose weight, to cough blood. They tried to ease her night fevers. But the disease was deadly, untreatable and easily spread. We can imagine Jane, at nine years old, scared for her older sister, and trying to keep little Bessie out from under her mother's feet. Jane was all too aware of the fears about paying the doctor's bills, the waiting, the struggles to make sure there was a meal on the table when the men came home from work. William, her brother, was only twelve but would also have been out working also as a messenger boy. It was Jane's job to run errands, or fetch groceries from the covered market.

Her father had an unpredictable temper. We know that in 1837, before Jane was born, he had been fined for assaulting a neighbour. It must have been more than just an exchange of sharp words, because the woman had reported him to the police. This was part of the background noise of her early life: Jane and her mother had to keep her father in good humour as they faced the difficulties of looking after a sick child, and trying to manage a household on a very small income. From a young age, Jane was learning how to cook, clean, sew, budget, shop, care for her sister, dodge her father, and make herself useful. It would have been hard to fit in schoolwork and friendships too. But she said later that she always loved to read. She craved stories and news from the wider world.

As Jane wrote in the 1870s, 'I still keep up my old habit of reading every scrap that comes my way.'[10] In the very few memories she shared of her childhood, there are these hints, these quick glances beyond her immediate poverty. She remembered standing on Hythe Bridge, overlooking the canal, and watching the boats casting off and leaving the city behind. She told Crom Price how 'I always thought when I was a little girl in Oxford how much I should enjoy a voyage on one of those barges . . . but it seemed like a dream I should never be able to realise.' In 1879, when she wrote this letter, they were planning an excursion along the river, and at last, 'the thing is within one's grasp.' She added, 'Crom, it must be a barge but not a very coaly one.'[11] This comment seems to sum Jane up – her hope and imagination tempered by practicalities. Like William, she knew that the 'embodiment of dreams' required a balance between the visionary and the realistic.

*

It is fitting that we first see Jane clearly at the theatre. In the summer of 1857 she emerged from the shadows of her background, and became visible as a potential artist's model. At the playhouse, Jane could immerse herself in alternative worlds, experience transformations and sudden revelations. The actresses of the Drury Lane Theatre Company on stage that night could choose how to present themselves to the audience. They could dress up, rearrange their hair, alter their posture, modulate their voice, step into the light. They could be a peasant or a princess. For a working-class girl like Jane, the theatre was full of possibilities.

The story of Jane's 'discovery' has been retold and romanticised many times. She is treated like a blank space, a nobody, as if she only became a fully formed person after she moved into the orbit of the artists. Very few people have tried to see the meeting from her perspective. Jane was already working, probably in domestic service, possibly for a college. She was already resourceful and imaginative. She was skilled in needlework and hungry for books. Yes, Rossetti and his friends were offering Jane the chance to try something new, to earn a bit of extra money. But at what cost? By scooping her up, they were asking her, in the first place, to risk her regular job. Maybe her employers would not want a model in their household, doing their cleaning, mending their laundry. Jane might upset the other servants with her fancy tales of artists' studios and what went on there. And, by drawing Jane into their circle, the artists were uprooting her from her family and neighbours. She no longer fitted into the fabric of her home. Was she embarrassed by her parents? Were they self-conscious, ashamed of their poverty and limited horizons? Or was there a row? Did her family assume the worst, and accuse her of loose morals, shameful behaviour? There is no record of Jane going home again after she married – not even to visit her mother in her last illness. She stayed close to her sister Bessie; this was the only connection she kept up. Jane does not seem to have faltered or looked back over her shoulder. She took this decisive step to change the direction of her life. But her new job, and the possibilities it offered, left her out of place.

How did it happen, this dislocation? In all likelihood, William and Ned had seen Jane before in town. But they had not looked closely at her, because she was in working clothes and wearing a bonnet. She would have been moving purposefully through the streets, clearly from another class, and nothing to do with the young men. This all changed on the night she went to the play. On that warm evening, she would have dressed more carefully. If she could afford it, she would have worn a lighter-coloured bodice and skirt, wrapped a more delicate shawl around her shoulders. Most importantly, she removed her bonnet inside the theatre. The artists sitting close at hand saw her fully for the first time. They could study her face. When she was out and about, Jane's bonnet would have hidden her hair, and passers-by would have struggled to catch a glimpse of her expression beneath the brim. But in the theatre, she was exposed.

Gabriel Rossetti was more assertive than his friends. He took pleasure in waylaying young working-class women. Ned described how he would follow Gabriel around the streets of London late at night, often after they had been to the theatre, and then go back 'to Gabriel's rooms, and sit until three or four in the morning, reading and talking'.[12] As middle-class men, they were free to roam the city at all hours. But for Jane and her sister, there was no such ease. Their presence at the theatre, and then their unchaperoned walk home, left them open to unwelcome attention. It was Gabriel who had noticed Jane's thick, dark hair and her strong face. He was struck by her tall figure and expressive hands. It was his idea to pursue Jane, to flatter her and to suggest that she would make the perfect Queen Guenevere for his mural design. He was pleased when she finally agreed to sit for him.

The following day, Gabriel and Ned waited in, drawing and chatting, expecting Jane to appear. She did not come. Instead, she went to her usual job and carried on with her chores at home. She thought the young men would forget about her. It was just a lark to them. But Gabriel had not forgotten. His designs for the mural were not strong enough. And he hoped that Jane's features and supple figure would make the composition more compelling. He fretted that Jane had not kept her promise to work with him. In the end, it was Ned who knocked at her front door. He had retraced their steps along Holywell Street, and asked some of the lads working there if they knew the sisters. They pointed to the narrow entrance of Brooks' Yard.

Ned saw the squalor surrounding Jane's home. He felt the oppression of the low ceilings and sparse furnishings of her living room as he stepped inside. He had grown up in the grimy city atmosphere of Birmingham. As a child, his own family sometimes struggled for money. His father's business was never a success. But they hung on to the very edges of respectability. Ned Jones was middle class – just. His upbringing was pinched, but his father always employed a servant. Ned grew up in a 'little house' which was 'destitute . . . of any visible thing that could appeal to the imagination; chairs, carpets, tables and table furniture each duller and more common-place than the rest'. Compared to William's spacious family homes, Ned had felt his background was very down-at-heel and colourless. Most of the things in his father's house were 'actually ugly'. Only 'some pieces of old blue china ... with a Sheffield-plated teapot and cream-jug of elegant design' satisfied the eye.[13]

But here was real poverty. Jane's life was restricted to these small rooms and airless yards and passages. There was no money for education, no hope of brightening her home with beautiful things, except the flowers in a jug by the window. Her best chance was to work diligently and develop her skills in domestic service and needlework. Above all, Jane would have to marry with care. She would hope to find someone in a good trade, with room for promotion, or even the opportunity to travel. (We can imagine an alternative version of Jane's story: one in which she sets out with her new husband for Australia or Canada, resilient and optimistic, like the family in Madox Brown's *The Last of England*.) She would prefer a man who did not drink and throw his weight about: she was tired of her father and his black moods. Now she is confronted by Ned Burne-Jones, suggesting another future.

He had tracked her down and was standing on the threshold, trying to persuade Jane and her mother that he really was a serious artist. He and Gabriel *did* want to draw her. Perhaps he brought some of their sketches, perhaps he offered to take Jane to the Union to show her the progress of the murals. Ned was persuasive, and at last she agreed. We do not know if she asked her sister Bessie or her mother to act as a chaperone. But the following day, Jane walked the very short distance to 87 High Street. She crossed the little garden, climbed the stairs, and began her career as a model.

*

Jane became one of the most recognisable women of her generation. But at the same moment that she was drawn into the Victorian art world, her own family slipped away into obscurity. We know from parish records that her father was buried, at the age of fifty-six, in St Cross Holywell in February 1865. Her mother was buried there too in February 1871. She died at sixty-six years old. We know nothing of their lives in the decade after Jane left. Her brother William also disappeared from view. Only Bessie stayed close to her sister. She enjoyed her own successes as an embroiderer and teacher, finding her place in the art movements that Jane, William Morris and their friends created.

The artists' studio was a completely new environment for Jane. She may have been in undergraduates' sets, if she was cleaning or working as a laundress. But this was a different experience. Normally she would try to remain as inconspicuous as possible in young men's rooms. A servant was expected to slip in and out of spaces, eyes averted, ears closed, silent, apparently oblivious to the private lives of those she was waiting on. This was the game that they all played – employers and employees. It was the only way to live and work together in one house. Like every woman in domestic service, Jane and her mother saw the dirty washing, emptied the wastepaper baskets, overheard arguments. Yet they were expected to remain mute and invisible, and not to interfere with the lives going on around them. It was a convenient fiction. Now Jane was taking centre stage. She was being paid to be looked at. The young artists wanted to talk to her, to get her to move and to pose.

What did it feel like on that first day? We can think our way through it. Gabriel Rossetti studied her closely. He asked her to sit by the window, then to turn her head and tilt her chin. He suggested she walk slowly across their sitting room. All the while his eyes, and the eyes of his friends, were fixed on Jane. Ned tried to make her feel comfortable. He understood how daunting it felt to be scrutinised by Gabriel. William, on the other side of the room, spoke little and fidgeted with his pencils and books. He had already finished his mural at the Union. He was now working on designs for the ceiling and roof-beams. Still, he could not help looking at Jane, considering her unexpected beauty. William made one or two hesitant sketches of their new model that summer, but he felt at a loss, unable to do her justice. So he folded them up and tucked them away.

Gabriel, on the other hand, was revelling in the possibilities of Jane's challenging looks. In his mural, the figure of Jane/Guenevere was placed at the heart of the composition. He imagined Lancelot seeing a vision of the Queen in a dream. Lancelot's adulterous love for her was a barrier between the knight and the Sanc Grael. In his early drawings, Gabriel imagined Guenevere seated on the edge of a well, her hair bound in a coif, and her hands cupped around her face, as if she were fearful or pensive. With Jane as a potential Guenevere, Gabriel altered his treatment of this central figure. He wanted to show off her hair and her long lean figure. He asked Jane to sit, with her arms outstretched, as if she were balanced in the branches of a tree. She holds an apple in one hand. The drawing he made, in pencil and brown ink, shows Jane leaning slightly forward, her hair rippling down to her collar, and tucked underneath. She seems to be wearing her ordinary dress, with a modest rounded neckline and gathered skirt, the long bodice fitted over her hips. This is a difficult pose. Jane is slightly twisting and tilted forward. Gabriel was already expecting her to work hard, so that he could create complex dynamics between his figures.

Over the coming weeks, his design continued to evolve, as he discovered how adaptable Jane could be as a model. He kept the idea of the apple tree behind her. But his finished mural showed Jane standing at her full height, with her arms held out, towering over the sleeping knight (modelled by Burne-Jones). Already, Jane was a commanding presence in Gabriel's imagination.

The painting of the Union was taking much longer than the artists had anticipated. Now the Long Vacation was over, the young men had to move to new lodgings on George Street. We do not know when Jane gave up her other jobs and began modelling more regularly. Her life for the next few years is hard to reconstruct, except through the art works and occasional anecdotes recorded by William, Gabriel or their friends. But during the autumn and winter of 1857, she was spending many hours in their makeshift studio. In October, Gabriel made a large pencil portrait of Jane in three-quarter profile. He must have given it to her, or possibly he handed it over to William shortly after, because Jane kept this image of her teenaged self to the end of her life, leaving it for her daughter at Kelmscott Manor. She looks solemn, with her eyes lowered. The drawing is related to Gabriel's studies for the Union mural but stands alone as a carefully observed portrait. Gabriel has dwelt on her strong jawline and long throat, her dark eyebrows and especially the rich waves of her hair, which she has caught up at the nape of her neck, just showing her earlobes. It is not a sensual image, but thoughtful. Gabriel seems to be considering the details of Jane's peculiar attraction.

Soon after he made this drawing, Gabriel left Oxford to join Lizzie Siddall in Derbyshire. And so Jane's role changed. She was no longer modelling for his Guenevere. William had taken an interest in her and was pondering his own Arthurian subject. This was a time of professional insecurity for William, as he had given up his architectural studies and was struggling to establish himself as a painter, alongside Ned. He was diligent, and especially concerned about the Pre-Raphaelite desire for 'Truth to Nature'. His friends remembered finding him in a garden in Oxford. He was trying to paint the trees, and he had ground his chair legs deep into the turf as he wrestled with the problems of getting the leaves and branches onto his canvas. William was more emotionally volatile than usual at this time. He became so unmanageable that at one point, even his dear friend Ned Burne-Jones nearly gave up on him. Ford Madox Brown recorded, in the New Year of 1858, that 'Jones is going to cut Topsy, he says his overbearing temper is becoming quite insupportable as well as his conceite.'[14]

Many of his mood swings seem to have been triggered by his growing affection for Jane. With Gabriel away, William felt able to ask her to model for his new painting. Gabriel was charming, but unreliable as a lover. William was glad when Gabriel seemed to rekindle his long-term, on-off relationship with Lizzie Siddall. By Christmas 1857, it was clear to the friends in Oxford how attached William had become to Jane. They laughed at him for his ways of wooing. He was so brusque, very different from Gabriel's smooth talking. He entertained Jane, hour after hour, in the sitting room overlooking Martyr's Memorial by reading aloud *Barnaby Rudge*. This was Dickens's historical novel, set in the 1780s, amid the upheavals of the American Revolution and the anti-Catholic riots in London. The plot revolved around an unsolved murder, and contained the usual assortment of disguises, near-deaths and a pretty girl called Dolly. There was also Grip the raven who, Dickens claimed, was the inspiration for Poe's poem.

For Jane, these readings must have been almost as strange as her modelling. Here was a wealthy young man, wanting to share stories and spend time in her company. Dickens's tale was peculiar and wide-ranging, showing her scenes far beyond her own experience. She later told a friend that she had never been to London and never seen the sea before she met William and the other artists. William wanted to offer her new worlds – revealing his pleasure in history, and leading her through the tumultuous, sprawling life of Dickens's metropolis. He hoped to open her eyes. Inevitably, he was talking, and she was listening. No doubt she was keeping her hands busy with small sewing tasks, and he would have seen her skills: William was starting his own experiments in embroidery. 'He had a frame made from an old pattern' and was stitching a bird and tree design in fine wools dyed specially in France.[15] Above each apple tree, he sewed his new personal motto – *If I Can*, adapted from Jan Van Eyck's 'Als ich kanne'. It was a promise to himself to pursue his art, in whatever form it might take, while keeping the medieval in mind. Did he explain his plans to Jane? Did she show him what she knew about handling textiles?

William and Jane were an odd pair. He was over-active, loud and bustling. William seemed bewildered by her appearance – not just her beauty but her poise and quietness. From our perspective, it makes sense for Jane to keep silent. She was learning her new trade as a useful model. But she was also hearing poetry and legends brought to life and fervently discussed. For a girl who hungered for every scrap of writing, every glimpse of imagined worlds, these weeks must have been a revelation. She was seeing paintings evolve, with her own face as the centrepiece. It was a time to absorb as much of these words and images as possible. Who knew how long it would last? Jane would also have been self-conscious about her lack of education. And her accent. When she spoke, Jane must have sounded different – her parents' rural Oxfordshire voices overlaid with modern phrases and tones picked up in town.

William's friends made fun of his fascination with this working-class girl, and he retaliated with wild energy. Crom Price wrote in December 1857 that 'Topsy raves and swares like or more than any Oxford bargee about a "stunner" he has seen.'[16] His boisterous language was not unusual. Algernon Swinburne was rather taken by William's manner: 'He swears awfully', Swinburne explained to a friend enthusiastically, 'and walks with a rolling gait as if partially intoxicated.'[17] Still, William's stormy behaviour intensified when Jane – and her various attributes – became the topic of male conversation over dinner. On one occasion, Val Prinsep gave his opinion of Jane, and 'everybody expected an outburst of fury. But by a prodigious effort of self-control Morris swallowed his anger, and only bit his fork . . . which was crushed and twisted about almost beyond recognition.'[18]

One of the difficulties of writing about this period in Jane's life is that all we can hear is the teasing that William experienced: we get very little sense of William's own feelings (apart from frustration), or of Jane's reaction to his affection. Did her parents encourage her new friendships? What about her neighbours? Presumably she was also getting provocative remarks about her work, sidelong glances and questions about how she spent her time in the studio. William's friends stressed Jane's aloofness. They made jokes about how she kept herself at arm's length, no doubt because she was worried about getting entangled in a short-lived romance that would leave her compromised and unable to work again. Swinburne seemed shocked that William would consider an alternative ending: William should be 'content with that perfect stunner of his – to look at or speak to. The idea of marrying her is insane. To kiss her feet is the utmost men should dream of doing.'[19]

*

Neither Jane nor William ever spoke out about why they married – or at least, their reasons for marrying were never recorded. Perhaps, in William's case, he was moved to marry her by a sense of chivalry. After all, he was steeped in stories of Courtly Love overcoming all obstacles, of gallant rescues and beautiful women saved from distress. William wanted to protect Jane from the taunts of their friends. He could understand the difficulties that her association with the artists had caused her at home. He wanted to do the decent thing, and not leave her stranded once he returned to London. But it was more than that. He certainly saw her potential as an equal partner in his plans to make art and poetry. This relationship was not just a headlong infatuation on William's part, although, clearly, he was deeply struck by her. This seems to have been William's first serious love affair; there is no evidence that he had ever been involved with any other woman before – not his sisters' friends, nor the models or hangers-on that came and went in Gabriel's rooms or Red Lion Square. Yet William saw beyond the immediate attraction of Jane's face and figure. He recognised that she was quick spirited, eager to learn, and willing to strike out into a new world, away from the narrow streets and yards around New College. Maybe he saw that she was also restless. He admired her practicality and lack of primness.

It is easier to explain why Jane would marry him. This was the best opportunity she would ever be offered. With William, she would no longer have the constant drip-drip of worries about money or how she was going to afford a decent pair of boots, or make her living now she was grown up. Jane's anxiety, the exhaustion of being poor, was made worse by a lifetime of inadequate food and damp bedrooms. This would all evaporate. She may not have been aware that William was considerably richer than Ned or Gabriel; the men were living a bachelor life, without luxuries of dining and fine lodgings, and William did not like to make a show of his money. But Jane would be looked after. She could travel, at least as far as London. William would give her security. And, as his wife, she would also be part of the larger network of his friends.

Jane enjoyed the company and openness of the artists, writers, thinkers that she had met while modelling. Their time working on the Oxford murals was remembered by the young men as a 'jovial campaign', and she had delighted in this ease and jollity, too. Yes, she was aware that they talked about her, criticising her looks, her 'exotic' colouring and her guarded manner, but this was no worse than the comments she overheard in the street or on the pub doorstep. To enter this world, not as a disposable employee, but as a wife, was an extraordinary opportunity. It was still daunting. Jane must have thought about the challenges. She would be leaving the only city she had ever known. She would have to learn how to present herself like a leisured woman. This would not be an easy task, if she was going to 'pass' among William's friends and family. But she was already learning how to move, how to chat about novels or pictures, how to adapt her manner and language to more polite society.

In the early spring of 1858, about six months after they met, Jane accepted William's proposal of marriage. Gabriel drew a swift sketch to commemorate the moment. Although it was made after the event, Gabriel captured William's urgent expression, his curls almost bouncing off his head as he leans forward and grips the edge of the table. He looks hard at Jane, trying to fathom her feelings. She lowers her eyes but seems to be smiling down at the new ring on her finger. It is hard to imagine how she could have refused him. She had no prior attachment that we know of. Jane is said to have admitted, many years later, that she had never loved her husband, although William himself married for love. But the poet Wilfrid Scawen Blunt, who recorded this remark, had his own reasons to downplay Jane's affection for her husband.[20] Jane probably made the decision to marry with her head, rather than her heart. But we should not criticise her for that. Many Victorian women married in the hope that love would come after, with children and shared lives. This was not unusual.

Jane may also have been reassured that she was not the only working-class woman to have joined Morris's artistic circle. Each of the couples chose their own path, negotiating the awkwardness of their position in the ways that suited them best. There was no clear-cut right or wrong way for Jane to behave; she could create her own new reality.

Ford Madox Brown's second wife Emma had also been a teenage model when she began her more intimate relationship with the artist. Blonde and robust, Emma came from a poor background – her father had been a bricklayer, and her mother was now widowed and in need. However, unlike Jane, Emma carried her more informal housekeeping and language into the marriage. She also had a problem with alcohol and could be unreliable with money. She did not marry Brown until April 1853, two and a half years after their first child, Catherine, was born. As far as we know, she never consciously changed her behaviour to conform with middle-class expectations. Even so, on good days, Emma's hearty hospitality was well loved by the young artists, and the rowdy dinners at the Browns' were remembered fondly.

Then there was Annie Miller, who was supposed to marry William Holman Hunt. She was a young barmaid when she started modelling for him. Like Jane, she had a wonderful mass of hair – corn gold, in contrast to Jane's rich black. By 1854, she was engaged to Hunt. He was keen for her to drop her working-class speech and manner, and Annie initially agreed to be educated into respectability. But when in 1854 Hunt left for the Holy Land to paint Biblical scenes with Pre-Raphaelite authenticity, she rebelled. Annie was too outspoken; she enjoyed her independence as a young working woman and was unwilling to be squeezed into a different pattern just for his benefit.

For other models, like Elizabeth Siddall, it seemed impossible to escape the gravitational pull of Rossetti and his friends. Lizzie Siddall was eager to learn. That is why she was willing to enter Gabriel's studio as a model; she hoped to gain experience as an artist in her own right, by watching, sharing materials and ideas, even exhibiting alongside Gabriel and the other Pre-Raphaelites. Throughout her career, she spent time away from London – in the South of France, in Derbyshire and Sheffield – in an attempt to find her own voice. Creativity was an essential part of Lizzie Siddall's character. Even when she was ill, she asked for her paintbox to be posted to her so that she could keep working on her watercolours.

For Lizzie Siddall, there was always tension. She wanted to be productive and self-reliant. Her writing and painting made her feel alive. But the doctors declared that her chronic ill-health was caused by her work: Lizzie suffered because her 'mental power' was 'long pent up and overtaxed' and she was advised to be 'absolutely idle'.[21] John Ruskin, who admired her pictures, called her 'wilful' and 'sickly headstrong' for pressing ahead with her own designs.[22] He treated

Lizzie like a lovely object to be preserved, rather than a living woman. He said he was looking after her, as 'I should try to save a beautiful tree from being cut down, or a bit of Gothic cathedral whose strength was failing'.[23] In 1855, Ruskin encouraged her to visit his friend Dr Henry Acland in Oxford, and recuperate under his care. It is worth pausing to consider how both Lizzie and Jane were treated by the men who hoped to 'improve' them.

*

After Jane and William became officially betrothed, we almost lose sight of her again for a year. By the time she emerges as William's bride, she is ready to be presented to his family and friends as a beautiful, slightly shy young woman. This is perhaps the most frustrating of all the gaps in her story: it was the turning-point of her life, the metamorphic moment, and it would be wonderful to see how she made it happen. How did she become so accomplished, so queenly, so capable of fulfilling the role as a middle-class wife, mother and hostess? To achieve her poise, she must have been coached. It seems likely that Jane and William agreed that she would be taken into the home of one of his friends, to be taught all she needed to know about her new role in society.

Various families have been suggested, from the architect G. E. Street to Ned's early patron, Archibald Maclaren. There is a hint that Sara Prinsep, Valentine's mother, might have guided Jane in these early months. In Mackail's notes we find the briefest reference: 'Prinseps kind in taking J up'.[24] That is all. The information seems to have come from Burne-Jones, who knew Valentine's family well. He was also a guest in their artistic home at Little Holland House. If Jane really did spend part of her transformative year with Sara Prinsep and her sisters, then this would have been an extraordinary setting to learn how to run a household, how to dress. The atmosphere at Little Holland House was welcoming, with an easy informality. It was a home filled with poets, painters and beautiful women. Sara Prinsep moved among her guests in the garden, or presided over dinners, wrapped in her glorious Indian shawls and long strings of beads. Had she been a visitor there, Jane could have learnt a great deal about unconventional artistic lifestyles.

It is most likely, though, that she stayed in Oxford. Perhaps Philip Webb's mother and aunt took her in to their tall house on Beaumont Street; a couple of Philip's younger siblings were still living there, too. This might account for Jane's close friendship with Philip, which lasted until her death. Of all William's friends, Webb seemed to understand her best. He sympathised with her reluctance to talk about her early life, perhaps because he understood how hard she worked to transcend the limitations of her upbringing.

It is also possible that Jane, like Elizabeth Siddall, was hosted by Dr Henry Acland and his wife Sarah. During Lizzie's convalescence with the Aclands, the family tried to 'introduce her into all the best society. All the women there are tremendously fond of her.'[25] Lizzie became a great favourite with a sister of Dr Pusey, and the Warden of New College offered to show her some rare manuscripts in the Bodleian Library. Lizzie did not enjoy being the centre of attention, and Mrs Acland complained to Ruskin that her guest seemed rather ungrateful. We do not know what Jane would have felt were she put in a similar position, to be treated like a pet, or a schoolgirl. It must have been difficult for any self-sufficient young woman.

Sarah Acland ran a far larger establishment than Elizabeth Speakman Webb, so the Aclands' might have been a better house in which Jane could learn her new skills, even if it came at a price. In 1858, Mrs Acland was responsible for the domestic comfort of four children, plus nine servants. These included a governess, nurse, cook, page and schoolroom maid.[26] Jane evidently had to stay with someone who had the space and time to devote to her education, and the inclination to bring her up to scratch socially. Mrs Acland had already shown that she was prepared to take in the Pre-Raphaelites' protégées, so it seems most probable that Jane joined her household in the spring of 1858.

While she was there, Jane was prepared for her new life. We can only infer her course of study from later descriptions of her self-presentation. Certainly, she must have had elocution lessons, so that she would lose her provincial, working-class accent. After her marriage, Jane was never criticised or mocked for using the wrong turn of phrase or a 'common' tone. She would also have been encouraged to read widely and learn to engage in polite conversation. Jane was already schooled in how to stand, sit and move, thanks to her modelling work. Now she could turn her attention to other ladylike pastimes, including music and languages.

We know that before her marriage, Jane was learning to sing and play the piano. William gave her a copy of his favourite traditional songs for her birthday in October 1858, in a two-volume edition of Chappell's *Popular Music of the Olden Time*. And certainly, in later life, she wrote to friends about her music-making on the mandolin. Training at the piano in particular was regarded as eminently lady-like. It was a way to fill the hours while the men of the house were working, and enabled a wife to entertain her husband in the evening. The piano developed the feminine attributes of dexterity and lightness of touch, which were also aligned with needlework. Alongside her musical studies, it seems that Jane learnt some French and German. In her surviving letters, we know that she was keen to discuss the works of Goethe. And her little manuscript books, made in the 1880s, included extracts in old French and Latin. Later, Jane also tried to learn Italian, writing to Gabriel about his sister Christina's translations, and asking to borrow a copy of Dante in the original. She was constantly pushing herself to overcome the narrowness of her schooling. Jane was unafraid of developing new skills, and confident that she could grow, not just during the year of her engagement, but throughout her life.

Although it was desirable that a young wife should be able to play and sing, and read modern languages, the real test would come when she needed to run a household of her own. Jane would be in charge of the housekeeping budget. She would also recruit and supervise her domestic servants. There were always potential tensions between mistress and cook, but in Jane's case, there would be the added awkwardness of her own background – would they see through her? Would Jane be able to maintain her position of authority, and set the appropriate boundaries between herself and her servants? There were various ways for Jane to learn the art of running her own establishment. She would have begun by shadowing her hostess: watching her discuss grocery orders and menu plans with her kitchen staff; sitting beside her as she wrote letters to friends, acquaintances and tradespeople; following in her wake as she paid morning visits or attended dinners; checking that the maids completed their work at the correct time of day. These were all tasks that had to be done firmly and tactfully, to keep a large house in order.

Jane could also take advantage of a new style of magazine, designed for young women like herself, who were unprepared for life as a middle-class wife. Perhaps they too had 'married up'. Or maybe they had moved from the country to the city, and could not rely on old friends or relatives for advice. Or they simply needed reassurance in the increasingly commercialised domestic world. Jane and her contemporaries could have looked to publications like *The Englishwoman's Domestic Magazine* for help in navigating the complexities of their daily lives. This magazine was founded in 1852 by Samuel Beeton, and in 1856 his wife Isabella became joint editor. At 2d a month, it was an inexpensive and effective resource for young women like Jane, who would be expected to nurse, clothe and feed their families. There was advice about cleaning a cut or curing a burn, with simple recipes, including one for 'A Good Cough Mixture': take half a pound of treacle, half a pint of vinegar and half an ounce of laudanum.[27]

Many of the instructions suggested that the wife would assist with the cooking, or would be working in the kitchen with a young or inexperienced servant. They include numerous ways to create a pudding using suet, breadcrumbs and dried fruit. And suggestions for dealing with gluts of garden produce – apples, vegetable marrows and especially rhubarb. There are nearly a dozen recipes for rhubarb wine, including one which promises to be 'equal to Champagne'.[28] These household hints and 'Things Worth Knowing' were tucked in between the longer essays, which gave readers a brief education in the arts or current political debates. In 1858, the articles ranged from 'The New Divorce Bill' to historical costume, a synopsis of a popular opera, 'London Prisons and Female Prisoners', 'Manners and Domestic Arrangements in Lapland' and 'The Mormons or Latter-day Saints'. There was a thorough and positive review of the recent exhibition by 'The Society of Female Artists', and, inevitably, a note on the 'Qualities of Rhubarb'.

The bulk of the magazine was devoted to serialised fiction. Much of it was light historical romance, but Beeton also reprinted significant contemporary works, like Hawthorne's *The Scarlet Letter*, published in the USA in 1850. As the plot revolves around the fate of an unmarried mother and her daughter Pearl, it was not a prim or safe choice. But the Beetons wanted to offer their young female readers new ways of looking at the world. Running through the magazine is a constant thread – the recognition that women were worth educating, that their voices should be heard, and their daily effort to maintain a healthy and happy household should be respected.

The editors also understood that readers would want to know about the latest fashions in London and Paris, but would need to make up their clothes at home, or with the help of a local dressmaker. There is, for example, an illustration and pattern for a 'Parisian Basquine'. This elaborate day dress has a three-tiered skirt, the flounces edged with a contrasting fabric. The sleeves of the bodice are also made up of three small tiers, decorated with tiny buttons, and a wide cuff, gathered to the elbow, and trimmed with velvet ribbon and fringing. The simple round-necked bodice fastens at the front (so that the wife could dress herself without help from a maid) and is finished with a narrow 'bertha' or shawl, also trimmed with fringing. The illustration and pattern implied that the reader would know how to fit, cut and construct a complex garment like this.

During the year of her engagement, Jane would have been preparing for her marriage by making and buying her new wardrobe. Presumably William gave her money for fabric, and would pay her bills with the Oxford seamstresses and milliners, as Jane had no settlement or trousseau from her family. She was learning to dress as a leisured lady, following the current fashions. Although William was never enthusiastic about dressing for dinner, as a bride Jane would expect, for the first time in her life, to have stylish evening clothes, fine undergarments and well-fitting boots.

We can see one of her day dresses in a drawing made in 1858 by Rossetti, when he returned briefly to Oxford. The bodice of this dress is a simplified version of the Parisian gown featured in *The Englishwoman's Domestic Magazine*. Jane has not added the fringing and ribbons to the edges of her bell-shaped cuffs. And she has a neat collar and wide ribbon tie at her throat, rather than the long bertha coming to a point at her waist. But her silhouette is very similar – the line of her shoulders elongated and dropped, the layered arrangement of her sleeves.

In this stunning large-scale drawing, Gabriel concentrated on the details of Jane's face and hair, and the outline of her dress and hands was pared down. With his pen, he worked intensely on the ripples of her hair and the curve of her lips. He showed the shadows at the base of her throat and at the corner of her eyes. It was probably made as a presentation piece for her wedding, but he never gave it to her: it was still in his studio when he died. Jane's expression is unreadable.

This drawing was made during a time of seismic change in Jane's life. She was preparing to let go of all her familiar surroundings, to say farewell to family. Of course, this was the experience of many women who married and moved away. But Jane was not just leaving her home city, she was expected to fit into a completely different domestic structure. William's income was £900 per year. A maid's wages, by comparison, were only £15 or £20. Jane would be joining the affluent middle classes – although as an artist's wife, she and William might choose to live on the more bohemian edges of respectable society.

It is interesting to consider how she shaped her own image, as part of this change. There are no written records of her engagement year. But, in addition to Gabriel's drawing, there are two photographs that were probably taken in 1858. They have been preserved in a Morris family album, now in the V&A Museum, together with larger, later photographs. These small pictures are the size of *cartes-de-visite*, and seem to have been taken in a commercial studio. They allow us the tiniest glance at her transformation in progress.

In the first, we see Jane full-length, enveloped in a heavy winter cloak, with a plain dark hooped skirt. She is posed in front of a painted backdrop, and stands in profile next to a conventional side table, with an unremarkable empty vase and a bust of a classical goddess squeezed into the far corner. Jane looks very young and hesitant, slightly stooping. Perhaps this was the official photograph, taken in February, that William showed to his mother when he announced his engagement at home. There is nothing here to give a clue to Jane's personality, or William's artistic intentions.

In the second photograph, which seems to have been made a little later in 1858, Jane takes charge of her self-presentation. She has learned from her modelling roles, and knows what the artists value. She shows off her hands and her neck, raises her chin and lowers her eyes. In the earlier photograph she seemed passive, reluctant. Now she is actively creating her own image. Rather than sitting demurely on the chair, she turns in the seat, so that her upper body rests against the chair back. This is a conscious pose, drawing attention to her clasped hands, the lines of her throat and strong profile. Jane is leaning into the picture. The photograph also allows us to study her dress a little more closely. She wears a summery day dress, with a very full tiered skirt. Jane has arranged a piece of lace as a collar, and fastened it with a brooch – a gift from William, maybe? The three-quarter sleeves are very wide at the cuff, gathered into a dropped shoulder, and finished with fringing and narrow lacy ribbon. We can also see the tight cuff-band of her white chemise at her wrist. The dress is made of a very finely striped fabric, but of course we can only guess at the colour.

Through these two small photographs, we can watch Jane as she begins to inhabit her new role. These images make it clear that Rossetti was not exaggerating Jane's extraordinary beauty. His 1858 drawing did reflect the real texture of her dark hair and the strength of her jawline. Growing up, she had been teased for her 'Gypsy' looks, the wild mane of her hair. Now she knew that her unusual appearance was treasured by William and his friends. He wanted to make her part of his magic circle of artists and poets. He had offered her a new life.

*

What was William doing, while Jane prepared for their wedding? His movements were erratic, and he did not leave many traces of his thoughts or hopes at this time. We think that he stayed close to Oxford for most of 1858. He was not in his lodgings in London during the summer of 'the Great Stink' when the smell from the River Thames brought the city to a standstill. He was too preoccupied to notice when Ned Burne-Jones became seriously ill, alone in Red Lion Square. Ned had to be moved to Val Prinsep's family home at Little Holland House to recover. Perhaps he talked of Jane while he was there, and piqued Sara Prinsep's interest in this beautiful girl who had caught the eye of the young artists.

We do know that William took the last of his bachelor holidays, in northern France. In August he travelled with Philip Webb and Charley Faulkner on a tour of great cathedrals, from Amiens to Beauvais and on to Paris. Then they set off in a small boat down the Seine towards Rouen, laden with three carpet bags and six bottles of wine.[29] William was often out of sorts. He lost his temper with his ink bottle, and a lock-keeper left them stranded after one of William's rages. It was an outdoors adventure, the last of its kind for many years. And it reinforced William's love of the Gothic, as he sketched buttresses and capitals, sitting in the stillness of the vaulted choirs, next to his friend Webb.

Together he and Webb started to map out a plan for the future, once William was a married man. With his inherited wealth, William could build his own house, something out of the ordinary, that incorporated their favourite elements of the medieval. On the back of William's battered copy of Murray's *Guide to France*, Webb jotted down an idea for a staircase tower. Their little boat, moored on the banks of the Seine, was the birthplace of Red House, William's 'Palace of Art'.

After several years of unrest, William was contemplating a settled life. He hoped that Jane's upbringing would mean that she was more practical and adaptable than a young woman of his own class. Together, perhaps, they could create an alternative to the rigid respectability of his family. It is less clear what William's mother made of his choice of bride. There is no record of their conversation about his engagement. In the past two years, Mrs Morris had been shocked, first by her son's resolution to give up his plans for ordination, and then by his decision to walk away from his training as an architect. We must assume that she was also surprised that he wanted to marry a very young working-class model who would bring no connections and no money to the partnership. Mrs Morris may initially have worried that they were marrying because Jane was pregnant. (No doubt, other friends and relations whispered about this, too.) But William's reassurance that there would be a year-long engagement, to allow Jane to prepare for her new position, laid that fear to rest. In due course, Jane became accepted as part of the Morris family. She visited William's mother and sisters, and, as far as we can tell, they never had reason to complain of her manners. Jane did not slip or give herself away.

Whether they approved of Jane or not, William was legally of age: he did not need his mother's permission to marry or to use the funds inherited from his father. He was also beginning to establish himself properly in the literary and artistic world. After his first forays into publishing with *The Oxford and Cambridge Magazine*, William had gathered together a full volume of his original verse. It was published in March 1858 by Bell and Dalby as *The Defence of Guenevere, and Other Poems*. He dedicated the collection 'To my friend, Dante Gabriel Rossetti, painter'. And he presented copies to other key figures in his circle, including one inscribed to 'John Ruskin from his friend the author'. A few of the poems, like 'The Chapel in Lyoness', had been published in the magazine. But most of the others had only been heard by his closest companions, as the 'grinds' he read aloud after dinner. There was no great fanfare around the publication, and sales of the two hundred copies were slow. But William was delighted when the poems were positively reviewed. Jane remembered how he 'came to her one day in a great excitement, waving the paper', overjoyed that at least one critic had recognised that his chivalric verses were 'not mere fantasy' but 'a living insight into the thought and heart' of the past.[30]

The first group of verses, including the title poem, were reworkings of the same Arthurian subjects that the young men had wrestled with on the walls of the Oxford Union. William cut across Malory's text, writing from unexpected points of view. The results are keen and bold, filled with primary colours, the sound of birdsong, the glint of metal. The other poems were also set in a Gothic world. But there is no sense of distance between then and now. The textures and tones are immediate, visceral, filled with raw images of harsh weather and vivid desire. William imagined the weariness of waiting, and the fear of sudden death.

'The Defence of Guenevere' itself hurtles the reader straight into the heart of the Queen's trial for adultery, beginning in mid-sentence:

> But, knowing now that they would have her speak,
> She threw her wet hair backward from her brow[31]

The verse is often inelegant, but filled with life – we feel the irresistible pull of Lancelot's body when she encounters him unexpectedly in the spring garden. We find ourselves face to face with William's ideal queenly woman, as she reminds the knights of her glorious, almost hypnotic beauty:

> See through my long throat how the words go up
> In ripples to my mouth;
> . . .
> And wonder how the light is falling so
> Within my moving tresses[32]

Guenevere's face and body are her defence. Her hair, her throat, her breast, her brow vouch for her. We do not know if William had seen Jane before he created this vision of female power and sensuality. So, it is hard to know if he became enamoured of her because she seemed to embody the qualities of his ideal, noble woman, or if the poem was a response to her physical presence.

In all of these poems, however, love is a struggle. There are no straightforward courtships. Instead, the thirty poems in the collection present romance as thwarted, violent or illicit. In 'The Haystacks in the Flood', the young woman, cold and muddied, watches as her lover is executed, and knows that she will be drowned as a witch, or raped by his enemy. The opening lines, 'Had she come all the way for this/ To part at last without a kiss?', make it clear that there will be no happy ending.

Even with the ballad 'In Praise of My Lady', which can be read as a portrait of Jane, there is a melancholy thread running through the work. Again, William itemises his lady's features. She has Jane's extraordinary hair, 'thick and crisped wonderfully'. It looks as if it were forged 'of some strange metal, thread by thread'. And Jane's 'great eyes, standing far apart'.[33] There is no peace in this relationship, no pleasure between the knight and his lady. The knight feels that he will 'choke and grow quite faint' in her presence. He can barely speak. He wonders who she is longing for.

Should we read these insecurities as autobiographical? Was William worried about Jane's love for him? Is there already a foreshadowing of her divided affection, with Gabriel Rossetti as Lancelot to her Guenevere? William and Ned were both aware of their friend's seductive manner, and his delight in Jane as a new type of model. It is possible that Gabriel deliberately tried to undermine William's confidence by continuing to work with Jane, perhaps to flirt with her. William had often been teased by Gabriel, and this might have intensified because of Gabriel's own unhappy love affair with Lizzie Siddall. He was jealous that William had found a beautiful, capable bride. But we should not stretch the evidence to suggest that Jane was already romantically attached to Gabriel before her marriage. In this whirlwind year, it seems more likely that she was glad of William's promise of security. And the tensions, the sorrowful themes of his verses could simply be a reflection of his medieval sources, rather than his own fears.

He showed his devotion to her, not just in his poetry, but in his paintings, too. William was determined to make Jane the heroine of his own Arthurian picture, as *La Belle Iseult*, yearning for her beloved Tristan. He had always struggled with drawing the figure. There is a heavily worked pen and wash study of Jane's head which he made in the first months that he knew her. The paper has been folded in half, with a crease running through her eye, but we shall never know if this was because William carried it with him when he was not in Oxford. Or perhaps he was not happy with the result, and folded it to hide his dissatisfaction. He must have concentrated long and hard on Jane's face, but this drawing shows that he simply did not have the same facility as Gabriel. We can recognise Jane's features, but there is none of the clarity of outline, or the delightful details of texture and shadow that we see in Rossetti's portraits. William was deeply frustrated that his friend could do this, and he could not.

There is a story, possibly apocryphal, that William worked himself up into a rage because of his failure to bring Jane to life on the canvas. He is said to have scrawled 'I cannot paint you, but I love you' on the back of *La Belle Iseult*. Even if it is not quite true, the legend sums up William's character as a lover. He wanted to rival the sensitive portraits made of their 'stunners' by Gabriel and Ned. But his image of Jane is stilted, and her pale skin looks almost waxen. We can imagine her in William's Oxford rooms, standing for hours at a time as if looking at her own reflection. She is posed before a tilted mirror, in the last stages of dressing. Jane/Iseult is fastening a belt around her hips. Her body sways slightly, and her legs are entirely hidden by the folds of her robe. She looks almost like a statue stepped down from the porch of a cathedral, or a figure cut out of a manuscript. There is little sense of the desired body beneath the patterned fabric.

The most sensual part of the picture is the tumbled bed, with a little greyhound curled into the warm hollow where Iseult has slept. According to the tale, the dog was a gift from Tristan, so it acts as a clue to Iseult's thoughts. She is also wearing a crown interlaced with long sprigs of rosemary, traditionally 'for remembrance'. It is in these elements that William shows his true, exceptional skills. *La Belle Iseult* is the visual equivalent of one of his poems. The emotions are restrained and melancholic. But the incidental details are alive. Our eyes are drawn in his picture to the bright buttons on Iseult's scarlet sleeve; her empty slippers embroidered with starbursts; the individual stitches in golden thread he picks out on her dressing-table cloth. Every surface is covered in medieval patterns and fabrics, lovingly observed. William pays as much attention to the folds and diaper weave in the linen runner under her mirror, or the fine threadwork of her bed curtains, as he does to Jane's hands and hair. These textiles are almost as expressive as her figure, falling and draping, or catching the light.

La Belle Iseult is a claustrophobic work. Jane/Iseult is trapped between the gaze of the viewer and her unmade bed. She stops with her belt in her hand and listens. The whole scene is overlaid with the singing of a minstrel and the sound of his psaltery. She is hemmed in by the cacophony of patterns and textures. She cannot escape the insistent details of the Turkish carpets on the floor and across the foot of the bed. On the far wall is a hanging which resembles the embroidered apple trees that William had stitched himself. He was piling all his antiquarian enthusiasm into this picture, showing off his knowledge of medieval objects. Some he must have collected himself. Others he knew from illuminated manuscripts, like the one beside Iseult's bed. He also included personal references that would have been recognised by his friends. In particular, William gestured towards his favourite painter, Jan Van Eyck, in his quotations from the *Arnolfini Portrait* (which was bought by the National Gallery in 1842). Details like the pile of oranges and the discarded slippers can be traced back to Van Eyck's picture. The most obvious connection is seen in the bagged bed curtains that hang behind Jane/Iseult, and above all, her pose. Like Arnolfini's bride, she stands in semi-profile, with her hand raised to her waist. But here she is alone, and without any means of escape – no window, not even the reflection of an open door. In many respects, it seems an unusual choice of subject to celebrate an engagement.

*

Did William tell Jane the story of Iseult and her ill-fated love, as they worked together on this picture? Did he share his delight in the material remains of the Middle Ages? This was the first time they were able to collaborate to create a beautiful interior. While it revealed William's sensitivity to flat patterning and the intricacies of textile production, it also played to Jane's strengths. She was able to bring her own understanding of stitching and dressmaking into William's studio. In their shy way, they could learn about the sort of home they might want to make together. As he painted *La Belle Iseult*, William discovered his own great strength. He could step away from easel painting and throw his energies into something bigger and more urgent – making a house beautiful.

Writing many years later, in his essay 'The Aims of Art', he outlined the lesson he had learnt as he painted Iseult's chamber: he saw the potential for delight in homely things. Art meant simply 'producing something which, when done, shall give pleasure to the user of it'. Art could be useful, domestic, and created by 'taking a genuine interest in all the details of daily life'.[34] In this essay, written nearly thirty years after his marriage, William thought back to his early days as a student and young lover. He remembered, clearly, regretfully, the old Oxford that he and Jane both knew:

> Oxford in those days still kept a great deal of its earlier loveli-
> ness: and the memory of its grey streets as they were then has
> been an abiding influence and pleasure in my life . . . There is
> another pleasure for the world gone down the wind; here again,
> the beauty and romance have been uselessly, causelessly, most
> foolishly thrown away.[35]

As so often in his writing, beauty was undercut by loss and longing. But he was still hopeful, and looked for pleasure, for 'splendours and beauties'. The idea was woven through his work. This was the point. It was why he carried on making and striving, loving the past as well as the present: 'whether it is to be called art or not, it will at least be *life*; and, after all, that is what we want'.[36]

William entered into his life with Jane in the same spirit that he embarked on every new venture. He hoped, as he put it, 'to be happy while I live' and to 'cherish with all my best endeavour' the possibilities of their partnership.[37] Jane had shown that he was right to put his faith in her. She had risen to the challenge of becoming a gentleman's wife. Jane's ability to transform herself was truly remarkable. Her voice, her posture, her dress, her reading and conversation, her ability to run a household had been questioned, turned inside out, and rebuilt from the ground up. In all this turmoil, Jane seems to have remained quietly receptive. She took what was offered and made the very best of herself. It was not just about 'marrying up', but about gaining an education, and using her skills. She had very little to lose. And here was a man who appreciated not just her looks but her intelligence.

It has sometimes been said that Jane's life story sounds like the tale of Pygmalion. This was certainly a favourite subject for Victorian art and poetry: a sculptor falls in love with the statue he has made, and Venus grants his wish to bring the marble to life. But Jane was not William's creation. She was not moulded into his ideal version of woman. Instead, if a literary parallel must be drawn, it might be with the story of King Cophetua, who fell in love with a beggar-maid, and made her his queen. (This tale appealed to Ned Burne-Jones, who in 1883–4 made a vast painting of the Beggar Maid on her throne.) It seems that, like the king in the legend, William recognised Jane's potential, and overlooked her origins. She was worthy of being his equal. They would live and work together. At every stage of his relationship with Jane, William demonstrated an open-mindedness and sensitivity that was extraordinary for a man of his time. Or indeed, perhaps, of any time.

*

It was a small wedding, held by special licence on 26 April 1859. Jane was still legally a 'minor', so her father and sister Bessie were there to support her. There were no banns read, no need for Jane and William to face the questioning glances of the congregation Sunday after Sunday. And none of William's family seem to have attended. There is no record at this stage of their reaction to William's choice of wife.

Jane was not married in her home parish of St Peter-in-the-East. She was shaking off her Holywell roots and moving formally into William's world. They stood together before the altar of St Michael's on Cornmarket. The most ancient of Oxford's churches, with its squat Anglo-Saxon tower, St Michael's is not prettily Gothic but reassuringly solid. William gave her a plain gold ring as they said their vows. The wedding was conducted by William's friend Richard Watson Dixon. Unlike Ned and William, he had completed his training for the priesthood, and was recently ordained. Charley Faulkner was best man. Ned was there in the background, but it seems that the coolness between the friends had not yet thawed. Or maybe Ned was still recovering from his illness and did not need the extra worry of supporting William.

We know very little about Jane's honeymoon. Both she and William were discreet about their six-week tour of northern France and the Low Countries. For Jane, there was the added anxiety (or thrill) of travelling for the first time, of seeing the sea and Paris, and William's favourite places. They stopped for a while in Bruges, staying at the Hôtel du Commerce. Here William would have shown her the quiet cloistered life of the Béguinage. As a student, he had talked about establishing a community like this with his friends, a refuge for work and prayer. Now he and Jane were contemplating a different future, just as radical in its way. They talked through plans for a family house in the country, somewhere hospitable where friends could meet, but where a young couple could also find peace. Webb could help them. He understood what mattered to William.

And so we can leave the bride and groom together for a short while. If we want to imagine William's honeymoon, we can follow the pair of lovers who, at the end of his strange story 'The Hollow Land', find a moment of joy and revelation. They come to a dreamlike version of Bruges, where they walk

through the golden streets under the purple shadows of the houses . . . at last we came to a fair palace, cloistered off in the olden time . . . so now it had its own gaiety, its own solemnity . . . We stopped before the gates and trembled, and clasped each other closer . . . for there among marble leafage and tendrils . . . were wrought two figures of a man and woman winged and garlanded, whose raiment flashed with stars . . . And then we walked together toward the golden gates, and opened them, and no man gainsaid us.

And before us lay a great space of flowers.[38]

Chapter 5

Red House, 1860

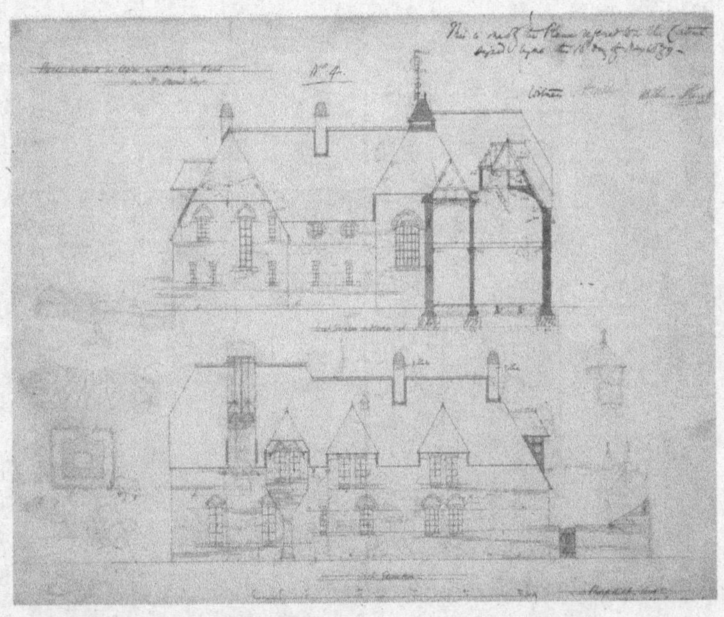

Philip Webb, *East and West Elevations of Red House*, 1859, V&A Museum

The friends arrived at the country station: 'A thin fresh air full of sweet smells met us as we walked down the platform.' Then 'a swinging drive of three miles of winding road' until they reached the garden gate. A path through the orchard, and there, beyond the trellis of climbing roses, they could 'see the tall figure of a girl standing alone in the porch to receive us'.[1]

Jane Morris welcomed the young couple to her home. She was only twenty years old herself, and mistress of a fine newly built house. Every detail of construction was designed for William and Jane by their friend Philip Webb – from the well and the wagonette that fetched their guests from the station, to the door handles and dog kennel.

Red House was both a 'Palace of Art' and a convivial home, built for long weekends of talking and painting, stitching and writing. They had chosen a site in the village of Upton, close to Bexley Heath on the edge of Kent. Here Jane and William could experiment with new ways of living. The sun seemed to shine on them. They played bowls on the lawn, or gathered apples, or shared plans for their next decorating project. The Morrises filled their spare rooms with artists and poets, who relished these visits as an escape from their grey, sooty London apartments. Georgie Burne-Jones remembered how Jane and William kept open house for their friends: 'The joys of those Saturdays to Mondays at Red House! . . . No protestations – only certainty of contentment in each other's society. We laughed because we were happy.'[2]

For a few brief years, their home was the hub of a new movement in art and collaborative labour. Many of the later works created by the Morrises and their friends can be traced back to these days. They had time and space to think through their ideals, reimagining textiles, stained glass, painted furniture, wall-coverings, storytelling and hospitality. Many of these projects drew on the colour and strangeness of the Gothic world, as Webb had done in his plans for Red House. But the house was no mock-medieval construction. Webb was not interested in embellishing his building with unnecessary details like lancet windows or archaic carving. Instead, it seemed to grow from the ground up. Red House felt organic, fit for its setting among the apple trees. It was loved by Jane and William. Their two girls were born here. And when they had to sell up, moving back to central London in 1865, they left many of their works of art here – painted on the walls and built-in cupboards. They abandoned the massive chairs, too big for a London townhouse, and the stained glass panels in the passageway. Jane and William never went back. As Georgie wrote, years later: 'When we turned to look around us something was gone, something had been left behind – and it was our first youth.'[3]

*

How can we rediscover the energy and imagination of those early years in Kent? Very few of William's letters from the early 1860s have survived, and Jane's words are even scarcer. We have to rely on the memories of their friends, and on the things they made together. The house itself remains, now in the care of the National Trust. And the objects also speak to us, helping us piece together the way that Jane,

William and the other artist families contributed their own skills. We can look directly at the needlework designs and panels they completed; that is, until other, more pressing sewing projects came along. We can walk upstairs and see the ungainly high-backed settle and the stencilled ceilings, and enter into the playful creativity of the place. We also have to bear in mind the works that were lost or went unrecorded. Many colourful wall and ceiling patterns were white-washed by the families who called this home after 1865. Red House was lived in for a century after William and Jane left for London, taking their dining tables, beds and curtains with them.

We can begin with the house itself, and the plans so lovingly drawn up by Philip Webb and his team. They outline the exterior and interior structure, including many details of metalwork, the placing of key pieces of furniture, and even planting in the garden. It was a holistic project, linking the outdoors to the spaces inside. A bench in a shady porch, a leafy view through a round window, the sound of birdsong from the orchard in the early morning: these framed the way the Morrises lived in Kent. And these experiences were carried with them into their later houses, and into William's imaginative worlds of design and storytelling.

Webb was one of William and Jane's most stalwart friends who remained close to them both throughout their lives. Forty years after building Red House, he was still writing affectionate, chatty letters to 'My dear kind friend Janey'.[4] And when William died, it was fitting that Jane should ask Webb to design the gravestone for his last resting place. As Webb said, William had been 'the very backbone of my poor life'.[5] He received no fee for designing Red House, although the Morrises offered one. Webb took the commission for friendship's sake. It was also a chance to establish himself as an independent designer, stepping out of the shadow of his mentor G. E. Street, as he set up his own architectural practice.

Webb's plans for this house are clear and carefully considered. We can still study them in the V&A Museum collections: the pencil outlines, with notes in ink about materials, cellars and plumbing, and watercolour details to show which floors were tiled, which were yellow timber. As well as the main formal plan, we find small sketches of chimneys and fireplaces, swiftly jotted down in corners of the building contract. We see the bold east elevation facing the garden, with strong gables and idiosyncratic circular windows in the bedroom corridor. Even the herringbone patterning of the bricks on the gateposts is defined.

One of the most distinctive features is the well, drawn by Webb in profile and cross-section, annotated with the exact dimensions of each oak timber scantling, and the chain for the bucket. The well with its fairy-tale turret roof was designed in July 1859, after Jane and William had returned from their honeymoon. Its timber framework echoes the arched doorway of the garden porch beyond. And the gentle splay of the tiled roof creates an overhang to shelter the servants who use it. But it was mostly for show, as water could be pumped directly into the corner of the scullery. There were also two flushing waterclosets in the main part of the house for the family, and one outside, next to the dustbins, in the service yard for the staff.

From Webb's designs, we also see how the house was divided. There were separate spaces for William, Jane and their guests at one end, and the servants at the other. As a gentleman's home, Red House required staff to keep it clean, prepare and serve meals, and tend the garden. The servants' part of the house, to the south, was substantial and well-lit, though over-warm because the afternoon sun came full into the kitchen. The cook worked on 'a capital Range', and there was also a 'Buttery Hatch, Large and Light Pantry, ample Closet Room for China and Glass, Large Store Room, Scullery, Larder, Housemaid's Closet, Watercloset, Beer and Wine Cellars', plus 'Commodious Outbuildings, excellent Coach-House and Two-Stalled Stable, with Loft'. The well was fed by 'an abundant supply of Spring Water, which has never failed in the hottest summer'.[6] And the house had its own cesspool, neatly marked on Webb's plans. Friends like Gabriel jokingly referred to Red House as 'the Towers of Topsy'; it was all so substantial, compared to their bachelor existence.[7]

At the time, by contrast, Ned Burne-Jones and his young wife were relying on a single maid, who sometimes doubled as a model when Georgie wanted to draw. The Rossettis had no kitchen in their rooms in Chatham Place, and ate out in restaurants like Solferino's and the Cavour in Leicester Square most evenings. Ford and Emma Madox Brown could barely afford a servant; they employed a teenager from the workhouse as their maid-of-all-work, but there were months when Emma 'the poor dear' was 'tired with no servant and char-woman'.[8]

William could afford to hire all the help his family needed, and to accommodate up to four live-in servants. Webb's plans show three large upstairs bedrooms for the family. Then, at the top of the back stairs, is a housekeeper's room and another long bedroom split into cubicles for three maids. The manservant slept in the loft above the stable block. This is how William had lived as a child, in a substantial house where another young person was paid to sweep out and lay the fires unobtrusively, or to polish the boots and knives. Even in his London lodgings, William relied on a housekeeper to clean and cook, or he dined out with friends.

But Jane had grown up in different circumstances. As a girl, she would have expected to be one of the semi-invisible figures moving quietly up and down the back stairs. Her family were in service. Her father worked in the stables and her mother washed other people's dirty linen. Their hands were roughened and reddened by their work. Yet, from the outset, William had reimagined Jane, the working-class girl, as Iseult the Fair, as Guenevere, in whose hand 'the shadow lies like wine within a cup/ Of marvellously colour'd gold'.[9] And she had grown into this new role. Morris's family money had given her security, along with unlooked-for responsibilities. She had become the mistress of her own household.

Jane and William lived alongside the cook, Charlotte Cooper, and housemaid, Jane Chapman. Thomas Reynolds worked as groom and gardener. It was a young establishment: at twenty-seven, Charlotte was the oldest person living there. We have no record of what Jane's servants thought of her, and what they guessed or whispered. One lady, who glimpsed Jane at a party soon after her marriage, remembered that she 'kept her bonnet, ready to depart in a rush to catch a train'. Jane was very visible, tall and lavish in her appearance: 'All we little women looked quite diminutive beside Mrs Morris.'[10]

We do know that the Morrises were talked about locally. One of their neighbours later recalled that 'she had heard, and felt sure it must be true, that Mrs Morris had been in a circus; no one could ride and manage a horse so beautifully'.[11] Not a circus performer, perhaps, but still Jane was a young woman who made a spectacle of herself as an artist's model. And as the daughter of an experienced stable hand, she had evidently learnt to handle horses as a girl.

Jane had shifted position, from one side of the domestic space to the other, and this shift was an integral part of her personality after her marriage. It did not weigh her down. Her friends passed over her upbringing, consistently describing her as noble and queenly. Still, she was always acutely aware of another life, what might have been, and sensitive to the intricacies of social standing.

Jane had recreated herself, and was now ready to step forward to greet her guests as they arrived from the station. They found her, like the house, new-made, fresh and full of potential. As William's first biographer describes it, 'the shell of the house was completed, and stood clean and bare among the apple trees.' But 'everything that was to furnish or decorate it had to be designed and made.'[12] Jane and William began without the lumber of inherited things or ways of living. In their sturdy, sparsely furnished house, they constructed the framework of their future together.

*

It was early August 1860 when Jane and William welcomed their first friends to Red House. Georgie and Edward Burne-Jones were newly married. They had arranged a quiet wedding in Manchester on 9 June, but then their plans had been spoiled by Ned falling ill. Instead of spending the first weeks of marriage in Paris, they returned to Edward's cramped London lodgings on Russell Place. Hemmed in by tall buildings, short of funds, Georgie began her new role as a wife. She was only nineteen years old.

It is not surprising that her visit to Red House was a revelation. The 'impression of ample space everywhere,'[13] inside and out, and the easy hospitality offered by Jane and William, were a relief after the anxious start to her marriage. The charmed weeks of late summer were spent chatting and working in the garden. They were remembered by Georgie especially with great affection. It felt like a honeymoon time for them all.

We can see it through Georgie's eyes as she found it that first evening. The grounds were already full of colour and movement. The flower beds were an integral part of Webb's designs for Red House, with planting marked on the plans. So, as the men unloaded the Burne-Joneses' few bags from the wagonette, Jane led Georgie past the ripening plum trees, and into the well court. White jasmine and bergamot scented the air. Climbing roses and passion flowers were trained up the wall, catching the afternoon sunshine. Two new pear trees were growing near the kitchen windows. They walked around a square herber of low hedges and rose-covered trellis, which seemed to have been transplanted from an illuminated manuscript. These small enclosures were an inventive element in the garden design. All around the house, the grounds were 'divided into many squares, hedged with sweetbriar or wild rose, each enclosure with its particular show of flowers.'[14]

Like the building itself, the herbers managed to feel both medieval and original. They were fresh and unsentimental. There was nothing pedantic or pastiche about Webb and the Morrises' new vision of the Gothic. It was substantial, consistent and organic throughout. As William explained later, he loved a garden to 'look both orderly and rich. It should be well fenced from the outside world . . . It should, in fact, look like part of the house.'[15] At Red House, the young people felt at home outside. And the new building never seemed raw, despite its unornamented red-brick surface. It was softened by green and growing things from the beginning.

Jane hoped her guests would enjoy the old-fashioned flowers, the promise of fruit, and fun on the bowling green lawn. She had grown up without a garden, in a narrow backstreet. For the first time, she had her own open space, 'with its long grass walks, its mid-summer lilies and autumn sunflowers.'[16] In her later letters, Jane carefully noted the changes as her garden was renewed each year: 'I love the English spring days,' she wrote, 'and watching things get greener every day.'[17] At Red House, she had time to sit in the archway of the garden porch, working and chatting with Georgie, and seeing the heavy blooms of the moss roses slowly opening.

The friends called this space the 'Pilgrim's Rest' porch; it was somewhere to pause before entering the long passageway connecting the garden to the heart of the house. The tiled floor of the passage was dappled with golden glints from the stained glass in the four windows. Webb drew the birds for these windows – squawking ducks and geese – to sit alongside William's simple daisies. It was the first time they had tried their hands at stained-glass design. They began by imaginatively reworking medieval models, creating small-scale, unfussy forms. The glass panels were likely painted at James Powell & Sons workshop in Whitefriars; this company went on to supply most of Morris's materials for his stained-glass production.

After the low-key Gothic details of the garden passage, Jane could lead her guests into the dramatic, high-ceilinged hallway. The newel posts of the staircase reminded her of tiny castle towers, with their pointed finials and miniature battlements. They were made of plain, unpainted oak. The banisters were just as austere in their design, with pierced roundels as the only decoration. This was the hub of the house. From here, Jane could see the front door and its deep-set porch. There was a waiting room to one side and a large dining room on the other. Behind the main stairs, the servants' area of the house began; here were the stores, the pantries and the kitchen passage, and then the tight back staircase.

The house was very much a work in progress when Georgie and Ned arrived. Webb had arranged to leave his scaffolding in place on the landing, so that William, Jane and their friends could decorate the open plasterwork between the beams with green and blue stencil patterns. Georgie described how 'the dining room was not yet finished, and the drawing room ... was being decorated in different ways, so Morris's studio was used for living in.' This spacious room was on the first floor, above the garden porch. 'A most cheerful place it was, with windows looking three ways and a little horizontal slip of a window over the door.' In Georgie's memory, the connections between inside and out, between nature and home life, were felt here too, with a view onto 'the red-tiled roof . . . where we could see birds hopping about all unconscious of our gaze'.[18]

This insistence on immediacy, on understated naturalism, was reinforced on the landing and in the upstairs passages. Here Webb left exposed brickwork arches and broad, unornamented lintels over the doors. There was a delight in the mixture of traditional materials and direct Gothic geometry. Jane and Georgie could see the turret of the well through the round windows, as they stood in the passage between the studio and Jane's bedroom. These windows, with their wide sills, were also filled with naïve stained-glass designs; each of the quarries showed a slip of a budding plant. They seemed to be lifted from a fifteenth-century herbal, and this conscious medievalism was reinforced by Morris's motto: *Si je puis* – 'If I Can' – his own expression of hope and perseverance.

Morris and Webb's fondness for the Middle Ages, and especially their focus on plant forms, chimed with recent writings by John Ruskin. In his exploration of *The Stones of Venice*, published 1851–3, Ruskin described how, 'to the Gothic workman, the living foliage became a subject of intense affection.'[19] His chapter on 'The Nature of Gothic' profoundly influenced William and his friends. They took Ruskin's suggestions to heart, in the rising and dipping of the roofs of Red House, in the placing of the porthole windows, in the pointed arches framing the porches and passages. They read, with enthusiasm, Ruskin's idea that Gothic architects were deliberately unconventional: 'If they wanted a window, they added one; a buttress, they built one . . . So that in the best times of Gothic, a useless window would rather have been opened in an unexpected place for the sake of surprise, than a useful one forbidden for the sake of symmetry.'

Ruskin showed how fourteenth- and fifteenth-century designers were constantly 'saying new and different things'.[20] Morris and Webb saw the potential for Gothic forms, Gothic preoccupations, to create a bold, modern home.

This applied not only to the house itself, but also to the objects inside it. Stepping into Jane's bedroom, Georgie could see how the couple had stripped away the usual layers of mid-Victorian furnishings. Georgie's own London lodgings were barely furnished because they lacked funds. (She and Ned only had £30 between them to begin their married life, and she had to sit on the dining table because they had no chairs.) But William was wealthy. So the limited number of things – bed, wardrobe, embroidered wall-hangings – was a deliberate choice. The effect was not bleak or inhospitable, although Jane's room faced north. It had a large window directly over the front door, a substantial fireplace and a spacious dressing room. Each piece of furniture was carefully considered, rich in colour and decoration.

Georgie recognised the wardrobe next to the window. She and Ned had given it to the Morrises as a wedding present. Ned had painted it with scenes from one of Chaucer's *Canterbury Tales*, including a portrait of the poet, and a vision of the Virgin Mary, surrounded by angel musicians, descending from heaven. In this comic-strip version of 'The Prioress's Tale', Mary, with her rippling hair, looked like an idealised portrait of Jane herself, bending down to perform a miracle. Both doors of the wardrobe and the side panels were covered with painted details: a busy medieval townscape, a flowerbed filled with poppies, a stand of trees in the distance, silhouetted black against a gold sky. William and Ned had been talking about what to paint inside the doors; perhaps the young women would model for the Four Seasons, or perhaps they would illustrate one of William's poems.

Around the walls were the heavy folds of deep blue wall-hangings. They were embroidered in white and red wool with stylised daisies and cowslips, adding warmth and pattern to the room. These hangings, which are still preserved at Kelmscott Manor, have gained an almost mythical status in the story of William as a pioneer in the decorative arts. And they show Jane's close involvement in their design choices. She finds the fabric. They stitch it together, using a corner of a fifteenth-century manuscript of Froissart as the model for the flowers. Or, as Jane wrote later to her daughter, May, 'The first stuff I got to embroider on was a piece of indigo dyed blue serge I found by chance in a London shop . . . I took it home and he [William] was delighted with it, and set to work at once designing flowers – these were worked in bright colours in a simple rough way – the work went quickly.'[21]

Even forty years on, we can still sense her pleasure in making their new home beautiful, in learning a new skill with her husband beside her. These hangings were extraordinary. They were practical, created from a substantial, unsophisticated material, and deliberately Gothic in their inspiration. They demonstrated the possibilities of remaking the Victorian interior. In this bedroom, and throughout Red House, Jane and William turned to medieval examples as a jumping-off point for something more radical: a rejection of the exuberant, mass-produced surface decoration that ran riot in British houses after the Great Exhibition of 1851. The rooms at Red House showcased the handmade and the personal.

Jane's bedroom can be seen as microcosm of the plans that emerged for the decoration of the house. Ready-made furniture, like the 'half tester bed hung with rose chintz',[22] was kept to a minimum. Her double bed was a wedding gift from William's mother. It was the bed he had been born in, and Jane slept in it to the end of her life. Bespoke objects, including the wardrobe, the hangings, and later, painted murals and Jane's dressing-table mirror, were preferred by the young couple. They were made with the help of friends like Webb, Ned and Georgie. Both the women and men contributed their skills. The whole house was a record of friendship and enthusiasm.

One of the distinctive features of Red House, and many of the later collaborative schemes, was the way the friends incorporated their favourite poems and tales into their artworks. They created a harmonious, multi-layered series of images and associations. Chaucer, for example, was woven into many of their designs. Even the daisies in the wall-hangings seem to look back to the opening lines of his *Legend of Good Women*:

> Of al the floures in the mede,
> Thanne love I most thise floures white and rede,
> Swiche as men callen daysyes in our toun[23]
> [Of all the flowers in the meadow,
> I love this white and red flower the most,
> which men in our town call daisies.]

The daisies might have looked artless, but in fact were part of the shared symbolic language of the group.

Did Jane and Georgie feel excluded from these visual and poetic intersections? After all, they had not been part of William and Ned's circle at university, when Morris read his first verses to his friends. They had not joined the young men with their glasses of wine, talking late into the night about Malory. But these texts became part of the women's personal history, too. Georgie's wedding was timed to coincide with the most significant date in Dante's life: 9 June was the day of Beatrice's death, commemorated in *La Vita Nuova* (translated by Gabriel Rossetti in 1848). And from her earliest encounters with the young men, Jane had been courted with tales of Guenevere and Iseult. The medieval stories became familiar to her. Later, when she was filling tiny keepsake books with the quotations that reflected her most intimate thoughts, Jane included verses from *The Canterbury Tales* and the *Divina Commedia*, Old French carols and Renaissance proverbs. These were part of her world too, shaping the way she thought and wrote and presented herself.

It is likely, then, that both couples were involved in the discussions that first summer about the books that inspired the decoration of Red House. Jane and William wanted to fill their home with stories and patterns. They planned murals for Jane's bedroom and the drawing room, and embroideries for the dining room. Georgie played the piano, and they all sang 'music of a simple kind – chiefly the old English songs published by Chappell, and the inexhaustible French song collection, *Échos du Temps Passé*'.[24]

Some of the projects were intended to fit around existing furniture, like the massive settle that William brought from the bachelor rooms he had shared with Ned. Others, including the painted cabinet in the hall, and the wall-hangings in the dining room, were created for blank spaces in the new house. Jane and Georgie spent many mornings together stitching these panels. Jane wrote later how they worked for months on the 'scheme for adorning the house [with] a series of tapestries for the dining-room of twelve large figures with a tree between each two, Flowers at the feet and a pattern all over the background'. She went on: '7 of the figures were completed and some of them fixed to the background.'[25]

The designs were drawn by Morris, initially in small sketches showing the relationship between the figures and the trees. Then they were enlarged and transferred onto linen panels. The theme of *The Legend of Good Women*, which Jane and William had hinted at in the Daisy hangings, was foregrounded in these embroideries. Rather than simply repeating Chaucer's choice of worthy women, William and his friends made their own list. Their mixture of pagans and Christians remained true to the Chaucerian model. St Catherine, Guenevere, Penelope, Lucretia, Hippolyte, Helen of Troy and Aphrodite (with a flower garland to cover her nakedness) were all stitched by Jane, Georgie or Jane's sister Bessie Burden. Artemis, St Cecilia and Mary Magdalene were designed but never embroidered. William imagined these 'Good Women' in their flowing gowns, holding books and swords and flaming torches, walking quietly in a grove of lemon and pomegranate trees.

The project gave Jane and the other women a chance to try out new needlework techniques. Each panel was ambitious – well over five feet tall – and relied on handwork that was beyond many domestic crafts-women. They stitched the delicate roundness of faces and hands. They created elaborate folds and textures of queenly robes. They worked in a wide range of stitches, adapting their size and smoothness to the demands of the design. They used chain and brick stitch, couched work, long and short stitches and darning stich. Then, when each figure was complete, they carefully cut it out and attached it to a decorative background. This appliqué method was time-consuming and created a softly three-dimensional effect. It was derived from a technique known as Opus Anglicanum, which was used for vestments in the pre-

Reformation church. Webb and Morris had learnt of these ecclesiastical examples during their time in G. E. Street's office.

The embroideries were best seen by candlelight, the fabric moving slightly as guests entered the dining room. Jane, Bessie and Georgie used coloured wools and silks, and golden threads that glinted. Many years later, Jane described how 'During the slow progress of this gigantic work, we were making experiments in silk and gold wools . . . emb[roidery] silks difficult to find of a good colour[,] gold thread of a good quality which would not tarnish had to be found.'[26] She also explained that the experience of working on the 'Good Women' panels underpinned their more commercial embroidery production in the coming years.

Georgie was so taken with the designs that she and Ned planned their own procession of embroidered figures for their home. They began to draw and stitch a series based on the Arthurian tales: unfinished panels showing King Arthur and Merlin are now in the V & A Museum. They are on a smaller scale than Red House's 'renowned ladies',[27] to fit the Burne-Joneses' more modest rooms. Although neither series was completed, Morris never lost sight of his ideal wall decoration. Twenty years later, he was encouraging his audience to create wall-hangings of greenwoods and gardens, and processions of ancient worthies: 'That surely was worth the trouble of doing.'[28]

William recognised that the work was time-consuming and troublesome. And time was running out for the young wives. That summer shone in Georgie's memory: 'Oh, how happy we were, Janey and I, busy in the morning with needlework or wood-engraving, and in the afternoon driving to explore the country round by the help of a map of Kent.'[29] But the bright, uncomplicated days were brief.

'One morning,' Georgie recalled, 'as Janey and I sat sewing (she was an exquisite needlewoman) I saw in her basket a strange garment, fine, small, and shapeless – a little shirt for him or her – and looking at my friend's face I knew that she had been happy when she made it;

but it was a sign of change, and the thought of any change made me sigh. We paid other visits to the Morrises after this, but none quite like it – how could they be?'[30]

*

Jane was already pregnant with her first child when she moved into Red House. By the autumn, plans for beautifying her home were in full swing, with friends often coming down from London to help. But there was an added urgency to their creative weekends. Ned and Georgie were frequent guests; they liked to travel to Kent with Gabriel and Lizzie Rossetti, who were married in May 1860. Philip Webb was another regular visitor, and so was Charley Faulkner. They all contributed to the decorations and the fun. They pelted each other with windfall apples, and played practical jokes on William.

Georgie recalled the spaces of the big house, its dark corners eerie in the half-light, and Jane's willingness to join in with the games:

> After work, when it was dark, sometimes there was a game of hide-and-seek all over the house. A fragment of one of these games remains in my memory; and I see that Edward, leaving the door open behind him, has slipped into an unlighted room and disappeared into its black depths for so long that Mrs Morris, who is the seeker, grows almost terrified. I see her tall figure and her beautiful face as she creeps slowly nearer and nearer to the room where she feels sure he must be, and at last I hear her startled cry and his peal of laughter as he bursts from his hiding-place.[31]

The rooms were full of surprises. One was a 'great painted chair', which had been brought across from Red Lion Square. It had 'a box overhead in which Gabriel suggested owls might be kept.'[32] Another was a settle, with a curved back decorated with embossed leather, glowing with gilded rose patterns. This was designed by Webb, as was the massive dresser in the dining room, with its oversized hinges, crenellations and three pointed gables. It seemed more architectural than domestic, and hinted at the scale of the entertainments that the Morrises planned for their guests: 'How is [he] looking?' asked one of William's friends. 'I trust well and rosy with good wine.'[33]

The strangest and most playful of the furniture was found in the drawing room. This was a majestic settle, with shelves and cupboards above. It was designed by Morris, again for the Red Lion Square rooms, and built by Henry Price of Hatton Garden, who described it as 'a large cabinet about 7ft high and as long, a seat forming a bunk'.[34] It was magnificent and very sturdy. When it was reinstalled in Red House, Webb and Morris enlarged it. They added an extra tier, with a panelled guard rail and a ladder, turning the upper platform into a gallery. They placed it against the south wall in the drawing room where, high up, there was a small hatch to an attic used as an apple store. This positioning made it somehow more marvellous, with a suggestion of a secret space beyond.

The settle became a central player in the Red House games. During one of the 'triangular bear-fights in the drawing room', Charley Faulkner 'surged up the steps into the "Minstrels' Gallery" [and] suddenly leapt clear over the parapet into the middle of the floor with an astounding noise.' It was also Faulkner who threw a well-aimed apple from his outpost in the gallery, giving William a black eye.

Georgie describes these antics as happening 'in the intervals between work'. So what was the work they were supposed to be doing in this room?[35] Some of them were stencilling the ceiling of the alcove with sunny yellow circles inside a simple grid, or stitching the gold velvet cushions for the window seat. Others, including William and Jane themselves, were painting the rest of the ceiling in a repeating scheme of brick red, yellow and brown. The pattern was made up of stylised teasels within a lattice framework. The lower part of the walls were also painted; this time, William designed flattened auricula flowers, each with a small scroll around the stem which read '*Qui bien aime tard oublie*' – 'Who loves well, forgets slowly'. The whole effect was complex and richly coloured; it was held together by an overarching system of grids and simplified flower forms. William's scheme was full of details derived from Gothic models. Some of them he had seen in illuminated manuscripts, while others he had read about in the fourteenth- and fifteenth-century poems and legends he treasured.

Words and images were intimately connected throughout the decorations. There were the mottoes wound around painted flowers, written on stained glass, stitched into hangings. And there were the more intricate overlaps between well-loved texts and the pictures that ornamented every space. We see them in particular on and around the settle, where two different medieval tales were reimagined – one on the wall and the other on the wood panels of the settle itself.

In the autumn of 1860, Gabriel Rossetti planned to finish his series of paintings on the flat cupboard doors of the settle. He had begun the pictures while the great piece of furniture was dismantled, in between Red Lion Square and Red House. He wrote in June 1859, 'I have done a whole picture in a week on one of Topsy's doors.'[36] The compositions were based on Gabriel's personal reading of Dante's *La Vita Nuova*, with the two outer panels showing the poet's encounters with his beloved Beatrice. On one side, Dante passes Beatrice on a stairway in Florence. They recognise each other, briefly, and then she moves on with her friends. On the other side, we see Beatrice after her death, as she greets Dante on the threshold of heaven. She pulls back her veil while he asks for her mercy.

In the first image, Beatrice is painted to look like Jane Morris, but by the time she reaches the Garden of Eden, Beatrice seems to be modelled on Lizzie Siddall. Like Ned Burne-Jones's wardrobe, where Jane appeared as the Virgin Mary, these panels were probably a wedding present to the Morrises.

When the settle was reassembled in Red House, Gabriel wanted to fill the central section with a winged figure of Love holding a sundial to show the hour when Beatrice died. This was, in Dante's eyes, her second birthday, the moment when she achieved perfection. The panel has the feel of an enlarged manuscript illumination, all red and blue and gold, with flat patterns and idealised portraits of Christ (looking down) and Beatrice (looking up). Christ's face is encircled by the sun, with rays, like fluttering banners, spiralling outwards. Beatrice's uplifted profile sits within a crescent moon, surrounded by greater and smaller stars. The whole design was titled *Dantis Amor* – 'Dante's Love'.

Gabriel himself did not seem to question Dante's vision of Beatrice as perfected by Death. But what about Jane and her friends? How did they see the young Florentine woman who died at the age of twenty-five? For the poet, Beatrice was a blank, an idealised figure. In many ways, she was more useful as an adored and flawless icon *post mortem*.

Jane, Lizzie and Georgie were well aware of Gabriel's translation of *La Vita Nuova*. We know Ned and Georgie planned their own engagement and wedding to coincide with the key date of Beatrice's death. Jane certainly owned several copies of Dante's work in later life, including 'a little Florentine copy printed in 1863' and one inscribed 'Jane Morris from D. G. Rossetti 1878'.[37] But it is harder to discover how she and the other young women felt about the representation of Beatrice, hovering somewhere between history and myth. Jane and Lizzie must have noticed that Gabriel used their faces interchangeably: in his eyes, both of them could potentially be seen as Beatrice. Did they laugh at this, or accept it without discussion, or feel uneasy that their own character, their individuality, could so easily be elided with another poet's dead love? Lizzie had already modelled for Beatrice in many of Gabriel's pictures and verses. Jane had become used to standing in for long-dead or legendary women. Dante's Beatrice was, in his words, 'so noble and praiseworthy', 'courteous', 'gentle';

these phrases were echoed in descriptions of Jane by Gabriel and others who met her.[38]

Yet here we find the dilemma for both Jane and Lizzie which has dogged them ever since. Their personal histories have been overlaid with the fantasies of the men who incorporated their distinctive features into their paintings. Their own voices have been drowned out by the verses written to venerate their beauty. They learnt to perform the parts of Beatrice or Guenevere, to move as a princess or an angel. Like Beatrice, they were defined and made visible by the male artists who loved them.

It might be convenient, then, to think of these working-class women as blank canvases, too. But we know that was never the case. They had their skills and opinions. They developed their relationships with each other, as well as with the men in their circle. It was always a balancing act, transcending the limitations of their upbringing, making sure no one was embarrassed by a slip of the tongue, or a *déclassé* gesture. But Jane was more alive playing hide-and-seek in her darkened spare bedroom than she would ever be, pretending to be Pandora. For her, the afterlife of Beatrice was a warning against the dangers of being transformed by art, erased as a real person.

We should remember that most of Jane's transformation came from within. She used her intelligence, her reading and her stitching to develop a new life, away from the slums of Oxford. Yes, these skills were coupled with her extraordinary appearance. But Jane was never a passive observer of her own change. She was actively creating her position within the circle of artists, as the presiding figure at the heart of a beautiful, welcoming home.

This joint enterprise, by Jane and William, was more sympathetically reflected in Ned Burne-Jones's decorations for the drawing room. His wall paintings wrapped around the settle. This meant that Gabriel's images of *Beatrice & Dante* were bookended by Ned's alternative tale of chivalric love, *Sir Degrevaunt*. Ned completed only three of his wall paintings. He had originally hoped to show seven scenes from the Arthurian legend, but in the end, he focused on the last section of the story: the wedding procession, marriage and wedding feast of the knight and his lady, Melidor. Dante's passion was unrequited, but according to the tale, Degrevaunt and Melidor were married for thirty years, after showing fortitude and chastity during their troubled courtship.

Ned's presentation of the bride and groom echoes the hopes of all their friends for Jane and her husband. Degrevaunt and Melidor are surrounded by other young couples, musicians and poets, good food and good cheer. In part, this is because Burne-Jones was adapting motifs from fourteenth-century frescoes he had seen on his recent visit to northern Italy. He lifted decorative details, and indeed whole groups of figures, like the minstrels in the *Wedding Procession* from Giotto's Arena Chapel in Padua. But these pictures were also hopeful, showing the rich and rare manner of living that his friends were trying to recreate, in a household filled with artists and their work. We see a rose trellis in the garden, and boldly patterned textiles, worn by the women or used as altar cloths or wall-hangings. Burne-Jones was reflecting back the way that Red House felt and looked to William's friends.

This effect is felt most strongly in the last mural of *The Wedding Feast*. In the first two images, the faces of Sir Degrevaunt and Melidor are generic, pretty but undefined. However, at their wedding feast, they are clearly portraits of William and Jane, turning graciously to one another. This was, in effect, another wedding present from Ned. It promised faithfulness and fellowship.

Throughout the autumn and winter of 1860, Jane and William encouraged the other young people to accept their hospitality. Their friends valued the clean air of Kent after the soot-laden dampness of the London streets. The coal fires that warmed the thousands of homes in the capital meant that clothes, curtains, even food and clean washing were quickly covered with airborne dirt. As one doctor described it, mid-century London had an 'opaque atmosphere' with 'deadened colours, obscured distance, smutted faces and black architecture'.[39] Women were advised to keep three hairbrushes – one to use today, one to be washed and dried overnight, one to lend to a friend – because their hair would become thick with coal dust if they walked or drove in town. 'Our brushes look black after once [sic] using,' as one lady explained in her advice book for young wives.[40] It is not hard to imagine Jane struggling to brush the gritty dust out of the masses of her thick hair.

Over Christmas and into the New Year, they played host to groups of friends. Ned and Georgie went home to their parents for Christmas itself, and then rejoined the Morrises soon after. Jane was now heavily pregnant, and Lizzie Siddall stayed with her for several weeks in December, to keep her company and prepare for the birth. Gabriel came and went. The cook and maid were busy preparing dinners (and breakfasts) for the assortment of guests. The 'bachelor's bedroom' by the garden porch was made over regularly, for Philip Webb, or Charley Faulkner, or the painters George Price Boyce or Arthur Hughes. It seems they slept on the sturdy, green-stained single beds that were designed by Ford Madox Brown. (A pair of these beds have survived in the attics at Kelmscott Manor.) Their utilitarian style reiterated the unfussy lines of Webb's built-in wardrobes, and even the great settle in its original unpainted form. Both Brown and Webb understood that medievalism did not mean quaint trimmings. The Gothic, in its simplest form, was forthright in its materials and construction, honest in its function.

Friends made the journey, even in the wet winter months, because they had the chance to share their plans with like-minded artists. They also relished William's boisterous welcome, his generosity as a host. 'It was the most beautiful sight in the world', one remembered, 'to see Morris coming up from the cellar before dinner, beaming with joy, with his hands full of bottles of wine and others tucked under his arms.'[41]

They drank the wine from beautifully simple glasses. These were designed by Webb especially for Red House. They were revolutionary in the clarity of their shape, with a fluted stem and a plain trailed line as the only ornament. The water jugs and tall tumblers were embellished with gilded bands, and tiny buds and stars in blue, white and brown. Webb thought very precisely about the shape of the spout, and the profile of the jug handle. The goblets and decanters that Morris commissioned were far removed from the weightiness of fashionable etched or cut glass. And he clearly expected to entertain many friends, ordering one and a half dozen each of the large and small wine goblets. They were displayed on Webb's majestic dresser, alongside water glasses, grace cups, and flower bowls with undulating rims. All the glassware was made by Powell & Sons in Whitefriars, like the stained-glass panels. They were uncomplicated and pleasing.

The fun of the dinners often involved jokes at William's expense. His friends knew that he had a short temper, and they would deliberately provoke him. These infuriating stunts – like refusing to speak to Morris at his own dining table – were a relic of the Oxford days. The men continued to lark about at Red House, as they had in the Debating Hall of the Union, or after a late night out in London.

Ford Madox Brown's young daughter Cathy remembered extraordinary scenes when the men stayed overnight with her family in Kentish Town, London. It sounded, she said, 'as if wild beasts were in the house'. She opened the door of her father's studio one night, to find William and Ned, Gabriel and his brother William Michael Rossetti, William Bell Scott and Peter Paul Marshall all pretending to be animals. 'The lion, hyena and donkey were the most energetic.' They only stopped when a policeman knocked on the door. Cathy's mother Emma put her back to bed and returned to her fireside chat with Lizzie Siddall.[42]

Tales like this reinforce the bohemian identity fashioned by the men, but they also highlight the networks of friendship created by the women. Emma Madox Brown and Lizzie Siddall spent a lot of time in each other's company, and when Jane moved into Red House, they visited almost as much as Georgie Burne-Jones. So Jane was able to gather a group of women around her who could share her hopes and her upheavals. Emma Brown, in particular, offered emotional and practical support when her friends were pregnant. In the last months of 1860, Lizzie was in the early stages of pregnancy, while Jane was preparing for childbirth early in the New Year. Having Emma in the house changed the atmosphere considerably.

Emma Brown, like Lizzie, was in her early thirties, ten years older than Jane. She was vivacious and unashamedly working-class. While both Jane (through her needlework) and Lizzie (in painting and poetry) developed their own artistic skills, Emma remained focused on the domestic. However, her liveliness and generosity were well known in the group. The Browns, when Jane first knew them, were chronically short of money. One Christmas Eve, they told their friends, they were at the end of their resources, until 'Emma found in her drawer 2 shillings and 3 farthings all in fourpenny pieces, pennys, halfpence, farthings etc left there at different times and forgotten, what a boon.'[43] Despite their own hardships, the Browns were open-handed, and there are several accounts of Emma befriending women she had found on the streets, including a seventeen-year-old with a tiny baby who was curled up on the doorstep.[44]

This easy-come, easy-go manner extended to their family life. Emma and Ford lived together on and off until April 1853, when they had a quiet wedding with Gabriel as one of the witnesses. Some of their friends thought they were 'too amiable and indulgent' to their children, encouraging Cathy and her little brother Nolly to roam widely and climb trees. At home, Nolly 'roved about in a rough pinafore' and wriggled under his father's chair while visitors tried to have a grown-up conversation.[45] Their casual approach to child-rearing was also coloured by Emma's drinking. In the early days of their relationship, Brown would note in his diary that Emma was 'unwell' or had 'a fainting fit'. But by the mid-1850s, it was clear that she struggled with alcoholism. Too often in Madox Brown's diary he would simply put 'E.D.' – Emma Drunk.[46]

We do not know how much Jane, Georgie and Bessie were aware of Emma's problem with alcohol. Certainly, Lizzie knew that her friend drank. She stayed with the Browns when her relationship with Gabriel was in crisis. In the later 1850s, Lizzie was fighting her own demons, too. Her habitual use of laudanum as a sedative and painkiller mirrored Emma's reliance on alcohol. Still, on their good days, both women enjoyed each other's company. (It has been suggested that they were friends from childhood.) 'Emma was the closest of Lizzie's intimacies,' according to the Rossetti family, and Gabriel was often agitated by what he saw as Emma's interference in his private affairs.[47]

Given Emma's unpredictability, and Elizabeth's intermittent ill-health, they might seem odd companions for Jane in the last weeks of her pregnancy. Maybe Emma enjoyed the change from her own cramped domesticity. And Elizabeth too would have preferred the quiet, unpolluted surroundings of Kent, after the smog and river stench of her London apartment. Perhaps Jane also valued their unvarnished conversations. On top of this, there was the shared sense that all three women were negotiating, in their different ways, the complex experience of upward mobility in their marriages.

There were also a great many preparations to be made, and Emma was the only woman in Jane and William's close circle with experience of childbirth. It was expected that female friends and family would share the tasks, especially as a mother-to-be was supposed to spend several hours resting every day: 'in the early months to prevent a miscarriage, and in the latter months, on account of the increased weight and size of the womb.'[48] We know that Jane remained active and hospitable throughout her pregnancy. And although she would have focused on her health, and the needs of her new baby, Christmas was still a time for merry-making. There is a portrait of Jane, her profile carefully outlined in pencil and Indian ink, made by Gabriel at this moment. It shows her thoughtful, but willing to set aside her tasks as a hostess, just for a while, to sit for him. Without the inscription – 'Upton, Xmas 1860' – we would never know that Jane was heavily pregnant. Her friends' desire to create and share artistic projects never waned, even when the mistress of the house was getting ready for the birth of her first child.

One marker of the eccentricities of the Red House circle has recently been revealed in Jane's bedroom. As well as the usual preparations, it seems that Jane's friends began a new mural decoration for her bedroom. In 2013, the conservation team at Red House discovered a painting beneath the layers of wallpaper. Although the surface is damaged, it is possible to make out the shapes and colours.

It was designed to look like a wall-hanging, with five large Old Testament figures, painted on the *trompe l'œil* folds, and stylised trees between them. Adam and Eve are by the door, naked except for their leaves; then come the stiffly draped figures of Noah, Rachel and Jacob. The mural raises a number of questions, not least why these subjects were chosen. After all, Jane was never conventionally religious. Perhaps they were imagined as a commentary on the tension between Jews and Christians that was depicted in the *Prioress's Tale Cabinet*, which was already in the room. Or perhaps, as Tessa Wild has suggested, the fictive hangings were designed in response to one of Burne-Jones's other contributions to the Red House interiors: the tale of Sir Degrevaunt and his courtship. The new paintings in Jane's bedroom might have recreated the atmosphere of Melidor's chamber, described in Degrevaunt's legend as richly decorated with Biblical figures, gilded archangels and azure blue textiles.[49] Jane's room would bring to life the many-layered beauties of a courtly love story.

Nor is it clear who painted the figures. It seems likely that William created the overall design, but different hands were involved in the execution. Ford Madox Brown and Ned Burne-Jones both seem to have helped, but presumably did less when Jane came closer to her confinement. We know that Lizzie Rossetti worked on the murals, as she wrote later, in May 1861, that she was having difficulties with her image. She asked Gabriel to 'come down here on Saturday evening' as 'I want you to do something to the figure I have been trying to paint on the wall.'[50] The upright female figure of Rachel, holding up her cherry-red robe, certainly resembles the distinctive elongated women in Lizzie's drawings. It is not surprising that she struggled to work on such a large scale. She usually created small works on paper, using watercolour and pencil. This design was a significant departure, being much more ambitious. Maybe Lizzie began her section as she kept Jane company during the long weeks of waiting for the baby.

Jane also had to oversee more ordinary domestic arrangements. One of the spare bedrooms would become a nursery, with space for the baby and the nurse, Elizabeth Reynolds. She was the sister of Thomas, the Morrises' groom, so would have known the family. She probably arrived soon after Christmas. It was her job to oversee Jane's recovery, and to help with feeding and changing the baby. And Jane still had to accommodate Bessie, Lizzie, Emma and, when the birth was imminent, Mrs Morris, William's mother. (Jane's mother did not travel from Oxford to look after her.)

It was usual in larger homes like Red House to set aside one of the bedrooms closest to the servants' rooms as a nursery. This meant that the rest of the household were less disturbed in the night. The 'bachelor's bedroom', on the ground floor, was certainly placed as far as possible from the potential disruption of a wakeful child.

We know that Jane made many of the baby clothes herself: Georgie had seen them in her work basket. A well-equipped nursery required a great number of new, carefully stitched items. These ranged from the towelling nappies (some households ordered six dozen) and their triangular flannel wrappers, to fine lawn shirts (a dozen), cambric gowns trimmed with muslin embroidery (at least half a dozen), and a large flannel shawl to keep the baby safe from draughts. A new baby also needed several binders – long strips of calico, linen or flannel – to wind around their tummy. This was believed to strengthen the child's spine, and keep their bowels warm. All these wrappings needed thorough washing and airing before use. The maid would have been hard at work, stoking and skimming the copper in the scullery in the weeks around Christmas, dealing with the laundry created by the impending birth, and the extra visitors.

What was Jane's experience of childbirth? William's brisk message, written shortly after the delivery on 17 January 1861 to Ford Madox Brown, gives very little away. It is not even clear if he was in the bedroom for the birth:

> My dear Brown,
> Kid having appeared, Mrs Brown kindly says she will stay till Monday, when you are [to] come to fetch her please . . . Janey and kid (girl) are both very well.[51]

The 'kid' was named Jane Alice, but always known as Jenny.

Although Jane left no record of her own, we can get an impression of what went on in those first weeks of 1861, by looking at a popular book of *Advice to a Wife* by Pye Henry Chavasse. His manual for young women in the early years of marriage was first published in 1839, and was regularly reprinted throughout the rest of the century. Chavasse outlined the current best practice for doctors and midwives. He used plain language to explain to his readers how to care for themselves and their newborns. He did not shy away from dealing directly with the possible problems of pregnancy and encouraged mothers to persist with breastfeeding for at least nine months. There was no need, he said, for 'false delicacy' in discussing bodily functions. He was clear about the realities of 'soiled napkins', 'flooding' and the exertions of labour.[52]

Advice like this would have been reassuring for Jane, as a very young woman facing childbirth in midwinter, without her mother to hand. We can imagine the stuffiness of her bedroom, with the coal fire blazing. William and the doctor waited in the drawing room next door. Perhaps Jane was offered chloroform; it had become acceptable after Queen Victoria used it in 1853 to ease her eighth delivery. However, we do know that Jane was very wary of opiates and other painkillers.

Jane would have been advised to remain in bed, lying down and 'perfectly passive', for 'the first five or six days, day and night'.[53] Then she might be helped into the drawing room to lie on a sofa for short periods, for another five days. The nurse, with help from Emma, would change, wash and dress little Jenny. Then Jane could feed her, lying on her side. It is likely that Jenny was breastfed, at least for a few months, as this was still the most common practice among Jane's friends. We know from Ford Madox Brown's diaries that Emma fed her son Nolly for nearly a year. And when the Burne-Joneses had their first child the following year, Ned wrote to a friend that 'Georgie is thriving on the kid, and the kid on Georgie, he is the fattest boy known'.[54]

By 21 February 1861, Jane was recovered, and ready to welcome many of their friends to a great christening party. Jenny was taken to Bexley church in the old-fashioned wagonette. The register shows that William gave his profession as 'artist', rather than 'poet'.

The celebratory christening dinner became the stuff of legend. Ned and Georgie were there, with both the Browns and Swinburne. Lizzie and Gabriel Rossetti also stayed, as did Peter Paul Marshall with his wife Augusta.[55] The dining room at Red House had been designed for a great feast like this. The two heavy trestle tables were moved to create a massive T, with Jane and William presiding. It was as if they were recreating the banquet from the tale of Sir Degrevaunt and Melidor. It was a scene that celebrated not just the birth, but Jane's own triumph as the mistress of Red House. The well-stocked pantries, larders and cellars, the bountiful hospitality, were testament to the success of William and Jane's partnership. Their friends wanted to be with them, to share their good fortune.

This was a pivotal moment for the group. Jenny's christening was the backdrop to many of the decisions and tensions that shaped the coming years. Georgie remembered the late-night fun of tiptoeing with Jane, as they took 'a candle to look at the beds strewn about the drawing room for the men. Swinburne had a sofa; I think P. P. Marshall's was made on the floor.'[56] But she also recalled Gabriel Rossetti's unusual melancholy. 'At dinner,' she wrote, 'I sat next to Rossetti, and noticed that even amidst such merry company he fell silent occasionally and seemed absent in mind.'

While the other guests were enjoying William's wine, Gabriel and Georgie sipped water.[57] His wife, Lizzie, was six months pregnant, and it was an uneasy time for the Rossettis. Lizzie's chronic ill-health was at the back of their minds as they rejoiced in the safe delivery of little Jenny. In Georgie's words, there was 'an impression which never wore away, of romance and tragedy between [Lizzie] and her husband'.[58]

Brown was more forthright. A few years previously, he had written in his diary that 'Miss Siddall has been here for 3 days and is I fear dying.'[59] And when Gabriel finally travelled to Hastings to marry her in May 1859, they had to postpone the wedding for a fortnight as Lizzie was unwell. As Georgie wondered, 'How was it possible for her to suffer so much without ever developing a specific disease.'[60] Her friends hoped that the imminent arrival of her baby would be the start of better days for Lizzie and Gabriel.

For all the young couples, parenthood inevitably brought new responsibilities. And this seems to have been at the core of the dis-cussions over the dining table that February evening. How would the artists support their families? Could they turn their art to more profitable use? Looking around at the glowing dining room, the boldly painted cabinets, the elaborate hangings decorating the walls, the friends began to plan. Jane and William were not the only new house-owners who wanted to furnish their homes from scratch. As Ned Burne-Jones described it, in those first months, 'The walls were bare, and the floors; nor could Morris have endured any chair, table, sofa or bed, nor any hangings such as were then in existence.'[61]

How could they offer their skills, the beautiful things they had created together, to a wider public? Red House was always imagined as more than a 'place to live in, but as a fixed centre and background for [William's] artistic work.'[62] By April 1861, William was writing to a friend about a new business venture. 'I have started as a decorator,' he said. 'You see we are . . . the only really artistic firm of the kind.' He and his colleagues could supply stained glass, wall-decorations, 'painted cabinets, embroidery and all the rest of it'.[63] The designs were no longer just for their own domestic delight. They could be bought and sold, part of a burgeoning market in interior decoration for new homes and churches. Gabriel, Ned, Ford Madox Brown, even Peter Paul Marshall wanted to contribute. They had already supplied architects or patrons as individual artists. Now they could pool their ideas and contacts, and advertise their work together.

'Morris, Marshall, Faulkner and Co., Fine Art Workmen' grew out of the late-night, wine-fuelled conversations and long days spent stencilling, stitching, drawing. The Firm, as it was known, profession- alised the projects that the friends had shared since the mid-1850s. As a result, it sidelined the women's contribution. Burne-Jones and Brown made regular notes of their income from Morris & Co. throughout the early years. However, as Linda Parry found, 'no payments to embroiderers appear in the accounts for the first years of production'.[64] Jane, Georgie and Bessie were not paid for their expertise. It marked the end of the easy overlap between home and paid work which the couples had enjoyed.

Jane was nursing her baby and then pregnant again by early summer 1861. She was very conscious of the shifts in her marriage. With the foundation of the Firm, William's focus turned back to London. He became a regular commuter from Red House to the offices in Red Lion Square.

Georgie Burne-Jones, normally so restrained in her writings, described this change – once the children came and the Firm was established – with heart-rending clarity. She had been used to 'sharing the life of the studio'. But now she, like the other women, was shut out:

I remember the feeling of exile with which I now heard through its closed door the well-known voices of friends together with Edward's familiar laugh, while I sat with my little son on my knee and dropped selfish tears.[65]

Chapter 6

Red House 2, 1861–1865

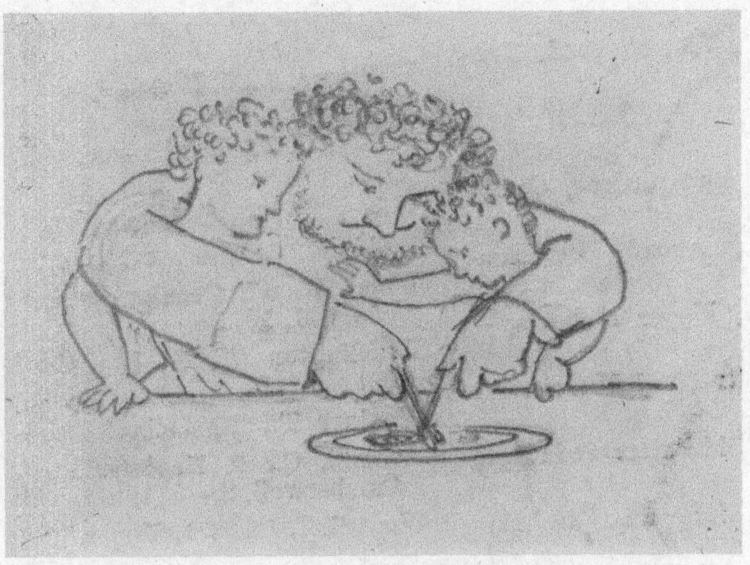

Edward Burne-Jones, *Caricature of William Morris with Jenny and May*,
original untraced, photograph by Emery Walker, c. 1865,
National Portrait Gallery

In the New Year of 1861, facing the future as a new father, William was contemplating how he might live differently. With a houseful of friends at Christmas and then the party celebrating Jenny's birth, there were opportunities for free-flowing, enthusiastic conversation, and moments to sit and make plans together. William was able to rethink how he should spend his time and money. He and Burne-Jones had declared that they would 'devote their lives to art' just before they quit their Oxford studies. But Morris was no fine artist, and although he had learnt a great deal in G. E. Street's office, he was not planning to become a professional architect. His literary magazine had strengthened artistic friendships, but it was not a commercial success. Now he saw another opportunity to use his energy, skills and contacts. William and Jane could reimagine their home as something bigger and bolder. The interiors of Red House would be the template for a new venture.

The 'Fine Art Workmen' had been discussing their plans for pooling their resources and generating income over many months. At last, these were crystallising. As Rossetti explained,

We are organising (but this is quite under the rose as yet) a company for the production of furniture and decoration of all kinds . . .

we are going to open an actual shop! The men concerned are Madox Brown, Jones, Topsy [Morris], Webb, . . . P. P. Marshall, Faulkner and myself. Each of us is now producing . . . things towards the stock. We are not intending to compete with Crace's costly rubbish or anything of that sort, but to give real good taste at the price as far as possible of ordinary furniture.[1]

William was fascinated with design and making, with materials and history. Jane was developing her talent for reinvention and gathering friends. The timing could not be better. The mid-Victorian boom in church and house-building was creating blank walls and windows that needed to be decorated. And there was a major international exhibition, showcasing the best in British and international products, expected to open in London very soon.

What was distinctive about the designs that William Morris and his friends could offer? It was a distillation of the avant-garde interiors of their artistic circle, mixed with a deep love of the medieval in art and literature. They did not just produce Gothic Revival designs. There were other objects that seemed simply old-fashioned or provincial. They chose homely things, often associated with eighteenth-century country interiors. Some of their first attempts at designing tables and cabinets were ungainly.

Where did they get their inspiration for the things they wanted to make and sell? What did they think an artistic interior should look and feel like? Ford Madox Brown's house was, for many of the young men, a foreshadowing of this ideal home. There they found 'Madox Brown and his wife seated at either end of a long table, and every guest a welcome friend who had come to talk and to laugh and to listen.'[2] It was at this dining table that William, Ned and Gabriel first recognised the quiet beauty of old blue and white plates. Soon after, when it came to fitting out the dining room at Red House, 'blue china or delft for vessels of household use' were among the few things 'then to be bought ready-made that Morris could be content with in his own house'.[3] They sat happily alongside Webb's simple glasses and jugs. This explained their love of old-fashioned ceramics, which they began to reinterpret as tile designs, with naïve swans and daisies.

A return to eighteenth-century patterns also shaped their decision to remake a range of elegant rush-seated chairs. The simplest were known as Sussex chairs, crafted from ebonised beechwood, with a spindle back. Jane and William ordered a set for Red House, and so did the Burne-Joneses. Soon they became a staple of the Firm's product list. They were light, and suitable for dining rooms, studios or bedrooms. A more decorative version, with a wheatsheaf back and a rounded rush seat, seems to have been modelled on an antique French chair belonging to Gabriel. And so it became known as the Rossetti chair.

But for their more substantial objects, Morris and Webb drew on other sources. Their time in Street's office, where they were trained in architectural Gothic, underpinned much of their early work for the Firm. There they had studied Street's designs for textiles and woodwork. Most had been produced for church settings. An unprecedented Church of England campaign saw 1,727 churches built or extensively reconstructed between 1840 and 1876.[4] These new buildings needed stained-glass windows, altar cloths, light fittings and pews. Designers like Street and his team responded to the surge in demand by producing furnishings that sat comfortably within these Victorian Gothic spaces.

The profound influence of William's time with Street can be seen if we look closely, for example, at the oak tables they both designed. Street made a virtue of plainness, in the visible joints and flattened legs. Street, in his turn, acknowledged his debt to A. W. N. Pugin's simplified Gothic; he wrote that Pugin's 'tables did not depend upon crockets, finials, and flying buttresses for all their character, but were real, simple'.[5] Pugin's designs were an example of form following function.

William had commissioned a round table, strongly indebted to Street and Pugin, for his bachelor rooms in Red Lion Square. This sturdy, plain wood table – firm and heavy as a rock, according to Gabriel – reflected one aspect of the new style of interior that William and his friends adopted.[6] When William moved to Kent, he and Webb translated these earlier examples into their own version of domestic Gothic. Webb described the long trestle tables made for the dining room in Red House, giving a striking sense of how large and robust they were: 'The shorter of the two . . . would be, if I am right, 8'6" long.' He added, 'both tables were bound round the edge with scoured iron fixed with clout-headed nails, to keep the impatient from whittling away the edge'.[7] William was very heavy-handed with the furniture in his house. He broke chairs with his constant restless wriggling. He stuck forks into the wooden table-top when dinner-time debates became heated. And he evidently could not be trusted with his knife either.

Webb's tables also help us to understand how the furniture was made, first for the house, and then for the business. Even from the earliest days of the Firm, William and his colleagues seem to have thought imaginatively about the manufacturing process. At a time when many companies would have turned a blind eye to sweat-shop labour, Morris's Firm took a different approach. Again, Ford Madox Brown was a key figure in this decision.

One of his patrons was Major William Gillum, who had retired from the Army after losing a leg in the Crimea. He had established an Industrial Home for Destitute Boys on the Euston Road. This was a refuge for homeless children, one of the Ragged Schools projects that were looking after 605 boys and girls in London in March 1860. The Industrial Homes were a lifeline for young people on the streets, giving them shelter and teaching them a trade. They were offered the chance to emigrate – to Australia, Canada, South Africa – or trained for domestic service.[8] Morris employed some of these apprentices to make the new designs for his house, and in due course, for the company.

Over the years, the relationship between Gillum's boys and Morris's circle continued, as William recruited young men into his workshops and encouraged them to develop their skills. It was a practical form of social enterprise, and it offered William an insight into the way that handcraft could transform young people's lives.[9]

This developing partnership with the boys' home also highlighted the shift in the Morrises' own life and work. The Firm drew William back into London. He was needed to oversee the business of designing, making and selling the products, and this was hard to do from Red House. The project had begun as an offshoot of the things their friends had created for Jane and William's home. But, as the new company took shape, it drove a wedge between the domestic and the professional spheres.

All the other original partners were based in town. They each had a £20 share in the company, and put their names to the first advertisement for the Firm in April 1861. Ned Burne-Jones, Charley Faulkner, Arthur Hughes, Ford Madox Brown, Peter Paul Marshall, Gabriel Rossetti and Philip Webb were all expected to attend the partners' meeting each Wednesday evening in central London. William, as the manager and drawing an annual salary of £150, had to stay overnight in town after these meetings. This was an exclusively male project. It brought the husbands together at the very moment when the wives were focused on their pregnancies and infant children.

*

As William wrote in the first advertisement for the Firm, they were offering furniture 'depending for its beauty on its own design' or in 'conjunction with Figure and Pattern Painting'. He insisted that, as a group, the artists had done their homework, having 'for many years been deeply attached to the study of the Decorative Arts of all time and countries'.[10]

This deep attachment to historical examples, as we have seen, included a sympathy towards some eighteenth-century designs. But, more often William built on the fashion for the medieval that had flourished in the 1850s. His delight in the Gothic was part of a wider enthusiasm that followed in the wake of the Great Exhibition of 1851. Pugin's colourful Medieval Court in the Crystal Palace had left an indelible mark on British taste. In the words of Charles Eastlake,

> moyen age mania [had risen] from Pugin's ashes . . . we see evidences of it more or less in every church, in every home, in every shop we enter . . . gothicizing the plates we eat from, the chairs on which we sit, . . . the shape of our beer-jugs, picture frames, candlesticks.[11]

Eastlake was criticising the applied decoration, the Gothic trimming on many conventionally manufactured objects.

At one level, Morris and Company were following in the wake of Pugin's 'gothicizing' fashion. They knew that there was a market for the medieval. However, they also wanted to make it clear that the things they offered were different: they did not rely on surface ornament for their 'moyen age' effect. From the outset, William tried to understand the processes of making, and used those inherent processes to create something that he saw as honest or appropriate. The way he decorated his own home – making 'work of a genuine and beautiful character' – would also apply to the business.[12] It was idealistic, and probably expensive.

Was William successful in setting the Firm apart from his competitors, the other companies that he labelled 'that curious nondescript mixture of clerical tailor and decorator'?[13] Did Morris and Company stand out from the crowd at the next International Exhibition? A massive showcase for art and industry was supposed to open in South Kensington in 1861, but it was postponed following the death of the Prince Consort. This, in fact, helped William and his friends, giving them extra time to prepare. By May 1862, they were ready to present their designs to the world.

We know what they exhibited in the new Medieval Court, and what else was there besides, because the displays were reviewed, some were catalogued and several were photographed. At least five images survive, taken by the London Stereoscopic & Photographic Co. These pictures offer a useful insight into the collections shown in 1862.[14] Firstly, they humanise the displays: in one, a small boy is posed on a plinth beneath a massive carved mantelpiece, his legs stretched out awkwardly. In another the boy is joined by a young man with a top hat; they are perched beneath some statues of Saints Peter and Paul, and an elaborate font.

Secondly, the overall effect is a jumble of ecclesiastical oddments. The whole display was curated by the Ecclesiological Society – it says so in a large banner above the boy's head. This Society encouraged the 'beauty of holiness' in churches, old and new, by championing more ritualistic services, alongside a return to Gothic decoration. But rather than displaying a coherent vision for a church interior, the curatorial team squeezed the objects in higgledy-piggledy: an eagle lectern in front of a fireplace, two painted organs separated by a carved Resurrection, with prominent labels advertising the manufacturers. Some of these juxtapositions are no doubt the result of the photographic process, which flattens the depth of the space. Nonetheless, the displays must have bombarded visitors with highly coloured and sometimes incomprehensible groupings of textiles, sculpture and carved wood. One reviewer, comparing this display with the Medieval Court of 1851, complained, 'There is less space, with more inconvenience.'[15]

For our purposes, we notice that the Firm's works were barely recorded in these stereoscopic pictures. In the five images that survive, we see designs by their colleagues William Burges and John Pollard Seddon, and church furnishings from their competitors, Cox and Son. The display by Morris & Co. was tucked into the far north-east corner. We catch a brief and indecipherable glimpse of one of Edward Burne-Jones's stained-glass designs – the St Frideswide window for Christ Church Cathedral, Oxford – but nothing else. Their metalwork, embroideries and painted cabinets did not merit the attention of the professional photographer. He focused on the more established architects and furnishers. As latecomers to the exhibition project, the Morris & Co. stand was not even fully catalogued. We cannot see the decorative textiles, candlesticks or the sofa designed by Rossetti, that were all on display.

We know, however, from contemporary criticism, that they showed the *King René's Honeymoon Cabinet*, made for J. P. Seddon's office. It was a cumbersome object. As a desk, it was 'satisfactory enough, barring the important fact that there is no place for the legs of the writer, and the table is too short to stand and write at'.[16] Bound with bold ironwork, and inlaid with chevrons and fleurs de lys, it was a statement piece to attract attention, rather than a useful thing. It highlighted the various techniques that the Firm could offer its clients.

The desk was designed as a frame for a series of painted panels that showed off the range of skills they had mastered. Using the legend of medieval King René as a starting point, Morris, Brown, Burne-Jones, Rossetti and their young friend Val Prinsep painted scenes demonstrating different arts. King René himself was seen in the large door panels as an artist, architect and sculptor. Smaller scenes showed other decorative and domestic arts. Both the choice of subjects and the way they were made reinforced the distinctive approach taken by Morris and his friends.

Firstly, the tale of King René emphasised the possibility that one person could turn his hand to many arts. Several arts are embodied by the king, and interlinked thanks to William's background patterning which created, as one reviewer said, a 'glow of harmonious colour'.[17] This reflected the experience of many of the makers in Morris & Co. Burne-Jones, for example, was at this point designing stained glass, tiles, embroideries and book illustrations, as well as murals and easel paintings.

However, despite their experience in working with the decorative as well as the fine arts, William and his friends still emphasised the entrenched hierarchies in artistic status – probably unconsciously. The images representing Painting, Architecture and Sculpture are large and masculine. The arts in which the women excelled – Embroidery, Weaving, Cooking and Gardening – are relegated to the smaller panels. These paintings show some of the young women with their sleeves rolled up, and their skirts kilted, as they focus intently on their work. The Cook with her pots looks like an idealised portrait of 'Red Lion' Mary, while the Weaver has Jane's heavy dark hair. The men recognised that these arts are essential for a pleasant life. But they were not elevated to the same status as the 'professional' arts practised by the men.

There is a clear distinction between the male arts of stone and paint, and the soft, mobile textiles, the feasts and the fruits produced by the women in their circle. This was reinforced by the physical distance in the lives of the artists, separating home and workshop, as design and production moved out of the Morrises' home and were concentrated in central London. The domestic spaces of Red House had driven the first enthusiasm for avant-garde creativity. Men and women had worked there side by side. Now Jane's home began to feel marginalised, out of touch.

The potential shifts and tensions within the circle were also reflected in the radically different designs for furniture that the group were producing. Alongside the massive Gothic desk was an ebonised sofa made to suit Gabriel's more sophisticated taste. Its delicate frame and red cushions were 'ridiculed by various critics, including Charles Dickens'.[18] They were unimpressed by the revealed construction and the Japanese-inspired detailing. There was musical notation embroidered on the upholstery, perhaps the most innovative element. Sadly, the sofa has not survived, and the original drawing (now in Birmingham Museum and Art Gallery) does not show the quavers and crotchets that were stitched on the cushions. We cannot say what music was chosen, and how it related to the overall design of the sofa. Even so, this feature hinted at a very different aesthetic from the rest of the works on display in the Medieval Court. It turned away from the sober Gothic of the church furnishings and chunky oak furniture, and gestured towards the lighter, more eclectic designs of a new artistic manner.

The playfulness and dexterity of some of the Morris & Co. works at the 1862 Exhibition caught the eye of the curators at the South Kensington Museum. They approached the Firm, hoping to buy *King Rene's Honeymoon Cabinet* for the collection of contemporary design. Unfortunately, J. P. Seddon was unwilling to sell; he had commissioned it for his own offices and was taking it back when the show closed. (The museum eventually acquired it from Seddon's daughter in 1927.) However, a little later there was another offer on the table. Would Morris & Co. undertake the decoration of one of the museum's refreshment rooms?

In his advertisement, William had promised that his craftspeople would produce 'work of a genuine and beautiful character' and could ensure 'harmony between the various parts of a successful work'.[19] The refreshment room would be a chance to showcase their skills to a wide artistic audience in the heart of London. Designing interiors for their friends was all very well, but how many people would see the tile panels and embroideries they made for their own circle? Here was a permanent shop window for their wares.

*

The space they created in South Kensington in the mid-1860s demonstrated a new, softer manner. The insistent geometric Gothic of the interiors at Red House was replaced with flowing lines and a simplified colour scheme. It became known as the Green Dining Room. The slate-blue wood panelling and mossy green walls were touched with accents of red and gold. Burne-Jones painted small inserts with young men and women representing the signs of the zodiac. Webb added little branches of fruiting trees, and a frieze of running hares and dogs. The ceiling was stencilled with golden sunbursts.

William and Webb divided the walls into sections. The lowest was the deep wainscotting, reaching to the height of a chair rail. Then came the narrow dado of zodiac and fruit panels. Above that, they created a broader green area of spreading foliage made of painted plasterwork, enlivened with tiny red flowers and blue berries. And then the cornice or frieze with chasing animals beneath the ceiling. This division of the walls – particularly the addition of the dado panelling – was at the forefront of the latest fashion. By the late 1870s, wallpaper manufacturers were making designs that incorporated all the different patterns in one drop. (The broadest area, known as the filling, was the least ornamented. It offered a quieter background for paintings hung from a picture rail.) But the Green Dining Room was an early example of a trend that would become commonplace within a few years. And as every element was handcrafted, it was an expensive and time-consuming business. Estimates for the work included £277 14s for 'colouring and gilding the plaster ceiling and painting the panelled dado', and £291 6s for seventy panels, painted 'with figures and patterns'.[20]

The Firm's accounts also show an estimate of £272 for stained glass, and Burne-Jones sent in a bill for £35 for the cartoons for these windows. Like the rest of the designs for this room, they demonstrated a shift in style. The girls are not allegories of anything. There is no story – of saint or Arthurian princess – to be told. The supple figures almost seem to be dancing between the rose bushes, swaying to the sound of the fountain. There is a suggestion of music: one of the girls holds an ancient stringed instrument. There are several notable differences between these windows and those Burne-Jones was designing five years earlier. Firstly, the colour scheme is much paler. Gone are the bold clashes of primary colours, to be replaced by gentle, sunlit effects. The setting has also changed. Burne-Jones is no longer conjuring up a specific medieval environment. Instead, the girls wander through an ageless space in their flowing robes. It may be Classical or Renaissance, somewhere or nowhere. This ahistorical landscape of the imagination, derived from Burne-Jones's travels and enthusiasms, but never dependent on a particular place or time, became the backdrop for his art for the next forty years. It is almost like a dream, composed of memories of Siena, Bruges and Oxford, Malory's Avalon and Chaucer's Tales.

Burne-Jones's eyes had been opened to the possibilities of new subjects and settings by his recent journey to Italy. In May 1862, just as the International Exhibition was opening, he and Georgie set out for Venice. They were travelling with John Ruskin, and as he was paying the bills, they journeyed in an unhurried, comfortable way. Georgie left her young son Philip at home with her mother and sisters, and Ruskin was surprised how 'she seemed to see everything through a mist of baby'.[21] Comments like these bring into sharp focus the different priorities, the different points of view of the men and women in William's circle. For Ned, the immersion in Italy, guided by Ruskin, revolutionised his manner of painting. Many years later, Burne-Jones recalled the mid-1860s as 'years of the beginning of art in me'. It was a time of bonhomie, with 'Gabriel everyday, and Ruskin in his splendid days, and Morris everyday and Swinburne everyday, and a thousand visions in one always, more real than the outer world'.[22]

Ned memorialised one of these visions in his watercolour *Green Summer*, painted in 1864 as a souvenir of the garden of Red House. Eight young women are seated by a pool in a flowery meadow, listening to a story. They have garlands in their hair, and the folds of their grass-green dresses are overlapping. The figures are not direct portraits of the young wives and sisters who stayed at Red House. But they represent a peaceful exchange of ideas, and a delight in the soft outdoors. For girls like Cathy Madox Brown, Red House was somewhere to read *Wuthering Heights* and *Sidonia the Sorceress*, in a garden filled with roses. In Cathy's imagination, William was the Beast, and Jane was Beauty.[23] This is what Jane's home and garden offered to the young women who came here. It was a place apart.

*

This dreamlike view of the group of friends did not tell the whole story. The early 1860s were also a time of bereavement, the end of hopes as well as the beginning of a radical enterprise. At the very moment when Morris, Burne-Jones and their colleagues were preparing for their debut at the 1862 Exhibition, they were also mourning the sudden and desperate loss of a dear friend.

Elizabeth Siddall Rossetti died on 11 February 1862. She had taken an overdose of the opiate laudanum. These bare facts are all that we can know for certain. Why she died, and how it affected the women and men who knew her well: that is harder to say. They had been concerned for Lizzie's health for many years. Ford Madox Brown had described her early on, in 1854, as 'looking thinner and more deathlike and more beautiful and more ragged than ever'.[24] By the spring of 1860, Gabriel was desperately worried: 'If I were to lose her now . . . I should have so much to grieve for, and (what is worse) so much to reproach myself with.'[25]

Jane and William did not leave any direct record of Lizzie's last months, although she stayed at Red House often. But Georgie grew close to her, and valued her as an artist and a friend. She sat with Lizzie in the Rossettis' apartment overlooking the Thames at Chatham Place, or sewed quietly at her side in the echoing rooms of Red House.

It is hard to interpret the silences and evasions that permeate Georgie's writings. However, we do know that during her pregnancy Lizzie was 'excited and melancholy', unable to find peace for her 'jarring nerves'.[26] Her visits to Red House became more erratic. Sometimes she took off back to London unexpectedly. Other times she bent to her work. She was trying to finish her section of the frieze in Jane's bedroom. It was not going well, and she wrote to Gabriel, 'I am too blind and sick to see what I am about.'[27]

Lizzie's ill-health increased after her daughter was stillborn on 2 May 1861, and she was left 'with empty arms'.[28] Her grief was compounded by Jane and Georgie's healthy pregnancies. Lizzie became more addicted to the painkiller laudanum, taking bitter doses mixed with wine or brandy. Georgie found her one afternoon, deep in depression, sitting by her 'childless cradle'. She hushed the visitors with a 'kind of soft wildness',[29] asking them not to wake the baby. Lizzie later suggested that Georgie take her dead baby's clothes, all the linens and flannels she had lovingly hemmed and aired. Gabriel was distraught: 'Don't let her[,] please. It looks like such a bad omen for us.'[30]

It was to Georgie that Gabriel turned early in the morning on 11 February 1862. He sent 'Red Lion' Mary to wake the Burne-Jones household. Lizzie had taken an overdose after an evening out with Gabriel and Swinburne. All Georgie could say was that 'our poor, lovely Lizzie was dead . . . There was nothing we could do – all was over . . . I leave you to imagine the awful feeling there is upon us all.'[31]

*

The loss of Lizzie's child, and then her own death, was a blow to all the circle. It damaged the fragile fabric of the 'beautifullest place on earth'.[32] Jane and William had started from scratch with his father's money, and the hand skills of their friends to bring it to life. Now the incomplete projects – the painted figures in Jane's bedroom, the unfinished stitching on the Good Women embroideries – reminded the couple that their home relied on the time and energy of the women, as well as the men.

The beauty of Red House was not just its bricks and mortar, its cabinets and chairs. It was brought to life by the cooperation of designers and doers, those who worked with the pencil and brush, those who threaded a needle, or planted and pruned, or oversaw the baking, those who made sure there were enough beds, and a place for everyone at the table. Jane's skills as a housekeeper had encouraged friends and acquaintances to return to this out-of-the-way corner of Kent. Now, in the wake of Lizzie's death, she and William tried to shore up what was left of this communal life. William in particular felt a pressing need to cement relationships with those who were left.

Ever since his Oxford days, William had toyed with the idea of an artistic community, a space apart. Originally, he had imagined living in a sort of monastic brotherhood. Now he and his friends had married, of course, it was impractical – although he never entirely lost sight of that dream. He wanted to experiment with new ways of organising family life.

In the spring of 1864, it seemed possible that Red House might really be the hub of a permanent artist's settlement. William and Jane had hopeful discussions with Ned and Georgie Burne-Jones. The L-shaped house could be extended to make a quadrangle, with the well at its heart. As the apple trees came into blossom, and the little herbers filled with flowers, Jane could look forward to her own children growing up alongside Georgie's family. The house seemed overlarge during the week, when William was away and she was left with the two little girls. Their younger daughter was born barely a year after Jenny, on 25 March 1862. This was Lady Day, the Feast of the Annunciation, so she was christened Mary, but always known as May. Jane's sister Bessie and the young nurse Elizabeth Reynolds worked alongside her, to keep the house in order, and help with the toddlers. Even so, the prospect of the Burne-Jones family being close at hand was something to wish for. They would enrich the possibilities of joint work.

It was this shared creativity, as well as 'certain dream-pictures . . . too intimate and tender for description . . . strangely intense' that May remembered from her infancy at Red House. She wrote later of 'work and play so interchangeable, so thoroughly enjoyed'. May believed that these days with his friends shaped her father's later vision for life and work. He longed to rediscover this joy and activity, and the laughter sounding through the 'half-furnished rooms' and 'the fragrant little garden'. There is a delightful caricature made by Ned at this time, showing William with his girls. He has an arm around each of his tiny daughters, as he tries to cut up their dinner. These were the scenes that May 'carried through the child-life' to her later days, when the 'beauty at last pierces the heart and they become a reality – dream and memory, today and yesterday, all strangely intermingled'.[33]

For Jane and Georgie, too, there was shared pleasure in work and play. Despite their different upbringings, they enjoyed each other's company. They encouraged each other to practise their artistic skills – Georgie with her drawing and wood engraving, Jane with her textiles – at least in the quieter moments. It was especially difficult to stay focused on these projects when friends like John Ruskin diminished them. Georgie respected Ruskin. She and Ned called him 'Papa' on their travels. It must have hurt when he wrote to remind her of her new responsibilities: there was no one more diligent than Georgie among all of Jane's friends.

Ruskin said he was 'delighted to hear of her woodcutting'. He thought it would be particularly useful if she could engrave her husband's drawings: 'without too much disturbance of feminine thought and nature. I cannot imagine anything prettier or more wifely . . . there is just the proper quantity of echo in it.' He finished by telling Georgie to 'Keep your rooms tidy, and baby happy – and then after that as much woodwork as you've time and liking for.'[34]

This was hard – and sounded harder in the wake of Lizzie's death. Elizabeth Siddall had tried to train as a professional painter. She had exhibited her watercolours, and coaxed unexpected images from old songs. Ruskin had acknowledged her as a 'genius' to rank beside 'Turner, Watts, Millais, Rossetti',[35] and had found her 'queenly-kind' when he saw her soon after her marriage in 1860.[36] But now she was memorialised as Gabriel's model, his lover, his shadow, when the women had known her as a bright creative spirit. Jane and Georgie had seen themselves with Lizzie, at the heart of the artistic activity of Red House. And before that, in Oxford and London, they had felt at home in the studio, discussing new ideas for paintings and poems, decorating their domestic spaces, entering into the radical spirit of the circle. Now the women seemed to be sidelined and separated. Meanwhile the men enjoyed the freedom to meet regularly, to talk and travel and build. Perhaps by bringing the two families together, these joint conversations and projects could be rekindled.

Philip Webb was delighted to return to the site. He drew up new plans. The families would have separate entrances and kitchens. But they could share the gardens, and work together as they wished. The new wings would be half-timbered, as if the original solid Gothic structure had been enlarged gradually in the sixteenth century. There would be a broad east window for Ned's studio on the first floor, and an oriel window in the drawing room. William was excited at the prospect. He was also very conscious that his friends lacked the funds for a substantial family home, so, he generously suggested that his own studio, and the downstairs 'bachelor's bedroom', could be incorporated in Ned's side of the house. Even with this reordering, the plan was too costly for Georgie and Ned: 'Enthusiasm had outrun our wisdom and modifications had sadly to be made.'[37]

Philip Webb pared back his ideas. In a new set of drawings, labelled 'the second arrangement for reducing the cost', he simplified the space below stairs and removed a bathroom. There were fewer bedrooms than in the Morrises' quarters – two on the first floor, with a nursery and servants' bedroom on the second floor. Both families were entranced by the scheme: 'Webb made a design for it so beautiful that life seemed to have no more in it to desire.'[38] Years later, after William and Ned had both died, Georgie wrote longingly about this turning point in their fortunes: 'The two sets of plans lie before me now, clean and unused, and it is curious to think how differently all our lives would have gone if this scheme had been carried out.'[39] She gave the plans to the South Kensington Museum, as a reminder of the strong hope they carried with them in the spring of 1864.

The families holidayed together in September that year, with Charley Faulkner, his sisters Kate and Lucy, and his mother. Georgie was six months pregnant, and the weeks by the seaside in Little-hampton seemed a joyful foretaste of the years ahead. 'Time passed lightly for Janey and me,' she remembered; 'the evenings were always merry with Red House jokes revived and amplified.' Even William's outbursts – when he broke his spectacles and threw them out of the window – were relieved by the presence of friends, and he 'burst into laughter'.[40] It must have been a blessing for Jane, who often had to cope with William's anger on her own.

As autumn set in, they returned to London. Then Georgie's son Philip developed scarlet fever. Georgie caught it too and her baby, Christopher, was born two months premature, on 28 October 1864. After three terrible weeks, little Christopher died, while Georgie was still in a 'delirium of fever'. Georgie recovered slowly, but the pain of losing her child lingered. She still carried the sadness in 1892: 'As every year comes round . . . I keep its birthday and death day, and a shadowy son of seven and twenty sometimes exists for a moment for me.'[41]

In these dreadful months, Jane struggled to support her friends. William was also very ill, bedridden with rheumatic fever. He suffered aching joints, chest pains, breathlessness and a high temperature, in the wake of a throat infection. It took a long time for William to shake it off, and the fever recurred over the years, particularly in bad weather.

By Christmas, all their hopes 'for building and living together' were ended. Burne-Jones wrote to William, explaining that he did not have the heart, or the resources, to commit to a new life in the countryside. William was still trapped at home when he received this letter. He wrote his reply from 'Bed, Red House':

> As to our palace of Art, I confess your letter was a blow to me at first, though hardly an unexpected one – in short I cried; but I have got over it now . . . I am only 30 years old. I shan't always have rheumatism, and we shall have a lot of years of invention and lustre plates together I hope . . . I had begun a letter to you but it read so dismal . . . that I burnt it.[42]

In his characteristic manner, William threw what strength he had into finding a solution for Ned and Georgie's sadness and insecurity. His plans were generous, as he felt that spending more time at Red House would help both families:

> Come and stay with me for a month or two, there is plenty of room for everybody and everything; you can do your work uninterruptedly; I shall have a good horse by then and Georgie and J. will be able to drive about with the kids jollily.

He added that he and Jane had been discussing what to do: 'Janey is exceedingly anxious that you should come and it is in her opinion the best thing you could do.'[43] Here was a chance for Jane to take her friend and their toddlers out in the wagonette, enjoying the quiet roads around Upton. They could offer a refuge at Red House, after the ravages of winter. But Georgie and Ned could no longer throw themselves into the convivial atmosphere. They were still too fragile to face the ghosts of what might have been. They did not come.

Their worlds had shifted. And practically speaking, the Firm could not be run from Kent. The workshops would not move out of the city, or at least not yet. This meant that William needed to devote more time to the business in London. In his long letter to Ned, he had suggested an alternative plan. The pair of them could get 'a studio in town'. Other friends could join them. He acknowledged that perhaps 'it would be too like the old way of living'. But part of him hankered for that collegiality of the old way. And he was tired after his illness. He did not relish the long hours commuting to Bloomsbury and back.

The men regrouped in the offices and workshops in Red Lion Square. They met after the day's designing and writing was over. William and Ned, Gabriel and Ford Madox Brown, Val Prinsep, Charley Faulkner, they all looked forward to their Wednesday evenings together. These meetings reinforced the sense that the workings of the Firm were based on personal sympathies as much as professional commitments. Thanks to a letter written by Charley Faulkner, we have one brief glimpse into these late-night gatherings:

Beginning at 8 or 9 pm, they open with relation of anecdotes . . . Topsy [Morris] and Brown will perhaps discuss the relative merits of the art of the thirteenth and fifteenth centuries, and then perhaps after a few more anecdotes business matters will come up about 10 or 11 o'clock and be furiously discussed till 12, 1 or 2.[44]

Meanwhile the work on the house slowed and finally stopped. The friends were caught up in paid jobs, drawing and setting stained glass and tiles, tackling new commissions for church furnishings from Bethnal Green to Scarborough. There was no time to complete the playful domestic decorations. One of the unfinished projects still stands in the hall at Red House, as a reminder of how William's dream of a 'palace of Art' came to an end. It is an inelegant piece of furniture, typical of their early designs. It has a bench and drawers, fold-down doors and hinged cupboards, and a pitched roof all in one. Some of the surfaces still glow with soft gilded decoration. And across the two largest panels is a painted idyll lifted from Avalon: an enclosed garden filled with fruit trees, where lovers embrace and make music.

The mood and medieval trappings link it back to the *Morte d'Arthur* wall paintings in Oxford. Like those murals, this cabinet seems to have been a collaboration, painted in stages by several different visitors to Red House. Gabriel Rossetti has been identified as one of the artists, but it is likely that William also helped with the backgrounds. We can identify 'Red Lion' Mary in an elaborate headdress standing to the far left. She seems slightly distracted, looking the other way, as if a latecomer to the gathering. Ned and Georgie are seated lovingly together on the flower-sprinkled grass eating cherries. Jane, with her unmistakable crinkled dark hair, sits on a bench close to a young bearded musician.

And here the story tails off. The face of the musician is indistinct. It may be William, or perhaps it is Charley Faulkner. There is a female figure standing by a tree near Ned and Georgie, but her action and her features are unclear. The last figures, a man and two women, have faces left completely blank. We can see some of the details of their clothing – the pointed slippers, the wide cuffs turned back to show the contrasting lining, the man's dark hood pushed far back. But the outlines of these three faces are empty. What do the gaps mean?

If this picture was supposed to be a celebration of love and companionship, like the *Sir Degrevaunt* series upstairs, then there is a couple missing – we cannot see the faces of Rossetti and Lizzie. When Elizabeth Siddall died, Gabriel could not go on with his portraits on the cupboard doors. It was too painful. Perhaps Lizzie was also one of the artists who had begun this project. The angular poses of Ned and Georgie suggest that she was painting this panel when she stayed with Jane. It was another relic of her presence, one of many artistic traces that she left around Red House.

The hall cabinet still stands, as it always did, in the middle of Jane and William's home. They had to pass it every time they climbed the stairs, or opened the front door, or went into dinner. It was a souvenir of their first delight in bringing friends together under the apple trees. It became a talisman, too, of what was lost in the years that followed, the people who were missing, the hopes diminished.

By the late summer of 1865, both Jane and William accepted that change was inevitable. William found the regular commuting was unsustainable. Jane knew that her close women-friends were scattered and preoccupied. William 'decided in his unflinching way that he must come up and live at his business in London'.[45] We do not know how Jane felt about this decision. It would be hard for her and the girls to leave the garden, to be confined in a townhouse, living above the workshop. They moved out in November 1865. Red House was sold the following autumn to James Heathcote, a retired naval officer. A new family was able to enjoy the massive furniture that had to be left behind. Heathcote's young daughter particularly liked one of the oak chairs, built 'like a throne with beautifully carved arms'.[46]

William never saw the house again: 'The sight of it would be more than he could bear.'[47] Jane never went back, as far as we know. But Georgie knew that Red House would not be forgotten. She wrote that 'some of us saw it in our dreams for years afterwards as one does a house known in childhood.'[48]

*

A few months after William's death, Georgie made a final pilgrimage to Red House. It is largely thanks to Georgie's love for the place that we can understand the role the house played in all their lives. It was the crucible in which they created their designs for living differently. Around the dinner table, in the quiet corners of the shady garden, up on the scaffolding, they shared their hopes for art and poetry.

In many ways, Georgie grew up at Red House. She had first visited as a new bride, barely out of her teens. She and Jane learnt together – how to be a wife, a mother, how to make a home, how to suffer loss. On her last visit Georgie found 'the fields around the garden untouched. The apple blossom was out.'[49] It was spring again.

Queen Square, 1865–1871

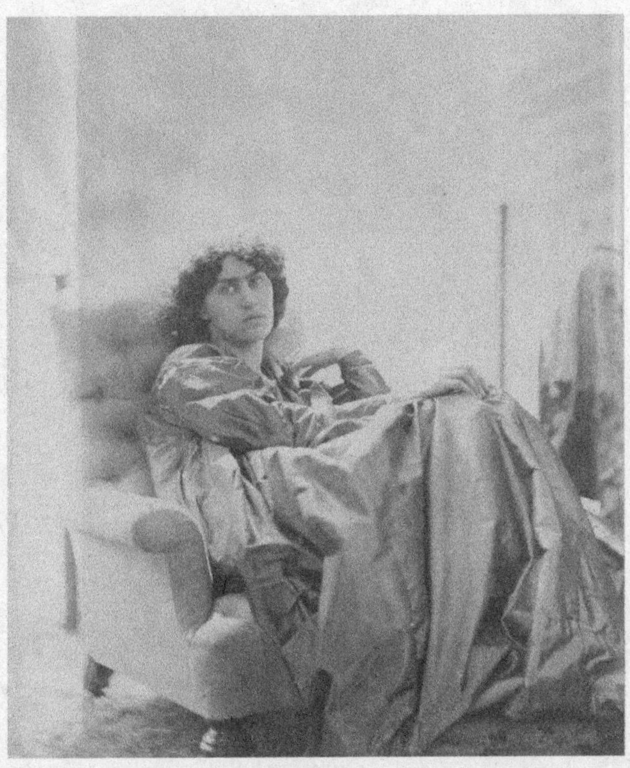

John Parsons and D G Rossetti, *Jane Morris*, photograph, 1865, V&A Museum

It is midsummer 1865, and Jane is curled up in the shade. She has been working all that long hot afternoon, and now she looks beyond the camera, out into the green of the garden. Her loose dress envelops her body. We concentrate on the turn of her neck, the tilt of her chin, her heavy eyebrows, the light as it catches the waves of hair framing her face, her flexed fingers. This is the last pose. Leaning against the button-backed armchair, her feet are hidden beneath the folds of her satin skirt. She is almost relaxed.

The photograph is preserved in an album, along with twenty-six other prints, made for her daughter May after Jane's death. Many of the pictures had been framed and on display in May's home when she was growing up, but they were showing signs of fading. She wanted to keep them safe, as a souvenir of her mother's presence.[1] Perhaps May had been there in the garden in 1865, a toddler just out of sight of the camera, tucked behind a screen, watching Jane as she folded and held her body.

The garden would have been an exciting place for a little girl. It was the haunt of exotic beasts and strange birds. Jane was modelling for Gabriel Rossetti in the large grounds behind his house in Cheyne Walk, Chelsea. Rossetti had moved to Tudor House by the river, in the autumn after Lizzie Siddall's death, intending to share it with Swinburne and his brother William Michael. He also began to fill the garden with creatures. At various points in the 1860s, Tudor House was home to

> a Pomeranian puppy named Punch, a grand Irish deerhound named Wolf, a barn-owl named Jessie, another owl named Bobby . . . rabbits, dormice, hedgehogs, two successive wombats, a Canadian marmot or woodchuck, an ordinary marmot, armadilloes, kangaroos, wallabies, a deer, a white mouse with her brood, a racoon, squirrels, a mole, peacocks, wood-owls, Virginian owls, Chinese horned owls, a jackdaw, laughing jackasses (Australian kingfishers), undulated grass-parrakeets, a talking grey parrot, a raven, chameleon, green lizards, and Japanese salamanders.[2]

Gabriel's menagerie was left to roam the house and garden, burrowing, hibernating in old cabinets, destroying trees, scaring the neighbours. For a while, he kept a zebu, or 'small Brahmin bull'.[3] Rossetti bought it because the bull's large dark eyes reminded him of Jane. He made no secret of his admiration for Mrs Morris. She had been one of his favourite models before her marriage, and she was becoming more visible in his designs again. He had arranged the photographic session to experiment with a range of poses and lighting effects. These images would become a repository of ideas for his paintings of mythological women.

Jane was a patient and flexible model, experienced in the ways of the artist's studio. But this was an unusual sitting, shifting from the bright lawn to the soft, filtered light of a large tent. She sensed the scuttlings and flutterings of the pets on the edge of her vision, as well as the gaze of John Parsons, the professional photographer hired by Gabriel.

Her movements were partly choreographed by Rossetti. Jane's

dresses obscured the outlines of her body, with voluminous sleeves and bulky floor-length skirts. But the masses of dark fabric accentuated her pale neck and face. Rossetti wanted to study her hands. Jane made sure they were visible, lying in her lap or on the back of her chair. Standing beneath the trees, she held a branch of heart-shaped leaves, taken from the avenue of limes behind the house. Then she gathered great folds of the antique robe she was wearing, creating elaborate swathes of fabric across her body. They moved inside the tent, where Gabriel had placed an incongruous sofa, a tub chair and a Japanese screen. Jane sat down, turning half-away from the camera lens and settled into a new position. She touched her necklace and rested her chin lightly on her hand. In each plate, she placed herself precisely.

The photographer had arrived in the late morning, to set up his equipment. They began in the open air. Jane was wearing a dark silken dress with very full sleeves and wide cuffs. She turned these back to show her wrists and the delicate decorative edging. This dress was fitted to her waist, not tightly, but pleated above and below her embroidered belt, with its flower-like buckle. The skirt still showed the creases from being kept folded in a drawer. She had left her hooped underskirt in the house, wearing just a couple of petticoats instead, so that the dress seemed more fluid, as it fell from the waist. Her mass of hair was smoothed and tucked behind her ears, secured by a large pin.

And so the session begins with some conventional, almost demure, arrangements. Jane is seated in a basket chair, with an Indian shawl gently swaying during the exposure; she stands quietly with her hands clasped; she turns her back to the camera and looks to one side, caught in profile against the garden wall. She goes inside to try on a different dress, an old-fashioned sack-back robe, with narrow cuffs. She needs help to fasten up the back – is her sister Bessie with her perhaps, keeping an eye on the little girls? Or does Gabriel ask

Fanny Cornforth, his housekeeper, to take Jane into one of the empty bedrooms, and give her some assistance?

The mood of the pictures changes. The poses become more complex, as Jane moves around the tent. She stands, her back resting against a tent pole, her hands held at her waist: Rossetti will memorialise her in this attitude as *Pandora*. She pivots and looks straight into the lens, her skirts crumpled. Next she goes to the sofa, and lies back uncomfortably, a heavy brocade cushion behind her head, a bangle discarded by her side. She looks up and away. Then she sits, bends, twists, leans forward. The back of her hair is messy, as it escapes the knot at the nape of her neck. It changes her silhouette, creating a wilder appearance, far removed from the neat respectability of the earlier photographs. As the afternoon light begins to fade, she drops into the armchair, tucks her feet under her skirts, and holds still for the last time. Then she can unwind her body, change back into her day dress, and think about going home.

*

Jane and William Morris were still living in Red House in the summer of 1865, when Jane sat for Gabriel. But their working lives were entrenched in London. Their move to 26 Queen Square in the autumn was an upheaval that could no longer be avoided. It brought Jane closer to her network of friends, and enabled William to realign his business and his home life. Still, it was hard to think of the 'beautiful Kentish home . . . deserted, and the sunny rose-garden with its fragrant rosemary and lavender borders' silenced.[4]

From her new bedroom, Jane could look down into the Bloomsbury square. For her daughters, the sooty communal gardens 'were big enough to be a place of mystery and adventure'. Hiding beneath 'the great plane-trees and thickly grown bushes', it seemed 'a wilderness of one's own fashioning' to Jenny and May.[5] Jane, however, missed the ease of the outdoor spaces of Red House, where she could sew or read in peace, or plan her planting and harvesting. Now she was mistress of another imposing house, but this one was hemmed in and uncomfortably tall, with four storeys, plus the basement kitchen and the attics. Her own room caught the setting sun in the evenings. Even so, it was sombre compared with the exuberant decorations of Red House. Medieval murals would have seemed out of place in this eighteenth-century space.

Jane had kept a number of relics from her old bedroom. The *Prioress's Tale Cabinet* stood to one side, glowing with gilded images of another age. She had an ebonised mirror, designed by Philip Webb, which was plain but pleasing. And beside her bed was a jewellery casket. This was a gift from Gabriel. It was decorated with miniature scenes, some of which he had painted. Other panels were made by Lizzie Siddall. The tiny pictures were filled with intense reds and blues, like the manuscript illuminations that inspired them. Inside the tight margins banded by iron fastenings, the figures swayed and gestured. Jane could trace the outlines with her fingertips. Here were three ancient goddesses, reimagined as Gothic queens, with Paris offering Venus a golden apple. On the lid, Siddall painted a couple in a fragile boat, sailing swiftly across a moonlit sea. And at one end, a group of young women make music and wait. The combined effect of the images was eerie and out of time.

The central panel showed a pair of lovers in a walled garden; the figures were lifted directly from an early fifteenth-century manuscript in the British Museum that Gabriel and William had both studied with great admiration. This *Book of the Queen* was written by Christine de Pizan. As Tessa Wild has pointed out, the work also appealed to Siddall, as 'a pioneering text on women by a woman'.[6] This casket was a reminder of how Jane and her friends had celebrated the possibilities of women's work at Red House.

The casket reflected the early intentions of the close-knit group of artists. It was a collaborative object, made by men and women whose creativity was steeped in Gothic tales and buildings. The move to London offered new opportunities for William, Jane and their circle to rethink their art. Jane and her girls could spend more time with neighbours like Kate and Lucy Faulkner, who found ways to work imaginatively.

The Faulkners lived with their mother at the south end of Queen Square, at number 35. Their brother Charley was one of the founding partners of the Firm, and Kate and Lucy were resourceful artists, who produced designs for the business. Lucy became particularly skilled in translating Ned Burne-Jones's designs on large tile panels. She painted the stories of *Cinderella* and *The Sleeping Beauty* on overmantels. Lucy worked hard to find the right glaze and touch to make Ned's complex visions of knights and ladies sit happily on the ceramic surfaces.

When Jane visited with her girls, the house seemed a wonderful mixture of activity and composure. The Faulkners' long drawing room on the first floor matched William's description of his ideal domestic space: it 'ought to look as if some kind of work could be done in it less toilsome than being bored'.[7] For little May and Jenny it was a 'precious place, full of old china and round mirrors . . . early drawings of Burne-Jones . . . and a dear little square piano'. It smelt good, too, with a 'delicious country atmosphere of freshness and roses about it'.[8]

Kate Faulkner, the older sister, played ballads on the piano. And she encouraged Jane's little girls to stand close by her side while she showed them the latest project on her work table. May remembered how they would 'watch her skilful handling of the long slim tile-painting brush'. From their earliest days, Jane and William's daughters learnt that this pleasurable making and doing was something they too could enjoy. Like Kate or Lucy Faulkner, they could grow to become 'a designer of ability and distinction'.[9]

From the Faulkners' drawing room windows, they could also watch the young women who were studying at the Female School of Art, on the south side of the square. These girls were being trained in design and drawing, not as a hobby, but as a way to 'obtain an honourable and profitable employment'.[10] This was very different from Jane's own upbringing. She had expected to earn her living as a college servant. But she too had discovered that access to the art world was transformative. Her experience as a model and maker had enriched her life, and introduced her to new friends. She knew that there were opportunities for women as well as men, to work and learn, and see the world with fresh eyes. Jane shared these opportunities with her girls. It was possible for women to work with their head and their hands, and not lose status. These were important days for May especially, and she remembered them with fondness. Above all, Jane was always reassuringly to hand, 'in soft silk gowns that we loved and stroked'.[11]

*

Their father, however, was busy with his poems and his customers. William was renting 26 Queen Square because it was large enough to accommodate both his work and his home life. On the ground floor, there was space for workshops and a showroom, and the family rooms were upstairs. The problem of his long hours of commuting from Kent had been solved, now he lived directly above the shop.

For several years, Red House had been an unofficial showcase for the wares made by the Firm. Jane's guests saw how Webb's candlesticks or Ned's stained-glass designs could be incorporated beautifully into an artistic home. In the early days of the Firm, they had also displayed a small part of their ecclesiastical and domestic designs in Red Lion Square. Morris would come in and out, talking through ideas with his colleagues, and explaining the virtues of their products to potential clients. Visitors would be struck by his vehemence in selling the products, demonstrating how Webb's wine glasses and tumblers 'would stand firm' when he put them on the table'.[12]

Gabriel Rossetti began to refer to Morris, rather scathingly, as 'The Bard and Petty Tradesmen'. He created a caricature of William, with his unruly hair and increasingly stout figure, his fists on the shop counter, uncompromising, belligerent even. It was around this time that William took to wearing informal working clothes every day, rather than the jacket, stiff collar and tie expected of a businessman. In his indigo blue linen blouse and heavy leather belt, he looked ready to get stuck into any job that came to hand.

William's blue smock echoed the traditional dress of working men. His idiosyncratic personal style became part and parcel of his creed: that craft and creativity were honourable callings and should be celebrated. For him, there was no disjunction between good work and pleasure. It made sense for production, sales and family to be brought under one roof. William sat at the heart of it, in his study upstairs which 'smelt pleasantly of tracing paper'.[13] The house was 'made to shine with whitewash and white paint', as a bright backdrop to the rich colours and patterns of the merchandise.

At the far end of the yard was an old ballroom. This was a souvenir of the heyday of Queen Square in the late eighteenth century, when it had been a more fashionable area, and there was still a suggestion of open fields to the north of Guildford Street. A century on, the extra-large space was repurposed for manufacturing. The Firm had moved their equipment from the premises at Red Lion Square. Furniture, ceramics and stained glass were all being made in Jane and William's back yard. The heat of the kilns, the smells of glue and soldering irons, the constant racket of a dozen men and boys were inescapable. After the quiet of Kent, it must have been a shock to the little girls especially. Still, there were moments of excitement, as when Jenny and May were given a glimpse of the 'shadows and the mystery of the kiln-house'.

They also liked to stand on tiptoe, peering through the windows of the covered wooden cloister that linked the house and the old ballroom. This was the hub for creating stained-glass windows to designs by Burne-Jones and Ford Madox Brown. The process was complex, like solving a jigsaw puzzle. May remembered 'the jewel-like colours of the glass . . . and the silvery network of the leading' as they were transmuted into saints and angels with ruby wings.[14] The Firm bought in sheets of richly stained glass from Powell and Sons in Whitefriars. The great skill was in choosing the finest pieces to fit the outlines. They had to match the subtle swirls and shading that were inherent in the material to the needs of the design. The results, when they worked, were a marvellous balance between the fluid colours, the brittle glass and the cobweb of lead-lines that emphasised the essential elements in the figures.

As so often in the artworks made by William and his friends, this was a collaborative process. Burne-Jones would draw an original design for the main subject in charcoal or pencil. Georgie described his process, how he 'made the designs without hesitation . . . these large free drawings' in the evenings after dinner, 'so quickly that it seemed as if they must have already been there and his hand were only removing a veil . . . He always stood at this work.'[15] Then he would pass them to William to add background details. On one drawing, for an *Adam and Eve*, Ned wrote a note by Adam's knee, suggesting that William 'put millions of flowers here as in the foreground of good women' (a reference to their earlier windows showing Chaucer's *Legend of Good Women*).[16] William's flowering plants would weave up and through the panels, creating a harmonious network that held the various Biblical figures together.

This is the secret of the Firm's success in making glorious, satisfying compositions – not just in glass, but also in textiles and wallpaper. William creates a sense of poise and flow through his handling of natural ornament. He guides the eye from one incident to the next, smoothing our path so that there is no jerkiness, no disruption in our visual pleasure. His treatment of the lead-lines in the stained-glass windows is also part of this process. Like the stylised, flattened figures or *millefleurs*, the bold leading makes it clear that stained glass is an artificial medium. William Morris and his colleagues liked to show their workings.

Soon after moving to Queen Square, it became clear that the yard behind the house was not big enough. Production spilled over into another workshop around the corner in Great Ormond Yard. Their new business manager, Warington Taylor, was concerned that the stained-glass commissions were turning little profit, despite their beauty and public visibility. They charged between £2 10s and £3 per square foot, plus the fee for the designer. This was considerably more than their competitors, like Heaton, Butler and Bayne, who rarely asked more than £2.[17] Warington Taylor felt that the Firm should put more resources into domestic furniture. The extra workshop space was ideal for making the ebonised rush-seated chairs that many of William's colleagues had at home. 'What about moveable furniture . . . something you can pull about with one hand?' he suggested. 'The old Sussex Black chair, the common chair of Red Lion Square . . . it possesses poetry of simplicity.'[18] The chair became a staple of the Firm's stock. It was important for the business to produce reasonably priced furnishings for the burgeoning middle-class market. They kept the finances buoyant, alongside the high-profile commissions. This tension between the everyday and the one-off projects was always inherent in the set-up of the company. In time, the elaborate stained-glass cartoons could be reused, with different combinations of figures and new colour schemes. The cost of design then could be spread over a number of clients. But this was not possible in the early days. It was only in the early 1870s that this started to make their glass more profitable.

There was also the issue of staff numbers. By the census of 1871, William was listed as an employer of eighteen men and boys. He believed that any bright lad could be trained to make himself useful in the workshop. However, when the company was trying to tackle several big commissions in the mid-1860s, it was clear that many of their team were young apprentices, or specialist glaziers or furniture makers. It was hard to find enough experienced decorators to create the complex wall and ceiling finishes in the South Kensington Museum: Webb calculated that it would take one person 243 days to complete 'the whole work above the dado' in the Green Dining Room, for example.[19]

The Firm had also been offered another spectacular new project: to decorate two large rooms in St James's Palace, the Armoury and the Tapestry Room. William had to subcontract much of the work to another decorator, S. & S. Dunn, based in Golden Square, a short walk away towards Regent Street. There was just too much for Morris's company to handle in-house.

The commission for the palace came to the company thanks to Gabriel Rossetti. He was dining with Georgina Cowper (later Lady Mount-Temple) and her husband, William, who was First Commissioner of Public Works. The Cowpers and Rossetti were all intrigued by the possibilities of Spiritualism, holding seances at home. (Gabriel had been trying to contact the shade of Lizzie Siddall.) Late in the evening, Mrs Cowper recalled asking Gabriel's opinion about their drawing room furniture: 'Well,' he said, frankly, 'I should begin by burning everything.' As Fiona MacCarthy said, his 'charm and audacity' persuaded Cowper to award the contract to this exciting new Firm.[20] Georgina Cowper's intimacy with John Ruskin, who was also hoping to find solace in Spiritualism, is likely to have helped, too. Ruskin was keen to promote the work of his young friend Ned Burne-Jones and his colleagues.

The St James's Palace project began in the autumn of 1866, and the first tranche of work was completed in the New Year of 1867. It was evidently seen as a success because Morris and his company were employed again, in 1880–1, to redecorate other parts of the palace. How did Morris and Webb treat these opulent spaces? They required very different handling from the usual townhouses and Gothic Revival churches they usually decorated.

They had to work around the objects that were on display in these rooms – a collection of eight suits of armour, together with dramatic displays of swords and pistols in one, and vast, faded tapestries in the other. They were also aware that these were part of the suite of royal apartments, seen by guests on their way to the Throne Room. Rather than holding back, the Firm responded with alacrity. Webb's designs filled the walls and ceiling with sunbursts and sunflowers. The surfaces were ebonised or painted with curling green tendrils and leaves. There was gilding on the doors and dados, and elaborate fireplaces. Fiona MacCarthy described these rooms as 'strange and magical, stagy, a bit preposterous, like the over-ornate palaces in Morris's fairytales'.[21] This commission reinforced the Firm's position among their prospective clients. Yes, a customer could come into the showroom, and buy a few tiles, or a couple of water glasses. But William and his colleagues were also prepared to think big, to create bespoke decorative schemes for grand houses.

In the years following the St James's Palace commission, the young company was employed by clients in some of the most fashionable parts of London, from Grosvenor Street to Belgrave Square and Prince's Gardens. They were also starting to develop connections with patrons further afield – working for George and Rosalind Howard at Naworth Castle in Cumberland, as well as their townhouse at 1 Palace Green, and for Isaac Lowthian Bell at Rounton Grange in Yorkshire.

For William, the years at Queen Square were a time of expanding vistas. His early potential, his dynamism, seemed to be coming good. He never expressed any nostalgia for the Red House days, although according to Georgie Burne-Jones, the family did not 'really take root' in their new home. Perhaps Jane found it hard to be flung back into the heart of a city – and one she barely knew. It was harder for her than William to find her feet here.[22] But he was able to plunge into his projects with renewed gusto, because everything here was easily to hand. He could be discussing wallpaper designs with a potential client one minute, overseeing the setting of a stained-glass panel the next, and then back up to his study, to pitch into his poetry. His daughter May described the mess of his workspace. There was 'a huge lump of bread with a small hole picked out of the middle, stationed on a chair or anywhere handy' – this was used to rub out mistakes on William's pencil notes – 'and the floor bestrewn with breadcrumbs'. She went on, 'The house . . . seemed pervaded by small rolls of printed paper, which I know now to have been proofs of "Jason" or "The Earthly Paradise".'[23]

In the summer of 1867, William published *The Life and Death of Jason*, a massive 13,000-line retelling of the ancient hero's quest. Swinburne described the poem as 'fresh as wind, bright as light; full of the spring and the sun'.[24] Some readers quibbled with William's archaeological accuracy. May acknowledged that 'it is doubtful whether the poet ever took the trouble to draw a map of the wanderings of the Argo'. Yet for many, including John Ruskin, this was all beside the point. *Jason* was a myth, and its shape was seen by William 'with as great distinctness . . . as a dream sent to any of us by night'.[25] The manner of writing in *Jason* was much less terse and frank than his earlier collection of poems, *The Defence of Guenevere*. Those verses had been intense and immediate. Now he had developed a more open-ended approach, with rolling lines, designed to be read aloud. William would test out new sections of the work on his friends. Georgie Burne-Jones described the effort of concentrating, as he shared the latest verses after dinner: 'I remember, with shame, often falling asleep to the steady rhythm of his reading voice, or biting my fingers and stabbing myself with pins in order to keep awake.'[26] She, like Jane, was tired from broken nights with a young family, and had her own needlework to occupy her evenings. Meanwhile, William always expected everyone around him to be as engaged as he was.

But even Ned could grow tired of Morris's insensitivity to his friends' discomfort. One of his most stinging caricatures shows Morris, thickset and insistent, grinding through another pile of poems, while Ned slumps pathetically in his chair, trapped.

William's pent-up energy found outlets in the constant bouncing from one idea to the next. In many ways, this was his greatest virtue. However, his business manager began to complain that 'Morris will start half a dozen jobs,' but 'they are put away, bits get lost, have to be done again'.[27] One of the difficulties, as ever, was the constant overlap between the personal and the commercial in the Firm's working practices. It was a business built on William's enthusiasms, and the partnerships between close friends. Morris and his colleagues often knew their clients socially, or they built up personal relationships with patrons as they worked together.

Wives and sisters were also intimately involved in the creative process: Burne-Jones's grand scheme for *The Romance of the Rose* embroideries at Rounton Grange, for example, would only come to fruition after Margaret and Florence Bell spent eight years stitching the figures in silks and gold thread. And on top of the handwork done by women in the circle, there were also the 'soft skills' they employed to create opportunities for sales and new projects: a productive conversation with potential customers over dinner, perhaps, or a picnic. Jane and Georgie enabled the men to meet and plan, through countless unmentioned actions. And William's freedom to be creative – his writing and designing – was also made possible through the work of four other women: Jane's sister, Bessie, and the three servants, Eliza Searle, Agnes Turner and Maria Hughes. William and Ned could enjoy their regular Sunday breakfasts, their river trips, their weekly suppers with Webb, because their households were being run efficiently, seamlessly, by their wives, cooks and maids.

We can catch only occasional glimpses of Jane's role as a successful hostess. We know of one memorable party, held at Queen Square on

27 May 1868. (It was Derby Day, and some of the guests had been to Epsom to enjoy the races.) Friends christened it the 'Earthly Paradise' banquet, after William's latest vast collection of poems which had just been published. This work rivalled Chaucer or Boccaccio in its scope, intertwining old stories from classical Greece and Rome, with northern folktales he had unearthed and come to love. On the flyleaf of the first volume William had written, 'To my wife I dedicate this book.' Jane's constant, quiet domestic organisation had allowed William to concentrate. He needed to find his way through the complex plotting and interweaving of the myths. At last, 'The spell works, the right mood comes, and . . . he is reading the new Prologue to his friends by the side of one of the beautiful reaches of the river above Oxford.'[28] Now the verses could be shared with the world at large. And it was time to celebrate an unequivocal literary success.

For the 'Earthly Paradise' party, Jane encouraged William to dress more conventionally. He wore an evening suit and tie to greet their guests. They had also made an effort, with 'Mrs Ned in a gorgeous yellow gown' and the poet William Allingham 'in velveteen jacket'. Many of the old Red House friends were gathered, including Gabriel Rossetti, Ford and Emma Madox Brown, Lucy Faulkner and Philip Webb. William's publisher, Frederick Ellis, and his wife, Caroline, joined the festivities. Jane managed to fit twenty people around their massive trestle table. It took centre-stage in the 'stately five-windowed room' overlooking the gardens. In the candlelight, it was a delightful sight, with 'the old silver and blue china . . . the greenish glass of delicate shapes' that 'gleamed like air-bubbles . . . and was reflected far away in the little mirrors set into the chimney-piece'.[29] There was 'a storm of talking' late into the night.[30]

During another dinner party around the same table, the loud conversations woke May, in her bedroom at the top of the house. The little girl felt 'utterly alone in the world – alone and in the dark . . . and they were laughing downstairs'. She remembered slipping into the dining room, fearful, in her nightgown and being 'received with kind laughter and applause'. There were 'a good many people there', who cuddled her and dried her tears. 'Swinburne is the only one among them I can recall', she wrote, many years later.[31] Swinburne's riotous behaviour was legendary among his friends, but he also understood how to cheer a little girl who was afraid of the dark.

After one of these parties, Rossetti joked that 'there was a room, a "blue closet", in the Queen Square house, entirely crammed with William's poetry from floor to ceiling'.[32] It was a barbed response to William's great productivity, his skill in finding verses at his fingertips. Gabriel's poems, by contrast, were the result of 'fidgetty fretting over old ground'. He aimed to make his 'little things' faultless by 'repeated condensation and revision', while William could 'spin endless poetry'.[33] This was a time of growing tension between the friends. And Jane was at the centre of the gathering storm.

*

Since the photographic session in Gabriel's garden, Jane had continued to model for him from time to time. Then in March 1868, William asked Gabriel to paint a half-length portrait of Jane. At one level, this could be read as a sign of William's confidence: he was feeling excited about the imminent publication of *The Earthly Paradise*. However, it might also have been an attempt to regularise the relationship between his wife and his friend. With this commission, William was creating a formal structure for Jane's visits to Gabriel's house in Cheyne Walk. William was invited for dinner after the first sitting, and Gabriel also suggested that Jane's sister Bessie might like to keep them company too; 'otherwise she would be very dull at home'. Gabriel added that Bessie could stay the night, in one of the many spare bedrooms. He also assured Jane that the pose would not be uncomfortable, and that 'the drawing of your head will take I expect two days'.[34] The composition was based on one of the photographs from 1865. Jane was seated, leaning slightly forward, her hands clasped beneath her chin. This initial arrangement was elaborated, with flowers, textiles and jewellery, to create a tactile, richly coloured image. Jane's skin glowed pale against the darker tones of her hair and intensely blue dress.

Jane was actively involved in the process of making her portrait. It was not just a question of sitting quietly, while Gabriel studied her face, her posture. She contributed to the splendour of the work, by making the deep blue silk dress, with a skirt that filled the lower half of the canvas. Jane and Gabriel discussed the details of the cut and decoration. He wanted added fullness in the sleeves, and suggested they could be 'lined with some soft material' but went on: 'of this you will be the best judge'.[35] He also asked Jane whether she might add some embroidery in gold thread at the neckline. He drew a little diagram of circular stitches and French knots to create gentle, glimmering lights on the dark silk. In the final arrangement, with Jane seated in profile, this embroidery was not visible. Instead, the dark fabric was relieved by a tiny ruffle of white seen at her wrist.

Gabriel Rossetti was concerned that the fabric should fall naturally. He encouraged Jane to 'wear the dress to take away the stiffness'.[36] This raises questions about how far the new dress was a costume, designed just for the picture. Or was Jane wearing unconventional clothing like this when entertaining family and friends? We know from her daughter May that Jane did wear this gown at home. May remembered it with great affection, the touch and sound of the fabric as an echo of her mother's physical presence. It was, she wrote, 'a delicious simple silk gown of shot blue and brown that was a great favourite with the little girls. It had some fragile ornament of gold thread at the throat and wrists, and was of delicate, faintly-rustling texture, that we never tired of stroking.'[37]

The blue silk dress was unusual in its choice of rich fabric, unadorned by traditional trimmings; there was no delicate lace collar, no contrasting buttons or braid on the bodice and skirt. It gave the impression that Jane might have stepped out of a portrait by Titian or Giorgione, with her gathered sleeves catching the light. From Gabriel's picture, it is hard to tell whether she was wearing the corsets and hoops that were de rigueur in polite society. Certainly, the skirt was full enough to cover these underpinnings, but her curved back and loosely defined waist suggest that she was not corseted.

It seems that around the time of this portrait – in 1868/9 – Jane began to develop her personal style. Her clothes and jewellery became more self-consciously avant-garde. There has been a great deal of academic debate about so-called 'Pre-Raphaelite' dress.[38] Costumes worn by models in the studio have been confused with clothes that were seen every day in public. Historically inflected gowns, like the sack-back robe worn by Jane for the photographic session in 1865, were 'fancy dress'. They were standard items kept in artist's wardrobes, to be played with, altered, shared with friends. But they were out of the ordinary, not for daily wear.

However, in her late twenties, Jane began to blur the boundaries between studio and home. She started to wear less structured dresses, not just when she was modelling, but also when she hosted informal parties in her drawing room. Jane was not the only woman in the Victorian art world who was doing this: Sara Prinsep (née Pattle) and her sisters, who welcomed G. F. Watts and Ned Burne-Jones to their homes in West London, were renowned for their *déshabillé*. The sisters' lives were closely entwined with the careers of artists that Jane knew well. It is possible that Jane also spent some time in the Prinseps' home before her marriage; Burne-Jones mentioned that they had shown an interest in William's beloved. Sadly we have no evidence that Sara Prinsep's sister, the photographer Julia Margaret Cameron, met Jane at this time.

In his correspondence, George du Maurier described the relaxed manners of the Pattles and their circle. 'Instead of dressing for dinner there,' he wrote, 'you undress; Watts without a shirt collar, and in long velvet painting jacket & list slippers.' On another evening in 1862, du Maurier was embarrassed by the low-cut bodices of many of the guests: 'all the women were *décolletées* in a beastly fashion – damn the aristocratic standard of fashion; nothing will ever make me think it right or decent that I should see a lady's armpit flesh folds when I am speaking to her.'[39] Other visitors admired the way that the Pattles brought together 'Parisian' *modes* and 'the draperies of Raphael into a happy combination for their own daily wear and use. To see one of the sisterhood float into a room with sweeping robes and falling folds, was almost an event in itself, and not to be forgotten.'[40] Having grown up in India, the Pattles also integrated exotic silks and jewellery into their ensembles, creating a look that was remarkable in mid-Victorian London.

The Pattles and their Holland Park circle established a repertoire of radical dress that was discussed, caricatured and envied. Their presence also encouraged other women in artistic households to experiment with their own styles. Jane never adopted the 'undressed' style that shocked du Maurier. Her appearance in paintings, drawings and photographs was deliberately modest. She barely revealed her wrists. Jane's flesh was seldom on display. Her bodices were high cut, so we only occasionally catch sight of her bare shoulders, or her *décolletage* in Rossetti's later 'goddess' paintings, like *Astarte Syriaca* (1876/7). She was not showy.

Even so, Jane appeared strange to others. Her dress and hair caused comment. It was partly her height and slenderness. Her figure was not fashionably curvaceous; she was rather flat-chested, and often she seems to bend forward in pictures, trying to look shorter, and obscure her true shape. It was also the lack of ostentation in her dress which was noticeable. The unadorned cut of her dress, without the usual trimmings; the draping fabric of her skirts, showing her natural outline; her unrestricted waist – these relaxations of the norm surprised visitors to Queen Square. And they contrasted sharply with the drama of her richly dark hair, her long white throat and fingers.

*

We have a remarkable description of Jane from March 1869, when the American author Henry James saw her at home in Queen Square. It is worth quoting at length. He wrote to his sister:

> She haunts me still. A figure cut out of a missal – out of one of Rossetti's or Hunt's pictures – to say this gives but a faint idea of her, because when such an image puts on flesh and blood, it is an apparition of fearful and wonderful intensity. It's hard to say whether she's a grand synthesis of all Pre-Raphaelite pictures ever made – or they a 'keen analysis' of her – whether she is an original or a copy. In either case she is a wonder.

He continued:

> Imagine a tall lean woman in a long dress of some dead purple stuff, guiltless of hoops (or of anything else I should say) with a mass of crisped black hair heaped into great wavy projections on each side of her temples, a thin pale face, a pair of strange sad, deep, dark Swinburnian eyes, with great thick black oblique brows, joined in the middle and tucking themselves away under her hair, a mouth like the Oriana in our illustrated Tennyson, a long neck without any collar and in lieu thereof some dozen strings of outlandish beads.

And then he went back to the theme that Jane was a work of art, brought oddly to life:

> On the wall was a nearly full-length portrait of her by Rossetti, so strange and unreal that if you hadn't seen her, you'd pronounce it a distempered vision, but in fact an extremely good likeness.[41]

This lengthy account of Jane's appearance has set the tone for most subsequent writing about her. Many of the later stories about her character and looks, her silence, her strangeness, grew out of this single source. So, what can we learn about Jane from this letter? How should it shape our understanding of her self-presentation, and her position at the heart of artistic London?

We should remember that James is himself trying to rise to the occasion, by becoming consciously artistic in his writing about Jane. This vignette is carefully fashioned, to be shared with friends back home in Boston, to be circulated and preserved. He had recently arrived in London. He was a young man, only twenty-five, and trying to establish himself as part of an exciting new artistic set. Seeing the 'flesh and blood' Jane in her own home was, for him, a rite of passage. He makes the most of it, as his writing moves back and forth between reality and art, between solid and flat surfaces, between the present and memories. James asks his sister to remember artworks she has seen by Rossetti and Hunt. He insists that Jane cannot be imagined separately from these drawings. He points to one, from the illustrated Tennyson published by Moxon in 1857. The figure of 'Oriana' in this edition was drawn by William Holman Hunt, and modelled on Fanny, his wife. It was not a portrait of Jane. Rather, James was suggesting that Jane fitted a recognisable 'type', with strong eyebrows and a bold mouth.

Would James or his sister, before the spring of 1869, have had access – through exhibition or publication – to any pictures with Jane as the model? This is unlikely. Except for the Oxford Union wall-paintings, the other works for which she sat had remained in private hands. *La Belle Iseult* was not exhibited. Three of Rossetti's finished 'presentation' drawings of Jane, made in 1865, were sold to Frederick Leyland, and he had also made a substantial half-length study, *The Golden Chain*, in coloured chalks. But he had not yet completed any large-scale oil paintings with Jane as the model, apart from the portrait commissioned by her husband. And Gabriel Rossetti was always wary of showing his work in public. So, again, Henry James was conflating Jane with images of other models, instead of presenting her as an individual. In his eyes, she resembles Fanny Cornforth, Lizzie Siddall and Fanny Hunt. He does not see her for herself. Yet she was, like Henry James, testing the boundaries of her new position in London. Jane too was in the process of self-fashioning.

Jane was at the forefront of the shifts in 'artistic' dress, taking it from the private space of the studio, to the everyday. Her semi-costumed appearance, her Indian or Middle Eastern jewellery, would later be adopted by advanced young women, and would become the subject of satire in *Punch* magazine and popular culture. But Liberty did not open his celebrated store until 1875. And Gilbert and Sullivan's opera *Patience*, which made fun of the *outré* outfits of fashionable souls, was first performed in 1881, many years after Jane began to greet her guests in her 'long dress of some dead purple stuff'.

Jane's decision to dress unconventionally seems to coincide with her greater visibility. Until 1865, and the move to Queen Square, she and her daughters were out of the public gaze, living quietly in Kent, and seen only by friends and family. But now, with a large townhouse that doubled as a showroom, she was on display too, as hostess, wife, maker and model in a burgeoning business. The shift towards her more avant-garde appearance came at a time when she knew she was going to be looked at. That is why Henry James wanted to visit the house. He was keen to speak to William Morris, as a poet and fashionable designer, but James also expected to see Mrs Morris. Her presence completed the scene, and her dress became part of the 'house beautiful'.

Jane chose to wear sumptuous, deeply coloured textiles, styled with a suggestion of the Renaissance, or of flowing medieval gowns. They were in tune with the soft woods, the glowing glass, that decorated her home. She could not hide, so she shone instead, and startled a little. Her relaxed robes were not unseemly for a small party at home. They would have been out of place at a formal dinner, or in a ball-room. But here, in her own space, she could experiment.

James failed to recognise Jane's agency in the way she appeared. He describes her in relation to the artworks made by the men around her. We do not see her move. We do not hear her voice. Morris, on the other hand, talks all the time, reading extracts from *The Earthly Paradise*, in 'a very loud voice and a nervous restless manner'. In another brief passage from the letter to his sister, James creates a memorable image of Jane's withdrawal into silence. He says that Jane, 'having a bad toothache, lay on the sofa with her handkerchief to her face . . . [a] dark silent medieval woman with her medieval toothache'.[42]

This vision of Jane has persisted, shaping later responses to her life and work. It is unsympathetic, refusing to acknowledge her pain – or the constant sound of her husband's voice. Jane would not take laudanum or chloral to dull the throbbing; she was resistant to any form of opiates, having seen the damage they did to friends like Lizzie Siddall. So, she endured the evening with the young American writer.

James, for his part, reinforces her sickliness by seeing Jane as almost ghostly, with her pale face and dark, deep-set eyes. She is presented in stark contrast to William, with his 'perfectly healthy body and temper'. She becomes a Gothic figure who 'haunts' him. In his letter, Jane is presented as an apparition, lifted from an old manuscript. And yet, he also appears very conscious of her body beneath her gown. He is mentally undressing her, wondering what underclothes she is wearing. Her skirt is not held out by hoops, as it folds against her legs. He looks closely and decides that Jane's waist and chest are uncorseted. Without the conventional armour of whalebone, her body is vulnerable to his gaze. There is also the unspoken feeling that Jane's loose clothes might imply loose morals.

Her status was potentially questionable, as a model who continued to sit for other artists even after her marriage.

*

By March 1869, when Henry James spent the evening in Queen Square, Jane's position as a respectable, faithful wife was indeed becoming equivocal. Her intimacy with Gabriel Rossetti was growing. The photographic session in 1865 rekindled Rossetti's interest in her as a model, and the *Blue Silk Dress* commission by William created more opportunities for Jane to spend time at Tudor House. She was not always alone. Her sister or William sometimes accompanied her to Gabriel's studio. But William, understandably, was often preoccupied with the demands of the Firm, or his writing. Gabriel, meanwhile, had been working on black-and-white studies of Jane's head since the summer of 1865. Some of these were highly finished, including one that was bought by the artist George Price Boyce. Next, Gabriel wanted to try out several possible poses for the portrait commissioned by William. And then, once that was complete, and hanging in the drawing room at Queen Square, he began another series of studies, with Jane as central motif. She became Tennyson's weary *Mariana*, trapped in her moated grange, and Dante's sad figure of *La Pia de Tolomei*, also waiting for release.

The private space of the artist's studio was always potentially disruptive. Gabriel and Jane must have been aware of this. They both knew of the turbulence in the Burne-Jones marriage, caused by Ned's passionate liaison with one of his models. She was Maria Zambaco, a good friend of Ned's patrons, the Ionides family, and recently separated from her husband. In January 1869, as Gabriel put it, 'Poor Ned's affairs have come to smash altogether.'[43] Georgie discovered her husband's infidelity and withdrew to Oxford with the children; her friend Rosalind Howard recognised that Georgie might be short of funds, and quietly left fifty pounds for her, just in case.[44] Burne-Jones physically collapsed. It was all very messy.

It is at this point that we begin to notice William's anxieties about his own marriage. He asked Jane not to visit Gabriel's studio while he was away, trying to look after Ned. This is the first time he voiced unease about her modelling. He was in a dreadfully difficult position: supporting his adulterous friend, while worrying about Jane's affections, and Gabriel's intentions. With the Burne–Joneses' marriage in peril, the whole balance of his personal and work life felt threatened. The easy conversations about Cupid and Psyche, the summers at the seaside, and evenings around the dining table, these had been the bedrock of William's partnership with Ned. And it was all damaged.

The structure of the Firm was also destabilised. It was built on mutual hopes and encouragement, an outflowing of shared creativity. The couples had worked together, the women as well as the men, to ensure that the skills and imagination of the friends could be turned into a successful enterprise. Georgie had been there at the beginning, alongside Jane. William was saddened. He wrote to Ned, apologising for his moodiness. 'I think you find it hard to stand me,' he said, 'and no great wonder, for I am like a hedgehog with nastiness – but again forgive me, for I can't on any terms do without you.'[45]

William was also distressed by the gossip about his own marriage. Rossetti had always teased his friend Topsy. But his jokes were becoming increasingly barbed. He drew little caricatures of William looking surprised at his pot-belly, discovering that he could no longer fasten his buttons.

In another letter, Gabriel said he had witnessed Morris 'threatening to throw a new piano of his wife's out of the window' because it had been delivered at dinner time.[46] These melodramatic scenes appealed to William's friends because they revealed aspects of his character that were usually downplayed when he was on public view. Henry James had described him as 'a delicate sensitive genius', blessed with good spirits. Those closer to William saw a more complex figure: his unpredictable temper, his singlemindedness which could make him blind to the needs of others, his appetite. Rossetti had watched Morris over many years, and could draw him, cruelly but accurately. These particular outbursts also reflected badly on William's relationship with Jane. She was portrayed as long-suffering, dealing with William's foibles patiently. It was her piano he wanted to destroy, her housekeeping that he mistrusted.

By contrast, Rossetti was often over-attentive to Jane, regardless of who was watching. His behaviour could be framed as acts of courtesy, in the traditions of Courtly Love. In this context, Gabriel might be permitted to admire his friend's wife, while she remained aloof. At a formal dinner in the autumn of 1868, for example, Gabriel became so distracted by Jane that the host complained that 'he acts like a perfect fool if he wants to conceal his attachment, doing nothing but attend to her, sitting side-ways towards her, that sort of thing'. Rossetti seemed oblivious to the presence of William and Bessie Burden, who were both watching from the other side of the table. But Jane was unflustered, 'a sealed book . . . cool'. [47]

On another occasion, we find Jane at an evening party, slightly withdrawn from the rest of the company, with Gabriel at her feet. He was offering her strawberries, 'carefully scraping off the cream, which was bad for her, and then solemnly presenting her with the strawberries in a spoon!'[48] There is something colourful, delightful and almost comical about this image. And perhaps we discover a similar mood in Burne-Jones's little drawing of Rossetti, trotting after Jane, carrying two enormous cushions under his arms. Again, there is a suggestion of chivalry, the ardent devotee in thrall to a remote, queenly woman. Certainly, Burne-Jones's image of Jane makes her seem untouchable: willowy in her long robe, clutching her shawl to her throat, she processes across the picture. She does indeed look like a figure out of a missal, compared with stout Gabriel, puffing in her wake.

Still, despite the jokes and melodrama, there were suggestions of a more serious understanding between them. And in the early summer of 1869, something happened that upset the balance of the Morris household. Jane was ill and William insisted that they travel to Germany together, so she could seek treatment. What was wrong with Jane? Was her disorder at some level triggered by a crisis in her marriage? Did William see this as an opportunity to repair their relationship, and put Gabriel at arm's length? If this was his hope, it did not work. William could not stop Gabriel from writing to his wife. And Jane's ailments, although alleviated by the treatment, continued to dog her for the rest of her life. She lived with chronic back pain that sometimes limited her movement.

The impression of Jane as a semi-permanent invalid began around this time. Georgie Burne-Jones noted, for example, that she saw less of Jane in the later 1860s because Jane 'was now so much out of health that I fear her share of the entertainments was more fatigue than pleasure, and gradually they came to an end'.[49] We have already seen her prostrated on the sofa in Henry James's account of his visit. And then she was whisked away by William to Bad Ems, a spa town in central Germany. She explained to a friend, Susan Sedgwick Norton, that she had recently become so unwell that she had 'been almost a prisoner' in her own home. She hoped she could 'muster enough strength' to travel. Jane revealed that it was 'with great difficulty' that she could 'sit up to write this' letter. Even so, she had not lost her sense of humour: 'Imagine My Husband at a fashionable German watering place!'[50]

They travelled with Lucy Faulkner and Bessie Burden for the first week, and then went on together. The journey was disorganised. They had no rooms booked in Bad Ems, so, as May described it, her parents were 'literally stranded at the station, and I scarcely know which to be sorrier for, mother waiting there alone in a state of collapse, or father, frantically seeking for accommodation'.[51]

It seems clear that Jane was struggling with the travelling, and in pain. But we must not think that poor health is her defining feature.

After all, many of the men around her were also frequently struck down by their own disorders. William often suffered from rheumatic fever, especially in cold weather, so that it was impossible for him to work or visit clients. Ned Burne-Jones made a virtue of his physical fragility; in his self-caricatures, he appears as a slight, stooped figure, prematurely aged. He was regularly tended by concerned women, like Sara Prinsep who 'swooped down and carried him off to be nursed' at Little Holland House,[52] his delicate health giving him access to some of the most advanced artistic circles. And Gabriel himself was often in poor physical and mental health. His insomnia and his dependence on opiates became severe problems, worsening in the early 1870s. Jane was not alone in needing medical attention. She was, however, unusual for refusing to become reliant on painkillers, and looking for alternative ways to ease her discomfort.

It seems likely that Jane's troubles were gynaecological. The lower back pain that she suffered may have been a catch-all term for pelvic cramps, fibroids or endometriosis. Her treatment at Bad Ems involved shower baths and doses of mineral water. As Fiona MacCarthy has shown, many of the doctors there specialised in *les maladies de femme*, and the bathing cabinets offered douches, vapour baths and the celebrated Bubenquelle, 'a fountain, applied strictly under medical supervision, [that] entered the body via the vagina'.[53] It was an intrusive procedure and did not seem to improve Jane's condition.

In Bad Ems, William struggled with the enforced leisure, complaining of 'sulks' and 'the fidgetts', and 'a fit of dumps at Janey getting worse now and then'.[54] It had been difficult to leave home, as he explained to his 'dearest Friend', Philip Webb. This was partly because 'Ned seemed more moved at my going than I should have liked to have seen him', and partly from the anxiety about Jane, and their future: 'It will be bad indeed to have to bring her back no better; I don't know how to face the fear of that.'[55] Trying make himself useful, he began to draft plans for a shower to be installed at Queen Square when they returned. He sent it to Webb, asking him to design 'a scooped-out wooden stool like those one sits on at the Turkish bath'.[56]

William took to walking miles up the valley and along 'cart roads through grain fields dotted all over with apple-trees'.[57] He rowed Jane across the river and encouraged her to rest in the shade. But the landscape could not soothe his fretfulness. William seemed to be spending his time dawdling or sleeping. These weeks of idleness were made harder because, for the first time in his married life, he felt short of money. The Firm had only made £300 profit the previous year. This was very little to share between the seven partners. The income from his father's investments was also diminishing, and William had decided to sell some of his books to raise cash.

The visit to Bad Ems came at a difficult time. In July 1869, just as William and Jane were setting out, their business manager Warington Taylor broke the harsh news that they would have to stop their dinner parties. He asked, 'What does an extra dinner cost: piece of salmon 5/-, leg of mutton 7/6, vegetable 2/-, pudding –, wine –, coals? – butter?' It was hard for William to contemplate a return to Queen Square when Taylor was standing over him. Jane was ill, but it seemed they could no longer afford to keep the house heated and lit, or to welcome their friends. They were spending too much on coal and candles. Even wine was now to be rationed to two and a half bottles a day.[58] William was hemmed in, oppressed by 'lonely and dismal' woods that were filled with horrible creatures. One of his letters to Webb seems to be crawling with ants and adders, and monstrous slugs.[59] He felt 'disgustingly well, and quite ashamed of myself'.

Jane was also stuck in the claustrophobic routine, hoping for a cure for her chronic pain. She was drinking daily doses of the warm spa water and being subjected to regular douches. Gabriel Rossetti made light of her predicament in one of the illustrated letters he wrote to her that summer. His cartoon shows Jane being pummelled by a great shower head as she sits, naked and resigned, in a bath. It looks like she is finding it hard to stomach the glass of mineral water she holds. And there are six more glasses lined up in front of her. Morris is in the background, trying to cheer Jane by reading aloud from his seemingly endless volumes of *The Earthly Paradise*. It is not lifting her mood.

The picture encapsulates the dynamics of the three-way relationship between Gabriel, William and Jane at this point. Of course, it is seen maliciously, from Gabriel's point of view. But it reflects Gabriel's jealousy of William, as a celebrated and prolific author. Verses seemed to gush from him easily. He did not have to scrabble around for inspiration, but plunged with enthusiasm into the legends of many lands, emerging with dozens of delightful rewritings of old tales. Meanwhile, Gabriel polished a few sonnets and fantasised about Jane – her pale neck and shoulders and a hint of bosom were all he dared to draw. But he was well aware of the rest of her body under the water. And then, how did Jane read this picture? Did she really feel trapped by her over-enthusiastic husband, who genuinely did want to help her feel better, and the enervating regime of the baths? It seems that she used this time to reflect. The summer at Ems highlighted the discords between Jane and William, and the difficulties at home. As William put it, he always found it hard to 'smother up my impatience'.[60] He needed to be busy: writing, walking, eating, studying new books, unpicking old textiles. Jane, in her current jangled state, found this wearing.

The tensions between William and Jane were only heightened by Gabriel's interference. He wrote to Jane constantly that summer, anxious about her health, her safe travels, and whether he would be in London when she returned. Only his side of their correspondence for this period survives. We cannot read her thoughts. But from July 1869, Gabriel was writing letters to Jane that were more than merely affectionate or fond. These were love-letters, written by a man who knew how to craft his lines. Reading them today, in the quiet of the British Library, we can still get a sense of Gabriel's desire to express himself. The urgency is made visible as he fills the pages with his swift, tiny handwriting. He calls her 'Dear Good Janey', 'Dear kind Janey', 'Dearest Janey'.

Gabriel began writing almost as soon as she had crossed the Channel. On 21 July 1869, he was urging Jane to wrap up well; it seems that he gave her several cloaks to wear on her journey, to warm and comfort her, to fold around her like an embrace.[61] Gabriel was already planning joint projects for when she returned. 'I want beyond everything to paint another portrait picture of you,' he wrote. 'I am sure I can do something more worthy of you.' He knew that William was not entirely happy with *The Blue Silk Dress*. William had sent it back at least once to be reworked and then complained, 'I don't think the frame suits it . . . a big, dark-toned picture like that.'[62] It was evidently not how he saw his wife.

For Gabriel, on the other hand, painting Jane was a revelation. He commemorated the long hours spent studying her face and hands in a sonnet, 'The Portrait'. Jane's person was swathed in sensual phrases, and buried beneath the layers of his art.

Here is a taste of the poem:

> O Love, let this my lady's picture glow
> Under my hand to praise her name and show
> Even of her inner self the perfect whole:
> . . . Above the long lithe throat
> The mouth's mould testifies of voice and kiss,
> The shadowed eyes remember and foresee.
> Her face is made her shrine.

Jane is presented as his Lady, in the traditions of Courtly Love. But more than that, he suggests she comes to life under his hand. Gabriel breaks her into fragments: eyes, throat and mouth, smiles, glances and kisses. William was right. *The Blue Silk Dress* was not truly a portrait of Jane as most of her family and friends knew her. It was Jane's image transformed, exaggerated. She had become, in Henry James's words, 'a grand synthesis of all Pre-Raphaelite pictures ever made . . . a wonder'.[63] At some level, she was complicit in this transformation. She began to dress audaciously in semi-public situations, drawing attention to her role as a model. In her blue silk, she was more than a mother or fashionable hostess. She continued to sit for Gabriel, to visit his studio, to welcome his letters.

It is hard to fathom Jane's feelings for Gabriel in the summer of 1869. But she could be in no doubt of his growing desire for her. In a letter written on 30 July, he oscillated between revealing too much, and too little, of his love. He acknowledged her commitment to William. But then Gabriel turned this on its head, claiming that his friend must know that Jane should be cherished, and not just by her husband. It is a very strange passage, trying to justify his devotion. Gabriel argued that 'dear Top' should recognise that

> the more he loves you, the more he knows that you are too lovely and noble not to be loved: and dear Janey, there are too few things that seem worth expressing as life goes on, for one friend to deny another the poor expression of what is most at his heart. But he is before me in granting this . . . I can never tell you how much I am with you at all times . . . But I have no right to talk to you in a way that may make you sad on my account when in reality the balance of joy and sorrow is now so much more in my favour than it has been, or could have hoped to become, for years past . . . Never mind what I could not help writing . . . Let me hear *something* from you, dearest Janey . . .
>
> All love to Topsy from your loving Gabriel[64]

We do not have Jane's answer to this riddling letter. It seems unlikely that she would have shared it with her husband. It was too close to a confession of love. She seems to have replied by deflecting rather than discouraging his affection. His next letter included a caricature of William with his braces dangling, in response to her tale of William's awkward encounter with a German chambermaid. Jane appears to have been treading a fine line between playfulness and open acceptance of Gabriel's devotion. She enjoyed some of the jokes at William's expense; his friends had always teased him, in Oxford and at Red House, so this was nothing new. But she sent Gabriel a 'grave rebuke' for his next drawing, showing William in the shower, looking furious and corpulent. It was 'the too naked truth' of this cartoon that upset Jane, and she asked Gabriel to leave William be.[65]

Drawings like this put Jane in a very difficult position. They made her complicit in belittling her husband, when he was trying to be sympathetic to her physical suffering. Sadly, William found it hard to compete with the emotional engagement, and the diverting news, that Gabriel shared in his letters. Rossetti was still encouraging Jane to return to the studio, so they could create another new picture together. He hoped to paint her as 'Fortune seated full-faced dealing cards', between 'a dove (or white peacock) and a raven'. He promised 'nice easy sittings'. He would be 'careful judicious and considerate'.[66] Gabriel also told her excitedly about his plans to create a new space in his stable block, with 'my studio . . . an ante-room for people to wait in, and I think also a bed-room for myself'.[67] It would give him greater privacy, away from the main house.

By early September, Gabriel was looking forward to Jane being back in London, refreshed by her treatment. He claimed her company and urged her to 'come to me soon and preside at a dinner in honour of your restoration'. And he wanted to introduce Jane to a new creature in his menagerie: 'What do you think? I have got a Wombat.'[68] Shortly after, Gabriel drew a fanciful little portrait of Jane leading the wombat by a ribbon. She approaches us, like a queen or saint. Her gown is distinctive; high-waisted, with vast sleeves, and falling straight to the floor, without hoops or voluminous petticoats. Both Jane and the wombat have delicate haloes. This cartoon betrayed Gabriel's sentiments for his model, and also for her husband. His friends would have seen that the wombat stood in for William: biddable, rotund, following in Jane's wake. (The poor wombat died on 6 November.) Gabriel gave this drawing to Jane, who kept it for the rest of her life. It is now in the British Museum.

Jane did start working with Gabriel again soon after she came back to Queen Square. Rossetti kept his word that Jane's modelling poses would not be taxing. As she explained to a friend, her stay at Ems 'showed me how ill I was and how to take care of myself at home'. But, she went on, 'it has not cured me. Still I am thankful to be at all better . . . What you say about Florence is very tempting. How I should like to pass one season in beautiful Italy.' In the same letter, she said that 'Mr Rossetti has been drawing from me but not painting . . . His work does not go on so rapidly as formerly, but every new thing he does seems to me to be more beautiful than the last.'[69]

The drawings that Gabriel made in late 1869, and in the following months and years, bear witness to the easy intimacy of their relationship. A few of them relate directly to bigger projects. But many are personal studies in pen or pencil. They show Jane relaxed, reading or sewing. Sometimes she is sleeping. Often we see her curled on a sofa, her feet tucked beneath her skirts. They look like sketches made on a quiet afternoon, while Jane and Gabriel chatted. Rossetti details the draping of her dress, or the angle of her head. He notes how her hair is loosened, how her hands are held, how she leans against a bolster cushion. These are sensitive studies, with echoes of the many drawings he had made, a decade earlier, of Lizzie Siddall.

*

Time and again, Jane stood in for Lizzie in Rossetti's imaginative world. He wanted to paint her as the dying Beatrice, in a reworking of a watercolour of 1856 of *Dante's Dream*. In the vast, new oil painting, Jane's raven-dark hair would replace Lizzie's red-gold. Jane's face would overlay his dead wife's. We do not know how Jane felt about this. She never mentions Lizzie in her own letters.[70] However, it is clear that Gabriel discussed Lizzie, both her life and her death, with Jane.

This was a very turbulent time for all those who had been close to Lizzie. In October 1869, seven years after her death, Gabriel arranged for her coffin to be dug up. This exhumation was, at best, disrespectful. At worst, it was mercenary, a violation of her memory and her physical remains. Her grave was opened so that Gabriel could retrieve a manuscript of his poems. He had placed the papers on her coffin and seen them buried with her, in an agony of grief and regret, but had mourned their loss almost immediately. He had no other fair copy of several significant works. Since William's successful publication of *Jason* and *The Earthly Paradise*, Gabriel had felt compelled to reinvigorate his own reputation as a poet, and keenly felt the gaps in his notes. Jane was one of the first friends that Gabriel told, when he decided to press ahead with reclaiming the manuscript.[71]

Gabriel tried to justify the desecration. He claimed that it was what Lizzie would have wanted: 'Had it been possible to her, I should have found the book on my pillow the night she was buried; and could she have opened the grave, no other hand would have been needed.'[72] This is a very uneasy image: Lizzie unable to rest in peace because of Gabriel's impetuous mistake. Writing to his brother, Gabriel seemed hardly to remember when the exhumation had happened: 'The thing was done, after some obstacles, on Wednesday or Thursday last, I forget which.' He was not present. But he could not avoid the questions about what was in the grave. He admitted that although 'all in the coffin was found quite perfect', the 'book though not in any way destroyed, is soaked through and through.'[73] The following day, he wrote, 'It has a dreadful smell – partly no doubt the disinfectants.'[74] And then, in a chilling phrase, he admits that 'the truth must ooze out in time'.[75]

Gabriel's treatment of his wife, even after her death, was very troubling to Lizzie's friends. The secrecy and the midnight digging, by the light of a bonfire, would have cut across Georgie's own strong patterns of behaviour and belief. It was even more complicated for Jane. As Gabriel's new confidante and model, she had replaced Lizzie. Jane's hair now flowed through his pictures, her lips and eyes were the focus of his new poems. How did she reconcile her intimacy with Gabriel, and her anxieties about Lizzie's memory?

Jane revealed very little, even after his death. To friends, she simply said that Rossetti was unwell – 'He is suffering from his eyes and from intense nervousness and general weakness.'[76] In the aftermath of Lizzie's exhumation, he became depressed and struggled to sleep. He began to take chloral for his insomnia. This was the start of a decade of addiction. It seems likely that Jane visited Gabriel partly for her own sake – she enjoyed his attention, and the frisson of modelling – but mostly to support him.

Gabriel's letters show how their relationship intensified that winter. By New Year 1870, he was writing to her as 'Funny Sweet Janey', and 'Dearest kindest Janey', and she was visiting Tudor House alone. In January, he wrote to her after they had dined together: 'The sight of you going down the dark steps to the cab all alone has plagued me ever since – you looked so lonely . . . Now everything will be dark for me till I can see you again.'[77] It is a telling image – she moves away into the night, while he sits and waits for their next meeting.

With the fervour of a lover, Gabriel wrote about his hopes to paint her well. But his words often seem fretful, demanding. 'No one else seems alive at all to me now,' he wrote, 'and places that are empty of you are empty of all life. And it is so seldom that the dead hours breathe a little and yield your dear voice to me again.'[78]

Gabriel's friends acknowledged his instability was tied up with his passion for Jane. William Bell Scott called her 'the sweet Lucretia Borgia', and blamed Jane for Gabriel's decline.[79] He was 'in the dumps, not painting . . . but lunging about the room . . . with his hands in his pockets because Janey was ill and unable to come'.[80] It is not clear whether they thought Jane should have been more loving, or should have left Gabriel alone to recover from his infatuation. As Wendy Parkins has pointed out, Jane's reserve left her open to 'unflattering interpretations'. Her discretion was read 'as a kind of conscious, knowing performance'.[81]

It seems that she cared for him deeply, but was understandably concerned about her own family, and her precarious position – as a model, as a working-class woman. What was most remarkable was Jane's ability to walk this tightrope. Her close friends stood by her. Webb and the Faulkners, Rosalind Howard and Ford Madox Brown never accused her of wrongdoing. Her intimacy with Rossetti was visible and talked about. It could have destroyed her. Still, to the very end of her life, Jane was described as kind and noble. She was not cut adrift like Maria Zambaco, the lover of Ned Burne-Jones, as a warning to beautiful women, a perpetual *femme fatale*. Jane remained a beloved and trusted friend, and a welcoming hostess to artists, poets, travellers, women and men. She was inevitably associated with Gabriel and his art. But this did not diminish her.

It helps perhaps if we look at the affair from the point of view of Philip Webb. He was one of William's dearest friends, and remained close to Jane to the end of her life. In the summer of 1869, during their visit to Bad Ems, he wrote to 'My dear Janey and Top . . . when you went away nearly my all was gone.' He continued, 'Ned & Georgie & Gabriel are part of the family but we look at each other in a kind of rage that the rest are not by.'[82] This was the inner circle. They were like family. When Maria Zambaco crashed into their world, she was an outsider. With Gabriel and Jane, their companionable intimacy was already accepted. They were often alone together at Cheyne Walk, and then in Hastings (for her health in February–March 1870) and for several weeks (April–May) in Sussex. William came and went. It was possible then to maintain the fiction that these visits were just an extension of Gabriel's long-standing friendship with him, and Jane's continuing role as a model. It was a reconfiguration, not a rupture.

We will never know the full story of their romance. Too many letters were destroyed, too much was left unsaid. William was bewildered and hurt, but remarkably, he stood by Jane throughout this crisis. He travelled with her to Sussex, and knowingly left her with Gabriel in the little cottage at Scalands, 'a goodish way from the seaside', lent by the artist Barbara Bodichon.[83] And then he went back to London.

If William had disowned Jane, it is hard to see how she would have fared as a 'fallen woman'. Jane would have lost her home and, almost certainly, access to her children. Her sister Bessie, who relied on Morris for bed and board, would also have been devastated. She must have seen what was happening. After all, she was frequently left behind to look after Jenny and May. Did Bessie question Jane's actions? Was she jealous of the attention lavished on her older sister, while she sewed in the corner, the reluctant guest, the spinster aunt? The cross-currents and tensions at Queen Square in 1869–70 were painful: Jane's unstable health, her infidelity, the flurry of letters from Gabriel, William's turning aside and deliberately not seeing.

*

The unspoken wretchedness surfaced, at times, in William's work. He had recently begun a new and life-changing project – learning Icelandic with a friend, Eiríkr Magnússon. Together they had started to translate the Völsunga Saga. In a letter written at Christmas 1869, William dwelt on 'the last interview between Sigurd and the despairing and terrible Brynhild'. He said it touches me more than anything I have ever met with in literature, there is nothing wanting in it, nothing forgotten, nothing repeated, nothing overstrained; all tenderness is shown without the use of a tender word, all misery and despair without a word of raving, complete beauty without an ornament.[84]

Tenderness, misery, despair and beauty: William's friends used to laugh at the torrents of words that poured out of him when he was writing poetry. But he was reticent on personal matters; he found it hard to speak directly about his own unhappiness. His fears found expression instead in these roundabout ways.

By midsummer 1870, the difficulties at home had become acute. Jane and William arranged for their daughters, Jenny and May, to go away for a break in Cumberland. At Christmas 1869, Jane had told a friend that 'they are dear little companions to me'. But she was worried about them: they were 'growing very tall but not very strong I'm afraid'. She was also concerned about their education. The girls were now eight and seven, and Jane felt that they 'want regular lessons and those I cannot guarantee'. Jane's own commitments (at home and at Cheyne Walk), and her occasional ill-health, meant that the lessons she gave them were 'at all hours, and sometimes they look so tired that I feel quite cruel'.[85] She might also have been aware of her own shortcomings as a teacher. Jane was very well read, and no one ever faulted her accent or grammar. She certainly learnt to understand some French, German and Italian herself. It is not clear how competent she was in mathematics or geography. Living with William, it is likely that both she and the girls had a good grasp of history, as a vibrant subject that coloured their way of looking at the world. Evidently Jane felt it was important that her girls should have the systematic education that she had missed.

They were both active girls, especially May, who could be boisterous. There are photographs of Jenny and May with the Burne-Jones children in the garden: they had all scrambled halfway up a tree. In one letter, William described the girls causing 'such a rumpus this morning. May enjoying a good tease and Jenny expressing herself in boo hoo.'[86] And like their parents, they were idiosyncratic in their dress and manner. One of their cousins laughed at them for their unladylike clothes. Their everyday dresses were stitched from indigo serge, a fabric like denim, made for running around and getting grubby. Their boots were sturdy and looked as if they were made for 'medieval brutes'. They wore chunky amber or glass beads.[87] This is how they appeared when they arrived at Naworth railway station in Cumberland in June 1870. They had been sent north for a summer break, staying with some new friends of their parents', George and Rosalind Howard. May was so excited by the journey that, she wrote, 'We were ready to jump out of our shoes.'[88]

We can read May's thoughts as she explored the Howards' home at Naworth Castle, because she wrote a journal detailing her summer holiday. May described herself as 'very untidy, and always very dirty and sometimes I am ashamed to say very naughty'. She went on: 'I will have my readers judge whether I am pretty or ugly'. This is a remarkable self-portrait by a young girl who 'shall be nine next twenty fifth of March'. It is written with gusto, and no real sense of self-reproach. May enjoyed being a little wild: 'The glen is most beautiful and the air smells sweet.'[89]

Jane was grateful for the chance for her girls to enjoy the open spaces of Cumberland for a while, after being constrained for many months in Queen Square. She feared that they would be a handful, and wrote to Rosalind Howard, worrying that they were 'sometimes unruly and will not do as they are bid'. May and Jenny had an ease and carelessness, which meant that 'they make themselves at home everywhere . . . [and] seem to take possession of a place as if they have lived there all their lives.'[90]

Were the girls truly 'very naughty' as May suggested, or was Jane overly anxious? It seems that they were more confident and self-reliant than many other middle-class girls. They had unusual access to the imaginative freedoms of artists' studios and the Firm's workshop. Their aunts and cousins had labelled them as odd. But that did not necessarily make them 'unruly', to use Jane's word. It seems that Jane was anxious about how her girls might appear to the Howards. She did not know Rosalind well – although they later became great friends. Jane was undoubtedly aware of their difference in class and upbringing.

George Howard was becoming close to William and Ned Burne-Jones because he was an artist himself, and a patron of the Firm. But George was also heir to the Earldom of Carlisle, and Rosalind's parents were Lord Stanley of Alderley and Henrietta Maria, daughter of Viscount Dillon. Jane must have felt at a disadvantage. Would the lack of refinement in her own childhood be visible in the behaviour of her girls? Jane did not want Jenny and May to be criticised as disruptive, or ill bred. Perhaps she emphasised their wilfulness to pre-empt this.

Jane need not have worried. Rosalind's children grew up even wilder. Her daughter, Dorothy Henley, wrote about her girlhood in a chapter called 'Rough and Tumble'. May's later enthusiasm for clambering around on the roofs at Kelmscott Manor may have begun in Cumberland. Dorothy described their access to 'the dangerous and often unprotected roofs at Naworth and Castle Howard. Freedom to play, romp, race, climb among them, was never given to us; it was simply ours.'[91] Little wonder that Jenny and May came home from Naworth 'so much stronger and fuller of life'. 'They seem to have been in Paradise,' Jane said.[92] 'They have inherited from their Papa that precious gift of enjoyment . . . Are they not merry things?'[93]

Why were the Howards so willing to welcome Jenny and May? It looks like Rosalind was aware of the difficulties at home in Queen Square, and offered to give William and Jane some breathing space. Rosalind was often an awkward woman. Her bossiness made her a successful campaigner for women's suffrage and the temperance movement. And her willingness to find practical solutions, meant that she was also a great support to friends in trouble. She had helped Georgie Burne-Jones when her marriage was struggling. Georgie had written to Rosalind thanking her for the 'tender thoughtfulness' of her words and actions. 'Forgive my reserve the other day when you came,' she said, 'but I am obliged to show it in time of trouble or I should break down.'[94]

Now Rosalind stepped forward to befriend Jane, and to reassure her that the girls were happy. In the meantime, William and Jane had the opportunity to talk. They needed to find a way to untangle the thorny problem of their marriage. We do not know exactly how they managed it. But they came to an understanding. William's untiring generosity, and Jane's discretion, helped them to rebalance their relationship. There would be no catastrophe. Instead, they would present a united face to the world, while each continued with their separate projects.

Neither of them spoke of it openly. But many years later, William wrote to his friend Charley Faulkner about how he envisaged a renewal in married life, as part of a political revolution. He hoped that a 'couple would be free', and 'being free, if unfortunately distaste arose between them, they should make no pretence of its not having arisen'. He went on: 'I should hope that in most cases friendship would go along with desire, and would outlive it, and the couple would still remain together, but always as free people.'[95]

Is this how he saw his own marriage – as an enduring friendship, a positive choice? It was not what he had hoped for on their wedding day. Still, when Georgie Burne-Jones was asked how she could stay with Ned, after the devastation wreaked by his passion for Maria Zambaco, she replied 'that there is love enough between Edward and me to last out a long life if it is given us'.[96] This idea resonated with William over the coming years, and sustained his partnership with Jane.

Jane continued to sit for Gabriel. Sometimes he drew her sensitively as herself, in *The Roseleaf*, for example. Sometimes she was transformed into idealised, allegorical figures, as we see in the chalk studies *Silence* and *La Donna della Fiamma*. These works reinforced her public image as a woman who was out-of-touch, dreamy and passive. They were Gabriel's constructed visions of femininity, steeped in his reading of Dante. But he and Jane knew that they masked her real character, as a compassionate friend and mother. In the meantime, William was busy with his poetry. He was hoping to publish Volume IV of *The Earthly Paradise* in time for Christmas. And the work of the Firm – the day-to-day conversations with colleagues and clients – continued to preoccupy him.

We can see a rapprochement in Jane and William's marriage in the last months of 1870. Evidently Morris's mother and sisters had no inkling that their relationship had been faltering, or at least, they chose not to make Jane feel uncomfortable. She spent several weeks in Torquay with Mrs Morris and Henrietta, apparently on good terms, and stayed on there for several days longer than expected. This dismayed her girls. On 5 December, William wrote, 'Your offspring are highly indignant at your bold step of not coming back; specially Jenny.'[97] For Jane willingly to extend her seaside holiday with her mother-in-law, without the rest of her family, suggests that she was content in the company of Mrs Morris. Or perhaps she was simply relieved to have some respite from her emotional obligations to both William and Gabriel.

William maintained his composure, most of the time. His letters to Jane were courteous and chatty. He was going to get his hair cut and had been measured for a new suit. But the churning worries about Jane and Gabriel surfaced in one revealing passage. It seemed as if the clouds of depression were closing in on him, and he wrestled to shake them off. Here we see William at his most resolute, determined to find an alternative to the blank misery that faced him.

I shall be so glad of you dear, when you come home ... I don't think people really want to die because of mental pain, that is if they are imaginative people; they want to live to see the play played out fairly – they have hopes that they are not conscious of – Hillao! Here's cheerful talk for you – I beg your pardon, dear, with all my heart.[98]

And with that apology, he shook off the muddle at home, and turned his face towards a new challenge, striding into a vast, elemental, vigorous world. His hopes, for now, lay in the Far North – in the language and landscape of Iceland.

Chapter 8

Iceland, 1871

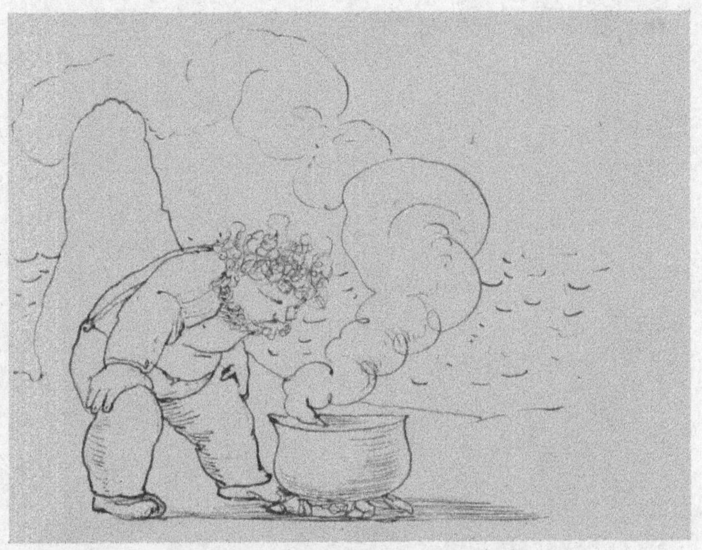

Edward Burne-Jones, *caricature of William Morris cooking in the camp in Iceland*, 1871, British Museum

Two tents, a fire, a kettle and a frying pan: the essentials of home. William stopped climbing and turned to 'look down on the little camp and the grey smoke'.[1] He was starting his journey into the heart of Iceland, exploring a dreamscape where the roofs of houses had become flowerbeds, and he rode through rivers, towards 'a great conical mass of black rock and ice'.[2] And yet here, in a small grassy space, William was at home. He clambered back down the slope to enjoy his tin cup of tea and a bacon sandwich. Then everything was strapped onto the little ponies, and they set off, across 'a huge waste of black sand all powdered over with tufts of sea-pink and bladder-campion at regular intervals, like a Persian carpet'.[3]

The soft turf, the bright flower petals, the uncanny blackness of the earth, these things were noted in his diary with wonder and delight. William was travelling with his eyes open. He was also escaping from family troubles, leaving Jane and the girls behind in England. Their life together had been fractured. He hoped this pilgrimage, or exile, would heal them all. This time in Iceland enabled Jane and William to redraw the boundaries of their relationship, to remake their home in unconventional ways which worked for them.

William also found a clarity of vision in the pared-down landscape.

The hospitality he enjoyed here shaped his future work. Entering 'the gates of a home-mead . . . big and rich-looking, up the lane between the smooth turf walls to the house door',[4] William was welcomed by people who seemed to understand his way of looking at the world. The Icelanders valued hand-skills and old poems. They opened their homes to strangers, sharing food, drink and stories. They lingered in William's imagination long after he returned to London. He remembered fondly his first lodging in

> a very clean room in one of the little wooden houses, which stands back from the road in its potato and angelica garden, with a hayfield, where they are at work now, at the back . . . Lord! how that little row of wooden houses, and their gardens . . . is wedged into my memory.[5]

These experiences forced him to face the question that was seared into all his work – what is a home? Was he happiest by a campfire in the fields, or in a little wooden house? What would he gain from returning to the bricks and mortar of Queen Square?

> Dead and gone is all desire
> Gone and left me cold and bare.[6]

In his tent, wrapped in thick blankets, William listened to the sleet on the canvas. It was early morning, the first day of August. His friend Eiríkr Magnússon lifted the flap and peered inside. Time to attend to the ponies, he said, and to try to light a fire. The men had eaten cold sausage and black bread for lunch the previous day, and cold mutton with cocoa for dinner. Now, with firewood scant and damp, they made do with more leftover mutton and cold water for breakfast. In his diary, William described their campsite: 'This waste is Ernewaterheath . . . where Grettir dwelt so long as an outlaw . . .

a most mournful desolate-looking place, with no signs of life as we rode up but for a swan that rose trumpeting from the lakeside.'[7]

William and his three friends had set out for the heart of Iceland in search of the sagas. He and Magnússon had translated *The Story of Grettir the Strong* two years earlier, and now William was experiencing at first hand the savagery and strangeness of the country: 'It gave quite a new turn in my mind to the whole story.'[8] He was travelling as a poet, a lover of language.

His daughter, May, later described how the Icelanders 'were tickled at an Englishman coming out, not to shoot their moors and fish their rivers, but to make pilgrimage to the homes of Gunnar and Njál'.[9] William began to understand how the past was very close to the surface, breaking through into the present in this volatile landscape. A few days later, at a farmstead in a valley beneath 'the stark bare side of the Holyfell',[10] William was shown 'a mound in the churchyard, which they call Gudrun's grave mound, as I don't see why it shouldn't be'.[11] Guðrun, the beautiful heroine of the Laxdœla Saga, lingered somewhere between legend and reality. For William, having ridden across the central wastes of Iceland, it was reasonable to find her buried here.

He had experienced the disorientation of lava caves, sulphurous rivers and 'black peaks sticking up out of the glacier-sea'.[12] He had watched eagles and sea-swallows overhead. Wind-chapped, his pony stumbling across jagged stones and quivering marshlands, he had been shaken out of himself. He veered between exhilaration and exhaustion, as one 'long dreamlike day' followed another.[13] Now, having seen Guðrún's resting place, he had the chance to write home, giving his letters to the captain of a Danish schooner bound for Liverpool.

He told Jane: 'I have seen many marvels and some terrible pieces of country; I slept in the homefield of Njal's house and Gunnar's.'[14] And yet side by side with these wonders were the delights of simple living:

I wish you could understand how jolly it is when we have got a good piece of road, and the whole train of 28 horses is going a good round trot, the tin cups tinkling and boxes rattling . . . I am dirtier than you might like to see me: my breeches are a triumph of blackness.[15]

His breezy tone suggests that all is well between husband and wife, despite the weeks apart. But William knew that his time away marked a crisis in his marriage. His wanderings allowed them both to take stock. William was only thirty-seven. Even so, this journey to Iceland became the midpoint of his life. As he told a friend on his return, it was a 'blessing and help . . . what horrors it saved me from'. His home life was in shadow, but Iceland gave him perspective: 'O how I long to keep the world from narrowing on me, and to look at things bigly and kindly!'[16]

Standing by Guðrún's grave, William recognised the distance from home. He remembered how Guðrún was loved by two men, foster-brothers. Their jealousy provoked violence and revenge. Guðrún never revealed the secret of her own heart, saying simply, 'I did the worst to him I loved the most.'[17] The parallels with Jane and William's own situation were uncomfortable. William had left his wife for the summer, so she could be with Gabriel, her lover.

And so William ended his letter home from the ragged edge of the North Atlantic: 'Goodbye, my dear, I have so often thought of the sweet fresh garden at Kelmscott, and you and the little ones in it, and wished you happy.'[18] Then he packed up his haversack and turned back towards the great rift of Thingvellir.

*

William wanted Jane to find contentment in the garden of Kelmscott. He repeated this hope in his letters all that summer of 1871, as he set out on his own quest in Iceland.

Jane was happy, and busy about the 'old stone Elizabethan house' deep in the Oxfordshire countryside.[19] Within a few weeks, she was writing to a friend, 'I am already so much better that you would scarcely recognise me.' The out-of-doors life suited her, catching the sun on her skin, so that she had 'some suspicion of red in my face'. She rose early to breakfast with her girls – Jenny was now ten and May was nine – to read with them and then walk down by the river: 'It is all delightful and home-like to me, and I love it.'[20]

Jane also saw where the house needed work. In a series of letters to Philip Webb, we hear her exasperation as she struggles to get a straightforward job done properly. There are the new corner cupboards and window seats to be painted deep blue-green. Jane asks Webb to send a selection of blue-and-white tiles to Kelmscott Manor, so that she can fix the 'broken mantelshelf' and fire-surround in the dining-room.[21] After a week of mess, she writes, 'I will never pull another fireplace down as long as I live.' She explained to him that she wanted to make progress while William was away, but that she had to oversee the work herself: 'They cannot make any great mistake provided I stand by to show them which [is] the right way of each tile.'[22] Jane was clearly knowledgeable about the designs made by the family firm, and how best to display them. She was also looking forward to beginning another embroidery project, 'in fine wool on blue serge' with 'different shades of blue for the flowers', from a pattern created especially for her by Webb.[23]

Stitching, or striding out, or standing over the handyman as he set the tiles in the hearth, Jane was enjoying her new summer home. There was a lack of formality, the sense of possibilities as room opened into room, the sunlight and scents from the gardens. The girls were happy here, too. May found her lessons tedious, but loved the world outside the 'wide mullioned windows', where 'the blackbirds were chuckling and feasting among the gooseberries: golden stacks were growing roof-high in the yard outside, and the huge barn was alive with busy men and women.'[24]

May loved to escape down to the water's edge. Her father was renting the 'beautiful and strangely naif house' for the family partly because it was 'within a stone's throw of the baby Thames'.[25] He enjoyed having 'a boat house and all things handy'.[26] May remembered that she and her sister 'took to the water instinctively', that summer, and 'could handle a boat or punt without losing our heads'.[27] Their mother was glad that they could spend time out of sight and sound of the city.

Already Jane felt settled. And this was in spite of the strangeness of the domestic arrangements. William and Gabriel had taken a joint tenancy of Kelmscott Manor to avoid gossip. We will never know exactly what William understood or felt about his wife's intimacy with his old friend. In public, he always treated Jane with 'gentle courtesy and affection',[28] and his decision to give her these quiet months with Gabriel was unusually generous, almost heroic. He had found a house, which he called 'a heaven on earth', the very first time he saw it. It seemed perfect, with 'such a garden!'[29] Yet as soon as he discovered it, he offered it to Jane, as a great gift, while he went away North.

What made Kelmscott such a peaceful, encouraging place? The pull of the house was so strong that it became a central character in the stories of many of the people who stayed there. It was not a particularly picturesque setting. Even Jane acknowledged that, from an upper window, 'when one looks far out, there is a sameness, a bareness of trees'. She was surrounded by flat, unimpressive farmland. But she recognised that 'every field is lovely by itself, and every house'.[30]

Kelmscott Manor was part of this ordinary beauty. It seemed rooted in the soil, at home itself. In his later novel *News from Nowhere*, Morris describes a young woman reaching out to embrace the stones of the house, loving it for being part of 'the earth, and the seasons, and the weather',[31] and it was this organic quality that delighted Jane and William and their friends. It was built of local materials, 'a mass of grey walls and pearly grey roofs' and with one wing 'buttered over, so to say, with thin plaster which has now weathered to the same colour as the stone of the walls'.[32] They enjoyed the sense of living quietly, in a place of deep history. The village was named after an Anglo-Saxon – it was the site of Coenhelm's cott – and the landscape around was dotted with ancient settlements and medieval churches.

*

Kelmscott Manor is not a grand building, though it is big enough for family and visitors, with gardens all round. There are meadows, a dovecot and barns between the house and the riverbank. Throughout its life, it has been updated and extended, to fit the needs of the Turner family who owned the house until the mid-nineteenth century, and then leased it to the Morrises. The main body of the house was likely built by Thomas Turner soon after 1600. A finer, more lofty room, with a chamber above, was added in the later 1660s. Then, in the early eighteenth century, a kitchen, buttery, brewhouse and dairy house were built out at an angle.[33] Jane and William added a larder and put in a watercloset upstairs.

When William and Rossetti took on the tenancy, it was a U-shaped house, with the grander family rooms in the middle and north, and the noisier, busier spaces to the south of the entrance passage. What would Jane have found, when she first entered the house in the early summer of 1871? Downstairs, the housekeeping areas – for preparing food and cleaning – were separated from the rest of the house by a wooden panelled screen, with the old kitchen on one side, and the hall, which she would use as a dining room, on the other. This screened passage showed how older building layouts had persisted in this tucked-away corner of Oxfordshire. It was a relic of a medieval way of life, still being used well into the seventeenth century to keep the draughts out. There was an outer door at either end: the front entrance under a small gabled porch, and another at the back, leading out to the little courtyard by the brewhouse.

Downstairs, beyond the dining hall, were two reception rooms. To the west was the green room, overlooking the mulberry garden, and to the east, the slightly grander room with white panelling, which was 'once the great parlour'.[34] Between the two was the north hall, and a side door out to the garden. Once they lived here, this was the way the family usually came and went.

Jane chose her bedroom – turning right at the top of the main staircase, and into an airy chamber with a large closet over the green room. She decided to decorate it with William's *Fruit* wallpaper. His bedroom was to the left, over the north hall. The girls, Jenny and May, would sleep in rooms in the centre of the house, above the dining hall.

And then there was the tapestry room which could only be reached by crossing William's room. There were a couple of steps up, in the far corner beyond his bed. William recalled 'the peculiarity of being without passages, so that you have to go from one room into another, to the confusion of some of our casual visitors'.[35] The tapestry room had been designed to impress. It originally had windows on three sides, with a small bachelor's bedroom or dressing room in one bay. This is where Gabriel Rossetti would work and sleep.

May Morris remembered sitting for Gabriel that summer, after she finished her lessons on 'those glowing August mornings'.[36] There was plenty to delight the child's eye, inside and out. Her father later wrote about the special charm of the tapestry room: through the south window you 'catch a glimpse of the Thames clover meadows and the pretty little elm-crowned hill', and 'if you sit in the proper place', the barn 'with its beautiful sharp gable, the grey stone sheds, and the dove cot' were also visible. Or her big sister Jenny would distract May by pressing her face against the glass of one of the windows in 'the flank of the earlier house'.[37] Sometimes Gabriel seemed preoccupied while he drew her, sometimes they chatted about friends in London. She remembered finding him, late one afternoon, 'sitting over the fire – alone'.[38] The house was filled with young people, laughing as they played hide-and-seek, and yet he was often melancholy, isolated.

How did these unconventional domestic arrangements work – with Gabriel and Jane living under the same roof, and William away for weeks? The façade of respectability that was maintained at Kelmscott Manor was based on William and Gabriel's long-standing friendship, and Jane's role as Gabriel's most important model. She was recognised as Rossetti's 'chief inspiration . . . a face in fact quite made to his hand. He has painted a dozen portraits of her – one in particular, in a blue gown with her hair down . . . an almost great work.'[39]

Gabriel's oil paintings and large chalk drawings of Jane were only part of the story. There were also dozens of informal sketches, made between the official sittings. Gabriel watched Jane with her embroidery frame, or as she curled up on the sofa, reading. She was relaxed in his company. In the small drawings, Jane is never idle: thoughtful, perhaps, but often occupied with some needlework or book. These pencil drawings give a clearer idea of the relationship between Jane and Gabriel than the haughty, almost obsessive images of her as a queen or goddess. As one young friend observed, 'I have always thought that one of the chief reasons for the great sympathy and attraction which she and Rossetti had for each other was their mutual sense of humour.'[40]

Jane herself reminded Gabriel, 'You know what a babyish hopeful creature I always am.'[41] They had looked forward to spending weeks together in the 'little house deep in the country'.[42] It was an imaginative solution to the thorniest of problems, made possible by William's open-heartedness, and Jane's discretion.

At first, Gabriel was pleased to be at Kelmscott with his beloved. He wrote to his mother about the gentle landscape, 'full of fat cut hedges'. He described strolling along the lanes between the farm buildings, which 'look settled down into a purring state of comfort, but seem (as

Janey said the other day) as if, were you to stroke them, they would move'.[43] Clearly, he saw no reason to conceal that he and Jane were spending the summer together. But soon after, he was describing the village as 'the doziest dump of old grey beehives'.[44]

The poems Gabriel wrote that summer veered between emotional extremes. There is the infatuated sensuality of clasp in 'Between Kisses', where the poet's 'worshipping face' is mirrored in his lover's eyes, 'grey-circled in a heaven of deep-drawn rays'. And then the broken promises of 'Down Stream', with an abandoned girl found where 'the summer river flows/ . . . With lilies meshed in tangled hair'.[45] Gabriel's seclusion with Jane, their outings on the river, their long August evenings together, were very close to the surface of his writing. Her face was essential to his picture-making. *Perlascura*, one of the pastels he drew at Kelmscott, was cherished by Jane. Her shoulders are bare, and she wears no jewellery at her throat or in her heavy hair. She seems aware of his gaze, but not meeting his eye. This very carefully finished work suggests long looking, a desire to memorialise their 'close-companioned inarticulate hour/ When twofold silence was the song of love'.[46]

But as the weeks passed, Gabriel's mood became gloomier. He was oppressed by the flatlands and meadows. He seemed out of step with the rest of the household. They were up and out before he came down for his solitary breakfast – he ate more eggs in one meal than young May thought possible – and then he spent long hours alone in the tapestry room. May felt the oddness of his position. She remembered him setting out in the twilight for a walk, sometimes with her mother, but often by himself. From a child's perspective, he looked terribly lonely. The sense of adventure and dalliance he had felt in the early summer was slipping away. Jane and Gabriel could walk out together, but they were observed – by the girls, by the caretakers, by the farm workers in the fields they passed.

Kelmscott was never a simple rural idyll. William was away, but he was not forgotten. When Jane wrote to a friend, a month after her husband had sailed, she sounded worried: 'I have no news of Topsy yet, Is it not rather odd'.[47] Although Gabriel could wander through William's empty bedroom after dark, and find Jane alone, their pleasure in each other was undermined by outside concerns.

Gabriel had published new poems including *The House of Life* sequence in 1870. He was keenly aware that these sonnets exposed his private life to critical attention. He had included verses titled 'Nuptial Sleep' and 'Supreme Surrender'. Those who knew him well were aware that many of these works were written since the death of his wife, Lizzie Siddall in 1862. Over the past months, there had been increasing tension between Gabriel and his friends because of his romance with Jane. Burne-Jones felt compelled to stand up for William, especially now his friend had gone into self-imposed exile in Iceland. In July, Burne-Jones admitted, 'With Rossetti I have had the skirmish I planned. First long letters and then a face to face row, but in each case I spoke my mind out in full'.[48] We will never know what was said, but these accusations and the feeling of friendships falling apart must have tainted the atmosphere at Kelmscott.

There is no evidence that Ned Burne-Jones blamed Jane herself. Having spent many years in Gabriel's company, he understood Rossetti's audacious and flattering manner. As Burne-Jones explained to his studio assistant, long after Gabriel's death, he 'was so fascinating, that he could bring over whatever man he chose, and . . . I'm quite sure there's not a woman in the whole world he couldn't have won for himself. Nothing pleased him more though, than to take his friend's mistress away from him.'[49]

Both William and Ned had felt the warmth of his enthusiastic notice when they were starting out. They understood why Jane had also fallen for Gabriel, relishing the charm and the energy of his attention. William was never an ardent lover. He was often distracted by making or writing. Gabriel, on the other hand, was intensely present with her, lavishly describing her eyes and lips in poetry or pastels. Still, Jane's relationship with Gabriel was complex and affectionate. Her fondness persisted long after the immediate passion had subsided. In the letters that have survived, she was encouraging and consoling.

The summer at Kelmscott was a turning point for Rossetti, too. His mental health was fragile, and Jane's 'truly friendly face' was one of the constants during periods of distress that afflicted him.[50] Their long walks in the dusk, their late suppers were the last remnants of his old life before it was shattered by drug dependence and paranoia. He maintained his tenancy of Kelmscott, living there sporadically until the late spring of 1874. Some of his furniture is still there. He never reclaimed his eighteenth-century satinwood writing table. He returned home without packing up all his things: Jane wrote to ask him whether he wanted his gilt chandelier and washstand back in London, adding 'The embroideries were all sent before, if you remember.'[51]

Gabriel left his mark on the house. He gave his opinion when Jane was choosing paint colours for the sitting rooms. When he died, he wanted her to take something from his house in Chelsea; she chose several convex mirrors, his Chinese red lacquer chairs, and a japanned corner cabinet, and reinstalled them at Kelmscott as tangible reminders of his presence. They still seem ill at ease, unnecessarily exotic, among the plain wooden tables and hand-stitched hangings. Beyond these relics, many of Gabriel's celebrated portraits of Jane, as well as his poems describing their intimacy, were inevitably associated with his quiet months in residence. For the girls, his shadow was sensed in the tapestry room long after he left. For all the Morris family, that first summer at Kelmscott was overlaid with memories of Jane and Gabriel's passionate but troubled liaison.

*

Gabriel was there when William returned from Iceland, with parcels of treasures from the North, and a pony called Mouse. He lingered in the background as William unwrapped his gifts – embroidered blouses and silver spoons – and told tales of the long trek across cold wastes, through green marshes. William made his girls laugh with descriptions of breakfast on shipboard: 'beefsteak and onion, smoked salmon, Norway anchovies, hard-boiled eggs, cold meat, cheese and radishes and butter'.[52] It all seemed so long ago and far away now, 'as if the old life of the saga-time had gone, and the modern life had never reached the place.' He spoke of the Faroes, and his first sight of those wild islands, 'not savage but mournfully empty and barren, the grey clouds dragging over the hill-top or lying in the hollows being the only thing that varied the grass, stone and sea'.[53]

Grass, stone, sea; everything in Iceland seemed to be clean and deliberate in William's memory. He had spent the summer trying to come to terms with the changes in his own household, while finding new ways of seeing the world and his purpose in it. He had pushed himself to extremes – of delight and fear, loneliness and companionship. He remembered the peculiar taste of mutton cooked in a volcanic hot-spring; the loyalty of his old friend Charley Faulkner who journeyed with him; the silliness of opening a packing-case of food supplies, and finding 'Fragrant Floriline and two dozen bottles of . . . Bond Street scents' instead of sausage; the wonder of meeting a girl who wore a beautifully wrought silver belt, three hundred years old; all these experiences tumbled together.[54] He appreciated the 'take it or leave it' hospitality of the Icelanders who had welcomed the travellers without fuss. William was moved by the apparent integration of handcraft and storytelling into everyday life. A loom in the living room, an old tale retold while crossing a stream, 'a piece of turf under your feet, and the sky overhead, that's all'.[55] The Icelandic way made sense to him.

Before he had left on his long journey, William and his daughters had built a makeshift hearth in the garden of The Grange, Burne-Jones's house. (They could never do such a thing in the fenced-off communal gardens outside their London home in Queen Square.) At The Grange, they had played at making tea with Burne-Jones's children, Phil and Margaret. Now William had gardens of his own at Kelmscott. He made a campfire in the late sunshine, and showed his girls how to clean and grill the fish they caught in the 'stripling Thames'.[56] He told them about cooking on a peat fire in Grimstunga, in 'a little shed with a hearth built up of dry stones, and a hole in the roof . . . the rafters black and shining with soot . . . I worked hard at my stew and soup: they really were both very good, or else we were very hungry'.[57] And another evening, frying trout in a kitchen, 'just big enough to hold me, my pots, the smoke, and a little girl whose name was Augustina', and then walking across the fields, 'till it was past one, and dawn was in the sky again', listening to the waves breaking and the 'unaccountable noises of the sea-birds'.[58]

Meanwhile, Rossetti was still refusing to leave Kelmscott, an unsettling presence sitting among the faded tapestries upstairs. It hurt William to feel him there. But mostly William, Jenny and May were outside, experimenting with a different way of living. Like the children in *News from Nowhere*, who 'play in the woods for weeks together in summer-time, . . . they learn to do things for themselves, and get to notice the wild creatures'.[59] William had discovered the importance of getting away: 'The less they stew inside houses, the better for them.' He had felt alive in the wilderness, clattering over the lava fields, 'with our faces turned towards the mountain-wall under which we were to sleep tonight'.[60] How would he settle at home again, with his wife walking across the meadow to call the girls inside, and her lover waiting in his studio?

At times on his journey William had woken up, 'puzzled . . . and with an unhappy feeling of being a long way from where I wanted to be'.[61] On his return, he and Jane decided to leave their lodgings in Queen Square, and find somewhere a little further out of town, where they could live on a smaller scale. They would create some distance between the family and the Firm. They could still escape to Kelmscott when the traffic noise and 'pea-soupers' became too much. Perhaps for Jane and William, this was a chance for a new chapter in their marriage.

William had been emptied out in Iceland. He had learnt that 'there was nothing mean or prosaic' in the places he had seen there.[62] 'Our joyous rough life' in camp had given him an opportunity to rethink.[63] Now he could use this clarity, the rawness, to rebuild his home life and shape his work.

Chapter 9

Turnham Green, 1872–1878

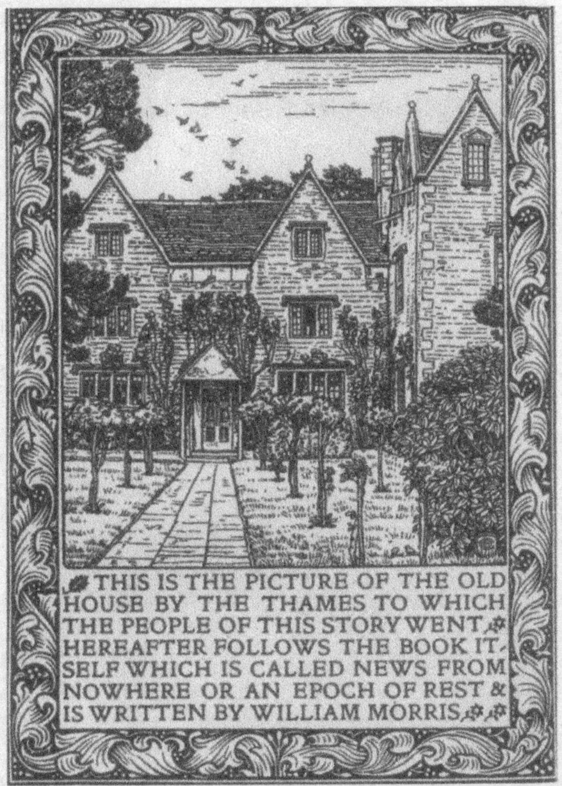

Charles Gere, *Kelmscott Manor: Frontispiece to 'News from Nowhere'*,
first published 1890, this edition, Kelmscott Press, 1893

As she stepped out onto the top of the tower, Jane caught her breath in the breeze. Downstairs, there were piles of cushions, mattresses and blankets, baskets of food, crates and bottles, all to be sorted. But up here she paused to remember why she had come. From the parapet, Jane could see for miles across the woods and sheep-grazed uplands of the Cotswolds. Harvest fields glowed in the early August sun. Looking down, she was able to trace the ancient track of Buckle Street, as it led north-east towards Chipping Camden, and south to Bourton-on-the-Water. She and May had arrived early to ready the place for the rest of their party. Jane loved the makeshift, light-hearted nature of these holidays. But she also enjoyed the quiet preparations, and time spent contemplating the bright sky, before all the fun and busy-ness began.

Broadway Tower was rented as a holiday home by her friend Cormell Price. He had been at school in Birmingham with Ned, and then became close to William at Oxford. They all called him Crom. When Jane wrote to him, he was 'My dear Crom', 'Dearest Crom', and even 'My dearest Brother'.[1] In the summers of 1876 and 1877, he offered his tower as a gathering place for the old set. Georgie Burne-Jones planned to come across, hopefully with Charley Faulkner and his sister Kate. William would join them, on his way to Kelmscott.

The tower was an ideal spot for picnics and exploring. It stood high on an exposed beacon hill, and had been commissioned as a folly in 1798 by the Earl of Coventry. It was a joint venture by landscape designer 'Capability' Brown and the architect James Wyatt. They claimed it was in the 'Saxon' style; in truth, it was a lively reworking of Gothic details, with three round turrets attached to a hexagonal central tower. It had neat arched windows with little balconies, and looked like something out of a fairy story. May Morris was very taken with it. Her mother said her 'excitement is tremendous . . . she wants to sleep in the top of the tower'.[2] Some of the men did sleep outside in the open air, and bathed on the roof, too, 'when the wind didn't blow the soap away'.[3]

In her letters to Crom, we see Jane away from the studio life of London. Here she is energetic and outdoorsy, rising early 'to enjoy the lark's song'. She strolls out before breakfast with May, stopping to say hello to an old farm dog who is waiting for them. Jane describes briskly and happily how they 'admired the hills, got very cold, and came in and got up a good fire' for their tea.[4] It is almost a camping trip. There is talk of setting up a tent, and walking to the inn at Broadway, and only cooking 'for amusement when we feel inclined'.[5] With no servants to hand, except for the caretaker who provided water and wood, Jane was in charge of housekeeping for the party. She took responsibility for finding blankets and pillows. She made sure there were enough hampers of food, kept an eye on the fires, and even tracked down the little wooden doorstops to keep out the draughts.

Jane liked being hands-on. She was resourceful and imaginative in her plans to make everyone comfortable. Like William, who had relished cooking for his friends in Iceland, Jane did not shy away from practical tasks of homemaking, wherever she might be. She corresponded with Crom, discussing who should sleep where. She offered to bring bedding across from Kelmscott. She even arranged for a sofa to be delivered, 'to use in daytime, having a vivid recollection of the legless one of last year.' This was not Jane fussing. It shows she was thinking ahead, and ensuring that she could play the fullest part in the activities they planned. Even if she was suffering from back ache, she would be present, visible, able to make the household run smoothly. But she hoped that the change of air would ease her chronic pain. She wrote delightedly to Crom when she arrived with May, telling him 'our beds are luxurious, being but the two of us'. The weather was kind and warm, and she was in good spirits: 'I believe I am getting fatter already.'[6]

*

Jane was especially grateful for the holiday this year. It was good to get some of their friends together, almost like old times. There were gaps, however. Ned Burne-Jones was not coming with Georgie. Gabriel Rossetti and her own daughter Jenny were too poorly. William was no longer on good terms with Emma and Ford Madox Brown. The loyalties within the group had shifted dramatically in the early 1870s. Some of these changes were caused by the growth of the Firm. Others were more emotionally complicated. In 1872, William had tried to resolve some of the complications, at least for himself, in a poem called 'Love is Enough'. The framework for the writing was itself very intricate – a play within a poem, and multiple verse structures – as he used pre-Shakespearean models. He hoped to show how love could heal, how finding and holding tight to a beloved was, as he says, enough. It was more subtle and carefully wrought than we might expect, from Ned's description. He wrote to a friend that William 'makes a poem these days – in dismal Queen Square in black old filthy London in dull end of October he makes a pretty poem that is to be wondrously happy; and it has four sets of lovers in it and THEY ARE ALL HAPPY and it ends well'.[7]

However, this was an idyll; it was wishful thinking. Ned, in the very next line of his letter, explained that there was a cloud lowering over their circle: 'As for Gabriel I have seen him but little, for he glooms much and dulls himself and gets ill and better and is restless.'[8] Gabriel's gloom became the dominant motif of the 1870s. It affected all his friends, especially Jane.

She was also having to deal with the disruption of moving house. In November 1872, the family began to pack up their rooms in Queen Square and settle in a 'little unpretentious house in Turnham Green'. She was no longer living above the shop.

Horrington House was described by May as having 'plenty of light and air and garden space'.[9] Inside, however, the house was considerably smaller than their rooms at Queen Square. It was also more out-of-the-way. It would be hard to imagine Henry James taking the Hounslow–Brentford bus and alighting at the stop by the Roebuck Inn; Jane's new home was next door to the pub, on the High Road. In her words it was 'a very good sort of house for one person to live in, or perhaps two'.[10] It seemed like a retreat from her semi-public life in the centre of London. A renewed focus on her domestic responsibilities. And a step away from the on-going business of Morris, Marshall, Faulkner and Company. This move felt very different from the excitement and energy of creating Red House, or their pragmatic relocation to the centre of London. Queen Square had its drawbacks. But at least Jane had still been close to the planning and making, and had contributed to William's artistic networks. Now she was adrift, in a house designed for cosiness, not for entertaining.

William seemed less unsettled by the move. In one of his letters, he almost seems to take pleasure in the disorder of the alterations: 'Janey's room has already got the workmen's benches in it: the big room is bare and painty; there is hammering and sawing and running up and down stairs going on.'[11] But he also looked forward to setting up a space for his own work. He told a friend that 'my own room is particularly cheerful and pretty'.[12] William was absorbed in calligraphy and illuminating manuscripts. May remembered the peace and concentration required for this art: 'the bare light room, the plain work-table; the splendid head bending over the gold, and the two young heads laid close, and the curly locks all mingling'. William and his girls were all caught up in the magic of making his intricate writings and drawings. He collected goose quills and crow quills, 'finely tempered knives and elegant rules and compasses.' Even the materials themselves might have been lifted from an alchemist's casket. 'There was precious ultramarine in a slim cake, there was pale gold in shells, and gold leaf in books,' and William would pick up the 'fragile glitter' by running his brush through his hair 'before laying it gently on the leaf of gold. That made us laugh.'[13] As he said, he spent many hours with 'my nose down on my vellum'.[14]

Several of these beautiful books were written out and decorated for Georgie Burne-Jones. William understood only too well how she suffered from Ned's liaison with Maria Zambaco. Both William and Georgie had chosen to weather the storms in their marriages. They relied on each other for uncomplicated affection. When William travelled to Iceland, his journal was written for Georgie's benefit, not for Jane. And now, having obsessively tracked down the finest vellum, the blackest oak-gall for his ink, he was creating manuscripts as gifts for Ned's wife, not his own. Some were collaborations, with Ned providing the images. These included the 'Book of Verse' given to Georgie in 1870, which contained his own poems and translations from Icelandic. Others, like the great romance of 'The Rubaiyat of Omar Khayyam', were all in William's hand. This was a heartfelt gift, tenderly decorated with gilded capital letters. Flowering branches frame the calligraphy. It is one of the great puzzles of William's life – that a man who often appeared so blundering, heavy-handed and unpredictable in his physicality could produce such exquisite and tiny beauties. He was patient and gentle with delicate things and fragile people. And yet his public face was often irascible, blunt and bear-like. His sensitivity was masked by his bulk, his vigour.

The intimacy between the Morris and Burne-Jones families was strengthened by the move to Turnham Green. It was one of the reasons William was happy with the new home – it was only half an hour's walk away from Georgie and Ned at the Grange in Fulham. Their daughter Margaret Burne-Jones remembered Horrington House as a place of warmth, where Jane would supply the children with 'quantities of crumpets'.[15] She and her brother Phil called her 'Aunt Janey'. In one of the chatty letters to Crom, we read how Jane's sweetness and concern extended to Margaret's little cousin Rudyard Kipling. He was alone in England, at the boarding school where Crom was headmaster, while his family stayed in India. She asked if 'he remembers his Aunt Janey'. She hoped he would 'look upon me as common property', as a friendly face, someone who might help to lift his loneliness. She understood enough about being separated from parents. She knew how it felt to be shy and out of place. She also had enough sense to say to her friend Crom that 'I suppose you never address a word to so small a boy'.[16] Jane recognised how the world worked, even if she chose to sidestep some of its customs.

'The littles', Jenny and May, also appreciated that their new home was closer to their young friends at The Grange. They enjoyed the Burne-Joneses big garden and their pets; Margaret had a succession of cats and, briefly, a green parakeet. They shared holidays and private games. Photographs of the girls, taken in 1874, show both Margaret and May apparently dressed in sturdy tunics and knickerbockers. Their tops have loose-fitting sleeves and the minimum of decoration – just a ribbon at the hem, and a necklace of plain beads. This was a radical choice, made by both Georgie and Jane. They were happy to let their girls climb and run, unencumbered by the calf-length skirts worn by their more conventional cousins. Theirs was an extraordinary girlhood, enriched by 'romping and skirmishing' as well as storytelling and picture-making.[17]

William enjoyed his renewed closeness to Ned and all the Burne-Jones family. As Ned explained, 'this was the beginning of the Sunday meetings' when William 'used to breakfast with us' and spend the morning in the studio at The Grange. It was a plan 'to bind us together'.[18] They were able to continue sharing tales old and new, recovering some of the freshness of their student days. They talked of poetry and paintings and travelling, to the icy North or the sunshine and shadows of Italy.

On weekdays, William returned to the old house in Queen Square fired up with ideas. The empty upstairs rooms seemed dismal and chilly, now his girls were no longer there. But he did not dwell on this for long. The drawing room could be turned into a formal showroom, and he would let the craftsmen move some of their workshops into the bedrooms. He thought he might set up 'a little dye-shop in the empty basement'.[19] There was a certain briskness in his attitude. He told a friend at the time that the move to Horrington House 'doesn't touch me very much . . . for this long time past I have, as it were, carried my house on my back'.[20] This seems strange, for a man so keenly associated with homemaking and decoration. But it seems to spring from his experience in Iceland, when he found a lightening, a clarity, a realisation of what was essential. Part of this realisation was that he needed some independent space, away from his family.

So, William did not give up his own foothold in Queen Square. It was important for him to be there, meeting clients or friends, and overseeing production. It made sense to keep a study and a bedroom, so he did not waste hours trekking across town every evening: as he told Aglaia Coronio in January 1873, 'I daresay, as time goes on, I shall live here a good deal.' Mrs Coronio, like Georgie Burne-Jones, provided some solace, while Jane was preoccupied with her own affairs. In William's letters to Aglaia we hear an urgency, a desire for her company:

so I could come on Wednesday or Thursday or Friday – the sooner
the better. It is a great disappointment to have missed you . . . an
hour or two with you would have helped me get along.[21]

It often seems as if we are catching him in mid-conversation:

Yes, truly letters are very unsatisfactory . . . the sheet is filled up
with trivialities . . . only there is something about the look of the
writing of anyone one is fond of that is familiar and dear and saves
one from utter disappointment, and one feels that the stiff awkward
sentences . . . have still something of a soul in them.

He went on:

Yes I think of you a great deal, my dear friend: as I looked out of
my window on Sunday, I pictured you coming into the little garden
till I could almost see you standing there.[22]

He reassured Aglaia that 'I can always see anyone I want at Queen
Sq: quite safe from interruption.' He wanted their conversations to
remain private, because he was more open with her than with most
of his friends. As Ned said, William did not often permit himself
to show the warmth of his affections.[23] It is not clear whether this
relationship with Aglaia strayed beyond flirtation, becoming a firmer
attachment. But William was habitually reticent with women. He
also knew first-hand about the miseries caused by infidelity. It seems
most likely then that this remained a fond friendship, and no more.

William's choice to preserve some space and privacy at Queen
Square reflected the realities of his relationship with Jane. Writing to
Aglaia about the new family home in Turnham Green, he agreed that
'it is a *very* little house with a pretty garden, and I think it will suit
Janey and the children.'[24] He did not include himself in this picture of

domestic life. William's sense of detachment was reinforced by Jane's entanglement with Gabriel Rossetti, which became more distressing and complicated in 1872–3 – just at the time that the Morris family were in the throes of moving house.

*

Gabriel's mental health had been unstable since a damning review of his poetry in the autumn of 1871. He had waited a long time to publish, fine-tuning and fretting over his verses. Now he was understandably nervous about their reception. Added to this was the risk of rekindling rumours that he had dug up his dead wife to recover his manuscript from her coffin.

It is worth unpicking the controversy around this review, as it reshaped Gabriel's relationship with Jane; several of the poems were written during their time together at Kelmscott. It also contributed directly to his suicide attempt in the summer of 1872. The article, titled 'The Fleshly School of Poetry', attacked the eroticism of Gabriel's verses. It also compared them unfavourably to recent poems by William, which were largely 'pure, fresh and wholesome'. Rossetti, by contrast, revelled in 'weary, wasting, yet exquisite sensuality; nothing virile, nothing tender, nothing completely sane'.[25] The women in his love poems were uncontrolled, animalistic. They were 'females who bite, scratch, scream, bubble, munch, sweat, writhe, twist, wriggle, foam, and in a general way slaver over their lovers'.[26]

The reviewer was Robert Buchanan, who wrote under the pseudonym Thomas Maitland. He was particularly agitated by Rossetti's description of 'Nuptial Sleep'. This was a sonnet describing the aftermath of lovemaking. Buchanan made sure to print it in full, so all his readers could see how unnecessarily sensual it was. It made him 'shudder at the shameless nakedness' of the writing. It was 'simply nasty' and unmanly.[27]

When the article was reprinted on the eve of Gabriel's birthday, 12

May 1872, Buchanan hinted that he knew about Gabriel's relationship with Jane Morris. There was no reason for him to be discreet about it. Gabriel's friends recognised his attachment to Mrs Morris as a private matter, not discussed outside their circle. But if Buchanan made it plain, then by implication, Jane would be one of the writhing, scratching female lovers in Gabriel's sonnets. We do not know if Jane was aware of the assertions at the time. None of her letters to Gabriel from these turbulent months has survived.

On 1 June 1872, there was a new article criticising Gabriel's 'utter unmanliness . . . at once so disgusting, and . . . so mischievous'.[28] The more he thought about it, the more Gabriel was convinced that one aspect of this 'unmanliness' was seducing a friend's wife. He also worried that exhuming Elizabeth Siddall's coffin to retrieve his poems was a cowardly and dishonourable act. As he had said to his brother, 'the truth must ooze out in time'.[29] Gabriel was scared that both these misdeeds were about to be made public. Now these fears tipped over into paranoia.

Gabriel had been using laudanum for months to help him sleep. And now, in a dreadful re-enactment of Lizzie's death, Gabriel took an overdose. On 8 June, his brother William Michael and Dr Hake found him in a 'lethal trance'. They managed eventually to revive him – after thirty-six hours – and pretended to his sisters and mother that it was 'suffusion of the brain' or perhaps a stroke that had caused his collapse.[30] They did not want word to get out that Gabriel had tried to commit suicide. Even so, the rumours started spreading. William Michael 'was told of somebody, a friend of somebody else being in the Solferino Restaurant and hearing Sandys and Swinburne going over the whole matter at one of the tables'.[31]

A few days later, a friend reported that Gabriel's 'delusions are more dreadful than ever',[32] and there was talk of moving him to an asylum. Emma and Ford Madox Brown offered to look after him in their own home in Fitzroy Square. But on 20 June, William Bell Scott whisked Gabriel up to Penkill Castle in Ayrshire. Scott felt that it was important to get Gabriel as far away from Jane as possible.

These events inevitably raise some difficult questions. It is clear that Gabriel was disturbed; he deliberately took an overdose of laudanum, expecting to die as Lizzie Siddall had died. However, he surely had some grounds for his feelings of paranoia – his work and his character were indeed being pulled apart by critics. He was desperate to go home but was being kept under very strict observation. Is it surprising he began 'crying out that he must leave the house' where he was being treated by his doctor?[33] And Scott and William Michael really were trying to remove him from the people he relied on, including Jane. They were concerned 'about his derangement being increased by thinking of her'.[34]

Seen from this angle, Gabriel's fears were not so far-fetched. He was right to feel he was being watched. He was deliberately separated from his beloved Jane. When she wrote to ask for news of Gabriel, his carers made a decision not to tell him. And his doctor burnt her letters.[35]

*

What was Jane doing and feeling during this distressing time? We only have Scott's word for how she took the news of Gabriel's breakdown. We must also remember that Scott disliked her, and that he passed on all kinds of gossip to his lover Alice Boyd. Jane therefore gave him no ammunition to use against her. She displayed her greatest reserve. When he arrived, rather gleefully, to tell her that Gabriel 'was getting into his worse state', she lay on her sofa, listening quietly. Scott thought that she was 'not discomposed by my intelligence'.[36] Jane refused to play into the hands of those people who blamed her for Rossetti's instability. She would not become a hyper-emotional female. She was no sensational *femme fatale*. Jane thanked Scott for taking the trouble to visit her, and let him go.

She retained her composure while Scott was there. But she wanted to do whatever she could to support Gabriel, without making their situation worse. It is at this point, when Jane was at her most vulnerable, that we see the great strength of her relationship with William. They worked together to help Gabriel. In doing so, William demonstrated his continuing care for Jane, and upheld her status as a respectable wife and mother.

Scott and William Michael Rossetti had underestimated both Jane and William. They expected Mrs Morris to arrive in a passionate whirlwind, 'rushing out to Roehampton or to Chelsea'. Instead, William brought her to see Gabriel. The next time he visited, William even offered to stay and help Ford Madox Brown look after his friend. Scott might have belittled William, calling him a 'more than amiable husband'.[37] But William saw what needed to be done. His forbearance, his loyalty, saved Jane from exposure and catastrophe. And by acting as a part of a couple, Jane could continue corresponding with Gabriel's carers – on behalf of her husband as well as herself – once he was moved to Scotland. She wrote, for instance, 'how glad my husband would be to see you to have a chat' about Gabriel's progress, and even followed up Gabriel's own suggestion of 'coming to us for a time' when he was more fully recovered.[38] However, these cheerful phrases masked the very real anguish she felt during these troubled months.

It was inevitable that she was worried, not just about Gabriel's physical and mental state, but also about the consequences for her own home life. Gossipy stories would be circulating among Gabriel's friends and rivals. Both he and Jane were usually private people, sharing their feelings within a very small circle. Jane was in a peculiarly difficult position, because she could not challenge the rumours. She could only imagine the connections that were being made between her modelling sessions and his sensual poems. In the letter she wrote to Scott, a month after Gabriel's overdose, Jane could no longer keep up her appearance of restraint. Her words seemed to overflow, stumble, in her hopelessness. She pleaded with Scott:

I have heard no news for so long that I dread all sorts of horrible things do please write and tell me even the worst, anything is better than the dreadful suspense. I am all alone and imagine such horrors as I sit in my room here that I despair of ever getting well let me have some news soon.[39]

She could barely sleep. 'I had such dreadful dreams last night,' she told Ford Madox Brown. 'I can't rest today without trying all means to get news.' Jane recognised that Gabriel's doctor and William Bell Scott were keeping her at arm's length.[40] Jane could not attend the wedding of Brown's daughter Catherine because, she said, 'I feel myself less and less capable of appearing in society . . . I am very weak and nervous still . . . Will you therefore kindly excuse me?'[41]

By the end of September 1872, the immediate crisis was over and Gabriel was brought to Kelmscott Manor to rest. Jane was surprised, given that Gabriel 'has said to me so often he would never go there again'.[42] However, it was now possible for her to visit him. Jane stayed with Gabriel on and off, during the autumn of 1872. William wrote in late November that she had 'just come back from Kelmscott last Saturday, and is very well apparently, and in good spirits certainly'.[43]

It is often difficult for us to follow Jane's movements during the years after Gabriel's collapse. In her few surviving letters from this period, she sometimes pleaded that she was unwell herself and found evening parties 'too fatiguing'.[44] Writing to his mother a few months later, William said that Jane was 'on the whole better but the hot weather is knocking her up'.[45] She was often away from home, staying with Gabriel in seclusion deep in the country. They were careful not to attract attention, but many in their circle knew about these arrangements. Jane was closely involved in the process of his painting, and not just as a model. She designed and made costumes – we know of one particularly elaborate robe because it was lost on the train, somewhere between Paddington Station and Lechlade. It was 'of crimson Chinese silk lined with yellow striped green'.[46] The time and care which Jane must have given to making the silk dress was considerable – sourcing the silks and threads, discussing the draping, cutting the pattern pieces, hand-sewing the slippery fabric, inside and out. And then it went missing. But she found an alternative, something equally rich and full of colour, and asked Gabriel's brother to take it down to Kelmscott.[47]

Jane's responsibilities were split between Turnham Green and Gabriel. Sometimes when she travelled to Kelmscott the girls were with her, sometimes not. It was a dislocated time. It seems appropriate that, at this point in their relationship, Gabriel chose to depict Jane as *Proserpine*. From 1872, he returned to the subject at least eight times, in chalk and oil. It became almost obsessive. According to myth, Proserpine spends six months each year in the Underworld, and six months back with her family. She can never settle. Jane/Prosperine stands, clutching a pomegranate, remembering her other life, as a shaft of sunlight briefly penetrates the gloom. Gabriel wrote about her unhappiness in a sonnet to complete the picture: 'Afar from mine own self I seem . . . And still some heart unto some soul doth pine'.[48] This seems to be the closest that Gabriel ever came to acknowledging how hard the situation was for Jane. She would not abandon him, when he relied on her. She valued his devotion, as a friend, as a lover. But she often felt torn.

Gabriel's arrival at Kelmscott was also a dreadful blow to William. In one of his most revealing letters, written to Aglaia Coronio, William wondered if he had been too weak in the eyes of the world. He felt low and was 'afraid it comes from some cowardice or unmanliness in me'. Again, this slur of 'unmanliness', of failure to conform to some masculine code of conduct, resurfaces. In William's case, it was because he allowed his wife to follow her own desires, rather than calling her to heel. He still loved her. He was 'so glad to have Janey back again; her company is always pleasant and good to me', but it was often hard to bear when she was away. This autumn was 'a specially dismal time' for William.

He directed his anger at Gabriel, not at Jane. It was a 'quite selfish business . . . that Rossetti has set himself down at Kelmscott as if he never meant to go away'. William had lost his 'harbour of refuge'. He loved to fish there, even in the floods and coldest weather. But with Gabriel unshakeably in residence, he could not go across, even for a few days: 'It really is a farce our meeting when we can help it.'

William rarely spoke about Jane's infidelity with his old friend. This is one of the few times he acknowledged the rift with Gabriel. Even so, he hesitates and turns aside, blaming his anger on Gabriel's attitude to the house itself. Gabriel did not appreciate the beauty of Kelmscott; he had 'all sorts of ways so unsympathetic with the sweet simple old place, that I feel his presence there as a kind of slur on it'. This is why William felt so 'very angry and disappointed'.[49] He was deeply hurt by the way Gabriel was treating the people and places that he loved. Of course, William longed for the peace of the old manor house. But he could not fully admit, even to a dear friend, how this feeling of sacrilege, of violation, was to do with Gabriel's treatment of Jane. Gabriel did not value her. So many things now seemed spoilt.

But William refused to be overwhelmed by his misery. His response to the crisis was to keep working, developing new skills, hoping. As he wrote to Aglaia: 'O how I long to keep the world from narrowing on me, and to look at things bigly and kindly!'[50]

*

As Kelmscott was out of bounds, Ned Burne-Jones suggested a different sort of holiday. William had never seen Italy, so Ned persuaded him that a springtime journey through the Alps and on to Florence would restore his spirits. It had long been a place of respite for Ned, and he wanted to share it with his friend. As William put it, he thinks 'that Florence ought to make a sick man well, or a stupid one bright'.

Instead, William was disappointed, not with Italy, 'but a good deal with myself'. He struggled, he said, to 'bring my mind up to the proper pitch and tune for taking in these marvels'.[51]

They arrived in early April 1873, during Holy Week, so 'the altar pieces are all covered' in the churches, and they heard the Miserere sung in Santa Croce. For William, the joy of the visit was in the unexpected beauties of handmade things, the places he 'stumbled on', the changeful skies, the mountains. He enjoyed the drive up to Fiesole on a 'queer wild showery afternoon'.[52] And he was particularly struck by the views as they came down out of the Alps, 'on the most beautiful of all evenings, and going (still between snow-capped mountains) through a country like a garden: green grass and feathery poplars, and abundance of pink blossomed leafless peach & almond trees'.

This was the Italy he remembered long after he returned home. He shared this vision with Jane, along with more down-to-earth descriptions of the market, with 'the lemons and oranges for sale with the leaves still on them: miraculous frying going on, and all sorts of queer vegetables and cheeses to be sold'.[53]

Ned grumbled that William wanted to 'pay more attention to an olive-tree or a pot than . . . to a picture'. And certainly, William's letters seem to bear this out. He wrote at length about the weather, the views, and little lead-glazed hand warmers, and 'flasks wickered, of all sorts of pretty shapes'. He placed an order for several dozen for the Firm to sell.[54] But there is not one sentence about frescoes, mosaics or easel paintings. As William explained, 'I understand more of pots than of pictures; and he is a painter professed, so it isn't quite fair'.[55] The magnificence of Renaissance Italy did not appeal to him. He wanted lovely things to hold in his hand. He looked for well-made, small-scale, pleasing objects to place on his dining table, to live with.

William returned to London after a fortnight, and left Ned to spend more time with Mantegna and Botticelli. William knew that his friend was entranced and refreshed by Italy. But he was drawn to the North. He wanted to see Iceland again. With Jane still entangled in Rossetti's emotional wreckage, William was keen to clear his own head. As soon as he was home, he started to make enquiries about ships and pack saddles and ponies.

This time his voyage to Iceland was wistful. There is an elegiac tone when he writes about it. On his original journey in 1871, William had looked for a breathing space, and perhaps some resolution to the difficulties at home. Sadly, Jane's involvement with Gabriel now seemed even harder to unravel: this was no light-hearted love affair. And William could not see how it would end. Still, as he sailed for Reykjavik, again with Charley Faulkner, he wrote honestly to Webb how strange it felt to be back in the same little cabin, on the same vessel – the *Diana*. 'I feel grave enough,' he admitted, '& not much as if this were a pleasant trip, but I hope to get something out of it.'[56] His letter to Jane, when he arrived in Iceland, was even more troubled. 'It is all like a kind of a dream to me,' he told her, 'and my real life seems set aside till it is over. Kiss my dear little ones for me.'[57]

He was writing as he waited for the overland journey to begin. There is a sense that he is following a path into the gales and snow, as if he is accepting his fate, but not willingly. In these letters, more than any others, William appears like a displaced person in one of his own tales. He becomes a tiny wandering figure in a vast, inhospitable landscape. He is searching for the answers to some riddle, he is waiting to be revived, to be restored to his beloved. In the meantime, he writes 'how wild and strange everything here is'. And then it seems as if he turns directly towards Jane: 'I am so anxious for you too, it was a grievous parting for us the other day.'[58] This is one of the rare occasions when we see the jarring unhappiness of their marriage laid bare. Even with Jane, he usually maintains his composure. But now, he shows his vulnerability. In this most private of letters, he also reveals his fears for Jane, his continued loyalty to her, and his unease about what he will face when he comes home: 'How can I help it, not knowing whether I am on my head or my heels.'[59]

And so Morris set out into the wastes. On the first evening, after a day's riding, he saw 'the great ridges and peaks of the Armansfell range with broken lights striking among the wildest and most awful gorges'. There is a moment of recognition: 'at last I remembered all I had come to see and the land conquered all my misgivings once for all, I hope.'[60] All, all, all is here as it should be.

He finds his way through the desolate pass beneath the volcano Hekla, along tracks made of 'lava and sand and ice-brought stones', until he comes to 'a space under high slopes . . . grown over with ground-willow and heath plants'. Despite his worries, and the emptiness of the wilderness, he is content, revived. Days that 'had been doubtful with showers and sunshine' were transformed, as 'the clouds break up everywhere in the most beautiful way and the sun shines hot and bright'.[61] As they travel on, Morris notices the details of tiny flowers, 'Loki's purse (money-rattle), buttercups, milkwort, white clover, cranesbill, one or two alpine flowers I can't name, and a most lovely little dark blue gentian'.[62] He watches the sheep running together, their fleeces coal black, rich brown or spotted. They are strange 'delicate little beasts'.[63] He can rejoice in the narrow strips of grass, vivid green against the black. He listens to the ravens 'making a sad noise' near the place 'where Gunnar dreamed'.[64] He finds a little tub of a boat and sculls across the lake at Grimsstaðir for a fishing expedition. There is a small island, 'all grown over with birch and willow', and a 'little bay quite full of young ducks just able to fly'.[65] They push north to Akureyri and Möðruvellir. The riding becomes rougher. His journal notes are more fragmented. His journal stops unexpectedly beside a 'small stream . . . among a grey wilderness of stones'.[66]

The tent canvas flaps in the wind, the drizzling rain comes down, there are ash-storms. So 'we shut the tent up and made ourselves snug and refused to be depressed, and so to bed and sound sleep'.[67] This is what he came for. Morris rediscovered his resilience. He slept well, overlooked by mountains that stood like dragons, splintered, cloven, crested, striped with snow.

*

William was away in Iceland for nearly two months. He returned in early September 1873, refreshed and glad to see 'all the dear faces of wife and children'. In a candid letter to Aglaia Coronio, he explains the changes that Iceland had wrought in him. He had been 'more unhappy . . . than I like to confess' before he travelled. The strain of Rossetti's illness and Jane's absences had worn him down. But 'the glorious simplicity of the terrible & tragic, but beautiful land . . . killed all querulous feeling in me.' He writes like a man who has achieved his quest. He is glad to be home, among 'friends dearer than ever to me'.[68]

Something has shifted for William. It is as if he has raised his eyes from the sadness and complications close at hand. He must let it run its course. He turns his attention towards other concerns, to his friends, his work. His letter to Aglaia ends with a remarkable passage, filled with self-awareness and renewal. He knows he must say farewell to his early dreams. He will set his course instead by the North Star, as a fixed point. It is a constant reminder of the simplicity of life in Iceland – flowing water, mossy earth, fishing, riding, poems, rocks, stars.

> Do you know I feel as if a definite space of my life has passed away now I have seen Iceland for the last time: as I looked up at Charles' Wain tonight all my travel there seemed to come back on me, made solemn and elevated, in one moment, till my heart swelled with the wonder of it: surely I have gained a great deal and it was no idle whim that drew me there, but a true instinct for what I needed.[69]

We can hear some of the lingering love for Iceland, a longing for the clarity he found there, in a letter he wrote the following spring. It was March 1874, his fortieth birthday, and a time for reflection. The letter reads like a manifesto for a new way of living. Morris is weighed down by the smell and dirt of London. After the raw beauty of the Northlands, the city is a 'sordid loathsome place'. He knows there can be a better, more sustainable life.

> Look [he writes], suppose people lived in little communities among gardens & green fields, so that you could be in the country in 5 minutes' walk, & had few wants; almost no furniture for instance, & no servants, & studied (the difficult) arts of enjoying life, & finding out what they really wanted.

At the time, he did not quite see how he could work towards this. 'It seems to be nobody's business to try better things,' he worried; 'isn't mine you see in spite of all my grumbling.'[70] But gradually the idea took hold of him, and began to crystallise, to form something tangible. It became his business. From the mid-1870s, his vision expanded, until he could conceive and then work towards an alternative form of society.

*

Morris had seen another way of life at first hand in the homesteads of Iceland. There people valued their domestic arts, stayed close to the land, felt at home with the ancient tales. He also believed it had been possible here in England, but many years ago. He thought himself back into the fourteenth century, as if he were walking alongside Chaucer, and seeing 'the strings of packhorses along the bridle-roads . . . the little towns well bechurched, often walled; the villages just where they are now . . . but better and more populous'.[71] He recognised that this was an idealised version of 'the face of mediaeval

England', but it was something to aim for, all the same. He wanted the people around him to regain access to the 'little land' that he loved, where 'all is measured, mingled, varied, gliding easily one thing into another . . . little hills, little mountains, netted over with the walls of sheepwalks: neither prison nor palace but a decent home'.[72] He hoped to share his desire for decent homes, decent livelihoods.

This germ of an idea, something that seemed just a throwaway line in a letter to a friend, took root in William's imagination. In time it would bear fruit. William was one of the creative spirits behind the 'Back to the Land' movement that blossomed from the 1880s. His ideas were also fundamental to the burgeoning 'Arts and Crafts' movement, as he encouraged more thoughtful design and making, on a domestic scale. His work emphasised the beauty of vernacular art, things that fitted naturally into their settings, with a focus on hand skills. William was not alone in his thinking. He was part of a generation of artists, architects and scholars who suggested radical ways to remake nineteenth-century cities, and who were prepared to criticise contemporary culture.

Many young men and women had grown up reading Ruskin and Carlyle. They were now in positions of influence, in business, in society, as patrons and makers. The shoddy consumerism and deadly industrialisation that Ruskin railed against had not been vanquished. William was a leader in this renewed rage against the machinery of Victorian culture and capitalism. But there were others, like him, who hankered for a better life, beyond the inevitable creeping urbanisation, the destruction of the old ways. As he explained in 1879, the 'tyranny' of the division of labour 'has turned some of us from being, as we should be, contented craftsmen, into being discontented agitators against it, so that our minds are not at rest'.[73]

We see the same desire for 'the simple life' in Edward Carpenter's decision, for example, to move to a smallholding in Yorkshire. Carpenter, like William, had trained for the Church. He was ordained in

1870 and served as a curate for a few years, but gave up his ministry in 1874. Carpenter found that working the land and developing his craft skills went happily hand in hand with his role as a writer and activist. They also helped him to hone his ideas about politics and society – so that he too embraced Socialism in the 1880s. Carpenter was a perceptive reader of Ruskin and Walt Whitman.[74] He took up their radical messages about engaging with nature and the potential of manual labour. And then he wove them into his own unconventional home life: Carpenter lived openly with his working-class lover George Merrill on their smallholding in Derbyshire.

At the end of William's life, Carpenter paid tribute to him – as 'one of the finest figures of this century' who 'in the midst of an era of finesse, sleekness, commercial dodgery' stood out as 'brusque, hearty, bold and manly'. Carpenter recognised how William fought against insincerity, and 'the ugliness and meanness of modern life'. He admired his character. William was 'energetic, stormy, a veritable Viking and seacaptain' with an 'immense power of work'. And his energy was 'most generous and humanly beautiful'.[75] William's ability to reimagine the world on a human scale encouraged fellow travellers like Carpenter in their own endeavours. Inspired by William, and mentored by Carpenter, projects like the Guild of Handicraft continued to marry art and social reform, well into the twentieth century. They looked to the Cotswolds, to the small towns beyond Kelmscott, as a refuge from life and work in London.

Other entrepreneurs were trying to transform the experience of living in the metropolis. Rather than decamping to the countryside, they integrated green spaces with new housing. Barely a year after William wrote his letter about living in 'little communities among gardens and green fields', Jonathan Carr began developing his own garden suburb at Bedford Park. The land Carr bought in 1875 was just north of Turnham Green station, less than a mile from William's home on the High Road. With architects E. W. Godwin and Richard

Norman Shaw, Carr established a cluster of red-brick houses, with steeply pitched roofs. They planned the layout of the streets and plots carefully, in order to retain the mature trees that were already on the site, as Philip Webb had done at Red House.

These new homes can be seen as little offshoots from Webb's experiments at Red House. The Bedford Park development was part of a wider reaction against High Victorian style and sensibilities. This reaction had been nurtured in the studios of Gothic Revival architects like G. E. Street and was now coming to fruition in the work of a new generation. Bedford Park became another gathering place for artists and authors who worked against the grain of the establishment. And inevitably they looked to William – as a writer and as a designer. Within a few years, the residents of Bedford Park became some of his most enthusiastic clients. As one visitor remarked, 'the majority of the residents have used the wallpapers and designs of Morris.'[76]

In the 1860s and early 1870s, most of the Firm's patrons were friends or came from personal connections. But by the time Bedford Park was built, William's designs were reaching a much wider audience – partly through church commissions and partly through their sales brochures. From 1877, customers could also see the wide range of products in the Firm's showroom at 264 Oxford Street. The wallpapers became especially popular. By 1881, William was so closely associated with wallpaper design that he could be described, only half-ironically, by Henry James as 'the poet and paper-maker'.[77]

Hanging Morris & Co. wallpaper in their homes was a quick and inexpensive way for families to bring their decoration up to date. It was much cheaper than other decorative schemes, like stained glass or tiling, with a few machine-printed designs priced at 2s 6d a roll. Most of the stock was hand-printed in distemper, creating a matt, chalky finish; they cost between 3s and 16s depending on the complexity of the print. Some more luxurious patterns, on gold ground, cost 40s a roll, but these were created for aristocratic clients, like the Howards at 1 Palace Green. The distinctive floral patterns were designed by William and his colleagues, and printed by Jeffrey & Co., established manufacturers who were willing to work to the Firm's exacting standards. William's hand-painted designs were often sent to the printers with precise comments about colour. In the notes that have survived for the *Lily* wallpaper, first produced in 1874, we see how carefully William paid attention to the individual flowers that he drew: 'wood sorrel, the outline a little stronger than in the drawing but not too brown . . . chrysanthemum, the tint of the right-hand flower, the seeds are the same colour as the stamens of the lily . . . wood sorrel leaves are three shades of green, the stalks and outlines being one'.[78] William clearly approved of the finished version of this paper, as he used it in his own bedroom at Kelmscott Manor.

From his earliest designs, like *Daisy* (1864) and *Fruit* (1866), William worked with two layers of pattern – a monochrome background, and a more colourful, bolder foreground. For *Daisy*, the background was a simple suggestion of tiny blades of grass behind the columbines and meadow flowers. By the early 1870s, William was producing more confident, fluid patterns, weaving two layers of tendrils and flowers across the surface. In some cases, like *Scroll and Branch* (c.1870) the simpler background pattern was successful enough to be available as a stand-alone design. But in most, the two patterns were overlaid with great precision and sympathy. In *Jasmine* (1872), for example, 'The background is an all-over pattern of hawthorn leaves, blossoms and branches on a disguised vertical meander. A scrolling tracery of jasmine, delicately but clearly defined, provides the foreground.'[79] Originally this design was going to be printed from twenty separate wooden blocks, but this was unworkable. Eventually it was created using eleven blocks, one for each colour or section of the pattern.

Some of his customers began to adopt the 'artistic' vogue for using several different patterns on one wall. William did not approve of this fashion for dividing the space into three horizontal bands – dado, filling, frieze – with another patterned paper on the ceiling. In his own houses, he used a single design from skirting to ceiling. Occasionally his rooms had a wood-panelled dado in the lower section, and a paper above. But he urged his customers 'never [to] stoop to the ignominy of a paper dado', and insisted that 'our wallpapers . . . are simple fillings; they imitate no architectural features'. He concluded that 'the practice of putting pattern over pattern in paperhanging . . . seems to me a very unsatisfactory one'.[80] In general, William often preferred simple paintwork or textile hangings as his ideal wall-coverings, rather than 'cheap recurring patterns in a material which has no play of light on it'.[81] However, he had a business to run, a family to support, and his wallpapers sold well. They were relatively affordable. Jeffrey & Co. managed the production, and by the end of the 1880s, William and his colleagues had thirty-two patterns in production, in multiple colourways. They became a staple product that could be updated from time to time, adding new shades to the standard repertoire.

We read, for example, in a note from Gabriel Rossetti that he was 'making a pattern for a new colouring of the marigold paper'.[82] This came in a letter written in October 1874, which mostly dealt with the troubled internal affairs of the Firm. The original partnership was being dissolved, leaving William as sole proprietor of the business. In the eager collaborative atmosphere of the early days, it had all seemed relatively straightforward. William was independently wealthy, so he and his friends felt he could bear any financial strain. All the partners had made the same initial investment, but some had done a great deal of work to make it a successful business, while others had faded out of the day-to-day affairs of the company. Ford Madox Brown and Gabriel Rossetti were both paid occasionally for piecework. They had been regular designers for stained glass when the enterprise began, and Gabriel was evidently still helping out from time to time. Ned Burne-Jones was far more prolific, producing dozens of drawings for church windows every year. But Charley Faulkner and Peter Paul Marshall, who had been involved at the outset, had made no substantial contribution for years.

The break-up of the business revealed the fractured relationships within William's circle. It was a painful process, taking several years to play out. In the early spring of 1873, William was clearly worried about money.

> I am working very hard at one thing or another [he explained to Aglaia], I should very much like to make the business quite a success . . . a smash in that side would be a terrible nuisance; I have so many serious troubles, pleasures, hopes & fears that I have not time on my hands to be ruined and get really poor: above all things it would destroy my freedom of work which is a dear delight to me.[83]

Morris, Marshall, Faulkner & Co. had been the perfect space for William to work. He could experiment with new materials, developing his skills as a designer and craftsman. He rarely felt hemmed in. As Edward Carpenter said, it was the ideal setting for a man whose 'chief recreation was only another kind of work'.[84] But as the Firm flourished under his direction, his annual salary of £200 seemed inadequate, given the vast amount of time and energy he was putting into the business. He did also get an annual bonus of 10 per cent of the annual profits. But this only added £30 or £40 to his income. It would not have mattered had his investments in the mining shares prospered. But his income from Devon Great Consuls was shrinking. He could no longer rely on his inherited wealth. William needed to earn his living. He was rather embarrassed when his Icelandic friend Eiríkr Magnússon asked for a loan: 'I will do my best to get the money £70 together in about a week's time . . . though I seem comfortably off I am always rather lacking of *cash*: my only important resource being what I can get from the Firm here.' He reassured Magnússon that it 'is a great pleasure to me to do anything in my power to pleasure you'.[85] But he did not want to be dipping into the business bank account for his friends.

It was this muddling of the private and professional parts of William's life that made the Firm so problematic. When the company had just started out, his friendship with the other designers, their personal contacts, their shared artistic ambitions, had been the Firm's greatest asset. Over time, however, their careers had developed in different directions. William hoped that the original partners would recognise that he was now *de facto* creative director, overseeing the making and selling of their products. When he raised this, however, it became clear that several of them felt short-changed by William's suggestion. They thought he was acting in a heavy-handed manner, disregarding their input over the past decade. By August 1874, it was clear that it would not end well. William wrote to the lawyer Theodore Watts-Dunton, saying that 'I find that two at least of our members wish to be out of the firm'.[86] At that stage, William thought that only Ford Madox Brown and Peter Paul Marshall wanted to be paid their portion of the value of the Firm. The men who had remained close to him, Ned Burne-Jones, Charley Faulkner and Philip Webb, refused their £1,000 share, and left the money in the business.

With Gabriel, the rifts in their relationship became even more strained. Rossetti had been making cutting cartoons of William for many years. But the caricature he drew during the dismantling of the Firm was especially upsetting. Gabriel called it *Rupes Topseia* or 'The Fall of Topsy'. He imagined William – very stout and hairy – being thrown down a cliff towards Hell. At the top of the slope sit the other six partners, sadly carrying a banner proclaiming, 'We are starving'. There are two bearded sages looking down on the scene from the centre of a blazing sun. Virginia Surtees suggested these were meant to represent Marx and Engels – and Karl Marx certainly did wear a monocle, but then so did Tennyson. Perhaps more bothersome for William was the presence of Jane, as a distant, unearthly figure, watching her husband's downfall, her face framed by the crescent moon. Gabriel believed that she would relish this image of William's humiliation. He sent it to Jane and she kept it until her death. May Morris, who inherited this and many other cartoons belittling her father, gave the drawing to the British Museum. It suggests that Jane took Gabriel's side, rather than William's, in the acrimonious split. At the very least, it seems that she was willing to indulge Gabriel's frustrations and laugh at her husband's unhappiness. It does not show her in a sympathetic light.

Unfortunately, we cannot hear Jane's side of the story, as none of her letters mentions the upheavals in the business. She was apparently still on good terms with Ford Madox Brown in September 1874, as she wrote to him about May – there had been talk of her sitting for one of Brown's pictures, but May's hair had recently been cut so it 'has not the same mane-like appearance on the shoulders'.[87] There is very little else to help us form an idea of Jane's response to the rancour that was growing among the group of old friends. Her involvement in the unravelling of their professional relationships was made more awkward by Gabriel's actions. He decided he wanted to take his share of the funds out of the business – £1,000, like Brown and Marshall. But to complicate matters, he intended to keep it in trust for Jane. In effect, he was setting her up with an independent income, with money extracted from the assets of William's company. At a time when William, by his own admission, was often short of cash, Jane now had access to her own funds, provided by her lover. It was a most unusual arrangement.

Gabriel's motives in settling this money on Jane are not clear, apart from his desire to antagonise William. It is particularly surprising, as Gabriel was often in need of money himself and harassed by tradesmen's bills and demands for rent. Maybe he wanted Jane to have something put aside in case she chose to separate from her husband. He was offering her the freedom to travel, or even to establish her own household. Or maybe Gabriel hoped this would bind Jane more closely to him, through financial as well as emotional ties. It is even possible that Gabriel saw this money as a way to reimburse Jane for her contribution to his art – she was the model for his paintings, the maker of his costumes, the inspiration for his poems, his carer when he was distressed. Perhaps he wanted to show his gratitude for Jane's loyalty, her kindness. We cannot say for sure. But it made the triangular relationship between Jane, William and Gabriel even more complicated.

On the day that Gabriel's share of the funds was paid out by the Firm, Jane went to stay with him in Chelsea. (He had finally moved out of Kelmscott Manor in July 1874, although many of his things were still there four years later.) Gabriel told Watts-Dunton that 'The Divine One and her offspring are likely to be staying here from tomorrow (Friday) till Sunday evening.'[88] Evidently, he thought that friends and colleagues would see nothing amiss in Mrs Morris spending two or three nights at his house, chaperoned only by her daughters. Watts-Dunton, of course, knew about Gabriel's decision to make Jane the beneficiary of his portion of the assets. And perhaps he was not surprised by Gabriel's pet-name for her. Gabriel's images of Jane were becoming less lifelike, more overblown. He exaggerated the curve of her lips, the column of her neck, the flexing of her fingers. He made a chalk drawing of Jane, which he showed to Watts-Dunton. They agreed that the picture 'expressed exactly the idea of one of the Oriental Venuses'.[89] In Gabriel's art, Jane's image was moving ever further from the face and body of the living woman. Her role as homemaker, seamstress, was constantly effaced. Once upon a time, she had stood in for 'Beatrice', or held a snowdrop to personify 'Spring', or a pomegranate as 'Proserpine'. Now he wanted to show her to the world as a goddess. But in her everyday life, she was still needed as a mother. Jenny and May were often with her as she sat for Gabriel, a reminder of her other life beyond the studio.

Occasionally she was alone with him. The girls were both in school when Jane spent several weeks with Gabriel in Bognor in November 1875. Jenny and May were now attending Notting Hill High School, along with Margaret Burne-Jones. It was a bold, uncompromising education. They were taught the same curriculum as boys at public school – with Jenny doing particularly well at Latin and English. The school had opened in Norland Square in 1873, with Harriet Morant Jones as headmistress. Jenny, May and Margaret were among the eighty or so girls who worked diligently as she patrolled the large classroom, dressed in purple velvet, her silk underskirts rustling. Miss Jones did not approve of teaching girls non-academic subjects like needlework. Instead, she encouraged them to aim for the new women's colleges at Oxford or Cambridge: 'She believed passionately in the education of women and in women working.'[90] William agreed with her faith in the potential of women, and Jane was glad that her bright daughters could benefit from the learning that she had missed. They both knew that the girls could catch up on their more hands-on education at home, surrounded by quills and vellum, embroidery silks, coloured swatches and dye samples.

*

In the winter of 1875–6, the Morrises were often apart. William spent a few days in November at Kelmscott Manor, living off bacon, pigeons and a tin of kangaroo meat (perhaps left over from Gabriel's time). He was glad to reclaim the wet, breezy pleasures of Thames-side life. It was 'almost as good as Iceland on a small scale'.[91] William was there again in late January, paddling about on the floods, noting the first flowers – violets, aconites and snowdrops. He wrote to Jane on 26 January that 'Mr. Butcher sold me a piece of steak and 2 kidnies.' He hoped it 'wont be tough'.[92] (There was some truth in the jokes his friends made about his appetite.)

William was also throwing himself into his next venture – dyeing and printing textiles – so he was spending a great deal of energy in these experiments. He was working with Thomas Wardle of Leek, trying to fathom the intricacies of the art. The two great difficulties were keeping the colours consistent – customers did not want curtains that were slightly different shades – and in fixing the dyes so they did not fade.

William told Wardle that he wanted to achieve, as a bare minimum of workable dyes:

> 1 blotch blue, 1 outline blue . . . 1 outline green which would be of an olive colour, 1 blotch yellow-green . . . 1 blotch blue-green to be diluted . . . 1 yellow greenish in character . . . 1 yellow, reddish in character, 1 brown . . . one might add a black . . . and a shade or two of rust yellows or buffs.[93]

This was in addition to the madder cloths and the indigo, which were essential.

William steeped himself in the history and technicalities of textile production. He sent Wardle a sixteenth-century copy of Gerard's *Herball or Generall Historie of Plantes*. It had been a favourite book since his boyhood, and it contained 'useful information about certain disused vegetable dyes'.[94] And from the early months of 1876, he was paying extended visits to the Staffordshire works, to learn the trade. He was keen to get his hands dirty. His eagerness to plunge into the dye vat was almost performative – as if he wanted to prove his worth to the working men who watched him.

This is where we find some of the most characteristic images of William, in his smock and clogs, blue to the elbow. He told Georgie Burne-Jones he was 'taking in dyeing at every pore (otherwise than by the skin of my hands, which is certain)'. As he told her, 'You know I like that.'[95] This was a time of great inventiveness. In April 1876, he registered three new textile designs – *Tulip*, *Marigold* and *Larkspur*. A week later, Wardle was making trial prints for *Columbine*, a block-printed cotton in muted green and salmon pink. All four patterns demonstrated the skills that William had learnt in designing wallpaper, based on the interplay between flowers and foliage: in fact, *Marigold* was available as both a printed silk and a wallpaper. William was engrossed by the complexities of creating these fabrics. When we look at his sixty surviving letters from 1876, twenty-six of them were addressed to Wardle, filled with long, meticulous notes about the samples he had been sent. And in most of the other letters, his friends and family had to put up with William's detailed descriptions of his dyeing experiments. Unpicking these processes, discovering the secrets of deep indigo, thinking about mordants, fents, dyeing vats, filled up his waking hours.

Meanwhile Jane was also often away from home. In the early part of 1876, she stayed several times with Gabriel at Aldwick Lodge, on the coast near Bognor. He had rarely been alone since he moved there the previous autumn. His family visited, and so did another regular model, Alexa Wilding. So Jane's presence was not seen as indiscreet. As he was working on a version of the 'Venus' picture, now titled *Astarte Syriaca*, May sometimes came with her. Jane's daughter was sitting for the attendant figures behind Jane-as-Goddess.

Jane's relationship with Gabriel disintegrated during these weeks in Bognor. We can hear the tension, the uneasy memories when, years later, she remembered sitting for this painting. She called it 'my old abomination, the study for Venus Astarte'.[96] Jane could not see herself in this image. In her eyes, it seemed to be a symptom of Gabriel's unsettled imagination. William Michael Rossetti described his state of mind at this time. He was often paranoid, suffering from 'perverted fantasy . . . an outcome of chloral-dosing'.[97]

It seems that Jane could no longer live with Gabriel's addiction. Perhaps he had tried to hide it from her when they were at Kelmscott. But in Bognor, he could not sleep without taking the drug, and he needed increasingly large doses. Chloral hydrate was first identified as a remedy for insomnia in 1869. Gabriel began taking it in 1870, washed down with whisky. He was soon hooked. His carers tried to limit the amount he consumed, but he became wary of letting them prepare his dose. By 1876, he was seeking medical help from Sir William Jenner for his combined alcohol and chloral addiction. Jenner advised him to take no more than 20 grains a night. By the end of the decade, he was taking almost lethal doses – 92 grains at a time. The chemist refused to make up his orders, saying they could not supply more than one bottle per day.[98] Gabriel was depressed and sluggish; rarely was he out of bed before one o'clock in the afternoon.

Jane had supported him through the ups and downs of his health crises. She had hoped that his symptoms would ease, that he would be restored. Sadly, in Bognor, she had to face the reality of his grave illness. He was deeply depressed, and had begun to make plans for his funeral – he was adamant that he wanted to be cremated, rather than buried at Highgate with Lizzie. This was an end-point for him and for Jane. She later explained that 'when I found that he was ruining himself with Chloral and that I could do nothing to prevent it, I left off going to him'. She added, almost as an afterthought '– and on account of the children'. Evidently, she could no longer explain away Gabriel's erratic behaviour to May. Her daughter was no longer a little girl; she turned fourteen in March 1876. It is possible that Jane gave Gabriel an ultimatum, saying that she would withdraw her intimate affection until he could control his addiction. That might be the reason he went to Jenner for help over the summer. But it was impossible. Jane remained a devoted, consoling friend for the rest of his life, but she no longer visited him as before. There were no more long weekends in Chelsea, or late evening walks in the lanes around Kelmscott. She missed Gabriel as he had been: 'he was unlike all other men'.[99] She could no longer bear the unhappiness of seeing him diminished.

Gabriel did not want to lose sight of her. He continued writing plaintive, devoted letters, reassuring Jane of his 'deep regard'. He said it was 'a feeling far deeper (though I know you never believed me) than I have entertained towards any other living creature at any time in my life'. He went on, seeming to reveal his love when it was too late: 'Would that circumstances had given me the power to prove this: for proved it *wd.* have been. And now you do not believe it.'[100] Did he really love Jane more than Elizabeth Siddall? Would he really have preferred to woo her, all those years ago in Oxford? Was it just the recognition of time passing, an attempt to rewrite his own history? It did not change Jane's resolution. She continued to write to him, sending kind letters about their shared interests, books she had read, the weather. His replies were tender. He thanked her for her 'affectionate zeal and care'.[101] He told her how 'it always rejoices me to see your loved writing, and know that your living loving hand has rested again on lines addressed to me'.[102] Gabriel longed for Jane's presence. He was left only with her occasional visits, and the many drawings and half-finished paintings of her face, her body, her 'living loving hand'.

It is also possible that Gabriel was more than usually lonely, because his long-standing companion Fanny Cornforth had also left him. Fanny had been Gabriel's housekeeper and lover, on and off, since Lizzie Siddall had died. Like Jane, she was a patient model, and Gabriel admired her matter-of-factness, her easy company. Hers was the 'kissed mouth' that was constantly renewed, the *Bocca Baciata*, painted by Gabriel in 1859. She had sat for *Fair Rosamund* and *Lady Lilith*, but now Fanny put the unreality of the studio behind her. Like Jane, she saw that Gabriel was too tormented by his own demons – she could no longer help him to recover himself.

*

Jane stepped back from her intimacy with Gabriel. And almost immediately she was facing another catastrophe, closer to home. Her eldest daughter Jenny became seriously ill with epilepsy in the summer of 1876. Her sudden fits were unpredictable and frightening. They changed her life for ever. Her condition also turned her parents' lives upside-down. They could not leave her alone, for fear that she would fall and hit her head – they had seen it happen, and every time it potentially caused further brain damage. It became hard for them both to go out for dinner, or off to see friends. Either William or Jane had to be home with Jenny. Her hopes of a place at Cambridge were swept away. She could never marry, in case her seizures were hereditary. She would need daily care for the rest of her life. Many epileptics were put away in asylums for the insane, but Jenny's parents preferred to look after her themselves and did their best to manage her *grand mal* convulsions.

There was no warning that Jenny would become a permanent invalid. Both the girls were occasionally delicate, missing school, looking pale. But her fits seemed to come out of a clear blue sky. She had her first seizure after a boating accident, but whether she was taken ill and fell in, or the accident triggered her illness, is unclear. Georgie Burne-Jones recalled the shock of receiving 'a note from poor Janey . . . because Jenny had suddenly fainted and frightened her very much. How little any of us expected the long drawn out pain and disappointment then begun.'[103] There was no cure. She was given potassium bromide, as a depressant. The drugs, and later the sporadic head injuries, changed her personality and appearance. William and Jane's sharp, scholarly daughter became increasingly drowsy, clumsy and forgetful. She put on weight, and her expression in photographs seems to suggest headaches or discomfort. It was a slow, dreadful transformation, year after year.

William and Jane both worked hard to support their girl, and to find the best care for her. She was never excluded from the family circle. William was worried that he was in some way responsible for Jenny's condition. It seems that his mother had suffered from mild seizures. And he was known for his own sudden unconscious actions – buffeting his own head, raging, apparently oblivious to those around him. His friends had noticed, even when he was quite young, that he could lose control. As an undergraduate, for example, Richard Watson Dixon witnessed one of his 'storms': 'I was made aware of a fearful cry in my ears, and saw Morris "translated". It lasted all the way home . . . I wanted to get him some wine: but he said he was all right.'[104] Was it possible that Jenny had inherited her condition from him?

William was deeply troubled by her illness, and tried to make amends by writing long, chatty letters whenever they were apart. He always treated her with peculiar gentleness and attention. She would not be left out. But as Mackail said, 'From this distress his mind was never henceforth free.'[105] Mackail was evidently embarrassed by the way that Jenny's well-being dominated William and Jane's correspondence. In his biography of William, Mackail refused to mention that she was suffering from epilepsy. He merely referred to her health breaking down, and suggested that the trouble 'can only be briefly touched upon'.[106] William, on the other hand, addressed the difficulty head-on. It is noticeable that in many of his stories, William included characters who were prophets, swooners and seers. They were able to experience wonders, and had a special place in his world order.

For Jane, her daughter's illness was a daily sadness, and with every seizure it felt 'as if a dagger were thrust into me'. She said 'it has been a dreadful grief for us all . . . I never get used to it, I mean in the sense of not minding.'[107] And a few weeks later, she admitted, 'I have been very desponding about Jenny.'[108] Jane has been criticised for complaining that the situation was 'worse for me than for anyone, as I have been so constantly with her'.[109] But there was a lot of truth in her grumbling. The worry about Jenny made Jane ill. Jenny was often Jane's responsibility. William loved his girl dearly, but he was regularly travelling to see suppliers, or spending weekends at Kelmscott Manor, or simply off to Queen Square for a day's work. He could concentrate on his latest designs and immerse himself in his writing.

Meanwhile, Jane was constantly looking for a path out of the terrible everyday sadness. 'We hope to get her cured by some new treatment we are about to try,' she wrote, 'but nothing is settled for her yet.'[110] This continued until the end of Jane's life. It was hard for their friends and colleagues to fully grasp the effect of Jenny's ill-health on those who loved her. It was not until 1907 that Georgie Burne-Jones finally recognised Jane's resilience in the face of relentless fears for her daughter: 'A week in Jenny's company', she wrote, 'has made me understand Mrs. Morris's life as I never did before.'[111] Maybe Georgie now appreciated why Jane could appear reticent, or even frosty. She was carrying the burden of Jenny's care, and had been quietly getting on with it for thirty years.

Jane was frequently on the move, for Jenny's sake, hoping that a change of air, a warmer climate, a different doctor, might stabilise her condition. She spent time, the first summer after the diagnosis, at the seaside in Kent with Georgie and Margaret Burne-Jones. And then as autumn approached, she took Jenny to Kelmscott Manor, where they were joined by Ned, Philip and Margaret. This was the first time they visited Crom's Tower at Broadway – they all signed the visitor's book on 4 September 1876.

Some of the party returned to the Tower the following year. Jane and May went ahead to make the place comfortable. They were travelling without Jenny, just the two of them, at least for a few days. Jane wanted to let May have some fun in this 'most inconvenient and most delightful place'. Her plan was a success because May remembered the 'great cheerfulness' of that short holiday. Even as a teenager, May also recognised how hard her mother worked to make other people feel at home. Jane was 'heroic on these occasions'. Mother and daughter were able to walk out together in the early morning sunshine, and 'the clean aromatic wind blew the aches out of our tired bodies'. May recalled simply, 'how good it all was.'[112]

Chapter 10

Italy, 1877–1878

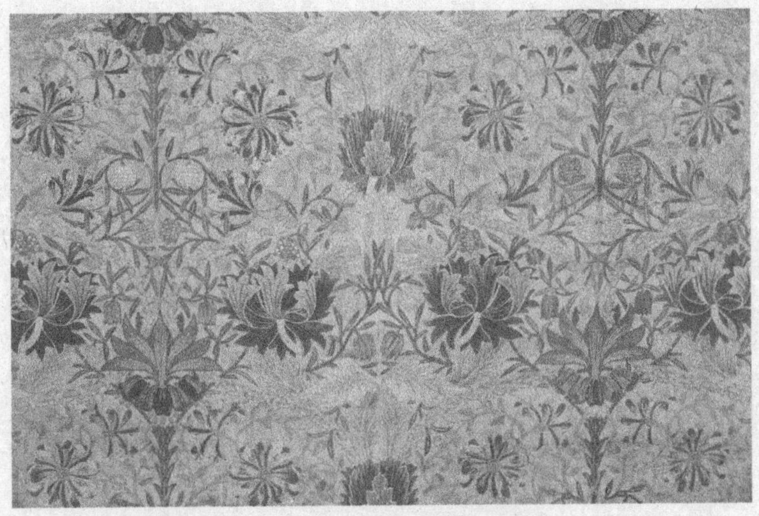

Embroidered by Jane and Jenny Morris, designed by William Morris,
Honeysuckle hanging, William Morris Gallery, Walthamstow, after 1877

Jane and Rosalind Howard were drinking tea on the terrace in the gentle sunshine. It was the early spring of 1878. They could hear Jenny and May playing with Rosalind's little ones in the greenery below. At the far end of the terrace, George Howard was working at his easel. He was studying the emerald and gold of an orange tree. Faded leaves drifted down from the vine above his head, and rustled at his feet. He had an idea that he would invite some local girls to sit for him here, with baskets of fruit. He imagined the washed-out colours of their skirts against the soft salmon pink of the garden wall. With the blue sky above, and the wooded hills rising behind the garden, it would make a pleasing picture.

Jane was grateful that spring was returning. The Italian winter had been bitterly cold, much harsher than she had expected. She found the mountain wind was 'piercing . . . it bites, it stabs, it strikes one dumb, it takes away one's senses'.[1] In November 1877, Jane had brought the girls to Oneglia, a small fishing town on the Mediterranean coast between Mentone and Genoa. It was another part of her sustained effort to restore Jenny to full health, another 'change of air'. The girls had travelled before. As Jane said, before they set off, 'Jenny and May are famous sailors'.[2] Morris had taken them all to Belgium in the summer of 1874, 'the whole bunch – Phil-and-Margaret and Jenny-and-May'. It had been an attempt at family harmony. On the train to Dover, as the children had squealed and squirmed, he had said 'with his heart and voice, "It's worth anything to take the kids a treat, Janey, and see the little rascals enjoying it."'[3]

This time, Jane left William at home, and struck out without him. She had never seen Italy, although she told a friend, 'I knew Italian tolerably well once.'[4] Perhaps it was one of the languages she had learnt in preparation for her marriage. Every so often, we get a glimpse into the hidden corners of Jane's life. But it is hard to reconstruct the details. We do not know now how she learnt to speak Italian, or French or German, although she certainly could read these languages. It is possible that Maria Rossetti, Gabriel's sister, taught her to understand Dante. But who was there to help Jane study Goethe? Who introduced her to medieval French verses? Jane clearly had an ear for language: she had proved that by softening her working-class accent, and modelling her speech on the voices of the poets and artists who had read to her as a teenager. She was eager to learn, to try out new versions of herself. Learning languages was a personal challenge. So was reading music and playing the piano. This journey to Italy was just one of her many experiments in living differently, in challenging preconceptions about what a girl like her could be.

It was a bold venture for Jane – to be travelling with her teenage girls, especially when Jenny's illness was so unpredictable and distressing. But she was encouraged by Rosalind Howard. It was Rosalind who had suggested that Jane should take the girls away for the winter. The Howards were renting a villa on the Italian Riviera, and Rosalind insisted that they could easily find a house nearby for Jane. She would have her own space, but there were friends close at hand. Jane was grateful to have her as an ally; Rosalind could be overbearing at times, badgering people, speaking her mind. She and William had a particularly lively relationship, after some initial misunderstandings. As she said, 'If he puts up with me, we shall jog along all right.'[5] Rosalind could see that Jane was struggling with her own ill-health, which was made worse by her worries about Jenny. In her practical way, she scooped Jane and the girls up, and smoothed their path to Italy.

We can hear Jane's excitement and thankfulness in her letter to Rosalind:

> of course my heart at once said yes, but . . . I felt it would be better to wait a day before writing. It is so good, so overwhelmingly kind and thoughtful of you that I don't know how to thank you enough. I must leave it to you to imagine what it will be to me to see Italy for the first time among kind friends, with the certainty of getting better health for myself and children.[6]

In her next letter, Jane told Rosalind, 'We shall place ourselves entirely under your care.' And she said that she had already worked out how to ease her own chronic back pain on the long railway journey from Paris. She explained matter-of-factly, 'I can do that quite easily lyeing down [sic].'[7] Jane was already thinking ahead. She would not be hampered by her bodily weakness, nor by her rusty Italian. She would find a language teacher for herself and the girls, and she discussed the 'servant question' with Rosalind. At times it must have made her pause: Jane, born into the servant class, was now corresponding with the mistress of Naworth Castle as a friend. Maybe they did not treat each other exactly as equals, but then Rosalind had an air of superiority with almost everyone, including her husband, George. She ordered him about, too.

Jane and William had been brought into the Howards' circle because of George's desire to be an artist. He had met them as a patron – he wanted someone to decorate his houses in London and the country. But George admired the collaborative work produced by

William and Ned Burne-Jones. He wanted to be treated as a fellow artist, not as an aristocrat. And so this unusual friendship had sprung up between the men, and then between their wives – Rosalind was a staunch supporter of Georgie Burne-Jones when her marriage was in trouble. For Jane, it was another example of art opening doors, allowing her access to people and places she could only have dreamed of when she was a child. As a model, as the wife of an avant-garde designer, as a maker, Jane's status was slippery, unfixed. It meant that she could holiday with the heir to an earldom. She could drink tea and watch the sun set over the Mediterranean, while the Howards gathered up their children, and said goodbye, until tomorrow.

*

On the wettest, windiest days of midwinter, Jane missed the 'coal-fires . . . & home comforts' of London.[8] But most of the time Oneglia seemed to her a 'Garden of Eden . . . a paradise of delights'.[9] She arrived in late autumn, before the orange harvest, and was astonished by the beauty around the villa. In an enthusiastic letter to 'My dear Crom', Jane told him about the flowers still in bloom, 'oleanders, camellias, cactuses all flowering out of doors'. May went out walking in the olive groves above the house, and brought back 'some enormous field daisies nearly as large as our ox-eyed daisies and quite red'.[10] The girls revelled in the outdoor life, sitting out in the warmth of a late November afternoon. Jane watched them from the open windows, a soft breeze blowing through the house. It was all unexpected and lovely.

From her few surviving letters, it seems that Jane did not venture far afield. She was often tired, but kept happy and busy in the villa. She and the girls tried to learn the language. We can hear the smile in Jane's voice when she tells Crom about the 'old Italian who goes on errands, with whom I hold a conversation daily (you should hear it) on the subject of getting provisions'.[11] And then there is her eye for detail, in describing the flowers and the small pleasures of domestic life. 'The food is cheap and good enough,' she says; 'Today we have got fish that look as if they had been taken from a Japanese dish.'[12] She is remembering the blue-and-white fish that swam across the painted surface of the bowls on Gabriel's dining table. Jane had little company, apart from George and Rosalind Howard. George came to paint in her garden, sometimes bringing his models with him. Jane described these local girls as looking 'quite commonplace', but 'they are all bright merry things, I like to have them about'.[13]

Her own daughters explored further afield, going down to the town on feast days. They enjoyed the ceremony of 'the blessing of the horses by the priest', Jane said, and she 'met them all coming from the Churchsteps largely decorated with oranges'.[14] She reassured Crom that they were not planning to convert to Roman Catholicism 'just yet'.

Although William had once trained for the priesthood, all those years ago in Oxford, he had gradually set his formal Christian faith aside. He was increasingly concerned about the present – what he could change with his own hands and heart – not the hereafter. William and Jane had brought their daughters up without religious teaching. Unlike most girls of their generation, Jenny and May did not see the world through the lens of Christianity. Rosalind Howard found this startling. On their first visit to Naworth, she had talked to May about the afterlife: 'She says the soul is "nothing but the imaginary part of her body" – that there is nothing left but bones after death – that it is the brain that lives. She has not been taught these things, simply brought up without Theology.'[15] For Jane's daughters, there was no Heaven, no Hell, only the here and now.

This is one of the most radical decisions that Jane and William made together – to free their girls from the conventional Christianity that shaped so much of British life at the time. Even though many of their friends only paid lip service to the Church and its traditions, still it overshadowed their lives. From politics to literature, from sexuality to monarchy, the teachings of the Church were woven through Victorian society. Morris, Burne-Jones and their colleagues made a living from beautifying church buildings, creating stained glass, altar frontals and furniture. In their student days, they had talked of taking vows, founding a brotherhood. But William had shaken all this off. Jenny and May read the Bible, just as they heard tales from Chaucer, or sagas from Iceland. They were old stories, filled with marvels, but nothing more. As Morris told his friends, 'In religion, I'm a pagan.'[16]

The Morris family could have been vilified for their atheism. Jane's reputation was especially vulnerable, given her intimacy with Gabriel Rossetti, and might have been muddied by her refusal to bring up her girls within the Church. Instead, she and William held their nerve. Maybe there were family arguments, perhaps William's sisters objected. Their own faith was very visible: Henrietta became a Roman Catholic, and Isabella was a deaconess who campaigned for women's ministry in the Church of England. But, as far as we can tell, they did not ostracise Jane or William for their lack of belief, or for the way that Jenny and May were educated.

Despite their refusal to remain within the Church, William and Jane celebrated Christmas as a family festival. Jane's own books of quotations included extracts from contemplative Christian verse. They respected and protected the ancient buildings of the Church. They valued the art created in God's honour. In fact, in 1877 shortly before Jane travelled to Italy, William was hard at work with a new campaign to save medieval sacred architecture that was being threatened by over-zealous restoration. In June, he had written to *The Times* repeatedly about proposals to reconfigure Canterbury Cathedral. He took issue with the plans drawn up by the Dean and the architect Gilbert Scott for an 'imitation, restoration or forgery' of thirteenth-century tracery. He feared that the work would result in 'the usual mass of ecclesiastical trumpery and coarse daubing.'[17] Three days later he wrote again, emphasising its purpose as a sacred space: 'A great building which is obviously venerable and weighty with history', he insisted, 'is fitter for worship than one turned into a scientific demonstration of what the original architects intended to do.'[18] He urged the Dean to embrace the many layers of history within the cathedral, rather than trying to tidy them up or obliterate them.

William was writing as Secretary of the newly formed Society for the Protection of Ancient Buildings. (He usually referred to it as 'Anti-Scrape'.) This was his first foray into public activism. But it began as a very personal project, as he cajoled friends to join him in campaigning against the aggressive remodelling of old buildings in the name of 'restoration'. Philip Webb was there on the committee with William, at the first meeting, held at Queen Square in March 1877. He persuaded Ned to sign up too, and George Howard and Thomas Wardle. Morris looked to John Ruskin for support, asking him in July if he could reprint a passage from Ruskin's *The Seven Lamps of Architecture*, which had advocated day-to-day repair rather than over-zealous remodelling, stripping and cleaning: 'Take proper care of your monuments, and you will not need to restore them . . . do this tenderly, reverently, continually.'[19] William reassured Ruskin that 'I feel ashamed at having to say anything else about it, as if the idea was an original one of mine, or any body else's but yours: but I suppose it is of service, or may be, for different people to say the same thing.'[20]

Both Ruskin and Morris were coming to the same conclusion: that a tenderness towards the art of the past, a care for authentic handwork, were not simply aesthetic concerns. Their study of art led them to agitate for political and social change. They saw the need for freedom of expression, access to nature, pleasing domestic design and architecture: they also knew these things would be beyond the reach of most people under the current systems of production and consumption. Ruskin attempted to reimagine the relationship between craft and the land in his Guild of St George, founded in 1871.

Ruskin also became closely involved in the campaign, with the SPAB, to save the basilica of St Mark's in Venice from destructive restoration. It appeared that 'each stone or mosaic' of the façade 'was to be removed, repaired, or scraped and then put back up again'.[21] A monumental painting commissioned by Ruskin from the artist John Wharlton Bunney in January 1877 showed that some of the weathered mother-of-pearl marble on the western façade had already been replaced by dead grey stone.

St Mark's and Canterbury were two of the most high-profile battles that were fought by the SPAB. But the majority of the work was local and less obvious. By the end of 1877, the London committee was dealing with over thirty cases, including churches in Duxford and Cherry Hinton in Cambridgeshire. By the early 1880s, they were considering 150 projects every year, hoping to save the 'living spirit' of these places from being turned into 'a feeble and lifeless forgery'. Restoration, in Morris's eyes, was 'wasted labour', and architects who took on this work were 'worthy of better employment'.[22] He was so convinced of the wrongness of this work that in April 1877, Morris announced the Firm would turn down commissions for stained glass, if the windows were to be installed in medieval buildings that were being restored or 'improved'. This new policy certainly damaged trade. But it showed William's resolve to stick to his principles. His company would lead by example, even if it meant sacrificing his own income.

*

'Anti-Scrape' was only the beginning. It was a project that played to his strengths, as a designer with architectural training, as a supplier of church furnishings, as a man who had nearly been ordained. It was no surprise that he launched himself into the movement. However, in 1876–7, Morris became involved in another, more overtly political cause, as he started to find his feet as an activist. He threw his energy into a new campaigning body, the Eastern Question Association.

Like many in his circle, Morris was concerned that Prime Minister Disraeli was preparing to support Turkey in a war against Russia. When the rumours of a military intervention began to circulate, late in 1876, Morris wrote an open letter denouncing Disraeli's plan for 'a shameful and unjust war', asking 'On behalf of whom? Against whom? And for what end?'[23] Throughout 1877, the rallies and committee meetings gathered momentum, as supporters of the EQA spoke out for peace. Charles Darwin, Anthony Trollope, Robert Browning and William Gladstone were all involved. This campaign was Morris's first attempt at public speaking. He added his distinctive voice, by calling on 'the working-men of England' to resist those who were leading the country towards war – 'greedy gamblers on the Stock Exchange, idle officers of the army and navy . . . worn out mockers of the Clubs'. He was deliberately using the language of class, of inequality. The 'richer classes', he said, aimed to silence the workers, to 'deliver you bound hand and foot for ever to irresponsible capital'.[24]

This was the moment when William's anxieties about class and capitalism finally took shape. The tensions he felt in his own position, his own responsibilities, had long been simmering. He was the son of a stockbroker, and the brother of an officer in the King's Royal Rifle Corps. As he began to work feverishly for the EQA, he made it clear that he was taking sides instead with manual workers and tradesmen. Morris was, after all, a shopkeeper himself. As he put it to Jane, 'picture yourself a 3 years war, and the shop in Oxford Street, and poor Smith [the shop manager] standing at the door with his hands in his pockets!' because all the customers had deserted.[25] But this was more than self-interest. Morris was trying to reshape the power structures within his society. He saw the 'Eastern Question' as a starting point, an issue that could encourage the working classes to organise and agitate for greater change. In his rousing song 'Wake, London Lads!', written for a mass meeting in January 1878, he called on the spirits of Cromwell's men to rise again:

> What! Shall we crouch beneath the load,
> And call the labour sweet,
> And dumb and blind go down the road
> Where shame abides our feet?
> Wake, London Lads! the hour draws nigh,
> The bright sun brings the day;
> Cast off the shame, cast off the lie,
> And cast the Turk away.[26]

It was certainly not his finest verse. But when it was sung by seven thousand voices, 'the burning words . . . thundered forth by the vast assembly', the effect was 'electrifying'.[27]

With the rest of his family away in Italy, William had no home life to distract him from the EQA cause. Even in his Christmas Day letter to his girls, he was caught up in politics. Disraeli and committees and a manifesto, and 'a big meeting before Parliament' and his own agitation: these things completely overshadowed his seasonal good wishes. He did admit that he felt 'a bit dull without you', but then roused himself to sign off with a cheerfully Dickensian 'Wot Larks!'[28] In the girls' absence, he was spending time with the Burne-Jones family at The Grange, and entertaining them with extracts from *Great Expectations*, 'reading Joe and Pip aloud'.[29]

His letter to Jane a few days later inevitably dwelt on the 'stirring' of the EQA. However, he was also concerned about her comfort, and especially about the cold weather in Oneglia: 'Mind and buy warm wraps against next month,' he encouraged her.[30] In many of his notes to Jane, William fretted that she might not be well supplied. He asked her about water filters and packets of tea. He sent over odds and ends that the girls had left behind. He urged her to buy decent wine: 'Don't let your celebrated thrift make you poison yourself.'[31] William also began to talk about giving up the house in Turnham Green, at least for the present. He would move back into Queen Square while she and the girls were away, and perhaps look around for a new home for all of them.

In March 1878, Morris wrote to Jane several times about his house-hunting. He had been to Hammersmith and Holland Park, in the hope of finding something larger and more convenient than Horrington House. He explained that new houses in Knightsbridge or Kensington Square were 'quite beyond our means: a fairish house in such places means £250 per ann and they almost always want a premium'.[32] He had to take into account the on-going expenses of retaining Queen Square and the new shop, in addition to the family home. And 'we might as well live at York as at Hampstead for all we should ever see our friends'.[33] None of them wanted to be too far from The Grange. He had seen a house at the corner of Earl's Terrace which might do. It was 'without gross vulgarity', but seemed 'both scrimply and dull, and the chief rooms look pretty much North'. There was no garden, just a yard. The best thing Morris could find to say about it was that it was 'delightfully accessible'.[34]

There was another possible house, on the riverside at Hammersmith. The poet George MacDonald had lived there, but now it was available for rent. The greatest drawback, in Morris's eyes, was its name. MacDonald had called it 'The Retreat'. William thought that sounded too much like an insane asylum: 'People would think something was amiss with me'.[35] Otherwise, he was very taken with it. He liked the garden. There was plenty of space to 'keep hens in it; or a pig, or a cow'. There was even an extra room at the back of the house, 'high darkish and ugly-windowed', which they could use as a 'larking room'.[36] What did Jane think? He would like to get it all arranged before she returned from Italy.

*

Jane already knew about the Hammersmith house. Gabriel Rossetti had been writing to her with some details about 'The Retreat' before

Christmas. He was also on the look-out for a new home, with his own tenancy in Chelsea coming to an end. Gabriel was not enthusiastic about the house. The garden flooded, he said, and the kitchens were 'frightful . . . perfectly dark and very incommodious – the kitchen stairs being a sort of ladder with no light at all . . . you would hardly get good servants to stay there.' He worried that 'the place is very damp', with 'masses of dead leaves forming a complete swamp in the garden'. And there was 'a very squalid slum' between the house and the nearest railway station.[37]

It is not clear why Gabriel was so off-putting about 'The Retreat'. Perhaps he wanted to save it for himself, or perhaps it was another melancholy symptom of his mental instability and drug addiction. He was also very troubled about Jane's absence in Italy: in January, he wrote, 'I have not heard from you . . . and am of course anxious . . . should you, by evil chance, be very unwell, perhaps Jenny or May would write me a line.'[38] A month later, Gabriel was fretful and dwelling on the past. Jane's 'very writing', he said, 'does not look like your firm hand but reminds me of poor Lizzy's in days gone by'.[39] It is rare to find him making comparisons between Jane and his long-dead wife. Gabriel seemed saddened that he had lost Jane, too.

Jane was trying to create some physical and emotional distance. She could not shoulder the burden of Gabriel's illness as well as Jenny's. Jane did visit him a day or two before she sailed, when Gabriel gave her some travelling expenses from the £1,000 trust fund he had set up in her name when the Firm was disbanded.[40] On that last visit, Jane was not relaxed as in the old days. She did not curl up on the sofa to chat and sew and laugh. Gabriel said she looked like 'a bemuffled banshee'.[41] This was hardly a compliment. Jane remained wrapped up and fierce.

These months in Italy marked a new phase in their intimacy. Jane did not give Gabriel up completely, but she was now his friend, rather than his lover. And Gabriel began to let go of some of his most personal portraits of Jane. This was partly, he explained, because he needed cash. He found a buyer for *Water Willow*, a little oil painting made in 1871, when they had been together by the river. As Gabriel said, 'You will be glad in one way and sorry in another to hear that I have sold both the Proserpine and the little picture of you painted at Kelmscott . . . I was really mortally sorry to part with the Kelmscott picture.'[42] This *Proserpine* was his first version of the subject, also begun at the Manor house. He was saying goodbye to relics of their time together.

Gabriel refused to exhibit his paintings at the fashionable new Grosvenor Gallery, despite Jane's encouragement. He was too fragile to face the critics again. However, in 1877 he began to publish photographic prints of his drawings. Most of these early autotypes were images of Jane; she had modelled for *Silence* and *La Donna Della Finestra*, which were among the first test proofs. He also planned to reproduce *Water Willow*, *La Pia de' Tolomei*, *Pandora*, *Mariana* and an *Astarte Syriaca* drawing. These were all portraits of Jane in various historical gowns and guises. In 1878, Gabriel suggested to her that he would produce a 'dozen autotypes of you in a book . . . I might call them *Perlascura: Twelve Coins of one Queen* . . . I should put a sonnet to each autotype.' He intended to use a motto from Dante with his translation: 'She hath the paleness of the pearl that's fit/ In a fair woman.'[43]

It was common practice for painters to earn additional money from reproductions. But Gabriel's plan was different. It was a celebration of Jane's beauty, an acknowledgement of their intense relationship. Jane would no longer be able to maintain the polite fiction that she was one of many models in Gabriel's art. This project would show that Jane was his obsession, his ideal woman: 'She is as high as Nature's skill can soar.'[44]

We might expect Jane, at this point, to try to avoid the extra attention. She was grateful when Gabriel reassured her that he had rechristened one portrait study of her, for 'I did not want it to be talked about among strangers by your name.'[45] However, Jane seems to have embraced the new project. She even arranged for some of the photographic reproductions to be displayed in her own home. Gabriel was delighted: 'How dear of you', he wrote, 'to stick to your old belief in me and my doings and to frame and hang up the auto-types.'[46] The real woman, the mother, the wife, would come face to face with Rossetti's image of her – transfigured – on the turn of the stairs, in the hallway as she greeted her guests.

*

As with so many of Gabriel's projects, the *Perlascura* autotype folio was left unfinished. The extra sonnets were never written. But Jane did not know that when she returned to England. The summer of 1878 was a time of readjustment. She felt unsure where she stood, perhaps even where she lived. William came out to meet her in Italy, and they took the girls together to Genoa and Venice. It was an unsatisfactory holiday – William was very ill at times, and Jane was often feverish and tired.

William enjoyed the few days he spent at Oneglia. Jane's villa 'really was a most lovely spot beneath the terraces of olive trees'. He wrote to Georgie Burne-Jones, that he liked 'to hear the jingle of bells as the carts went by . . . nothing can be imagined more beautiful and soothing'.[47] As they travelled on to Genoa, however, William's gout caught up with him. It must have been distressing for May, seeing her energetic father rendered helpless. She was with him when he collapsed. (Jane was looking after Jenny.) William described how he 'could not walk or even hop well, so I got stuck'. A local man tried to lift William onto his back, but 'things began to dance before my eyes'. He explained that 'I woke and found myself on the ground in the centre of an admiring crowd'. At length, he was carried up to the hotel room. Given their experience of Jenny's terrible seizures, it is understandable that May was 'very much frightened'.[48] It does seem that this was more than pain in William's foot. He lost consciousness, and his response when he came to – 'chuckling with laughter' – does not appear to be embarrassment, but instead, a lack of self-awareness. There are parallels with the rages and 'transports' described by his friends when he was younger.

Perhaps William's unstable bodily reaction to the reunion with his family is not surprising. They had been separated for five months, and in the meantime he had thrown himself whole-heartedly into political and SPAB campaigning work. He had barely given himself time to breathe. Looking back, May recognised that 'we girls . . . little realized the mixture of loneliness and real hard work and anxiety in which he passed that winter. But we can surely never forget with what emotion he greeted us as he stepped off the train in Oneglia straight into our arms.'[49]

William never felt comfortable in Italy. He had not enjoyed his awkward visit with Ned Burne-Jones a few years before. Jane and his girls knew that he preferred the bracing barrenness of Iceland. Morris admitted as much in a letter he wrote from Verona:

I really have had more sympathy with the North from the first . . . with the later work of Southern Europe I am quite out of sym-pathy. In spite of its magnificent power and energy I feel it as an enemy . . . I long rather for a heap of grey stones with a grey roof that we call a house north-away.

In the 'infernal furnace-heat' of the Italian summer, he was pining for Kelmscott, the rain and the river.[50]

There were a few moments when the loveliness of Italy shone through for him. We catch sight of William relaxed, in Padua, when he and the girls were caught in a rain shower. 'The pavement was clean and dry,' he said, so 'I sat down with great content with my back to the wall.' There was a dyer's cart near by, with a load of deep blue cotton, and William wished that he could talk to the man about his work. In the evening, he went to a 'botanic garden and heard the birds sing'. That was a good day: 'How sweet the hay smelt!' Even his visit to the Arena Chapel, to see Giotto's paintings, was remembered simply for its 'beautiful garden of trellised vines, all as green as the greenest just now'.[51] This is what mattered – birdsong, and bright leaves, and simple things well made. William was eager to head home.

Jane, on the other hand, was reluctant to leave Italy. It seems that she was worried about what lay ahead for her – Jenny's illness, Gabriel's unhappiness, William's agitations. By the time she started the journey home, as William said, 'My wife is quite poorly . . . I think she has picked up a touch of fever somehow'.[52] She loved their week in Venice, although William was virtually housebound. Perhaps she found it easier to see the city at her own pace. William was very gloomy. On the few occasions that he was able to explore, he struggled with the signs of restoration at every turn. He wrote mournfully to Georgie Burne-Jones that 'it is sad to think that our children's children will not be able to see a single genuine ancient building in Europe'.[53]

They stayed in 'a queer ramshackle old house: very cheap, but attendance bad: it has a nice platform of its own over the water'.[54] This meant that Jane could slip away quietly, and be carried along the canals. It was much more comfortable for her than the jerks and rumbles of the railway. As William said, when they turned for home, 'Janey . . . never ceases longing for the gondola and its easy travelling'.[55] Rosalind Howard and her children had also come across to Venice, and Jane wished she could stay longer. As she told her friend, 'I might perhaps have been of some little use to you with the children . . . at any rate you might have lent them to me sometimes . . . but I could not let the others go without me'.[56] Her responsibilities were leading her back to London.

This letter from Jane to Rosalind reveals a great deal about their relationship, and especially Jane's reputation for being reserved or uptight. It shows how hard it was for Jane sometimes to speak openly. She was afraid of being over-emotional, out of control. She was constantly having to check herself. She needed to be sure that she was not giving herself away. Jane still felt that her social position was precarious, even after nearly twenty years of marriage. This meant that some people misread her manner, including Rosalind Howard, who was famously blunt. If we listen to Jane's explanation, we can hear her authentic voice, and her fear of losing a well-loved friend.

She begins regretfully:

My dear, dear Mrs Howard,
I can't tell you how much I am saddened by your letter . . . it was all my stupidity and clumsiness. When I was parting from you at Venice, if I had attempted to say any one word more than the ordinary good bye, I should have broken down and been unfit for the journey before me, I thought you must have understood how fond I had grown of you, and how very sorry I was to leave.
[. . .]I enjoyed being with you more than you can possibly have enjoyed being with me, you can't think what a magical effect a bright presence like yours has on so quiet a creature as myself, I enjoyed every visit you made me, and every day that your husband painted near us more than I can say, it seems impossible that you should not have known this all along and trusted my affection just as I trusted yours.

She was so upset that she had been sleeping badly, suffering nightmares.

[I] hated myself whenever I woke up, my dullness and ill manner seemed unpardonable, pray forgive me and remember me only as someone who loves you, is most grateful to you.

The letter ends with thankfulness that Jenny's health problems seem to have eased, with Rosalind's help. And the earnest last line: that Jane would 'always as long as I live . . . remember our stay in Italy as one of the happiest bits of my life'.[57]

Jane rarely opened her heart to anyone in this way. It is a measure of how much she liked and trusted Rosalind, that she was willing to share her insecurities. With some people, like Henry James or William Bell Scott, she could maintain her façade, retreat into *froideur*, because she did not care to be understood. Rosalind was different. Jane described a conversation with 'Georgy and Ned [who] dined with us Friday'. They agreed that Rosalind and George Howard 'were the only real friends we had made of late years, who had entered what your husband one day called our "magic circle"'.[58] She looked forward to welcoming them to her new home.

For William had arranged to take the house at Hammersmith. In early April he had written to her, saying that he believed 'people will come to see us at the Retreat (fy on the name!) if only for the sake of the garden and river'.[59] Jane was on the move again, to a house she had never seen. William had spent many hours there, and wrote about the place in great detail, trying to reassure her, hopefully walking her through the rooms and garden in his enthusiastic letters. Even so, it was a complicated homecoming. Gabriel was dead set against Hammersmith, and blamed William for 'making so mistaken a move towards a house in town even damper than the old one'.[60] And he said the interior décor was atrocious: the long drawing room had 'blood red flock paper and a ceiling of blue with gold stars!'[61] But it was too late now. The agreement was signed while Jane was still sitting on the terrace at Oneglia, watching George Howard painting baskets of oranges.

And so Jane came back to London, more fragile-looking and slender than before, and with her dark curls thinning: 'A good deal of my hair came off after I got a slight fever,' she explained to Gabriel.[62]

At least the Hammersmith house was not as frightful as she had feared. It would be good to have a garden again. Jane had not been able to tend her own fruit trees and flowers since the Red House days. She told Rosalind that 'a great deal will have to be done to bring it into reasonable order, I foresee much work for myself there.' Yet, it was hard to settle after Italy. She had been hopeful that the English springtime would soothe her, but in late May she was writing, 'How I long for the warmth, and Venice, and gondola! I am shivering at this moment close to a large fire.'[63]

Hammersmith, 1878–1883

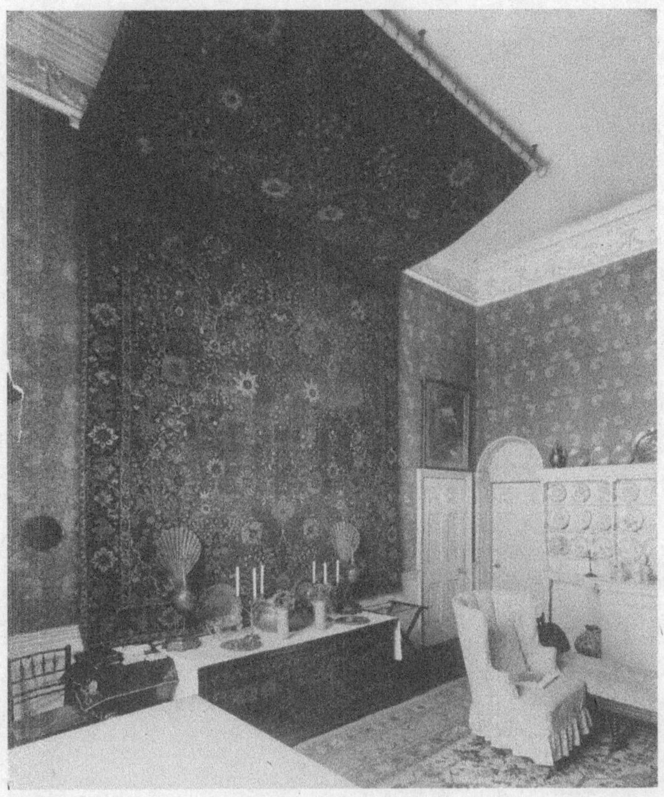

Emery Walker, *Dining Room, Kelmscott House, Hammersmith*,
photograph, 1896, V&A Museum

Jane leant against the tree trunk, her book open in her lap. It felt good to be sitting in the green shade beneath the canopy of leaves. Jane was reading poetry, piecing together unfamiliar Italian phrases. From time to time she lifted her eyes to look at the shrubs and raspberry canes near by, and asked herself: what would else grow well here? Later she wrote to Cormell Price, telling him about her new home in Hammersmith. 'It is a heavenly garden on a hot day,' she said, a delight to spend the morning 'in an appletree reading Tasso'[1].

Jane's letter to her friend gives us an insight into the contradictory ways in which her life has been portrayed. From the moment she began modelling, her life was doubled – she became an artefact, as well as a flesh-and-blood woman. For her, the new garden was not simply a place of retreat. She wanted to concentrate on serious reading, stretching herself, while keeping out of the way of the builders. Jane also took time to consider what would need to be done to tidy, to reorder and restock the flower beds and orchard. And, as she told Crom, she did not want to be thought of as 'a lazy fool': 'I have the new house on my hands,' she said, and that was why her brain felt 'like a pudding'.[2] She was busy planning, learning, supervising.

And yet, the idea of Jane sitting in a tree carries other associations – of idleness and distraction. One of Gabriel Rossetti's most famous pictures of her, embowered in the branches of a sycamore, is called *The Day Dream*. The pose was developed from a drawing called *Reverie*, made at Kelmscott. Both titles imply an absence. Jane is presented as passive, uninterested in her book, barely able to summon the energy to hold herself upright. In the sonnet written by Rossetti to accompany the picture, he dwells on her silence and dreaminess: 'till now on her forgotten book/ Drops the forgotten blossom from her hand'.[3] But Gabriel himself knew the effort that Jane had put into creating this work of art.

Jane discussed the details of the commission with Gabriel. She suggested flowers that would be in season when the sycamore was budding. She offered to send snowdrops and anemones, and then, later in the year, honeysuckle cuttings. She provided the shimmering green dress made of tussore silk. We can almost feel it in Gabriel's hands as he arranged the folds of drapery. He missed Jane's presence. He told her how the dress 'is replete with your memory, empty as it is now'.[4] Jane was the essential part of the picture – her face, her body, her hands. She had sat for him many years before, to be photographed, and then drawn. But he needed her back again, to perfect his image of the woman whose 'Dreams even may spring till Autumn'.[5]

In the finished picture, however, he effaced Jane's work. Gabriel made her appear unresponsive, deathly pale. In truth, although her health was shaky and she was in pain – at times, she said, 'I have fainting-fits still if I sit up for more than a few minutes'[6] – she was always thinking practically about how to improve her situation. She was clearly trying to make Gabriel smile when she wrote about the 'sea-weed baths at Ramsgate for people of a delicate constitution'. Jane told him, 'One is made into a kind of pie with seaweed, when it is supposed that one absorbs vast quantities of Ozone.'[7] And Gabriel liked nothing better than swapping stories with his friends about their ailments. Illness and money troubles dominated his correspondence in his later years. His paranoia made him an uneasy companion. His letters were often plaintive and upsetting. Jane had to tell him that she did not want to receive any more 'Jeremiads', and he apologised: he had been 'subject to depression'.[8] With Jane he could be vulnerable. In one unexpected moment, Gabriel shared his sadness about the death of Lizzie Siddall and their stillborn child. He wrote of the 'aching core of my babylessness'.[9] Nearly twenty years after they lost their baby, Gabriel continued to mourn the life that might have been. He wanted Jane to remember and mourn with him.

Our impression of Jane has so often been shaped by the words and images created by Gabriel. However, in her correspondence with friends like Crom Price, we rediscover a more rounded view of her personality. Jane writes and thinks about her life now, rather than dwelling on the past. She often sounds more relaxed, more sociable, as a busy wife and mother. In 1878, May turned sixteen, and she wanted to enjoy the fun of being young in London. Jane took her to garden parties, art galleries and concerts.[10] May was also accepted as a student at the Government School of Design in South Kensington. There she would have a vocational training in the decorative arts – textiles and ceramics, jewellery, wallpaper and book illustration – as well as access to the vast collections of the South Kensington Museum (later renamed the Victoria & Albert). May had grown up surrounded by people creating things. Now she was preparing to earn her living as a designer and maker. May's decision to follow in her parents' footsteps was bold but not unexpected. Still, it came at a particularly hectic moment, just when the Morrises were moving into their new house in Hammersmith. Jane wrote, in comic despair, to Crom, how 'everything is topsy-turvy; no one can find anything, not even their temper'.[11]

Jane knew that taking on the new house was a significant financial commitment. She joked with Crom that the family 'have all begun to think of what we could turn our hands to, in case of absolute failure in the Art line'. She told him, 'Top suggests shoemaking for the men, and plain sewing for the women', but Jane said she would 'refuse, I won't try to be respectable'. If they ended up in the workhouse, she threatened to 'tear up my clothes all day'. She wondered if her next letter would be 'dated from Hammersmith Union'.[12]

It is a strange image – Jane and William and their girls reduced to nothing. Fear of destitution had hung over Jane's childhood, with her family shifting from one poor lodging to the next. She had grown up in the backstreets of Oxford, and now she was moving to a house in the prettiest situation in London.[13] Her comments to Crom are a reminder that Jane had not played by the rules as a young woman, when she became a model and married William. Her close relationship with Gabriel also showed she was willing to sidestep convention. All too often, William has been portrayed as the rebellious one in their partnership. But in this letter, we hear Jane's own defiant voice. This was the spirited side of her character, the woman who 'roared with laughing'.[14] She was happy to sit in a tree with a book of poetry, not from idleness, but from a desire to 'keep up my old habit of reading every scrap that comes in my way'.[15] She was open-minded, eager for knowledge, amusing. And willing to take on the challenges of a big house in need of renovation, while her husband ploughed on with his new projects.

*

What did Jane find when she saw the Hammersmith house for the first time? William had sent her letters filled with descriptions and diagrams. She knew where the walnut tree, the horse chestnuts and the weeping ash stood in the garden, and she had already begun to think about what they could grow in the greenhouse. Jane and William had talked about a trellis in the kitchen garden, to hide 'those b---y new houses [and] the new chapel' just over the wall.[16] The girls liked the sound of Hog Lane on the other side. Like their father, they were glad not to be 'cut off from the Neds' at The Grange.[17] And he had assured Jane that there were '2 nice airy rooms (though they needn't be very big) for our dear maidens . . . and a good & quiet room for you, my dear' overlooking the garden. Morris would have a study and bedroom on the ground floor.[18]

Standing by the river now, looking up at the handsome four-storey house, she understood why William was so eager to move here. With the Thames on their doorstep, they felt connected to the Manor in Kelmscott. This was a good enough reason to rename their new home: it became Kelmscott House. As she crossed the road, and went in through the front door, the hall and landing felt grand, compared with their cramped house on the High Road in Turnham Green. William wanted her to see the drawing room on the first floor. This was the glory of the place – with five tall windows looking towards the river, and the elm trees at the water's edge casting a soft green light. Here was a house they could enjoy with friends. And everybody could have their own space. There was room for three servants on the top floor. William could meet clients and suppliers downstairs, and he was talking about using some of the outbuildings as workshops. Above the stables were two bedrooms. William thought Crom Price might use one, when he came to stay, and the other 'would be a general sulky-room'.[19] Given how William and those around him struggled with his tantrums – as Ned Burne-Jones said, Morris was often 'tempestuous and exacting company' – a sulky-room seemed like an excellent idea.[20]

In the main house there was a 'little den of a bathroom with gas and water laid on', a linen closet upstairs, and a good-sized pantry on the ground floor. The downstairs spaces were better than Jane expected. The back-kitchen had a copper for laundry, and the main kitchen faced south towards the river.[21] Then, further down, were the cellars.

Their friend Webb was confident that the house itself would not flood, although water had come into the cellars a few years back. He had taken a good look at the drains. Webb and William wanted to dispel all of Rossetti's rumours that the house was damp and unsuitable. Yes, it was, as William said, 'in very bad repair', but it 'could easily be done up at a cost of money'.[22] This was why William had been able to rent it at £85 a year. It was only a few pounds more than Horrington House in Turnham Green and far cheaper than a place closer to town. He had thought seriously about one in Earls Terrace, Kensington, but the rooms were 'very *small*: [and] the garden like a prison yard & very *tiny* . . . I don't think either you or I could live there.'[23] And most importantly, he had 'established the fact that the house [in Hammersmith] was quite dry . . . there was no smell about' and 'even the dreary room could be made habitable'.[24] William had high hopes that their new home could become another showcase for his designs. As he said, it might 'be made very beautiful with a touch of my art'.[25]

What did his art look like now? By November 1878, when the family moved in, William's approach to decoration had matured considerably. As he and Jane refurbished the interiors at Hammersmith, they created a home that looked very different to the Gothic, flat patterns of Red House. The medievalism of the early 1860s was now overlaid with a multitude of other sources: natural forms, in the bending stems of fritillaries and tulips; occasional references to elegant eighteenth-century shapes; the sophisticated woven brocades of Renaissance Italy; and cherished objects from Damascus or Constantinople. The designs were less literary, less reliant on the well-loved texts William had shared with Ned and Gabriel twenty years ago. Now the effect he created was fluid, tactile, multi-layered.

William made the most of the high ceilings and substantial floor-space in the new house. He could use the rooms to display his own designs, and the many beautiful things he and Jane had collected. The drawing room and dining room appeared rich, but not busy or over-loaded. It was while they were arranging the interiors of Kelmscott

House that Morris summarised his rules for decorating. He was asked to supply some notes for the Manchester Literary Club in February 1879. William wrote down:

a few things that have occurred to me.

1. Do not have anything in your house that you do not know to be useful or believe to be beautiful. (If this rule were carried out, we should be rid of most upholstery.)
2. Never have anything which is not good and sound in workmanship . . .
3. A thing (house, piece of furniture or the like) if it is essentially ugly, is made uglier by any attempt to decorate it with surface ornament . . . I do not think that there can be any other general principles than these.[26]

In a watercolour made by his daughter May two years after the family moved to Kelmscott House, we can see how William's principles worked in practice. She drew her mother practising at her new grand piano. Jane is concentrating on the sheet music, and we cannot see her face. May's attention is focused on the things in the room, and how they live harmoniously together. Most noticeable are the textiles, enlivening every surface – only the piano is undraped. Jane found that 'the hangings in the room ruin[ed] its lovely tone', so after a while they had to move the instrument out of the drawing room.[27] Its place was taken by bookshelves. There are no paintings on the wall, but instead a heavy blue fabric hangs in slight pleats from the picture rail, instead of conventional wallpaper. From May's writings, we know that this is Morris's *Bird* design from 1877–8, a jacquard-woven woollen cloth. William described this design as 'intimate and friendly . . . the most adaptable to the needs of everyday life'. It suggested, for him, the home of a man who lives with 'the few beautiful things he has collected slowly and carefully'.[28]

In May's watercolour, we also see the faintest outline of a figurative textile – perhaps an embroidery or old wall-hanging – near the piano. It must be summer, because the fireplace is covered with a curtain, embroidered or woven in pinks, blues and greens, to stop draughts. There seem to be several different carpets in the middle of the floor: we can see their overlapping borders. And another rug, smaller and more precious, is placed on the heavy table. Morris was following the common practice of the Tudors, who imported richly decorated carpets from the Eastern Mediterranean – and spread them on tables as they were too valuable to walk on.

This end of the room is not cluttered with furniture. Beyond the piano are two chairs: an adjustable recliner upholstered in green velvet, and a light rush-seated armchair. Both are in ebonised wood. There is plenty of 'quarter deck', as May called it – empty floor space for her father to stride up and down, when he was in animated discussion with friends. Most of his collection of ceramics is carefully stowed away in the built-in cabinets, painted sage green, that flank the fireplace. It is hard to see their details, but the shelves are filled with pale shapes. On the mantelpiece, some of the most beautiful plates and vases are on display. We can tell from the outline that William or Jane has chosen a tall-necked Iznik vase to take centre stage. Overall, May's picture gives the effect of muted colours playing off one another, shiny ceramics against warm woollen hangings, old and new sitting comfortably together, and her mother's music enveloping the whole scene.

We can get a sense of the other end of the long room from a photograph taken more than a decade later. There is, of course, no colour. This time a fire is blazing in the hearth. The fire surround was designed by Philip Webb, and again acts as a display area for William's collection of ceramics. There is a plain round workbasket on the floor by the daybed, as if Jane has put her sewing away and stepped out of shot. This part of the room has a cosiness, created by familiar furniture brought from Red House. The *Prioress's Tale Cab-*

inet stands against the far wall, and the settle with its curved hood is drawn close to the fire. Both would have gleamed with gold and umber by candlelight. There are piles of books on the table by the windows, ready for William to draw up his chair, and begin to read aloud. And over in the corner, we can just see an antique chest, with a large metal tray and ewer balanced on the lid. The mellow sheen of these imported objects, in chased and inlaid brass, perhaps from Persia or India – it is hard to tell at this distance – was matched by the brass candleholders on the other side of the cabinet. They were designed by Webb. Again, there are no pictures on the walls. There is plenty to delight the eye in the carefully chosen decorative objects.

*

Throughout the 1870s, William had been paying more attention to art from India and the Islamic world. He was buying and studying carpets and woven textiles, sometimes unpicking them to understand how they were made. His fascination with Persian rugs was clear to anyone who visited Kelmscott House. They were spread all over the floors and tables upstairs. And William transformed the 'dismal' dining room by hanging a huge carpet from the ceiling, so that that it created a canopy or cloth of honour. This carpet is now in the V&A Museum. Jane sold it when William died, as it was too big for any other home. It was, no doubt, one of the 'magnificent carpets' bought by William in Venice. May remembered the scene in the store, when as her father 'grew excited over them, the dealer grew more nonchalant'. George Howard, 'who went with us to do the bargaining in Italian', May recalled, 'had also to play the diplomat' as Morris became 'hotter and hotter' over the haggling. Even their gondolier got involved, wondering why Howard's friend was so angry. Eventually they struck a deal, and William was able to bring his treasure home.[29] As so often, William could not understand why people were indifferent to the things he passionately cared about.

He did not mind making a fuss, even if the rest of his family were squirming with embarrassment.

Back in London, he hung one of these marvels up in the dining room, its dusky pink ground contrasting with the blues of the *Pimpernel* paper that covered the walls. In this tall room – sixteen feet high – there was only a plain dado to break the floor-to-ceiling patterns. Beneath the carpet William created a spectacular grouping of objects. There was an Italian cassone of carved cypress wood. This was covered with a pale runner, with two peacocks perched on top. Between them were platters, candlesticks, glass serving dishes and vases filled with fresh flowers. The Persian peacock incense-burners were particularly eye-catching. They stood nearly three feet high, their tails of pierced brass, their long necks splendid with turquoises. Jane and May took these to Kelmscott Manor when William died. May loved how 'this side of the room had more than a touch of the Thousand and One Nights', with its 'table of Eastern riches' and the 'carpet spread like a canopy across the ceiling'.[30]

As curator Quisra Khan has said, William integrated Islamic motifs and objects so seamlessly into his own work that we have rarely acknowledged his debt to the artists of Persia, Syria and the Ottoman Empire. In Ned Burne-Jones's words, 'He loved everything Persian', not just the objects, but the poetry.[31] William started to make a verse translation of the *Shahnameh*, the epic eleventh-century 'Book of Kings', written by Ferdowsi, but it was never finished. However, the influence of Islamic art played out in other projects. Just before he began decorating Kelmscott House, William saw a reconstructed interior, 'a room complete from Damascus, walls, ceiling, window and all'. This experience influenced his work well into the 1880s. He described a visit to the dealer Vincent Robinson, where he immersed himself in the 'vermillion & gold & ultramarine' of the display. There were tiles, and engraved bowls in brass and copper. Among all the glitter and colour, he singled out 'one little casket of the 13th century' as 'the finest piece of metal-work I had ever seen on that scale'.[32]

William loved boxes. He enjoyed collecting and arranging them in his study on the ground floor. They were the only decoration on the plain trestle table in his own room, apart from the piles of books. May remembered his personal space as uncarpeted, 'almost frugally bare'.[33] We see, at the heart of his home, the pull towards emptiness and simplicity he had felt in Iceland. And yet, he could appreciate the colour, the delicacy, the abundance found in the art of the Islamic world. He recognised that, as a decorator and designer, he had much to learn from these imported textiles and pots. They were a rich source of ideas that he could reimagine for the homes of his clients, the deep reds and golds, the ogee curves, the carnations and tulips.

Sometimes William made it clear that he had been looking at designs from the Alhambra, for example; in 1884, he named a textile design *Granada*. On other occasions, however, the relationship was less obvious. The popular *Flowerpot* embroidery kit (c.1878–80) has sometimes been attributed to his study of Italian textile panels. However, Quisra Khan has shown that the vase and flowers could equally have been drawn from the carpets of Kerman in south-east Iran. And William had a spectacular example of this design tradition in his own home. The massive carpet that hung in the dining room at Kelmscott House encouraged William to experiment with new forms and materials. As he said, in a lecture on textile production, 'It is hardly worthwhile as an artist going into the history of this art in Europe: since whatever was really fine in it was little more than a literal copy of Indian or Persian originals.'[34]

William took time to read his dining room carpet, to get to grips with the underlying structure that restrained the floral decoration. As the V&A catalogue explains, there are three interconnected grids, 'blue-black, thorny white, leafy blue' creating a network of diamond-shaped trellises. These holding patterns sprout as if they were alive.

They give a framework to the profusion of flowers; we can see irises, and tiny starlike clusters of white meadow flowers, and Solomon's seal, and leaves as they unfurl. There are multitudes of colours, from blue and pale turquoise, to a fine yellow, all created in wool on a silk and cotton weft. The lavish flower decoration means that we almost miss the grid system that lies beneath. But it is this balance between geometry and naturalism that makes the design so effective and pleasing. As William had discovered in his work with stained glass, the most satisfying patterns are based on firm foundations.

*

William's study of the Kerman carpets and Iznik ceramics went hand in hand with developments in his own business. From the late 1870s he was experimenting with woven textiles and carpet making. He was also working closely with the ceramicist William de Morgan, who was trying to recover the art of lustreware, to create pots that rivalled the Hispano-Moresque glazes of the fifteenth and sixteenth centuries. Together they wanted to find a space to manufacture their products. The workshops at Queen Square and Hammersmith were too cramped to create fabrics on the scale that William envisaged.

For several years William had concentrated on dyeing and printing at Thomas Wardle's printworks in Leek, Staffordshire. But by the end of the 1870s, William wanted to bring production under his direct control. The Firm had to supply customers at the Oxford Street store, as well as substantial private commissions. He hoped to experiment with weaving damasks and brocades. He needed space to create knotted carpets using Turkish techniques. However, the looms that he had installed in the outbuildings behind Kelmscott House were sometimes in danger of flooding. May recalled a particularly high tide, when the river rose and covered the road, and the yard, and the floor of the weaving room. It happened on a Sunday afternoon, and 'all the household and all the guests' had to help save the 'finest and largest of the carpets' which was being woven for the Howards at Naworth Castle. They managed to lift it 'out of harm's way, with only one corner of it slightly wetted'.[35] This was another reason to look for new premises.

William also had a yearning to re-establish the techniques of indigo dyeing, to produce the intense blues he had seen in samples of Indian cotton. In pursuit of this perfect colour, he spent days at the dyeing vats in Leek. He often emerged, as his friends said, 'in roaring health and . . . with two dark blue hands'. Rosalind Howard thought it was likely that he had dyed more than his hands: 'I am now prepared to see him blue altogether,' she told Georgie Burne-Jones.[36]

Early in 1881, William wrote to Jane about a dream, 'how we were making carpets by the riverside & yet in Red Lion Sq: the rooms very large and desirable'.[37] This vision of a spacious factory became known among his friends as the Fictionary. With de Morgan's help, William visited many possible sites around London, until they found an old silk-weaving workshop near Wimbledon. The original factory, as de Morgan explained, had been set up by Huguenot refugees on the banks of the River Wandle. 'Seven acres of land went with it' and in the grounds were 'the remains of an ancient well' from the twelfth-century Augustinian monastery where Walter de Merton had been educated.[38] It ticked all the boxes – plentiful clean water, airy weaving sheds and the added romance of a medieval backstory. By Christmas 1881, William had moved production out of Queen Square, and across to Merton Abbey. He was delighted to be able to work beyond the reach of the city, the 'world-without-end-for-everlasting hole of a London'.[39]

*

In his first years at Merton Abbey, William designed a series of printed furnishing fabrics which were all named after tributaries of the Thames. *Wey* was a cotton velveteen, *Kennet* and *Evenlode* were indigo-discharge prints, *Windrush* and *Wandle* were both bold diagonal patterns. The names of these designs underlined the importance of waterways in William's life and work. The new site at Merton Abbey relied on the purity and reliability of the river there: dyeing and washing the textiles consumed vast quantities of water. And in Hammersmith they had the river on their doorstep. As a sort of grand housewarming, the family invited ninety guests to watch the Oxford and Cambridge Boat Race on 5 April 1879 (Cambridge won by three lengths). This was no elegant garden party. Georgie Burne-Jones remembered William and the young people playing an energetic game of 'Prisoner's Base' – a form of 'tag', which had been a favourite among the boys at Marlborough College. May could invite her school friends, and students from the School of Design. It was the largest party Jane had hosted since the Derby Day dinner at Queen Square. After her years of semi-exile in Turnham Green, Jane returned to a more visible social life, welcoming May and William's artistic friends and potential patrons.

For Jane and especially for William, one of the joys of Hammersmith was its sense of connection to Kelmscott Manor, at the headwaters of the Thames. The silver thread of the river linked the various parts of William's life: his London home, his workshops and his quiet days, fishing on the floods around the Manor. In the summer of 1880, the family were able to strengthen this bond between their two houses by making a pilgrimage upstream by boat. Jane helped to organise the food supplies, with Crom Price bringing the drink. As Jane said, he was an essential companion on this expedition and 'the originator of the plan'.[40] May asked her friend Bessie Macleod to come along. William de Morgan and Richard Grosvenor, a young member of the SPAB, made up the rest of the party.

The whole voyage was wonderfully eccentric. Their hired boat was named the *Ark*; it was described by May as 'an insane gondola' and by William as 'biggish', and with a cabin that looked like 'a small omnibus'. William was childishly excited at the idea of rowing and towing all the way to Oxford and beyond. On the first morning, he and Jenny went out to inspect their 'odd but delightful' craft, and to see the sun rise: 'The sky is one sheet of pale warm blue.'[41] William was particularly looking forward to sleeping on board, with 'the stream rushing two inches past one's ear'. He and Crom mostly stayed on the boat, but it was too small to house the others. Jane and the rest of the party slept at inns by the waterside or 'scattered all over the village' wherever they stopped at dusk.[42] There were picnic teas, and wasps, and an invasion of swans, and a regatta at Maidenhead, where the ungraceful *Ark* and its crew were teased by the crowds of spectators. The boat ran aground at Wargrave, and William de Morgan went barefoot onto the mudbank to push her off. Jenny remembered how 'Everybody perpetually gave orders in a very loud voice and . . . nobody ever paid the slightest attention to them.'[43]

William wanted to cook for the company, tucking himself into the tiny galley which was 'fitted up luxuriously . . . with two shelves and a glass rack' and then emerging triumphant with a steaming dish, 'like the high-priest'.[44] He needed to be busy – rowing or cooking or steering. He had left London with his head full of 'small necessary work at Queen Square', but as he told Georgie, he hoped the 'river will wash all that away'.[45] He was right. As William travelled further from London, the water worked its magic. He found new stretches of the river that were 'full of strange character in many places . . . enormous willows' and afternoons 'one can scarcely hope to see again for brightness and clearness'.

Walking back to the boat after supper in Marlow, William suddenly 'saw the streamers of the Northern Lights flickering . . . it was very mysterious and almost frightening to see them over the summer leafage so unexpectedly'. They jolted him back to his Icelandic voyage, when he watched the night sky above the mountains. The next day, he felt at home again, wandering around a higgledy-piggledy collection of Gothic buildings, once a monastery and now a farmhouse. He was delighted by the huge fifteenth-century dovecot. That was Friday.

On Sunday they reached Oxford, and left the *Ark* at Bossom's boat yard. They pressed on in a smaller rowing boat, past the harvesters in their punts who were gathering sedge for winter fodder. William said it was 'very pleasant' to see people 'hay-making on the flat flood-washed spits of ground and islets all about Tadpole'. It seemed to him a timeless task, and a long way from the grubbiness of London. They carried on upriver, and night fell. 'We fastened our lantern to the prow of our boat', making slow progress beyond Radcot Bridge.[46]

Jane had left the party at Oxford, and gone ahead to the Manor. She needed to make preparations to welcome the tired travellers, to be sure the beds were aired, the pantry was well stocked, there were kettles on the stove for hot drinks and bathing. William described this homecoming simply and irresistibly. The tired travellers approaching the house through the darkness, seeing the lamps and the woman at the open door – this heartfelt image resurfaces again and again in his writing, to the very end of his life. In his questing stories of hard journeys and uneasy encounters, this is what William's heroes were seeking. As he explained to Georgie, after the voyage, 'The ancient house had me in its arms again'. He recognised that this was Jane's doing, that it required forethought and kindliness. 'J. had lighted up all brilliantly', he wrote, 'and sweet it all looked you may be sure'.[47]

*

Jane was always busy behind the scenes. Even on the boat, she was not idle. She could not take the oars herself, but she sat in the stern, sewing. As William said, 'There was Janey lying down and working quite at home'. She had been, she told Crom, 'too decrepit for anything' earlier in the year.[48] She was suffering from neuralgia on and off, and the stabbing pains had forced her to stay in bed for several days in January. Then she had caught 'a violent influenza cold' and could not face being seen by friends 'with a red nose and the rest'.[49] But now she was on board the *Ark*, with her embroidery to hand, enjoying the good companionship of friends old and new. She seemed unbothered by the haphazard lodgings, the 'very hot and waspy' lunches, and their inexpert handling of the boat, which drew the attention of people strolling on the riverbanks.[50] She was, after all, used to being observed.

William never handled it well, when they were stared at. They were a conspicuous couple. William was so broad, and when he wore his unstructured blue working clothes, he was sometimes mistaken for a sea-captain. Jane was tall and slim and somehow foreign-looking. May remembered an outing in Burford, a few years earlier, when they were walking in their 'usual easy, happy-go-lucky manner'. As she said, 'Father and Mother were always striking figures wherever they went.' But there was, she recalled, 'a little hustling and laughing and a remark or two made' and William reacted with 'an instantaneous – what shall I call it? – a Berserker mask of rage and threat . . . the laughter simply crumpled up, startled into silence'.[51]

William saw nothing funny in his own appearance, or in Jane's. But she undoubtedly seemed out of place to some people when they met her for the first time. Her looks suggested an otherness. As Letitia Bell Scott told her husband, 'I can't think what countrywoman Mrs Morris is like, not an Englishwoman certainly.' She was too eye-catching: 'All us little women looked quite diminutive beside Mrs Morris.'[52] There is undeniably something more than jealousy in these comments. They imply a low-key prejudice that was not about class, but instead about Jane's dark looks, her obtrusive body. She seemed somehow foreign, or gipsy-like. Of course, Jane was anything but 'exotic' to those who knew her. She was down-to-earth, handy, and thoroughly rooted in Oxfordshire and then London. She could be brisk or elusive when she felt someone was taking an indecent interest in her personal life. But equally, she could write, with a smile, that 'I am extremely well just now. I think Xmas pudding is a good medicine.'[53]

Friends of her daughters remembered Jane with a mixture of

fondness and awe. They were impressed both by her extraordinary looks and by her industry. Helena Sickert, for example, recalled her pleasure in visiting May at Hammersmith, where she had

> the chance to see Mrs Morris reclining on a couch in all her strange beauty, her long pale hands moving deftly over some rich embroidery; to watch for the slow raising of her stone-grey eyes from under the brooding brows and listen for the delicious chuckling laugh with which she would greet our youthful extravagances.

Jane would enjoy the drama of showing off her skills with the needle, providing her young audience with 'exciting moments when she would rise and fling the great portière down and spread it out, so as to judge whether the general effect was what was intended'.[54] Sometimes she embroidered over a printed fabric, like the *Honeysuckle* hanging she made with Jenny, stitching in silk on linen. For other projects, she made coverlets and borders, following the faintest outlines pounced through the paper pattern. Jane learnt to choose stitches and blend colours to enhance the overall design. She knew that she was making something beautiful: she was quietly rejoicing in her own creativity and expertise. She kept at it, even 'when I am lying down flat on my back, I find it hurts my eyes less than reading constantly'.[55] Jane never stopped working.

Until 1885, Jane was not just doing her own embroidery for the Firm. For more than twenty years she also managed the women who stitched the hangings and fire-screens that were sold in Oxford Street. Bessie Burden, her sister, had become such an accomplished needlewoman that in 1880 she was appointed chief technical instructor at the Royal School of Needlework. Although Bessie had not been living with the Morrises since their move to Turnham Green, it must have been a relief to Jane that her sister now had independence and status as a teacher. The other embroiderers were a small team, often making samples to demonstrate techniques and colours. They also began the corners of the 'do-it-yourself' kits, like the *Rose and Olive* pattern designed in 1880 by William. This helped customers to understand what stitches to use – long or short, stem or glossy satin or feathered – and how to work with the colours provided.

Embroidery was a gendered activity in the firm. All the needleworkers were women, and so were the vast majority of their clients. There were occasionally female employees like Kate Faulkner who designed and painted ceramics. And later, William hired young women to work on the carpet looms. But the embroideries were exclusively made by Jane's female colleagues. It was flexible employment for women who had domestic responsibilities and, as Jane proved, could be accomplished even when the artist was limited in her movements. Stitching could be done at home, as piece work. William negotiated directly with some of the most talented women, like Catherine Holiday, when Jane was away. In 1878, for example, William had a long correspondence with her about a spectacular door-hanging, possibly the *Sunflower* design now in the V&A. He asked her if she would 'put another just like it in hand: I know you don't like doing repetitions: but this is such a beautiful thing that I should think it a great pity if there were not more than one of it in the world.'[56] But Jane monitored most of the day-to-day work. Sadly, Jane's letters to her team do not seem to have survived, so we cannot track the progress of smaller projects, or study her relationships with the rest of the women.

However, we do see Jane writing letters about other aspects of the business on behalf of William. There is a note, for example, asking for some letters of introduction for George Wardle, who was planning to travel to America in the spring of 1880. William was concerned about Morris-style goods being sold that were not 'the genuine things', and as Jane explained, 'at last my husband's patience has worn out'. She was using her network of female acquaintances to find a way around a sticky problem for Morris & Co.[57]

A little later, Jane was in touch with another well-connected lady, Louisa Powell Macdonald, about sourcing some stock for the shop. Jane had met Louisa in the early spring of 1881, when she was invited to spend several months with Rosalind and George Howard on the Italian Riviera. On this occasion, as Jane explained to Gabriel Rossetti, 'the invitation was only for me'. Jenny and May stayed in London, 'to keep house for their Father . . . I think it does them good to be made responsible sometimes'. Moreover, Jane's health had been very poor. Before she left, she was unable to step outside the house for days, and 'the talk of going to Italy . . . seemed like a ghastly mockery'.[58] But here she was 'only a few minutes' walk from the sea', with a 'garden facing the south in a stream of sunlight' and 'olives, lemons, oranges everywhere, blue mountains – blue sea and such sunsets'.[59] She was very pleased that the Howards welcomed her as a friend, and gave her the chance to recover.

Lousia and Jane's paths had almost crossed before – the Macdonalds had lived in the Hammersmith house before the Morrises moved in. When Jane arrived back in London, Louisa sent her 'two little presents' – one of which was a 'blue cup with little trees on it'. Jane remembered seeing pottery like this in a shop on the road to Ventimiglia. She explained that the 'cup so won my husband's heart' that she wondered if Louisa could arrange to buy and pack '3 or 4 dozen cups and saucers' of this style.

It was a bold request. It also showed that Jane had been paying close attention to the small-scale, homely products around her. As well as the blue pots, she also hoped that the village shop might still be selling 'some brown glazed thick saucers . . . also some little basins', or indeed any of the 'common things of home manufacture used by the peasantry'.[60] William wanted to offer his customers these authentic, unspoilt objects, the pottery equivalent of an unrestored medieval building. But of course there was always the dreadful dilemma at the heart of his business – he was lifting 'peasant' products out of their original context and selling them to a sophisticated urban market.

These anxieties rise to the surface more and more. We see William and Jane's increasing engagement with political and ethical questions throughout the 1880s. Jane, for example, wrote from time to time to the American Unitarian minister Moncure Conway, who was now a neighbour in Hammersmith. Although several of the letters ostensibly dealt with William's to-ings and fro-ings, it is clear that Jane was also playing an active role in showing him the Firm's ware. In May 1880, for example, she invited Conway to Kelmscott House to see the carpet-making workshops.[61] There is a blurring of the boundaries here, between home and business, private space and semi-public showroom, and her roles too – oscillating between 'wife of the poet and papermaker' (in Henry James's words), and skilled craftswoman. Unlike James, Moncure Conway appreciated Jane for more than her 'aesthetic hair'. Conway thought she was 'a superb lady, great hearted and sincere'.[62]

In a letter she wrote to Conway a few years later, Jane's focus had turned from interior decoration to practical politics. She and William were fundraising to send aid to people affected by the Iceland Famine – their crops and cattle had been devastated by bad weather, and families were facing starvation. As she said, 'We are getting up a Committee . . . would you kindly give your name to it?'[63] Although she had never visited Iceland, this was a joint concern, something that Jane wanted to help with, by putting in her time and calling on her friends. She was taking an active part in campaigning.

Throughout the early 1880s, it seems, Jane was working alongside William to promote the Firm, and to raise awareness of the causes that he was championing. She sent out tickets to his SPAB meetings and invited friends to hear his lectures. This was more than mere secretarial help. Jane was rallying support, helping William's radical ideas to gain traction.

*

The move to Hammersmith coincided with a visible shift in William's political outlook. He tried to explain to Georgie Burne-Jones how he seemed to be saying farewell to all the old assumptions about his art and his life. He wrote to her from Kelmscott in the late autumn of 1879:

> I am sitting now, 10 p.m., in the tapestry-room, the moon rising red through the east-wind haze, and a cow lowing over the fields. I have been feeling chastened by many thoughts, and the beauty and quietness of the surroundings, which latter, as I hinted, I am, as it were, beginning to take leave of. That leave-taking will, I confess, though you may think it fantastic, seem a long step towards saying good-night to the world.[64]

As so often, William's innermost thoughts seemed to flow from his contemplation of the world outside the window. He offers Georgie a moonrise, before telling her what is on his mind. He felt that his days of peace and quiet were behind him. He was entering a time of activism, of outspoken lectures, of awkwardness. He had become convinced that the political systems within Britain and the Empire were rotten. Initially he had seen it in the need for a transformation in art and architecture – that had been clear as long ago as the Red House days. But increasingly he believed that the failure of art to flourish was a symptom of a greater malaise. The Society for the Protection of Ancient Buildings, for all its good works, was not enough. He did not just want to preserve the past, but work for a bolder, more equitable future.

He now talked openly about his 'Hopes and Fears for Art'. He had developed his public speaking during the Eastern Question Association campaign, and had learnt how to hold an audience. The EQA had been a single-issue project. William was now thinking much more broadly. He outlined his uncompromising vision in a lecture on 'The Art of the People'. In February 1879, he was asked to speak to students and supporters of the Birmingham School of Design in the massive Neoclassical setting of the Town Hall. When he took to the stage, the makers and moneymen in the audience could not have anticipated the whirlwind that William directed at them. They had expected a neat speech on the structure of flat patterning, or setting up a successful interior design business. Instead, William presented a robust criticism of the structure of capitalism and 'so-called commerce'.

William was convinced, as he said, that 'it is not possible to dissociate art from morality, politics and religion'.[65] It is all connected – how we decorate our houses, treat our workers, ply our trade. These things show what we value in the world. In his arguments, he was following in the footsteps of John Ruskin, who had stood before a similar audience in 1864. On that occasion Ruskin had said to the merchants of Bradford, 'Tell me what you like, and I'll tell you what you are.'[66] William had been reimagining Ruskin's ideas for many years. In some respects, he was stepping into Ruskin's shoes, as a lecturer and agitator. This was a necessary role, now that the older art critic was *hors de combat*, after a prolonged battle with mental health crises. As Ruskin himself put it, he was 'down in dreamy scatterment and bewilderment'.[67] Early in his career, William had responded to Ruskin's enthusiasm for the natural ornament, the fancifulness and freedom of movement found in the Gothic. Now he summed up Ruskin's central argument: 'That thing which I understand by real art is the expression by man of his pleasure in labour.'[68]

William had also, through designing and managing the Firm's products, reached his own conclusions about the relationship between makers and consumers, about what art is, or might be. In William's words, art 'is to be made by the people and for the people, as a happiness to the maker and the user'. The creation of art was totally bound up with the 'two virtues much needed to modern life, if it is ever to become sweet . . . honesty and simplicity of life'.[69]

As many of William's critics have pointed out over the years, it is of course an uncomfortable paradox that a man who made his living by selling expensive textiles and wallpaper should state that 'I have never been in any rich man's house which would not have looked the better for having a bonfire made outside of it of nine-tenths of all that it held'.[70] Still, the point is that he was hoping to empty out, and start again with fewer, more carefully chosen pieces. Luxury, to his mind, 'is either a gathering of possessions which are sheer vexations to the owner, or a chain of pompous circumstance'[71] which encumbered the rich, and squandered materials and the labour of those who made all the unnecessary stuff. William saw this cycle as unsustainable. He wanted to persuade his wealthy clients to be part of the solution. They could use their influence for the bettering of the world, 'for if you are rich', he claimed, 'your simplicity of life will go towards smoothing over the dreadful contrast between waste and want'.[72] It all sounds too good to be true. But William was speaking from a position of authority. He understood the nature of creating and consuming. He knew what was necessary in a home, and what was there for the joy of making or using. Or just because it was lovely to look at. He argued that 'though simplicity in art may be costly as well as uncostly, at least it is not wasteful'.[73]

In his own Firm, William was striving to change the nature of work. Inevitably, he did not always succeed. We may question his employment of young teenaged boys and girls on tedious work at the looms – but these apprentices were trained, valued and paid more than the going rate. We may of course ask why he sometimes under-valued the skills of the needlewomen who supplied his shop. We may wonder how far the average worker in the Merton Abbey sheds was allowed to express their own creativity. After all, Morris was notoriously controlling about his designs, and often hard to please. However, he had chosen those sheds because they gave him and his workers access to fresh air and orchards. He encouraged his dyers and weavers to spend time in the gardens around the workshops, to dig the soil or sit quietly by the river. He educated his workers. And above all, he recognised his own limitations. William knew he was imperfect. On his own he could barely scratch the surface of the problem.

William acknowledged that in any society, in any work, there were difficult or tedious jobs to be done. But at present, 'the blindness and hurry of civilisation' led to 'that enormous amount of pleasureless work – work that tries every muscle of the body and every atom of the brain, and which is done without pleasure and without aim'.[74] He pointed to the wastefulness of 'the toils which makes a thousand and one things which nobody wants, which are used merely as the counters for competitive buying and selling.' This was much more degrading than the 'rough labour' that kept the world turning – 'to plough the earth, to cast the net, to fold the flock . . . carried many hardships', but would be good enough 'for the best of us' given 'certain conditions of leisure, freedom and due wages'. Similarly, in a more equitable society, 'the bricklayer, the mason and the like – these would be artists, and doing not only necessary but beautiful and happy work'.[75] It all comes back to beauty and pleasure. William believed that his audience felt like him – that making art is 'the thing that we love . . . the bread we eat and the air we breathe'.[76] He wanted all workers to relish and use their natural gifts, as horses love to run, and birds to fly. He was hoping for a new system of production which was in tune with nature, as 'the earth and the very elements rejoice in doing their appointed work . . . as the spring meadows smiling, [and] . . . the countless laughter of the sea'.[77] All William's experience – as a potential priest, and as a poet, as well as a designer and maker –

seemed to be crystallised in this lecture. The lucid imagery and the rolling phrases surged forward, suggesting a hopeful change of heart in his audience.

However, William recognised that he was pushing against the tide of the times. The rot was spreading. In this lecture, William voiced his concerns about British imperialism undermining the deep-rooted cultures of India and South East Asia. He had looked to India to learn about textiles, to unravel the most sophisticated dyeing, weaving and pattern-making techniques. He had relied on the collections in South Kensington to see what wonders could be done in cotton and silk. William knew that he was witnessing the ruin of these skills, with 'Englishmen in India ... in their short-sightedness, actively destroying the very sources of [our] education – jewellery, metal-work, pottery, calico-printing, brocade-weaving, carpet-making – all the famous and historical arts of the great peninsula'. This was the 'grievous result of the sickness of civilisation'.[78] In the name of competition and conquest, Britain was destroying beauty and 'pleasure in our daily labour', even on the far side of the world.

William called on his listeners to ask themselves whether they cared what the state of art was telling them about the state of society. In India, he pointed out, art was now subject to the interference of the British government. They had begun to arrange the manufacture of 'cheap Indian carpets in the Indian gaols'. He went on: 'The government being ... in full sympathy with the English public, has determined that it will make its wares cheap ... and nasty'.[79] There was something very sordid about these transactions.

Even in Britain, where overt war and tyranny seemed to be kept at bay, 'with all foes conquered', men still had 'to sit down and labour for ever amidst grim ugliness'.[80] Then they returned after their toil to 'houses which have become a byword of contempt for their ugliness and inconvenience'.[81] William saw this as the reality of working life for many of his fellow citizens. He seemed almost defeated by the scale of the misery. 'The stream of civilisation is against us,' he said, 'and we cannot battle against it.'[82]

William did not only blame the 'leaders of modern thought [who] . . . for the most part sincerely and single-mindedly hate and despise the arts'.[83] He pitied, but expected little of the 'vast number of people, who (poor souls) are sordid and brutal of mind and habits, and have had no chance or choice in the matter'.[84] He was, however, furious with those closer to home who wanted to avoid the hurly-burly of the fight, and withdraw into a closed artistic corner. He directed his anger at the artists, poets and critics of the Aesthetic Movement, calling them feeble, narrow and cowardly. For William, the motto 'art for art's sake' was not harmless. It was the slogan of 'the few' who 'despise the common herd, . . . hold themselves aloof from all that the world has been struggling for from the first . . . [and] guard carefully every approach to their palace of art'.[85] William chose his words deliberately. He knew that he and his friends, including Ned Burne-Jones, would be classed among the clique who made the idea of 'art for art's sake' fashionable. William's close affiliation with the Ionides family, with the artists who exhibited at the Grosvenor Gallery, even with Gabriel Rossetti, made it necessary for him to spell out the differences.

This modern school of art was distinguished by its esoteric delight in the quaint and the unworldly. It celebrated sensory pleasures, and seemed to disregard craftsmanship. William feared it would create a culture in which art 'will seem too delicate a thing for even the hands of the initiated to touch; and the initiated must at last sit still and do nothing'.[86] William could not bear the idea of the arts withering, too refined to be useful, beyond the reach of those who needed beauty most. He called his audience to action: 'At least do not let us sit deedless, like fools and fine gentlemen, thinking the common toil not good enough for us, and beaten by the muddle.'[87] There was no straight path through the problem. But at least he would strive.

The 'fools and fine gentlemen' included Oscar Wilde and James Whistler. They were the darlings of the Aesthetic Movement. Their approach to art seemed to William to be a twisted version of the message he and Ruskin were preaching. They too took to the lecture circuit and talked loudly about beauty and nature. But Whistler, in particular, turned Ruskin's arguments about craftsmanship and value inside out. Whistler insisted that visible work was the enemy of art. He rejected William's focus on striving. He wrote, for example, that 'the work of the master reeks not of the sweat of the brow – suggests no effort'. In his own pictures, he constantly wiped back and reapplied the oil paint, in fluid, almost transparent glazes, until he was satisfied that the effect seemed spontaneous. As he said, 'Work alone will efface the footsteps of work.'[88]

Whistler envisioned the role of the artist in very different terms to the 'common fellows' praised by William. In his Birmingham lecture, William said that most of the art he loved was made by people who were not 'highly paid, daintily fed, carefully housed, wrapped up in cotton wool'. For Whistler, however, an artist was by definition set apart, not a man of the people. He told his audiences that, from the beginning, other men would go out each day, 'some to do battle, some to the chase; others again to dig and to delve in the field'. These were the effortful activities that William celebrated in his writings – the warriors, the herdsmen and homemakers. But they were not good enough for Whistler. His ideal artist was different, 'a dreamer apart'. He was the first artist, and was 'chosen by the Gods'.[89]

Whistler told his origin story in a lecture given in London in February 1885, as an after-dinner talk to a fashionable audience in Piccadilly. Whistler was always immaculately dressed, but for this event, he was especially well turned out with a glossy opera hat and walking cane. The whole performance was worlds away from William's own gruff, unpolished appearance on stage. William had unceremoniously squashed his own top hat, sitting on it deliberately, when he had retired as director from his father's finance company in 1872.[90] It was an early sign of where his allegiances lay.

*

Appearances mattered a great deal to the artists who pioneered Aestheticism, and to their critics. Outré costume and posture contributed to the controversy around the Movement, as did the suggestion that there was something unhealthy or queer about their self-presentation. There was a feverish popular fascination about their looks and lifestyle. The more these writers and painters separated themselves from the 'common man', the more they became recognised as celebrities.

William initially disapproved of the Aesthetes because they seemed to want to retreat into their palaces of art. But by the early 1880s, the visibility of Aestheticism became a personal issue – Jane herself was increasingly singled out for satire and disapproval. Jane had once said she looked like a 'Scarecrow', after a bout of illness. But her unconventional dress and her role as a model for Rossetti made her a target for the caricaturists. Her distinctive features had been exaggerated in Gabriel's paintings. Now they were more cruelly parodied, as a version of her body appeared in cartoons alongside Wilde's velvet jacket and knickerbockers, or Whistler's monocle and walking cane.

It was George du Maurier who focused attention on Jane and her circle. He had drawn parodies of Pre-Raphaelite images for *Punch* magazine in the 1860s. And now he directed his attacks on the next phase of modern British art. He created a long-running series of sketches in *Punch* about a poet called Jellaby Postlethwaite and his painter friend, Maudle, mocking the affectations of Aestheticism. They were ridiculed as effeminate, and for their 'language of intensity' – beautiful objects were 'exquisite', 'consummate', 'utterly utter'. But it was female dress and deportment that often received the most attention in these cartoons. It was particularly hurtful when du Maurier turned on Jane, since he had been a good friend of the

Burne-Joneses in the early days when they were all newly-weds. Now he rebranded her as 'Mrs Cimabue Brown', a leading lady in the 'Mutual Admiration Society' of the Aesthetic Movement. Mrs Cimabue Brown featured in at least ten *Punch* cartoons from 1879 onwards, marking her out as one of du Maurier's most recognisable characters.

Jane had always stood out as tall, slender, dark-haired, strong-featured. Du Maurier emphasised these most dramatic elements of her appearance until they became overblown and graceless. Mrs Cimabue Brown looked unkempt. Her mounds of thick hair were frizzled like a bird's nest. Her slim figure became gaunt. She stooped. Jane's firm chin and bold mouth were made heavier, so her features lacked finesse. Her taste in clothes made her seem even more peculiar and peevish. Mrs Cimabue Brown's dresses accentuated her straight-up-and-down figure. She appeared uncorseted, and swathed in bold floral patterns. The cut of her costumes sometimes included vaguely historical references, or balloon sleeves, or trains and ruffles. They mimicked the robes in which Gabriel dressed his models – designs that were suitable for the artist's studio, but outlandish if seen at a dinner party.

The contrast between conventional fashion and Aesthetic dress was made explicit in a drawing published by du Maurier in *Punch* in April 1881. To most people's eyes, du Maurier suggested, the fashionable lady was elegantly turned out, with a smooth, controlled waist and bust. But to Aesthetes, this same costume appeared unnecessarily trimmed, artificial in its curves and drapery. The 'woman of fashion' looked like an overstuffed piece of upholstery. On the other hand, devotees of Aestheticism's 'cult of beauty' preferred a more natural silhouette. Ideally, a lady would wear a dress that allowed movement, with an unrestrictive collar and sleeves, and a fluid skirt. For most *Punch* readers, however, the Aesthetic model was anything but elegant. Du Maurier clearly references Jane Morris's appearance in his depiction of the heavy-jawed, thin-cheeked, drooping woman. Her hair is straggling over her forehead, and she wears a dress covered in a sunflower pattern. (The sunflower was Oscar Wilde's flower of choice in his publicity photographs.) She looks absent-minded and frankly ill.

Was there any truth in this depiction of Jane? Is this how she did appear to those who met her? We know that an acquaintance who saw her in Italy in 1878 thought she looked 'haggard and wistful-eyed, with a heavy bush of black hair'.[91] Of course she had taken her girls to Oneglia because she was in pain herself, and concerned about her daughter's health. It was not surprising that she seemed pale and thin. Perhaps we can learn more from a couple of photographs taken on Jane's next journey to Italy in 1881, when she travelled to Siena with two sisters, Jane and Anne Cobden, and Anne's fiancé, Thomas Sanderson. These *carte-de-visite* images, taken in Paolo Lombardi's studio, help us to understand the reality of Jane's appearance. She is significantly taller than her friends, and stands in a slightly hunched way, as if she is protecting an aching back. She holds an umbrella. She leans on it a little, like a walking stick. Jane looks tired and worried, especially compared to Anne, small and pretty, who gazes confidently down the camera lens.

Jane's costume in these Italian photographs is unusual only in its practicality and plainness. She was not dressing to be noticed. Her dark gown buttons down the front, so she does not need a maid's help in the morning. It is a single quiet colour, with a hint of trim at the cuffs. She seems to have a small pocket sewn onto the outside of the waist, perhaps to carry a watch. Apart from that, the only decoration is a simple silk scarf twisted and tucked into the front of her dress. She seems deliberately less dressy than the Cobden sisters. Jane Cobden wears a long jacket trimmed with fur over her striped dress, and her hair is carefully arranged. And Anne's gown is a fashionable Artistic cut, with a sash belt, turned-back cuffs and a small collar of white ruffles. Meanwhile, Jane Morris in her unobtrusive, unadorned travelling costume would pass unnoticed, if it weren't for her extraordinary rich hair and mournful eyes. She seems a long way from home.

Du Maurier himself, when he sat opposite Jane at a party in 1885, said he was 'depressed' by her 'old Florentine costume and old Florentine face above it'.[92] But we can hardly blame Jane for her haughtiness in the presence of the man who had created such a distorted version of her beauty. We do not know what she thought of the *Punch* cartoons. Neither she nor William seems to have spoken openly about it. But she knew that this image of her was partial, perverted even. Du Maurier implied her sickliness was a performance, while for years she had been trying her best to feel healthier. And she had kept working. She was no idle, artificial person.

*

Jane was also the target of du Maurier's satire because of her association with Gabriel Rossetti. In a cartoon of June 1879, Mrs Cimabue Brown sits on a Morris and Company ebonised chair and asks a resolutely un-Aesthetic guest, 'Are you intense?' (Reading Jane's letters, it is the sort of phrase that she would never use.) She folds her hands, just like Jane does in many of Rossetti's fancy portraits of her – as Beatrice, or La Pia de' Tolomei, or La Donna della Finestra. In another *Punch* cartoon, Mrs Cimabue Brown whispers adoringly about the painter Maudle, whose work is only revered by a clique of patrons. Gabriel, like Maudle, preferred his pictures to circulate within private networks.

Gabriel and his works acquired a cult status, known by initiates. As *The Times* explained, 'Only a few old friends used to frequent his studio in the quaint Elizabethan house.'[93] Jane was one of these old friends, writing to him regularly, and still visiting him from time to time, at least until August 1881. By then, she said, 'I gave up seeing much of him owing to chloral drinking.'[94]

Their correspondence helps us to keep track of Jane, as she writes to Gabriel from Hammersmith, and from the Howards' at Naworth Castle, and from Bordighera. She heard from him so often that, she said, 'to wade through a drawer-full of your letters' to find an address, 'would be the work of a day'.[95] Her notes are chatty, thoughtful and practical. She continues to send him costumes to help with his pictures, 'an old blue cachemire gown, and a cloak'.[96] Jane knows how his pictures are progressing, and what she can do to support him in his work. She tells him about the loveliness of the garden at Kelmscott House: 'I never saw so many birds in a town garden, they come in scores to be fed', she wrote in March 1879, 'and reward me by singing sweetly in every tree or bush.' She began that letter with 'a line of congratulation on the return of spring, or more correctly on the disappearance of the horrible darkness of winter . . . I can breathe without gasping, you will paint without bad language'.[97] Jane's tone was affectionate, but unsentimental.

Gabriel was thankful for Jane's 'gentle kindliness', especially when she found him in what he called 'my dullard state . . . I have become so subject to depression' that he fretted about her constantly.[98] She understood, and always tried to keep in touch with him, especially if she was travelling. When she arrived in Cumberland she sent 'just a line to say that I have got here safely'.[99] And a few weeks earlier she had written 'a line as you ask though but in lead pencil. I am still confined to my sofa.' He wanted to know all the ebbs and flows of her health, so she told him how she had 'just managed to sit up to eat my dinner, the violent pain in the back is gone'.[100] When she was most poorly, she had to write with a pencil – she could only use a dip pen and inkwell when she sat at a desk.

In return, Gabriel wrote about his painting and his patrons, or gossip he had heard about mutual friends, or the books he was reading. He copied out sonnets to send to Jane. He gave her advice about framing pictures and medicine (which she mostly ignored).

While Jane's letters were simply friendly, Gabriel's were more often demonstrative or anxious. There were hints of humour. But these were becoming rare. Early in 1880 he wrote to 'Dear suffering Janey' and went on, 'I have just kissed your handwriting, the most welcome thing in the world . . . I don't know how I should have got through the night if I had not heard . . . I have got to look on everything as an omen.'[101] At the end of that year he reiterated his regard for her. In a passage that is almost painful to read, he wrote that

> the deep-seated basis of feeling . . . is as fresh and unchanged in me towards you as ever, though all else is withered and gone. [. . .] This you wd never believe, but if life and fate had willed to link us together you wd have found true what you cannot think to be truth when – alas! – untried.[102]

We do not know what Jane made of this declaration. Did she imagine herself taking Lizzie Siddall's place as Gabriel's life-companion? Her next surviving letter was business-like. It made no mention of what might have been. Gabriel's words carried her back to their quiet times together at Kelmscott Manor in the early 1870s. Was there an implication that if Jane had been able to devote herself entirely to Gabriel, then he might not have struggled so much since? But Jane had stayed close even as he slid away from reality, into the twilight world of addiction. She had not abandoned him, although their intimacy had been more muted. Jane must have realised that she was in a better place, with William still supporting her. Her husband's continued care made it possible for her to travel, to think, to work.

Gabriel also reminded her of where she had started, rather than what she had become. He wrote to Jane about a new housemaid who 'will be 17 in September'. She seemed to resemble the young girl with astonishing hair he had seen in an Oxford theatre many summers ago. His maid said she had gone into 'service at 11, but used to sleep at home till she was 13, since when she had earned her living entirely'. This had been the shape of Jane's life and her sister's, before her encounter with the artists. As Gabriel said, 'It is difficult to think of such a kid as being only a year younger than your stately self when I first met you.'[103]

William did not hark back to their beginnings. Instead, he was perpetually looking to the next enterprise. William refused to retreat from the harsh words and ugly things that existed in the world beyond the studio. Gabriel on the other hand would not use his status, as an artist and writer, to agitate for change.

*

'Morris never faileth', Ned Burne-Jones wrote to a friend in the spring of 1883. But Gabriel by then had been dead for nearly a year: 'I wonder if any man ever made such a hell out of this little earth for himself as he did.' The death of Rossetti, on Easter Day 1882, left, in William's words, 'a hole in the world'.[104] Gabriel had been staying in a bungalow at the seaside near Margate, attempting to recover from a stroke which had left him paralysed in his left arm and leg. His doctor insisted that he stop taking chloral – and instead he was treated with a cocktail of laudanum, whisky and morphia. In recent years he had suffered from an uncomfortable swelling in his groin, as well as chronic insomnia. And since his latest collapse, he was cared for partly by a young admirer, Thomas Hall Caine, and partly by his mother and Christina, his sister. They had expected him to linger longer. But he died there at Birchington, just as spring arrived.

Both William and Burne-Jones had lost faith in Gabriel in his later years. Still, as William said, he 'was very kind to me when I was a youngster'.[105] He had seemed 'the centre and light of it all' to these hopeful artists in the 1850s and '60s. As Ned explained, 'Those first things of his were such miracles to me.'[106] But for the last decade, Gabriel had been increasingly exiled from his old friends. William, on the few occasions he referred to Gabriel publicly, was admirably generous in his response to his wife's lover. However, he was not afraid to criticise Rossetti's 'arrogant misanthropy' and to blame his early death on his lack of 'the grain of humility which makes a great man one of the people, and no lord over them'. As a result, in William's eyes, 'he lost the enjoyment of life which would have . . . sweetened all his work for him and us'.[107] These comments reveal as much about William's own preoccupations, and his insistence on art for all, as they do about Gabriel's character. They also imply that if Gabriel had been less egotistical, then he would not have caused so much pain to those around him – including William and Jane.

Jane's reaction to the loss of Gabriel was a mixture of shock, regret and thankfulness. She was grateful for what they had been to each other, but also glad that he had ceased to suffer. 'I had mourned him as one dead 6 or 7 years ago,' she told Crom Price, and had not expected to be so shaken by his loss. However, 'The effect on me at the sudden news of Gabriel's death was quite unlooked for . . . he had written and appeared to be working as usual up till the last few weeks'.[108] It was a hard time of grieving. Jane was caring for her daughter Jenny when she heard of his death. Jenny was experiencing seizures, and Jane needed to be on hand. So, neither she nor William attended Gabriel's funeral. Ned intended to go to the funeral but only got as far as the station, and turned back, too upset to say his final goodbyes. As he wrote to a friend, this was a very worrying period: William's 'eldest girl is ill and grows weaker and fills him with almost constant alarm'.[109] A year later, in March 1883, there was little sign of improvement, as Jane explained that 'Jenny is very ill still, I am almost in despair about her'.[110] William admitted to Swinburne that he felt more worn than before: 'You see I am getting an oldish fellow now, and bear on my back a wallet of disappointments & "tacenda" [secrets]'.[111] These things that were left unspoken – the half-hidden intimacies between Jane and his old friend – seemed rawer than ever in the wake of Gabriel's death.

To add to the troubles at home, there was also the inevitable flurry of interest about Jane's connection with Gabriel. The first biographies were published very swiftly. Hall Caine's *Recollections of Dante Gabriel Rossetti* was in the shops before Christmas 1882. His book coincided with major exhibitions of Rossetti's paintings at the Burlington Fine Arts Club and the Royal Academy in the winter of 1882–3. Jane lent her portrait *The Blue Silk Dress*, and a large drawing of May. *Water Willow*, with Kelmscott Manor in the background, was also on display.

For the first time the public were able to see the way that Jane's face and body had become embedded in Gabriel's art. Until now, almost all his works had been kept in private collections and were known only through reproductions. It must have been extraordinary to walk through the galleries and see Jane's painted image repeated in picture after picture. She was invited to one of the Private Views, in late December 1882, but it seems she did not attend. 'I want to go very much,' she explained, 'but if weather is bad I should not attempt it.'[112]

The reviewers recognised Gabriel's obsession. For Harry Quilter, it was clear that his fixation had begun in 1857, during the Oxford Union project: 'For the last twenty-five years of his life everything he wrote or painted could be traced to her.' He seemed to blame Jane for the 'unfortunate coincidence which gave him a model of a physical type which . . . forced him into one groove of thought and held him there like a vice.'[113]

In another review, Sidney Colvin agreed that Gabriel had 'become a slave of his own predilections'. Again, Jane's appearance was singled out as the source of his artistic narrowness, 'with lips at once full and pining and eyes overshadowed by a great thunder cloud of hair'. He went on: 'The length of throat, the litheness of limb . . . almost degenerates into caricature.'[114] They implied that Jane herself was a kind of Astarte, an enthralling figure out of time, whereas those who met her discovered that Jane was a straightforward woman who happened to look extraordinary. She was a great model. She could present as Mariana or Pandora. However, this was only one facet of Jane's character.

Friends of Jenny and May remembered her as a mother who presided over a beautiful home at Kelmscott House, where they were made welcome at a simple trestle table, with a tea of honey and homemade bread served on blue-and-white china. They recognised the 'exquisite cleanliness of the house (for Mrs. Morris was a notable housekeeper)'.[115] Her down-to-earth manner in her private life – even in her relationship with Gabriel – counterbalanced the eroticisation and otherness of her public façade.

In a letter to Theodore Watts Dunton we hear, all too briefly, Jane's opinions about Gabriel's art and his life. Even here, though, she was discreet. She said, 'I don't know why I am writing this to you, but I feel that I want to talk to someone about him.' She was spending the winter in Lyme Regis for the sake of Jenny's health. Sitting in Dorset, looking out to sea, she felt estranged from the world she and Gabriel had created together. She acknowledged that 'Gabriel was mad . . . no one knows that better than myself.' And she agreed that his earliest work was the best, but felt that 'the same might be said of most men's works' when 'there is a freshness in everything, a wealth of invention'.[116]

We know Jane read the reviews of the exhibitions. Watts Dunton sent them to her. She did not refer to the criticisms of her own role as model. But she did express her anger on Gabriel's behalf. She felt the articles 'would have enraged the painter himself! Fancy his hearing it said that his finest work was done about 1866!'[117] She was clearly upset by the 'swinish tastes' of Quilter, and had hoped for more sympathy from Colvin. It was especially hard as Rossetti was not able to defend himself, or her. But she was naturally curious to hear the chatter about his life. She had 'seen neither of the books' that came out at the end of 1882. Jane said 'I imagine from all I hear that

[William] Sharp's must be ludicrous' and she was 'rather curious to see Caine's'.[118] She asked Watts Dunton to send her a copy so that she might know the worst. Gabriel had been careful to keep Hall Caine and Jane apart. His biographers were working largely from hearsay and surmise. However, he did talk to Hall Caine about her on the day before he died. He wanted Jane to have anything of his she cared for. Their friendship had endured. As he told her, 'Your sweet faithfulness in the value you set on what I do is most touching to me . . . but you are always faithful, and always will be, I know.'[119]

Jane, like Gabriel's other friends and family, was concerned about stories that might surface now that he was gone. She worried about the letters that she had sent him. He had kept them in various cabinets and cases around Tudor House. Were they safe? Could they be circulating now, seen by prurient eyes? Had his housekeeper Fanny Cornforth found them? Would she sell them? Jane knew that Gabriel's brother, William Michael, had been to Cheyne Walk soon after his death, to tidy up any indecent letters that were lying around – Swinburne was notoriously lewd in some of his correspondence. We will never know how much was burnt by William Michael. Jane destroyed many of the notes Gabriel had sent her. Others she considered building into one of the walls at Kelmscott Manor, and letting history deal with them. But she could not part with them just yet.

There were other, more public, souvenirs of their time together. Gabriel made sure of that. In his Will, he left Jane the 'largest and best of the chalk drawings . . . now hanging in my studio'.[120] She would be able to have the presentation drawings of *Perlascura* and *Reverie* at home, alongside studies for *The Day Dream* and several other works. Gabriel also gifted her the costume jewellery worn by some of the models in his pictures. They were unusual pieces which he had found in bric-a-brac stalls and sale rooms. Each one showed Gabriel's fascination with sinuous lines and rich colours. There was the silvery girdle that had hung low on Jane's waist in *Astarte Syriaca*, made up of interlinked flowers with a large central rosette. This had been fashioned in Germany sometime before 1750, but in Gabriel's eyes, it was so beautiful it could encircle the body of an ancient Venus. He saved her other treasures: a Burmese bangle made of plaited gold, decorated with dragon's heads and rubies from *The Beloved*, and a heart-shaped brooch, set with three artificial stones – two red and one green. This was the most distinctive piece and had been worn by Fanny Cornforth in *The Blue Bower*. It was the closest thing to a love token.

We do not know if Jane ever wore these gifts in public. However, after his death she seemed to be more willing to dress the part, to encourage the association between herself and the pictures, to take pride in her role as a celebrated model. She certainly enjoyed choosing unorthodox accessories and robes. Shortly after Gabriel died, she was seen wearing 'dark dull red with a garnet necklace and cross'.[121] And a few years later, she was described by a young acquaintance as standing 'tall before me, draped in a simple white gown which fell from her shoulders down to her feet. She looked a veritable Astarte.'[122] On this occasion, she did not need the girdle to give the impression that she 'did not belong to our common mortal mould'. But although she looked like a goddess, although sometimes she liked to make an entrance, and move uncorseted, in trailing velvet, this was only half the story. In her doubled life, this was her public face, her performance as 'Janey Morris', her tribute to Gabriel.

Rossetti had helped her to see herself differently. As a girl, Jane had felt gangly and too much. People had stared in the street and called her names. Gabriel had encouraged her to embrace her unconventionality, to own her looks, to appear 'more queenly than any Guenivere'.[123] They worked together to create masterpieces in painting and poetry. And Jane showed him affection. She knew that he could be great company. She wanted to bring him back into the daylight world, to relieve his melancholy. Jane recalled the very last evening they had spent together, having dinner, gossiping, talking about art. Gabriel took her home in a cab. Jane tried to persuade him 'inside the house to see the children'. The girls were waiting up, hoping to see him. He had 'already half crossed the courtyard' towards her door, when he turned back and disappeared into the darkness. 'He was in high spirits that day,' she remembered, 'but I never saw him again.'[124]

Chapter 12

The Coach House, 1883–1890

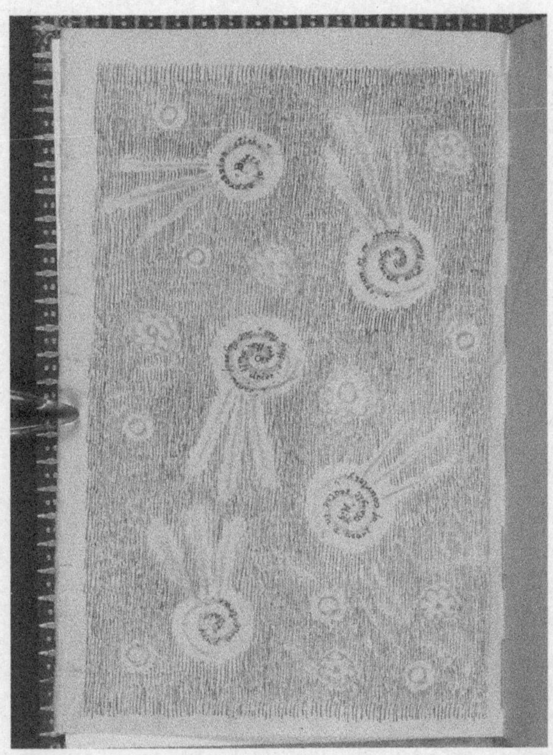

Jane Morris, *Page from a commonplace book*, around 1885,
British Library

William stood on the doorstep of the miner's cottage. The man invited him into the cramped living room so they could talk about the strike. The miner – we do not know his name – bore dreadful scars from an accident at work. He had lost one eye, and the other was badly damaged. He explained how the men in his village were now only working four days a week, and the pit owners were planning to cut their pay by 12½ per cent. That was why the collieries were silent today, and the men were sat at home. The miner's wife and daughter, 'tidy and good-tempered women', made William welcome as he listened to the 'Northumbrian smack' of their accents and looked about him.[1]

The doors of all the cottages down the street were open to the spring sunshine. Inside each front room, a 'swell but ugly bedstead' took up most of the visible space, polished and covered with colourful quilts. William noticed how clean the cottages were inside, compared to the sad coal-stained exteriors. They seemed the 'most woful looking dwellings' set in 'a miserable back yard to the collieries'. He recognised the hard work of the womenfolk as they tried to keep their homes unpolluted, their constant battle against the blackness that covered the countryside. For William, as a man who had enjoyed a comfortable upbringing on the back of the daily discomfort of miners in the Devon Consuls, this was an unsettling encounter.

It was the spring of 1887, and William was in Sedgehill (now known as Seghill), just to the north-east of Newcastle, for a Socialist rally. He wanted to talk to the miner and his family before moving on to the mass gathering near Blyth. As he walked the six miles down to the field, he and his friends fell in with a band and banners and a lot of other men and women on the way. The whole scene seemed out of kilter. It was a beautiful April morning, with 'the bright blue sea forming a strange border to the misery of the land'.[2] William readied himself to address the crowd.

William was raised above their heads, balanced precariously on a plank on the back of a waggon. There were nearly seven thousand people waiting to hear his call for a general strike. He urged them to remember that 'they were many, and the masters were few. Masters could only attack with a certain instrument, and what was that instrument? A part of the working classes themselves.' He believed that if the rebels were organised, 'the cannon would be turned around . . . the swords and bayonets be sheathed' and the soldiers would say, 'let us all be honest men like yourselves'.[3] William wanted to hasten the revolution. All his talk of striving and fighting, his desire that an artist should be a man of the people: this is where it had led him. The rhetoric had become reality, in a cacophony of scuffles and heckling and protests.

*

William could have chosen to embrace a different kind of Socialism. As he told Georgie Burne-Jones, this agitation led him away from his own 'love of ease, dreaminess, sloth, sloppy good-nature . . . All these would not have been hurt by my being a 'moderate Socialist'. But he explained that this would have been self-deception.[4] Time and again, he had to tell his friends, 'I cannot help it.' William wrote to Georgie that he needed to get to 'the root of the matter' and work 'in the thick of . . . trying to do something'. He could not stand on the edges and watch.[5] William had begun reading a French translation of Marx's *Das Kapital* in 1882, and joined the Democratic Federation a year later. This was the first Socialist political party in Britain founded on Marxist principles. William signed up to their policies in *Socialism Made Plain*. Their manifesto included promises on better housing, free compulsory education and free school meals, an eight-hour working day, the nationalisation of banks, railways and the land, and co-operative reorganisation of agriculture and industry. For William, there were the additional concerns about art and home life. In a letter to the *Manchester Examiner*, he made it clear that in future, his lectures would show that 'the question of popular art was a social question . . . What business had we with art at all unless all can share it?'[6]

Increasingly William presented himself as a tradesman and an employer, rather than a gentleman-poet. He recognised that he was only ever going to change a tiny corner of the world. But still he went on preaching and writing. And trying to persuade his friends. He was convinced that 'the contrasts of rich and poor are unendurable . . . I am bound to act for the destruction of the system which seems to me mere oppression and obstruction'. That would only come about 'by the united discontent of numbers'. As a member of the 'shop-keeping class', William was all too aware of the 'waste and disgrace which is the essence of our present system of Commercial War'.[7] To Georgie, he stressed the importance of education, but he was often almost in despair at 'the struggle for bread, and lack of leisure, and squalid housing – and there we go, round and round the circle still'.[8]

Many of William's friends saw his Socialism as an aberration, a distraction. Certainly, that is what Ned Burne-Jones felt. He asked that *The Commonweal*, the Socialist journal edited by William, should be sent in future 'to *Mrs* Burne-Jones, not to "Mr"'. Georgie and Philip Webb were supportive of William's conversion, but the earliest biographies tend to marginalise this period of his work. Mackail's *Life*, written under the close eye of Ned, stressed the effect that the long days spent on Socialist journalism, the late nights out lecturing, had on William's art and poetry. The Burne-Joneses were both saddened to see less of William during the week. And, although their Sunday breakfasts at The Grange never faltered, the conversation was often overshadowed by William's political preoccupations.

More recent biographers, especially E. P. Thompson in the 1950s and Fiona MacCarthy in the 1990s, have traced the complexities of Morris's Socialist career with greater sympathy. They have shown that his political life was an organic development: as he said, I 'have really been a Socialist for a long time'.[9] It can be seen as the culmination of all his projects, from his ideals of Brotherhood in the 1850s to the move to Merton Abbey twenty-five years later. He began his work for this new Cause as a foot soldier in the Democratic Federation, which was led by Henry Hyndman. As so often happens, internal squabbling led to the break-up of this alliance. Hyndman wanted to work towards parliamentary change, while William and his allies saw parliamentary government as part of the problem. William joined the Socialist League in 1884 and set up a meeting room in his own coach house at Hammersmith. Even this was only a short-lived enterprise, as in 1890 William had to step away from the main League, which had been taken over by anarchists within the movement. He could not support fellows who advocated opening the prisons or setting fire 'to the slums and getting the people into the West-end mansions'. At least one of the other members, Franz Kitz, had been experimenting with bomb-making.[10] William remained at the helm of the renamed Hammersmith Socialist Society, with its 120 members. The coach house continued to be the focus for talks and readings until his death.

William's commitment to consciousness-raising meant that he could be travelling to events three or four times a week, in addition to the regular Sunday evening talks in Hammersmith. It was grim and exhausting work. He gave speeches in the snow. He went into the smoky back rooms of working men's clubs, where the 'coming and going all the time, the pie-boy and the pot-boy' carrying jugs of beer, made it hard for him to concentrate on his message about 'Monopoly'. All too often the meeting room turned out to be a 'dirty wretched place'[11] or 'a tumble down shed ... amongst the woful hovels'.[12] He had to snatch his dinner where he could – in a railway refreshment room, on the top of a bus, a few biscuits, three penny-worth of potted shrimps, a bottle of ginger beer. He tramped miles on marches. He sold copies of *The Commonweal* from his satchel. He dealt with drunks and rowdies.

At the tail end of 1887, when the protests were becoming violent, William was part of a mass rally heading for Trafalgar Square. He and 10,000 others faced more than 2,500 police and cavalry and foot soldiers, armed with live ammunition. This event became known as Bloody Sunday. *The Times* reported that 'the police, mounted and on foot, charged in among the people, striking indiscriminately'.[13] The little column of the Socialist League tried to stand their ground, but as William watched, they were attacked from the front, the flank and the rear by police wielding their batons: 'It was all over in a few minutes.'[14] For William it was a stark lesson in brutality.

Within a month, William was acting as pall bearer for a young man, Alfred Linnell, who had died in a demonstration a few days after Bloody Sunday. Linnell was killed by a kick from a police horse. His funeral procession started in Soho, and as the hearse carried him east to the Mile End Road, followed by banners and bands, more and more people joined, until it became over a mile long. It was raining and almost dark as he was buried. William spoke at Linnell's graveside, honouring a man who had 'a hard life and met with a hard death'. He urged the crowds to recognise that they were all 'engaged in a most holy war, trying to prevent their rulers ... making this great town of London nothing more than a prison'. He hoped they would work together to transform working lives, so that they might be delightful, beautiful, happy.[15] One of those who stood beside him remembered William throwing 'his whole soul into his speech. There was a fearful earnestness in his voice.'[16]

The marching, lecturing and long days took their toll. His gout returned frequently, especially from 1885, and made him house-bound for a time. The pain was so severe that he could not even hobble from his study to the dining room in Kelmscott House. He needed to be wheeled around on a sofa. He quite enjoyed spending his days 'reading trashy novels'.[17] At least this enforced rest gave William time to catch his breath. For a short while, he could lie in bed 'in the morning and let the sun creep over me and watch the clouds'.[18] On these days he almost envied Edward Carpenter's simple outdoors life. In a Christmas letter to Georgie, he told her how he 'listened with longing heart to [Carpenter's] account of his patch of ground, seven acres . . . they grow their own wheat and send flowers and fruit to Chesterfield and Sheffield markets: all that sounds very agreeable to me'.[19] There was a pared-down calm to this vision.

William recognised that he could not step away from his family responsibilities or the men and women at Merton Abbey who relied on him. He knew it would be 'dastardly to desert'. Instead, he tried to refashion his own approach to the everyday. As he said to Georgie, 'It seems to me that the real way to enjoy life is to accept all its necessary ordinary details and turn them into pleasures by taking interest in them.' He blamed modern life for the tendency to 'huddle them out of the way, have them done in a venal and slovenly manner till they become real drudgery'.[20]

Finding beauty in the daily, homely tasks – this was at the heart of William's work. It tied together his desire to improve the lives of all workers, and to create delightful decorative objects, filled with natural forms and made in humane conditions. It should not have been a radical message, but it was. He would educate, agitate, organise to hasten the new world order.

*

William insisted that his ill-health was unrelated to his 'knocking about to meetings' on street corners or cold club rooms.[21] His friends were not convinced. But it is true that he sometimes faced a tougher crowd at Oxford University, for example, than in the East End of London. When he gave a lecture in 1885 at the Holywell Music Room, just a few yards from the lodgings where Jane had grown up, it ended in stamping and uproar. A handful of undergraduates let off a stink bomb and Charley Faulkner, who was in the chair, had to close the meeting early. William spent the rest of the evening more quietly, with a moonlight stroll in New College Cloisters. Being in Oxford inevitably heightened his sense of distance – from his own upbringing, from dear friends like Ned.

At William's first public lecture in Oxford, in November 1883, the Fellows had refused to believe that he would really preach Socialism. The Master of University College, where the lecture was to be held, had vetoed an invitation given to Hyndman: he was leader of the political Democratic Federation, and might stir up the students. William tried to explain 'the fact that I am quite as much a Socialist as he is', but his talk on 'Art and Democracy' was seen as safe, and it was allowed to go ahead. William did reassure his audience that 'as a Sec. of the SPAB' he would not allow Hyndman 'to blow up any *old* building in Oxford'.[22]

It was a strange evening, memorable for the force of William's oratory, and for the consternation he caused. John Ruskin was in the chair; he had returned, for now, to public life after a severe mental health crisis. Some of the early passages of William's speech sounded almost Ruskinian, as he argued for the stewardship of resources and access to the beauty of Nature. William argued that our system of government had a duty

to keep the air pure and the rivers clean, to take some pains to keep
the meadows and tillage as pleasant as reasonable use will allow
them to be; to allow peaceable citizens freedom to wander where
they will, so they do no hurt to garden or cornfield; nay, even to
leave here and there some piece of waste or mountain sacredly free
from fence or tillage.[23]

William's call to action emphasised the need for a sustainable agricultural landscape alongside areas of wilderness. He advocated the 'Right
to Roam', nearly fifty years before the mass trespass of Kinder Scout. He
insisted that those who bore 'such heavy tasks of grinding labour' were
most in need of leisure and green space. He saw that his generation
were 'surely and not slowly destroying the beauty of the very face of the
earth'.[24] Ruskin would have welcomed this intervention: he was in the
throes of anxiety himself about pollution and the impact of industrialisation on the wellbeing of the earth and its inhabitants. Ruskin's own
lecture on 'The Storm Cloud of the Nineteenth Century' (1884) shared
several themes with William's speech. But he stopped short of declaring,
as William did, 'I am one of the people called Socialists.'[25] Ruskin was
always a conservative, but, for all his 'looking back', William was not.
He could not believe that small-scale philanthropy like Ruskin's Guild
of St George, with its emphasis on 'back to the land' and an underlying
Christian sentiment, would break the deadlock.

To William, 'The very essence of competitive commerce is waste;
the waste that comes from the anarchy of war.' Capitalism looked tidy
and well regimented from the outside, he argued: 'The very orders
for destruction and plunder are given with a quiet precision . . . this
is the mask that lies before the ruined cornfield and the burning cottage.'[26] The fight was very real to William. As he explained a few days
later, 'We are but minute links in the immense chain of the terrible
organisation of competitive commerce, and . . . only the complete
unriveting of that chain will really free us.'[27]

William often had to answer pointed questions about his own personal circumstances. On one occasion, when he was asked why he did not just give his money to the poor, he responded with such emotion and earnestness that the crowd were won over.

For a moment he stood speechless, glaring down at the interrupter like an angry lion. Then the resentment died in his eyes, giving way to pity, and he made his defence:

> I started in business for myself over thirty years ago. I am as rich now as when I began, despite my ability and industry. I have paid my men good wages – better, indeed than they could get anywhere else; I have taught them to make beautiful things, and some of the work which has passed through our hands will last even after our bones have mingled with the dust. I have treated my workmen not as an employer, but as a comrade . . . Even if Rothschild gave away his millions tomorrow, the same problems would confront us the day after.[28]

There was another compelling argument that William sometimes used. Ruskin, for example, could choose to give away his fortune. He could gift his pictures to the universities, and sink money into museums and farmsteads. Ruskin had no family to support, apart from his cousin Joan. He did not have to worry about keeping dozens of employees in business. Ruskin's money, like William's, came from his middle-class father's industry. It was his to keep or to hand out. But William could not afford to take this route. He had one chronically ill daughter, another just starting out in her career, and a wife who was also often in poor health. He admitted that 'we ought to be able to live upon £4 per week, & give the literary income to the revolutionary agitation.'[29] William would not mind cutting back. He rather relished the austerity of simple meals and plain furniture. After all, £200 per year was the salary he offered many of his best workers, like Kenyon the colour mixer, and Goodacre the foreman dyer. William expected them to get by. But he had to think of 'his wife and the girls', and how could he put upon them'.[30] There were some cuts he could not afford to make: Jenny often relied on a live-in nurse to save her from accidents and support her when she had seizures. With William away on Socialist League business, Jane needed more help.

*

William also had to bear in mind that his home was now an important meeting place for the Socialist comrades. From 1884, Kelmscott House became a hub where radicals from many different backgrounds could debate and dine together. The looms had been moved out of the workshops, and now the campaigners could move in. William himself attracted poets and artists, who sat alongside refugees, anarchists and veteran Chartists on the long rows of benches and kitchen chairs in the converted coach house. Providing hospitality for these gatherings was part of William's commitment to the Cause.

When he and Jane had first settled in Hammersmith, William calculated their household expenses at £1,200 a year. He reckoned they would need to pay £100 rent and £100 on rates, taxes and insurance. He expected to spend £500 on general household outgoings and the rent at Kelmscott Manor. The rest of the sums are more revealing of their priorities as a family. William estimated they would spend £100 a year on books (for William) and another £100 on travel (for Jane and the girls). The budget also included £100 a year for 'Dress for 4 persons'. This seems high, bearing in mind that William never wore the tailored suits expected of a gentleman, and Jane and May designed and made most of their own clothes. But May wanted to socialise with college friends, and Jane often needed to chaperone her. It is also a substantial amount compared to the total bill for keeping four servants at £80 a year, or an average salary of £20 each. As live-in staff, they would be provided with bed and board, and some clothing allowances. Even so, these figures highlight one of the fundamental disparities in nineteenth-century society – servants were low paid, and their positions could be precarious. Young women's labour was cheap. It was also the essential groundwork on which all William's own activity relied. All his designing, campaigning, writing and gathering of political fellows was built on the constant household vigilance of Jane, her maids and cooks. They were up and down the stairs all day, as they prepared the meals, laundered the linen and lit the fires. Meanwhile William agitated, debated and lectured.

William always enjoyed entertaining. His expense sheet included £50 a year for his wine merchant. This sum would inevitably rise as he brought more men and women into the Socialist fold. A scant few embraced teetotalism and vegetarianism. Many others enjoyed the lively dinners after the Sunday talks, as William poured the claret and pounded the table: 'why do people say it is prosaic to be inspired by wine? . . . Has it not been made by the sunlight and the sap?'[31]

*

The evening meetings in Hammersmith seemed a long way from the miner's cottage in Sedgehill. It was hard to imagine that they were part of the same project. William's reputation as a poet and fashionable designer meant that people came to see him and his remarkable family. The chance to spend an evening in the presence of Jane and May encouraged a diverse audience for these events. They would sit through a chilly lecture in the coach house, its barn-like interior barely relieved by hessian hangings and a few framed prints. They would listen to enthusiastic calls to overturn the current system of wage-slavery, and to sing William's Socialist hymn, 'The March of the Workers', for the sake of being near his beautiful wife or daughter at supper.

A select group of Comrades and admirers would process from the frugal meeting space, with its bare boards and hard chairs, to the dining room. They would be welcomed into the richly patterned room overlooking the garden. There, beneath the canopied carpet, they would arrange themselves around the trestle table: undergraduates and activists, Austrians, Russians and Scots. The poet W. B. Yeats found himself sitting among a strange assortment of guests, including 'more or less educated workmen, rough of speech and manner, with a conviction to meet every turn'.[32] When H. G. Wells visited, he was struck by William's emphatic conversational style, and the 'sprinkling of foreigners, who discoursed with passion'.[33]

Oscar Wilde appeared from time to time, sporting a dahlia in his buttonhole. William was unimpressed by this young writer, calling him 'an ass ... and clever too'.[34] A few years later, in 1891, Wilde published his own manifesto for *The Soul of Man under Socialism*. He presented William's earnest endeavours to lighten the load of the poor in almost flippant phrases. He laughed at altruistic and emotional responses to distress: 'They try to solve the problem of poverty, for instance, by keeping the poor alive; or, in the case of a very advanced school, by amusing the poor. But this is not a solution: it is an aggravation of the difficulty ... Charity creates a multitude of sins'.[35] Wilde said he sympathised with the poor, who had 'no grace of manner, or charm of speech, or civilisation, or culture, or refinement in pleasures, or joy of life'. He thought 'a poor man who is ungrateful, unthrifty, discontented and rebellious is probably a real personality, and has much in him. He is at any rate a healthy protest.' But the 'virtuous poor ... must be extraordinarily stupid'.[36] Whether or not he had a serious message, Wilde couched it in such condescending terms that he undermined any political intent. He would never reach the audiences that William touched.

Although William was sometimes shy of speaking man-to-man with individual workers, he did try to frame his arguments in ways that would appeal to people of all classes. His writings were well loved and continued circulating in the homes of the working poor until the Second World War. William's Socialist historical novel, *A Dream of John Ball* (1886–7), was still kept safe 'in house after house' in Northumberland mining villages during the Great Depression, even when most of the furniture had been sold.[37] William's visionary narrative of past and present spoke of hope for the future. It was a fable that opened up possibilities, using the backdrop of the Peasants' Revolt of 1381. William was so steeped in the medieval world that his landscapes and relationships did not seem forced. Instead, he helped his readers to stand beside him as the archers loosed their arrows, or to walk with him past 'the church with its new chancel and tower, snow-white in the moonbeams now', encountering sights and sounds that were 'a wonder to me, and affected me almost to tears'.[38] Yes, there were hardships, and the hedges, orchards and meadows of England became a battleground. But the narrator returned to a house filled with wildflowers, jugs of yellow blossoming flags and white poppies. The walls were hung with 'loosely-woven stuff of green worsted with birds and trees woven into it'. And a dinner of broth and meat, bread and cherries was on the table.[39] As they ate, 'wide open were the windows, and the scents of the fragrant night floated in upon us'.[40] William believed that such simple pleasures could be available to all. The atmosphere of this supper – the urgent conversation, hearty food and cheerful surroundings – echoed the mood he and Jane created at their Sunday evening meals. We can almost hear William raising a glass of wine with the rebels and drinking a toast to 'Tomorrow, and the fair days afterwards'.[41] This was good fellowship.

*

What food did Jane serve to her Sunday guests? There is a file of family recipes still kept at Kelmscott, which records their favourite dishes. Most were written out by Jane and May. Others – including instructions for making Icelandic waffles – were sent by friends, and they were all gathered into a leather folder. Some of the recipes were clearly intended for formal dinners, or days when one of the family felt delicate, like the consommé maigre, an easily digested clear vegetable soup. Others were for teatime, when May could invite friends to sample her mother's syrupy orange cake. The collection includes recipes for picnic food, too, or perhaps the 'Cornish pasties / Sufficient for four good-sized' were made to sustain William when he was out on the road. Then there are the dishes that would have been relished by the comrades at supper: a creamy haricot bean soup, and a substantial meat hotpot. All the recipes reflect the Morrises' comfortable life in Hammersmith, with a well-stocked larder, and ample domestic help. None of them is over-luxurious, but they are signs of plenty, designed to be made in good quantities and shared with friends. The hotpot sounds particularly nourishing and delicious, an ideal meal to serve after sitting in the unheated coach house. Jane liked to flavour the stew with apples, half a cupful of port and redcurrant jelly, as well as parsley, thyme, cloves and a teaspoon of curry powder. The garlic-infused vinegar was perhaps an ingredient that she learnt to love on her Italian journeys, especially when mixed with sprigs of thyme: she picked herbs on her rambles in the countryside near Bordighera. Jane told a friend how flowering thyme reminded her of the sunshine and sea air: 'I always think it conveys such a strong idea of out:door life.'[42]

JANE MORRIS'S HOT POT

Ingredients: meat, chopped parsley, 2 apples, 1 bay leaf, ½ leaf balm, a few peppercorns, 1 clove, 3 large Spanish onions, 3 grated carrots, 1 teaspoonful of garlic vinegar, same of curry powder, 1 gill port wine, pint of stock, teaspoonful redcurrant jelly, thyme.

Cut the meat in small pieces, taking away all fat and gristle, put in the jar, add the herbs & apples chopped & spices; onions & carrots *fried* separately – then pour in the stock in which the jelly, curry powder & wine has been stirred. Stew gently for 2 hours.

Some of the men and women at her table would be grateful for Jane's substantial dinners. The Russian Nihilist exile who styled himself Sergius Stepniak (or 'a man of the Steppes') was 'so massive and striking in appearance that he suggested comparison rather with some fact of nature – a rock, a vigorous forest tree – than with another man', according to a girl who met him at this time.[43] Born Sergey Mikhailovich Kravchinksy, Stepniak had fled Russia after becoming involved in anti-Tsarist agitation. He not only wrote about guerrilla warfare, he was also an assassin who killed the head of Russia's secret police. His stories of repression published in *Underground Russia* moved William. He said they made his blood boil. Stepniak became a close associate of William, although Jane explained she did not know him personally. He is said to be the model for the Russian refugee who was cared for by *The Railway Children* in E. Nesbit's book. Edith Nesbit and her husband Hubert Bland were also active in the early Socialist movement, as co-founders of the Fabian Society, and were well aware of Stepniak and his history.

They would also have met Peter Alexeivich Kropotkin, a Russian prince and Cossack officer. He had been imprisoned in St Petersburg for spreading revolutionary propaganda, but had escaped to Switzerland. He came to Britain in 1886 and worked on *The Anarchist* newspaper. Jane and William both counted him as a friend, and he was frequently invited to speak in the coach house. Like William, he was not just a political radical, but was fascinated by the natural world, especially geology and map-making. Jane told one of her correspondents that she hoped 'you would like him as much as we all do'.[44] She looked forward to evenings with Kropotkin. He was a compelling storyteller.

The Hammersmith dining room rang with many tongues, many accents – the Viennese gilder and furniture maker Andreas Scheu comparing notes with George Lockner, a Socialist from Berlin. Sometimes Bruce Glasier would visit from the Scottish Land and Labour

League. William admired their club room in Edinburgh, which was 'decorated with fine taste and furnished with specially designed cane-bottom chairs'.[45] Glasier worked in an architect's office but had grown up on a croft. He was campaigning for land reform, and making links with radicalised industrial workers to create a distinctively Scottish programme.

It was often an oddly mixed crowd at Kelmscott House. Eleanor Marx, who was a frequent visitor, celebrated the international flavour of the meetings. As Karl Marx's daughter, she was a central figure in building Socialism in Britain while maintaining links with activists in Germany and France. She rivalled William in her energy, as a tireless leader of the Cause. Her biographer Rachel Holmes describes her 'sending off 600 pieces of correspondence since the morning, as well as cleaning the grate and getting food from Shepherd's Market' for dinner.[46] Unlike William, she did the double shift of woman's work at home, too. She was there beside William when he was heckled in the Holywell Music Room, and together they drafted the manifesto of the Socialist League. Rachel Holmes suggests she was 'Morris's perfect political partner'.[47]

We get a sense of the risks faced by all involved in the Cause when we see Eleanor standing shoulder to shoulder with William in court, to defend their Socialist League colleagues. The men had been arrested at a rally at Dod Street, Limehouse, on 20 September 1885, when police seized the League's banners, even as the crowd tried to disperse. A sentence of two months' hard labour was imposed on Lewis Lyons, a Jewish tailor, living in poverty in the East End of London. There were cries of 'Shame!' from his comrades. In the uproar, the police 'commenced an assault upon all and sundry'. Eleanor was singled out and hit hard. William tried to restore order, 'remonstrating at the hustling and thumping'. *The Commonweal* reported that they had 'rarely seen anything more brutal than the way in which two or three able-bodied men fell upon the author'.[48]

William was himself arrested for hitting a policeman and breaking his helmet.

William told the judge that he was hustled. 'When you are pushed,' he said, 'you naturally push again, but that is not resisting.' He also argued that the policeman 'was very rough and I am quite prepared to bring a charge of assault against him'. The judge let him go, after hearing William describe himself as 'an artist, and a literary man, pretty well known, I think, throughout Europe'.[49] William tried to make light of it to Jane. '[T]here was a funny scene in the police station where they charged me,' he said, 'the inspector and the constable gravely discussing whether the damage done to the helmet was 2d or 1½d.' But clearly he was rattled by the 'bullying and hectoring'.[50] He and his fellow Socialists had to face the fear of police interference and beatings every time they marched. As for Jane, she seems to have become resigned to the constant upheavals, the comings and goings of countless comrades, and the threat of William's arrest. Jane wrote to a friend a couple of years later that 'my husband is not in prison yet, but I should think it would not be long before he will have an opportunity of writing the longest poem ever penned by man'.[51] She could see that he would never stop pushing back.

Eleanor Marx and William both travelled to a major conference in Paris in 1889, where she acted as 'chief interpreter from French and German into English' and 'translated a long speech by an Italian professor on anarchism'. Eleanor had found that Hyndman, as leader of the Social Democrat Federation, fomented suspicion between home-grown radicals and refugees from Europe; he had, in her words, 'endeavoured to set English workmen against "foreigners"'.[52] William, on the other hand, was keen to meet fellow travellers from many different backgrounds.

Through Eleanor, William was introduced to Friedrich Engels. He was almost a generation older than William, and the two men never became close. Engels also hosted Sunday evening gatherings for like-minded Londoners, which often lasted until the early hours. It seems that William was not invited, never part of the inner circle, and of course these meetings clashed with his own Socialist League lectures. However, he did visit Engels' home in Kentish Town from time to time. The two men seem to have talked about their love of language as much as politics. William, roaming the room in his characteristic manner, spotted a copy of the Old Norse *Edda* on Engels' table, and shared some of his own verses from Sigurd. But William admitted to a colleague that Engels thought that the League was 'weak in political knowledge and journalistic skill'.[53] And, perhaps more to the point, William was not used to being told what to do. He bristled at being 'summoned to go up to Engels on Saturday morning on important business'.[54] This was an uncomfortable dynamic, unprecedented in William's adult life. He had rarely been treated as an amateur. Still, in Engels' eyes, William had a lot to learn. He and his comrades, Edward Aveling and Ernest Bax, were, according to Engels, 'the only honest men amongst the intellectuals – but men as unpractical (two poets and a philosopher) as you could possibly find'.[55]

Eleanor was also wary of William's naivety and misplaced enthusiasm. She was particularly concerned that 'Neither Morris nor Bax, nor any of our people know really what these Anarchists are.' She said they were being taken in by foreign members, 'half of whom I suspect to be police agents'.[56] The thread of anarchy that wound through many of their conversations concerned some of the more experienced activists. Eventually it led to a split between William and Eleanor. But while they worked together in the League, Marx contributed more than simply her political and intellectual clout. Like William, she wanted to win hearts as well as minds. Together they created entertainments, like the 'Art Evening' in Bloomsbury, with recitals of music and poetry, including William's reading of *The Passing of Brynhild*. Eleanor was a skilled actress and translator, and she put on a two-handed performance of a new play, *In*

Honour Bound, which focused on the limitations of conventional relationships.

Eleanor's style and strength appealed to May Morris. She revered Eleanor as a heroine of the new age, a woman who was unafraid of speaking her mind and living out her hopes. Marx was a little older, and far more worldly-wise than May, but they became friends. May loved this 'gifted and brilliant woman, who worked long and valiantly for Socialism'.[57] They organised a Christmas Tree Fund and a children's summer party. And they acted together in one of the first English performances of Ibsen's *A Doll's House*, for Eleanor's birthday at Christmas 1886. The staged reading was held in Eleanor's living room in her flat near the British Museum. The dark interiors were enriched with Morris embroideries and printed textiles, all eager presents from May. (It seems that William also helped Eleanor out with gifts of money, when she was in difficulty.)

For both women, Ibsen's interrogation of claustrophobic domesticity seemed to speak directly to their own lives. They wanted to find an alternative to the 'bourgeois property-marriage' that failed so many families. We do not know how much May knew at this stage about her own parents' relationships, and the difficulties faced by others in their circle. But from a distance, it is clear that many conventional marriages were a mirage – we can see Jane's infidelity and William's emotional reserve; Ned Burne-Jones's affair with Maria Zambaco and his ongoing intimacies with young women; Elizabeth Siddall's suicide; Emma Madox Brown's alcoholism. Even Rosalind and George Howard chose to live apart.

Eleanor set up home with her Socialist comrade Edward Aveling. They could not marry. He had a wife from whom he was separated but not divorced. Eleanor was prepared to ignore the expectations of the age, by living with him in a 'free union'. She helped to draft the Socialist League's manifesto clauses on marriage, which stressed that conventional marriage was in itself immoral, 'maintained as it is by its necessary complement, universal venal prostitution'. She did not look away from the harsh lives of the women on the streets. For Eleanor – and for William, too, as he showed in his later writings – there was a hopeful alternative: 'kindly and human relations between the sexes. Marriage would become a matter of simple inclination' and would be 'freed from mere theological views as to chastity'.[58]

Sadly, both Eleanor and May's chosen partners were unfaithful and manipulative, taking advantage of the women who loved them. Edward Aveling, who lived with Eleanor, was described by May as a 'strange little lizard of a man'. 'In money matters and sexual relations', Aveling was 'almost incredibly shameless, conscienceless and heartless.'[59] In the spring of 1898, Eleanor discovered that Aveling had married another woman, actress Eva Frye. On 31 March, Eleanor took her own life, drinking prussic acid. She was forty-three years old. Eleanor was found dead by her servant Gertrude Gentry, who wrote a few weeks later, 'Oh how we do miss her, and it nearly breaks our hearts when we go out into the garden and see all the flowers coming out that she was so fond of.'[60] Her death was a dreadful blow to May and all the extended Socialist family. It came at a time when May was mourning the loss of her own father, and facing the demands of maintaining his legacy, as Eleanor had cherished Karl Marx's memory and life's work.

*

Eleanor's death also brought into focus May's personal struggle to find a loving life-partner. Although May did not officially 'come out' into society, by the summer of 1878, when she was sixteen, May was asking her mother to accompany her to concerts and garden parties. Jane wrote to Crom Price about their socialising, and asked him, 'Do you happen to know a nice youth who would like to marry a very nice girl?'[61] But May was in no hurry to be married off. As she told the writer George Bernard Shaw towards the end of her life, 'I'm a remarkable woman – always was, though none of you seemed to think so.'[62] She did transcend the expectations of many of her friends, even those who were embedded in the world of radical politics, as she was.

When May first met Shaw, he was 'a raw, aggressive Dubliner'.[63] William offered to publish some of his writings in his Socialist newspaper, and Shaw became one of the regular guests at dinner after the Sunday lectures. May was then in her early twenties, and 'astonishingly handsome': she had a 'pure Greek profile, with hair short on her neck; wore a long dark fur-trimmed cloak and Tam O'Shanter cap of velvet'.[64] By Christmas 1885, she had taken over the management of the embroidery department of Morris & Co. from Jane. She was also thoroughly immersed in the activities of the Socialist League. May organised the little library and reading room for members, which she set up in one of the outbuildings in Hammersmith. She felt confident to step into her father's shoes when he was unable to give one of his Sunday evening talks. And as a fine musician, she ran the Socialist Choir on Friday nights.

There is a photograph of May playing her guitar, taken in the mid-1880s. She is standing outside Kelmscott House, resplendent in her long uncorseted dress and over-gown, with trailing sleeves. May had a taste for the dramatic, as we know from her performance of Ibsen with Eleanor Marx. In *A Doll's House*, May played opposite George Bernard Shaw. And we can see the electricity of their exchanged glances in photographs taken as they rehearsed for the League's entertainments.

Shaw was excited by May's frankness, and by her undeniable physicality. In his words, 'It happened that among the many beautiful things in Morris's two beautiful houses was a very beautiful daughter, then in the flower of her youth.' He described passing close to her late one evening, after one of the Sunday suppers: 'I was on the threshold of the Hammersmith house when I turned to make my farewell . . . I looked at her, rejoicing in her lovely dress and lovely self; and she looked at me very carefully and quite deliberately made a gesture of assent in her eyes.' Shaw called their intimacy a Mystic Betrothal. But there was no formal engagement, and this connection did not stop Shaw seeing other women. He said, apparently without irony, that he had 'no doubt that the thing was written in the skies for both of us.'[65]

For a while May enjoyed the excitement and freedom of their affair. But in the winter of 1885/6 she became tired of Shaw's teasing: 'You keep me in a constant state of terror by your sarcasms . . . you credit me with subtleties and coquetries,' when she always preferred plain talking.[66] May distanced herself from Shaw, and within a few weeks was becoming entangled with another young Socialist. Henry Halliday Sparling seemed even less promising. Shaw described Sparling unkindly as 'a tall slim immature man with a long neck on champagne bottle shoulders and not athletic'.[67] He seemed rather startled to have been taken up by May.

By the spring of 1887, May and Sparling were engaged to be married. They were short of funds and William refused to let them live together at Kelmscott House. Jane looked on with concern. She wrote to Rosalind Howard that 'they are as much in love as ever and no nearer marriage as far as one can see. May rightly insists on employment being found for her fiancé before she marries, and I strongly uphold her.'[68] To other friends, Jane was apparently more forthright. Sparling, she said, was 'stupid and helpless'. But there was very little she could do to prevent their marriage, as May 'has been brought up in the mill of socialism. She is 25 and has a will of her own.'[69]

As William and Jane's daughter, May understood how to make the best of it. In the late summer 1887, she was 'away at Kelmscott Manor alone learning cooking and how to live on a few shillings a week'. Jane was exasperated, telling Rosalind Howard, 'I have said and done all I can to dissuade her, but she is a fool and persists.'[70] The engagement dragged on. Eighteen months later, Jane was writing, 'May is not married yet . . . I don't mind confessing that I hate parting with her.'[71] Eventually, on 14 June 1890, May and Henry were married at Fulham Register Office. They spent their brief honeymoon at Kelmscott Manor, and then moved into their own home close to her parents at 8 Hammersmith Terrace. It was a good-sized eighteenth-century house, overlooking the river, with space for May's needlewomen and apprentices. They worked together in the drawing room, all dressed in white uniforms, spotlessly clean, and had their midday meal around May's dining table.

For Jane, the wait for the wedding was 'like a bad dream, but it must end sometime like all dreams'.[72] Sadly the marriage also came to an end within a couple of years. Shaw moved in with the new Mr and Mrs Sparling, partly drawn by his desire for May. He claimed that 'everything went well for a time in that *ménage à trois* . . . it was the happiest passage in our three lives'.[73] Jane had a very different perspective on her daughter's household: 'May's position is this, she has been seeing a good deal of a former lover, and made her husband's life a burden to him. He refuses to bear it any longer . . . they will go separate ways'.[74] Sparling and Shaw both left her.

By June 1894, May was alone in Hammersmith Terrace. Jane was 'in a heart broken condition . . . although we always expected some catastrophe or other in that direction, the blow is not less heavy'.[75] In 1898, May sued Sparling for divorce on grounds of desertion – even though he was in reality the injured party. She hoped that Shaw would finally recognise their 'Mystic Betrothal' but by the time May was divorced, Shaw had married someone else. May became 'the most pitiful personification of grief'.[76]

Many years later, Shaw walked back into her life. According to his account he simply knocked on the door of Kelmscott Manor and was welcomed inside. May was editing her father's Socialist lectures, and she asked Shaw to write on 'Morris as I knew him'. In this essay, Shaw established some of the most persistent myths about Jane. Even now they continue to shape perceptions of her as unnaturally quiet and almost inhuman in her beauty and bearing.

Shaw remembered his first sight of Jane in her drawing room at Hammersmith. He said that 'in her strangely beautiful garments, looking at least eight feet high, the effect was as if she had walked out of an Egyptian tomb at Luxor'.[77] She seemed to him resolutely un-English, otherworldly. This judgement of Jane, as strange and out of time, has been hard to shatter. Shaw amplified the impression that Jane was all surface and no depth with the comment that she was 'the silentest woman I have ever met. She did not take much notice of anybody, and none whatever of Morris, who talked all the time.'[78]

And so, almost certainly, did Shaw. Why would Jane interrupt their conversation? She had her own views, but she did not readily share them with impertinent young men. Shaw's snapshot of the dynamics between Jane and William has been accepted for nearly a century. It airbrushes the complexities of their relationship, denies their care and understanding of each other in private. In fact, it highlights the difficulties of carrying on personal, homely conversations in the semi-public space of their drawing room. The Sunday night activities were part of William's 'work'. And she had no affection for Shaw.

Jane's contempt for him, which Shaw recognised at the time, grew stronger as she watched him hurt May repeatedly. However, Jane picked her own means of expressing her dislike. One evening she simply 'pressed a second helping' of pudding on Shaw, knowing he was a vegetarian. He was hungry, and ate with relish: 'Then she said "That will do you good: there is suet in it".' Shaw did acknowledge that Jane 'had a certain plain good sense which had preserved her sanity perfectly under treatment that would have spoiled most women'.[79] Perhaps he recognised the neatness of her quiet revenge. She used her own domestic knowledge, her authority as housekeeper, her sense of humour and turned these against his undeniable appetite.

In the mid-1880s, when Shaw became a regular fixture in the Hammersmith coach house, Jane was often restless and insecure. Like many of William's friends, she felt unable to follow him into the Socialist fold, and could only watch from the sidelines as he became more and more enmeshed in the movement. Then in 1885 her role in the Firm was reduced. May became the head of the embroidery studio, teaching sewing skills to young women and establishing herself as an accomplished designer. Jane was still constantly stitching, as she worked on textiles for her own home and for clients. But she had to relinquish her position within the business. There was an unspoken suggestion that she was becoming redundant, as the Firm grew and May grew with it.

Increasingly even Jenny's care was taken out of her hands for long periods. Jane and William were constantly searching for ways to manage the epileptic attacks: Jenny was in a nursing home for the last months of 1885, and then they tried moving her to the little house at Merton Abbey, where William sometimes stayed overnight. The family hoped that she would prefer to be out of London. Her father could keep an eye on her. Jane wrote that her girl 'likes Merton, likes living there . . . she is interesting herself in the work and in the people and I have begun to hope that her life may be a useful one'.[80]

At Merton Abbey there were kitchen gardens, and a long border filled with 'tall blue larkspur and orange lilies' at midsummer. Jenny could watch the fabrics being washed in the Wandle, and dried in the open air between the almond trees and the willows. May described the prettiness of the process, on 'the bleaching ground, a meadow Father had set with poplars, how charming it looked when yards and yards of coloured chintz lay stretched on the grass!'[81] But this hope was short-lived. Jenny could not stay there long – soon she was on the move again, to Kelmscott Manor, to Malvern, back to a nursing home. The constant anxiety wore Jane's spirits, until she was told by her doctor that she 'must never live with Jenny while she is in her present condition': 'my brain is suffering from it', she said.[82] The ups and downs of Jenny's health punctuate all Jane's correspondence: she is a little better, a little worse, very ill, not at home.

Jane's New Year letter to Crom Price in January 1886 was more than usually glum, although she tried to laugh at her own middle-aged woes. 'I have not seen Ned for a long while, he has had shingles,' she said, 'and I have had mungles.' She went on, 'Perhaps you don't know what that is, it is made up of grief and temper and various aches.' Jane recognised that 'it may be called incurable at my age';[83] she was forty-six, and as Shaw had noted, 'her wonderful curtain of hair was touched with grey, and the Rossetti face ten years older'.[84] It was very hard to be condemned to age, when her face in Gabriel's portraits remained eighteen or twenty-five or thirty-five, or ageless as a goddess. But Jane would not resign herself to inevitable decline. Yes, William was gouty, May was engrossed in an unsuccessful love affair and Jane was 'making frantic efforts to keep myself warm'. Still, she looked around for fresh challenges; 'In spite of it all,' she said, 'I am learning to play on the mandoline, which is a great resource – it goes with May's guitar and we make noises together that please me, and I hope don't annoy others much.'[85] She was not afraid of the new, not bound by what she had been – as a working-class girl, as Gabriel's lover, as a careful mother. She was open to unexpected encounters.

Jane's unsettled moods were partly caused by the complications at home. But they were undoubtedly increased by her growing intimacy with the poet Wilfrid Scawen Blunt. She met Blunt in 1883, and by 1887, he was her lover. As with Gabriel, she carried on corresponding with him as a friend long after the spark had faded. He kept her letters, allowing us to hear her voice as she writes to him about family, pol-itics, books and travel. She sounds almost girlish at times, breathless and overwhelmed by this late-flowering emotional attachment. Jane is eager to see him; there is little of the melancholy and navel-gazing that she experienced with Gabriel. As she tells Blunt, shortly after they first met, 'I am often amazed at the capacity for enjoyment still left in me, and I have never felt it more strongly than in your house. I shall like to come again some day if you will have me.'[86]

*

Jane's affair with Blunt might appear vulgar or immoral. Perhaps it would be more accurate to say that she lacked originality. Blunt was one of the nineteenth century's great philanderers. His list of conquests, carefully recorded in his *Secret Diaries*, included at least a dozen aristocratic or artistic wives. In the *Dictionary of National Biography*, Blunt's article begins 'hedonist, poet and breeder of Arab horses'. And Elizabeth Longford's memoir of his life and career is titled *A Pilgrimage of Passion*. But Blunt was in many ways the ideal lover for Jane. He was charming and discreet, he sent her poems, and talked to her about his remarkable visits to Egypt. There were no histrionics, no 'if onlys', no declarations or catastrophes. Jane clearly enjoyed their flirtatious meetings and the passionate moments when they could be alone. But she also valued Blunt's conversation and concern for her. William was too preoccupied to take his time with Jane. Here was a man to flatter and arouse her. He made her feel fascinating, even though she was only one in a long line of beautiful women who had fallen for Blunt's bravado, his impetuous kisses, his delightful whisperings.

Blunt was a diplomat and an aspiring politician as well as a poet. He was known for his 'advanced' ideas; an anti-imperialist, he campaigned against British interventions in Egypt and Ireland. Parties at his home in Sussex could end with the guests camping out under the stars, skinny dipping and playing naked tennis. He chose his *amours* with care, preferring to dally with women who were attached to men he admired. His greatest catch was his wife Anne, daughter of Ada Lovelace and granddaughter of Byron. To marry into Byron's bloodline was thrilling for Blunt. He carried on a serious relationship, over several decades, with Minnie Pollen. Minnie was a beautiful, pious woman who modelled for Burne-Jones, and married John Hungerford Pollen. He was the artist who had helped to complete the Oxford Union murals, when Rossetti had given up and gone back to London. Blunt said that Minnie was 'the longest love of my life, and perhaps the strongest'.[87] He liked to hold civilised conversations with the husbands, while making love to their wives. And it eased his access to house parties and dinners where he could cast lingering looks at the hostess.

Blunt was attracted to Jane not just for her own famed beauty, but because of her connections to Gabriel Rossetti, whom he idolised, and William Morris, as a fellow writer and agitator. At times, in his diaries, it seems that his romance with Jane was merely a pretext for getting as close as possible to her previous lover and her husband. There is a strange pitying tone in some of his memories of their time together: 'There are moments', he wrote, 'when she is still a beautiful woman and I wish I had known her in the old days.'[88] A few years later he acknowledged:

> we have little really in common on the outside of things, and she is so silent a woman that except in the physical senses we never could have become intimate. As it is, though we have been so long on these terms, we have neither, that I can remember, ever called the other by our Christian names. I wonder whether it was so with Rossetti. The result is in any case a very excellent and worthy friendship, unbroken by a single unkind or impatient word.[89]

In hindsight, this does sound like a kindly, unencumbered romance, which allowed Jane some ease and pleasure at a time of strain in her family life.

Jane might have seemed quiet compared to many of Blunt's other lovers, but her letters to him are livelier, less measured, than some of her correspondence. Through these notes we can follow her thoughts from the mid-1880s. She sent him little bits of family news, and snippets to keep him amused. It is in one of her letters to Blunt that we hear a delightful story that overturns all notions of 'Jane as Goddess'. She was visiting friends in Wales, in 'a most romantic valley . . . I see different effects of sunlight every day'. Jane paints a delightful picture of 'taking their little baby in my arms, he is quite happy playing with my hair, and making gigantic efforts to swallow it all'.[90]

*

Jane was introduced to Blunt by her friend Rosalind Howard on a visit to Naworth in August 1883. Rosalind had an idea that Blunt would be excited to meet the woman to whom Rossetti addressed his *House of Life* sonnets, and that Jane might appreciate an affectionate tête-à-tête. Jane wrote to Crom Price on her return about the fun she had there with May. She told him that the visit 'cheered me up . . . there were wild expeditions into the wildest loveliest country, temperance gatherings at the Castle, political talk and flirtation'. She adds, as if she needs to clear her own conscience, 'the last I need not say, I had no part in'. She signed the letter, 'always your affect: and not despairing Janey'.[91] Blunt was more realistic about the flicker of connection with Jane: he noted in his diary that he 'spent a week in her company, and we made friends'.[92]

The following summer, in July 1884, Blunt visited Jane and William in Hammersmith. Blunt argued with William on 'his scheme of the universe . . . Still, we agree on many points.' He appreciated the 'nice old-fashioned garden full of flowers, pinks especially . . . the space is all made use of'.[93] Later that summer Jane wrote to him from Kelmscott Manor, telling him about the shape of the quiet days she arranged for her guests. Jane was on call constantly as hostess, welcoming a regular stream of visitors who valued their retreat into the Oxfordshire countryside. Jane tells Blunt,

> My house is beginning to fill, we shall have someone or other with us all the time. I am already very tired . . . which is odd, for the life is very pleasant here, we spend most of the day in the garden, or reading by the river-side where there are endless varieties of wild-flowers and strange plants that I never see anywhere else – books and work and chat make up the day.

She finishes with a sentimental hope: 'Farewell, send me a bit of heather if you write from Scotland – and think of me sometimes.'[94] Those last words reveal a great deal about Jane's emotional attachment. She rarely wrote to Gabriel in such a tender manner, needing reassurance, encouraging the continuation of their correspondence, hoping for a love token.

When she travelled to Italy with May early in 1885, Jane wrote regularly to Blunt, sending him 'a Valentine of violets', and a few weeks later, 'a bit of flowering thyme I picked close by the sea in my walk this morning'.[95] He was very much on her mind, partly because her 'time here is passed in walking and idling, for I must not read too much . . . I am used to reading in bed and find it difficult to sleep without, but this is strictly forbidden.' Instead, she told him, 'I think of you often and wish I could see you and talk with you and wander about these valleys with you – of course I know this is impossible and utterly foolish', but she was enjoying the experience of being loved again. As Jane wrote, that summer, 'It is re:awakening in me the old interest in such things which I had long ago thought dead within me. I thank you for all this with all my heart and shall be Ever your affect: friend.'[96] Even when she was at home, and simply walking in her garden in Hammersmith, she could not help 'thinking of the last time you were there – you seem to haunt that little plot'. Her eagerness spills over: 'When will you come in earthly form?' she asks. 'I shall be quite free for the next three afternoons – I should prefer Wednesday as being the earlier.'[97] Her letters to Blunt show a new side to her character, one that we barely see in the rest of her correspondence. Reading her dreamy, optimistic notes, we can reimagine her as the young woman who caught Rossetti's eye, the romantic teenager who won William's heart.

Jane's attachment also led her to become warmly involved in Blunt's political concerns. She was vocal in supporting his campaign for Irish Home Rule, especially when he was imprisoned for protesting at an anti-eviction meeting. Jane wrote in unusually outspoken terms to Jane Cobden about the injustice of the situation. She felt that William should be more focused on the Irish Question, and was upset that he saw it as a diversion from his Socialist activism. She told her friend that 'I taxed him this morning with not caring about Home Rule. He says he does as one of many things, but that there are more evictions in London in a week than there are in all Ireland . . . we can't convince each other.'[98] She also noted that Minnie Pollen and her husband John were trying to raise awareness of Blunt's poor treatment in prison. There may, of course, have been a certain amount of suspicion in William's mind when he saw Jane caught up with Blunt's cause. Even if he did not fully recognise the extent of Jane's attraction to this other man, he must have questioned why she became so heated in discussing Ireland, when she was far less animated when it came to politics closer to home.

Through her relationship with Blunt, Jane found an opportunity to speak her mind, to engage with ideas that took her into new territory, beyond William's art and Socialism. She was able to connect with an independent network of thinking women and men, including Jane Cobden and Minnie Pollen. And she used this intimacy as a chance to develop her own artistic skills, by designing a cover for Blunt's *In Vinculis*, a series of sonnets written in prison. She wrote to him excitedly, 'I don't know how it looks in colour. I fear it is not very like a shamrock.' Although it was only a slight design, with none of the flourishes created by William or May, it showed Jane's desire to be considered an artist in her own right. In the same letter she said she was inspired by Blunt to read Charles Montagu Doughty's *Travels in Arabia Deserta*, saying, 'It is delightful . . . we read it aloud on foggy days, and almost imagine ourselves in sunshine once more.'[99] Blunt brought a new vivacity to her life. She wrote to him as 'Caro mio' (my dear) and told him how 'I wish we could meet oftener when you are in England, but I know it is simply impossible – still it is such a very great pleasure when it does happen that the sweetness remains always.'[100] The following summer, Jane was still enamoured of Blunt, revelling in the unexpected joys he brought. In one brief note she said simply, 'I can't write you a letter my soul is in too great a turmoil, whether it will ever calm down again Heaven alone knows,' and ten days later, from Kelmscott Manor, she wrote, 'I move about in a sort of dream, as if a spell has been cast over me and the whole place.'[101]

*

Blunt was first invited to the Manor in October 1888. Jane was nervous about how he would find the backwater life: 'I fear though you will be bored as there is nothing to do but fishing.' She apologised in advance that the house was not as grand as his country estates, explaining that 'the place is barely furnished, it will be a sort of continual pic-nic.'[102] Blunt returned several times to the Manor, visiting again in the summer of 1889. He left a vivid account of his relationships with Jane and with William. In his diaries, Blunt recorded how 'at Kelmscott Manor . . . and at her house in Hammersmith, I found with Mrs Morris a quiet resting place of affection'. He said that this affair replaced 'in some measure what Minny [Pollen's] house had been to me. It was at this time that I first became intimate with Morris.'[103]

Like George Bernard Shaw, Blunt emphasised the emotional dis-tance between husband and wife. To his eyes, William appeared 'uniformly kind but without tenderness treating her in a certain off-hand way peculiarly his own. She was a loveable and noble woman, but he knew he had never touched her heart.'[104] Again, he seems to have underestimated the continued care that sustained Jane and William's relationship. Undoubtedly, Jane found in Blunt something that William could no longer offer: not simply physical attraction, but playfulness and suspense. And time. William was constantly being pulled in different directions, by his Socialist colleagues, his commitments to the Firm as designer and manager, and his own desire to write. There was also the continual strain of keeping Jenny safe. Blunt witnessed one of Jenny's seizures when he visited Jane in Hammersmith: 'The girl had fallen suddenly backwards, her head (a tragic circumstance) striking the panel of that well-known and most beautiful cabinet' which had been a wedding present from Burne-Jones.[105] To watch her daughter fitting and suffering a head injury, at the tea table, must have shaken Jane, and made the whole family increasingly reluctant to expose Jenny to criticism, to keep her sheltered within the domestic circle. Blunt called her 'this poor hardly sane girl'.[106] No one wanted her to be judged like that.

No doubt William's offhand behaviour towards Jane in Blunt's presence was also sparked by his unspoken jealousy. Blunt recognised this: 'What had taken place between her and Rossetti he knew and had forgiven. But he had not forgotten it.' Blunt went on, 'I used to think too that he suspected me at times (for her intimacy with me was not very explicable).' At least with Gabriel there was always the cover-story that Jane was his model. Blunt noticed that 'more than once, after having left us alone together ... [William] had returned suddenly on some pretence to the room where we were, blundering with loud footsteps and as if ashamed of a suspicion which he had not been able to control.'

But the lovers made sure that William found nothing untoward. 'And yet', as Blunt said, 'there was reason.' We can imagine William stomping up and down the old wooden stairs, 'like a Norwegian sea-captain', coughing as he entered the sitting room and hoping that he was mistaken.[107] Blunt was careful. And he was only too aware of the dangers of being caught out, especially in a house where 'every movement was heard plainly from room to room'.[108]

Kelmscott Manor, he found, was 'a romantic but most uncomfortable house with all the rooms opening into each other and difficult to be alone in'. Sometimes he slept downstairs, when there were lots of guests, and sometimes upstairs, in 'a passage room connecting the main house with the servants' quarters'. But for him, 'such midnight perils have always been attractive'. He enjoyed tiptoeing through to Jane's room 'at the end of a short passage at the head of the staircase'.[109] She would leave a pansy on the floor by his bed when she hoped he would come to her room – a symbolic *pensée*, 'think of me'. It was an echo of the flower-filled acrostic poem that he wrote to her, overflowing with 'Jacinths and jessamines and jonquils sweet' and ending with the question, 'In thy shut lips, what secrets! Who am I/ Should seek a sign at that sad sanctuary.'[110]

Blunt remembered how 'In the darkness of the night it was a ghostly place, full of strange noises.' The house resonated with memories. 'Rossetti seemed a constant presence there, for it was there that he and Janey had their time of love some 14 years before.' And now we start to get close to the root of his excitement, Blunt's reason for entering Jane's lonely bedroom, ardent, wordless: 'I came to identify myself with him as his admirer and successor.'[111] He loved Jane because Gabriel had loved her first. He even admitted this to her later, saying, 'I think I loved you for Rossetti's sake. He is the one modern poet who interests me.'[112]

Was Jane saddened by this admission? Did she too feel haunted by Rossetti's shadow and memories of old times? We know that Jane trusted Blunt with her remembrances of Rossetti. And she also trusted him with the letters that Gabriel had sent her – although Blunt returned them before she died. He described a summer visit to Kelmscott Manor, when 'we slept together, Mrs Morris and I, and she told me things about the past which explain much in regard to Rossetti.' She confessed, 'I never quite gave myself as I do now.'[113] How do we interpret this revelation by Jane? Perhaps she was simply reassuring Blunt that he was the better lover, that he stirred her, that she was able to relax into his embrace. No doubt he would have hoped to hear that. Perhaps Jane was always aware of Gabriel's insecurities, and was also conscious that she was taking Lizzie Siddall's place in his bed. These underlying anxieties might have made their love-making more complex. It might, more prosaically, be a matter of timing. In 1889, Jane turned fifty, and for most of her time with Blunt, she was almost certainly menopausal. She would no longer be so worried about an ill-judged pregnancy. She could not have risked bearing Gabriel's child, but with Blunt there was no fear that this calamity might happen. (Did she know that Minnie Pollen had miscarried Blunt's baby? Probably not, but Jane was wise enough to know that an affair carried greater danger for her than for her lover.)

Blunt's response to Jane's disclosure was unsympathetic. He saw the relationship from Gabriel's point of view rather than hers. He thought that if Jane had given herself more fully to Gabriel, 'he might not have perished in the way he did'.[114] He suggested that her hesitancy was selfish. We would see it now as self-preserving, maintaining her own boundaries in a passionate but fraught affair. Jane could not be responsible for Gabriel's peace of mind. She had to look after her own children, her own body.

Although Jane and Blunt remained close to the end of her life, after a few intense years the heat ebbed away. Blunt accepted this as part of the natural rhythm of intimacy. He noted in his diary in 1890 that he had 'spent the day yesterday with Mrs Morris, the last I fancy in a quite intimate way – She felt this and said it, and I did not contradict.' The end of the affair, if that is what it was, seems to have been muted rather than tumultuous. Blunt 'lunched with her and Jenny in their melancholy house' and then they went out together to see Ned Burne-Jones about a tapestry.[115]

But Blunt's friendship continued to carry Jane through times of depression, pain and worry. In the autumn of 1892, he recorded that 'Mrs Morris came to lunch with me, looking ill, poor woman. She tells me she is really threatened with "melancholia", that it has been gradually coming on . . . I did what I could to console her, and she told me that I had been a great comfort to her . . . She will perhaps come to Egypt in the winter.'[116] The Egyptian visit did not happen just yet, but Jane was evidently thinking about ways to manage her low spirits. She recognised that she was happier when she could escape the cold and damp of London: 'I should like warmth to be so great as to make me forget all but the present moment,' she wrote in her Christmas letter of 1892. 'From what you say I fancy that would be possible for me in Egypt, one day I hope to see it before I pass away from this earth.'[117]

*

Jane's intimacy with Blunt encouraged her to think about what was possible, how she might reinvent herself. William was constantly shifting from project to project – from priest to architect, from painter to poet, from business manager to Socialist leader. Jane could also see how far she had transformed her own life, through reading and music and travel. And friendships. We have already seen how she took up the mandolin as a cure for 'the mungles'. Surrounded by writers, she also could not resist telling stories to herself. She recognised that she might still have a lot to learn, but she told Blunt that 'I am always inventing plots for novels, and if I ever find myself anywhere in peace I believe I should develop them, but I daresay they would be bad and would not sell.'[118] This was not a throwaway line, or a bid for attention. Jane had mentioned it before. At Christmas 1888 she had sent an upbeat message to Blunt, telling him how 'The streets are full of violets and wallflowers in large bunches . . . I long to get away into the Country.' She went on, 'I shall have to find something to occupy my time if I keep as well as this. I can think of nothing but novel writing, one of my sisters-in-law suggested standing for Poor Law Guardian. I wonder which I should do worse.'[119]

The idea of standing for election was not as far-fetched as it sounds. In 1875, Martha Merington had been elected in Kensington. Since then, other women had served as Poor Law Guardians. They helped administer the local welfare system, visiting workhouses, schools and asylums, providing support to the unemployed and homeless.

With Jane's own childhood experience of life of the fringes of poverty, the role might have suited her more than she liked to admit. Certainly, the Unitarian minister Moncure Conway, one of Jane's neighbours, remembered that they had worked together to 'clear away some of the evils of Hammersmith'.[120] Presumably this refers to her attempts to relieve the needy families that were very visible – and audible – near their home. Kelmscott House was just a few doors away from a 'poor overcrowded quarter between the town and country'. May described how the children – 'ragged mites from the neighbouring riverside slum' – would play on their doorstep, shouting and squabbling. They were a great distraction to William, 'driving home the galling differences between man and man', while he prepared his Socialist lectures. He was only too aware of the absurdity and privilege of his situation, as he went outside to 'beg them to give him a little peace.'[121]

William knew that his attempts to change the children's lives for the better were often theoretical and long-term. His sister Isabella Gilmore, however, was tackling the problems in much more immediate ways. It was probably Isabella who suggested that Jane become involved in local committees – she was an ordained deaconess in the Church of England, and saw at first hand what needed to be done. In her own way, she was just as radical as William in using her influence to transform lives. As William said, 'I preach Socialism, you practise it.'[122]

Through her quiet persistence, Isabella created a sisterhood who acted as nurses, housing officers and counsellors to the poorest families. They dealt with domestic violence, tackled destitution and disabilities. Isabella's projects did not appeal to Jane. The deaconesses were tied to the institution of the Church, while her own efforts to assist the families in her area were private. But Jane could see the value in women using their talents and education outside the home. After all, her own daughter was marching, performing and speaking out for Socialism, as well as running a successful branch of the family business. Jane was enthusiastic about her friends who chose to put themselves forward in more formal roles. In her New Year letter to Jane Cobden in 1889, Jane said, 'I am so glad you are standing' for election to the newly formed London County Council.[123] Through these limited channels, at city or parish level, women were establishing footholds in public life. And they were demonstrating that they could do the jobs – as administrators, campaigners, fundraisers, legislators – on a local scale. Jane Cobden won her seat to represent Bow and Bromley. However, in William's letter to Jenny telling her about their friend's success, he was also only too aware of the resistance to women taking their place in politics: 'Yes, Jane Cobden has got on to the County Council; though I suppose there will be a fight about whether she and the other lady will be allowed to sit on it.'[124] As the first women to put their heads over the parapet, Jane Cobden and Lady Sandhurst were targeted by Tories and anti-suffragists who complained constantly until both women were unseated. But it was a start. Electors had voted for them. Jane Cobden had proved her professionalism.

In later years, when the suffrage debates became much more heated, Jane admitted, 'I can't make up my mind about our vote.'[125] This might sound strange, coming from a woman whose home was a meeting place for radicals of all backgrounds. She acknowledged that 'it is of course absurd that I should not have a vote while many a drunken working man has one.' Still, she hesitated to give her support to the Suffragists:

> I object to these noisy women having any increased power because they only want to reverse things and spitefully trample on the men. I want both sexes to have equal rights when the women are better educated companions and housekeepers.[126]

These arguments go right back to the heart of William's political thinking. It was essential to put education first, in order to change the status quo. As he said in 1883,

> I want an educated movement . . . the discontented must know what they are aiming at when they overthrow the old order of things . . . it is all the more necessary that the revolution . . . should be, not an ignorant, but an intelligent revolution.[127]

Democracy would only work with an electorate that understood who and what they were voting for. And he fundamentally mistrusted the parliamentary system. William did not believe that MPs would support the root-and-branch change that he believed was needed. The 'Votes for Women' agitation looked to him like a distraction. And he was not alone in this.

Eleanor Marx and Edward Aveling had pointed out the limitations of the Suffrage campaigns in their essay on 'The Woman Question', published in 1886. They said that it was a 'perfectly just aim', and that there were many 'excellent and hard-working folk' who were campaigning to change the political landscape for women. But it was only one piece in a complicated jigsaw. The Suffragists were mostly of 'the well-to-do classes' and they expected the vote only to be offered to women of property, like themselves. This would never 'get down . . . to the bedrock of the economic basis . . . of society itself'.[128] As Marx and Aveling explained, 'we will support all women, not only those having property, enabled to vote . . . Without larger social change, women will never be free.'[129] As Jane said, many years later, 'I detest the Spankhursts and all their works.'[130] In her opinion, their violent protests did nothing to further the cause of women's freedom. They undermined the hard-fought efforts of campaigners like Millicent Garrett Fawcett, who insisted that women were responsible, rational, useful in public life. It seems that Fawcett knew Jane and William, but sadly there are no surviving letters to throw more light on their shared opinions.

*

This gap in the story reminds us that there are still many unanswered questions about Jane's life. We have to work from snippets, the relics that were preserved, or pick our way through the self-confident memories of outspoken men, to find fragments of her voice. Can we believe what Blunt said about Jane? Should we listen to George Bernard Shaw?

Very occasionally we can get close to Jane – there are a few intensely personal objects that almost let us read her thoughts. In the late 1870s and 1880s, she made at least four little books, filled with words and images. They appear to let us see what mattered to Jane, as she carefully created these small manuscripts. They were, in some ways, similar to the calligraphy projects that William worked on. Like him, she was copying cherished poems and proverbs onto neat folded pages, and decorating the borders with her own designs. But the results look very different. She chooses her own quotations, showing her extraordinary range of reading. And the pen and ink decorations have a remarkable graphic quality, much more abstract than William's flowering tendrils. Some of them seem closer to the geometry of Vanessa Bell's art. They are startling, intimate objects. And yet, they create as many puzzling questions about Jane as they solve. Perhaps this is why they have rarely been studied. Only Johnanna Amos has written at any length about them. Her essay on 'Meaning and "Material Reality": Jane Morris's Keepsake Books' was published in 2019. No other studies have tried to unpick their making and significance.

We know that the first book was made as a gift for Rosalind Howard in 1878. It was inscribed 'Oneglia' and was probably a New Year present created while Jane was staying near the Howards in Italy. Rosalind Howard's book is the least remarkable. The texts are conventional, well-loved extracts, including Shakespeare and Tennyson. Jane embellishes 'Ariel's Song' from *The Tempest* with harebells and a trailing blue border. It is the sort of thing that many leisured ladies might exchange with friends, vaguely pretty but not revealing much about the character of the maker. It feels very 'safe'. Perhaps Jane was not sure of Rosalind's tastes, and how she might be judged or found wanting.

But the other three keepsake books are more of a mystery – we know that they were found among May's papers when she died. But for whom were they originally designed? And what do they reveal about Jane's way of looking at the world? They are beautifully bound, one in ivory vellum, another in olive green velvet, and the third in red leather tooled with gold leaf. Jane has used silk on the inside covers of this book, also richly gold. Each one suggests a different purpose, perhaps a different recipient.

The little red book seems to contain several individual manuscripts bound together, including one dated Christmas 1885. Jane has copied out an extract from Swinburne, celebrating the birth of the Messiah, whose 'presence is alive in the unseen air'. The decorations are made in red pencil and black pen strokes, highlighted with gold ink. Jane has set her initials within an outline that resembles either a shamrock or a pansy flower – both had associations with Blunt. As we turn the page, we see a bell-shaped flower. A line from Keats's poem 'To a Friend who sent me some Roses' is written on each petal. And opposite that, a row of little cherub faces, very simple, above a verse from an old French Christmas carol, 'Dieu parmy les pastoureaux', about the baby in the manger. Already it is clear that Jane feels comfortable quoting modern poems alongside songs from long ago and far away.

Jane includes the same French carol in another little folded manuscript bound inside the green cover. She pairs this with a 'Hymn for the Nativity' by Ben Jonson, and a joyful acclamation offering hospitality and greeting the 'heavenly King': 'Welcome all and make good cheer/ Welcome all another year/ Welcome Yule'. This little verse floats in a cloud above a string of cherubs holding hands and drifting skywards, over her distinctive flecked pen-and-ink background. Jane anchors the double-page spread with a monogram JM, formed into a golden crown. It is a charming design, rather naïve but almost humorous, like a children's book illustration.

These Christmas books are relatively straightforward in terms of content and design, even if we do not know who Jane had in mind when she made them. The little ivory bound book is also, on the surface, a simple structure. It was conceived as an Alphabet, with texts arranged according to the first letter of their first line. The design is minimal, with the header letters picked out in gold, and embellished on occasion with restrained decorative touches. The big Z on the last page, for example, has rings dangling from its tail, and tiny stars and golden dots between the zigzags. The centre of the large V is filled with lines, like the rungs of a ladder. And the O becomes a dynamic ring encircling three little mottoes, including 'Our last garment is made without pockets' and '*On ne dit rien – mais on est ensemble*' – 'We say nothing – but we are together'. Much of the excitement of the design comes from her experiments with layout, the texts pointing in differing directions, some slanting across the page, some sitting in little corners, or almost disappearing into the gutter. The quotations are interspersed with golden ruled lines, spirals and dots.

As for the content, this seems to have been a personal object, made for Jane's own contemplation. It looks as if she added to it over several months or years, which partly accounts for the changes in handwriting. It is likely that she showed it to Blunt; when he sent her the acrostic verses in June 1893, he offered to 'write them in your white book'. But they are not there under J. Instead she copied out a sixteenth-century French verse, also dwelling on flowers and their meanings: '*J'aime la belle violette/ L'oeillet et la pensie aussi*' – 'I love the beautiful violet/ The carnation and the pansy too'. Many of the texts she chose are melancholic, seeming to mourn lost love, emphasising patience: '*Chi dura, vince*' – 'Those who endure, win'. Her inclusion of Tennyson's *In Memoriam* is of course commonplace; it was a favourite poem for many of Jane's generation. But there are other, less obvious quotations that speak to her situation, even from Tennyson: 'Give her the glory of going on, and still to be'. And then there are the two extracts from Swinburne's poem 'A Dead Friend': 'What may sorrow send/ Toward thee now from lips that said/ "Friend"?' And simply, '*Memor et fidelis*' – 'Remembrance and Faithfulness'.

For all those who criticised her quietness, Jane could remind herself of the motto *Faire sans dire* – 'Do without speaking'. For those few who recalled where she had been born, and how far she had come, she included quotations from Dante and Newman, Chaucer and Langland, Gabriel and Christina Rossetti, Heine, Spenser and Suckling. There was even a smattering of Greek. We see flashes of her self-assurance and self-knowledge. We can imagine her resolve as she thought of Gabriel, or Blunt – or William – and wrote out the lines from Landor:

> Proud word you never spoke, but you will speak
> Four not exempt from pride some future day
> Resting on one white hand a warm wet cheek
> Over my open volume you will say
> 'This man loved me'! then rise & trip away.

It was good to remind herself that 'This man loved me'. There are other phrases which spoke to her practicality and strengths: '*Ayons le Coeur et l'esprit hospatiliers*' – 'Have an hospitable heart and spirit', and 'Hospitality is the most important part of Divine worship'. And then suddenly Jane revealed her love of the absurd, as she transcribed '*Petit Bo-Bouton/ A perdu ses moutons*' – 'Little Bo-Peep has lost her sheep', and '*Questo piccolo porco/ E endato al mercato*' – 'This little piggy went to market'. The Italian nursery rhyme was tucked in next to more solemn sayings: '*Que le Coeur fait parler*' – 'If the heart could speak', and '*Qui n'a liberté, n'a rien*' – 'If you do not have liberty, you have nothing'. She seemed happy inscribing French or Italian quotations, moving easily from one language to another. This little book demonstrates how far Jane had travelled from her birthplace in St Helen's Passage, almost better than anything else that has survived. It shows her willingness to experiment with new forms of self-expression and to relish her love of poetry. It was also an opportunity to remember the loss of Gabriel and other friends, through mourning verses. There are even some passages that seem to look forward to the hope of an afterlife, although only in the most general terms. There is little here that is overtly pious. Instead, Jane chose open-ended, vaguely Christian commemorative verse.

Several of the other manuscripts are more complex and strange. One of the little books bound in the red leather cover contains conventional extracts – from Ruskin, Wordsworth, Tennyson, Arnold – as well as a dozen shorter mottoes under the title 'Posies'. These are tokens of affection: 'Kepe Faythe tille Dethe', and 'Bel 'ame, bel 'amy/ Fayre soule, good frend'. This is a collection destined, it seems, for a lover. Jane includes the declaration, 'God's will is done & I have mine,/ My heart at rest in having thine', and 'Knotts of love Are knit above'. These little lines are written out in various styles, some in Jane's usual handwriting, and some in a more formal Gothic text. And they are placed at right angles to the rest of the quotations.

On the last page, one of the short extracts is incorporated into the border, each word placed within its own red pencil ring. This is a carefully designed object, which integrates the text and images into a pleasing whole. The images do not illustrate the words, but there is a sense of balance and visual delight, an intention to the design, even though it is limited to black, red and gold.

The first and last pages are highly decorative. On one sheet Jane has created a series of interlocking circles, filled with tiny flowers, teardrops and butterflies. The rest of the page is ornamented with little gold 'x's and twirls; we have already seen these in the Alphabet book. She develops an idiosyncratic technique for the border, using small dashes and hatches of black pen. This gives a sense of gentle texture and depth as she creates a breathing space around each line of red pencil. It is almost as if she is drawing stitches on the surface of the paper, as she would with embroidery. Jane is working with a pen rather than her needle, but with the same delicacy. On the inside pages there are decorations, drawn like ribbons, placed across the page horizontally and diagonally. We find another effect – borrowed from stitching instead of traditional pen skills – in the green-bound book, where the edges of the pages are ornamented with running patterns that look like fringing, or loops of thread, or cross stitch, or French knots.

The opening pages of the red keepsake book are even more unexpected in their style. They bear no resemblance to William's organic forms, or May's soft textiles. What should we make of the circles within circles, grids and repeated 'x's that Jane has created? They are very much her own visual vocabulary. The opening page is extraordinary, with each short quotation written on a spiral, whirling like a comet, tumbling down through a void punctuated with flowers. One reads, 'Fair, kind and true'; another, 'Patience lighteneth what Heaven forbids us to undo'. Like many of the quotations, Jane seems to focus on her choice of who to love, and her recognition that she will have to bear the consequences.

But then what about the initials on the second page – ACS, AE and SBS? The first seems to relate to Algernon Charles Swinburne, an old friend of Jane and William, but the others are less clear. They do not seem to relate to any of her obvious friends. We know that Jane stayed close to Swinburne after Gabriel's death. Jane offered to introduce Blunt to him, hoping the two poets would find each other amusing. She later described one memorable lunch with Swinburne; he was putting 'so much action into his reading and things roll off the table making noises, all the same we enjoy our visits, he is so friendly'.[131] The romantic nature of many of the quotations makes it impossible that Jane intended to give the little book to Swinburne. So why include this reference to him? Does it help us to understand the repeated motifs of crosses, circles and the unusual little shapes – the chalices and swirls? These seem more than simply decorative. They begin to look like symbols to decode, a puzzle that Jane has set. It is odd to think that Jane might have incorporated esoteric signs into her manuscripts. But it is hard to explain these away. They seem so deliberate, placed on the ribbon decorations, contained within the borders.

The symbols are hard to decipher at this distance. There are more, larger examples within the green velvet binding, given a page to themselves, as if challenging us to understand their meaning. They include a solar cross, and something that resembles either the Greek letter Φ (phi) or a butterfly. Attempts to decode them are still speculative, and lead us down rather odd paths. The symbols have some elements in common with the alchemical shorthand developed in the Renaissance. But the gold dots might equally suggest a link to the so-called 'celestial alphabet' that was also in use from the sixteenth century in arcane circles; it was designed to contact angels. We know that W. B. Yeats, who sometimes joined the meetings at Kelmscott House, was a member of the Hermetic Order of the Golden Dawn, an occultist offshoot of the Freemasons. This Order based its rituals on a collection of manuscripts written in code, which certainly bears some resemblance to Jane's notation. Or perhaps she and Blunt made up their own playful cipher, their alphabet of desire? He certainly told one of his mistresses that she should not refer directly to their lovemaking in her letters, but merely indicate it with an 'x'. Maybe that accounts for the profusion of little crosses in Jane's manuscripts. At present, we cannot say for certain. What we do know is that Jane was far cleverer than her critics would ever acknowledge, and she still evades our attempts to pry into her most personal life.

In creating her little books, Jane produced beautiful works that were utterly original, and set apart from the designs made by the rest of her family. They might only have been on a small scale, and, of course, they had to be constructed within the confines of her domestic duties. But they were distinctively hers. The spareness of her style and many of her motifs, particularly the interlocking circles and other geometric forms, have more in common with early twentieth-century art. In some respects, they seem to foreshadow the books and textiles of the Bloomsbury group. They make us reconsider our assumptions about Jane, encouraging us to look at her as an experimental artist.

*

Jane's desire to try new things never faltered. In this, she and William understood each other. But Jane also saw the world differently from him. She wanted to continue exploring Southern Europe, for instance, while he was drawn to the North. And so we see her journeying again to Italy in the early spring of 1887, going a little further, meeting new friends, keeping company with Rosalind Howard, just Jane and Jenny and a maid (whose name is not recorded). Ostensibly, they were travelling in the hope that the 'complete change would benefit Jenny'. But Jane was also loving the 'pure warm sunshine . . . I shall get young once more if only I can stay long enough.'[132]

There in Rome she saw things that William and his friends never saw – including Ned Burne-Jones's massive mosaic designs. Ned had always hoped to work on a public scale. He once exclaimed, 'I want big things to do, and vast spaces, and for common people to see them and say Oh! – only Oh!'[133] He achieved his dream with a commission from the new American Church in Rome, St Paul's Within-the-Walls. Jane visited on several occasions, so that she could see it 'by all lights now, and it shows splendidly among the best early things'.[134] Ned wanted it to be as fine and stern and legible as the most beautiful medieval mosaics in Ravenna, and clearly Jane thought he had succeeded.

Only the first section of the mosaic had been finished when Jane was there. This was the *Heavenly Jerusalem* in the apse above the main altar. Ned wanted to show a vision of Christ in Glory, with a rainbow at his feet, and the water of life flowing down towards the congregation. On either side stood the archangels, ready for Judgement. It was everything Ned had hoped for. In many of his works he tried to recreate the sensation of heaven 'beginning six inches over the tops of our heads, as it really does'.[135] And here it was. Sadly, he was never able to travel to Rome to see it for himself. But Jane saw it instead, and loved it. She could encourage him, knowing that the great project did indeed rival the sacred art he had revered since he was a young man, just setting out.

Here in Rome Jane could linger and look with understanding and friendly eyes on Ned's work. She could step aside from the rumbling arguments among the Socialists in her cold coach house. She could let May worry about embroidery orders, her apprentices and the colour matching. Jane felt warm. She could drive out to the Campagna or listen to Vespers in St Peter's. And she could reassure her old friend that his angels, 'their faces sweetly pale', looked well in their new home.[136]

Chapter 13

Into the Garden, 1890–1896

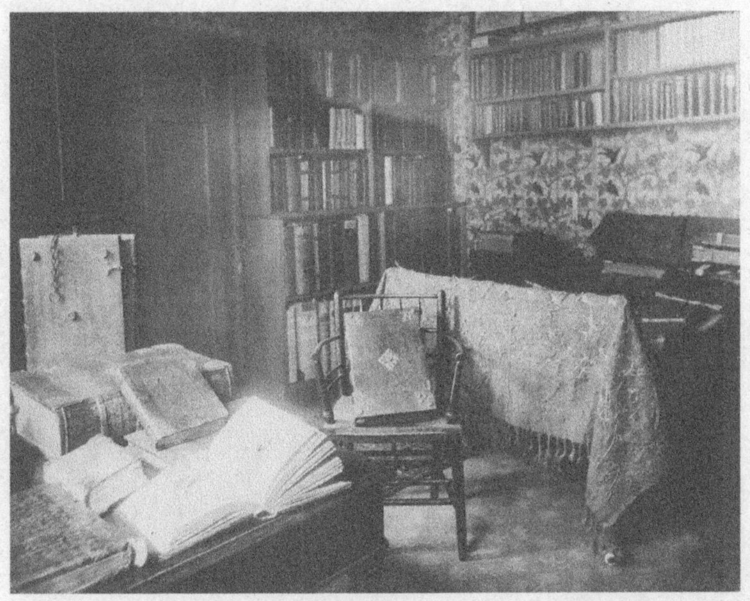

Emery Walker, *William Morris's bedroom at Kelmscott House, Hammersmith*, 1896, William Morris Society, London

'This has been a jolly world to me and I find plenty to do
in it.'[1]

William was walking slowly round the garden in Hammersmith, with
an old Socialist comrade. They had fallen out, and made up, and now
both hoped for better days. It was mid-July 1896, and William was
far from well. But here, under the apple trees, he was able to rejoice
in the work he had completed and look forward to a new journey.

William's home and garden were never entirely private spaces.
He and Jane entertained, debated and worked here, showed clients
around and welcomed friends. But their house in Hammersmith had
become more talked about and scrutinised in recent years. William
was subjected to a spate of interviews in the 1890s. He was a celebrity,
and a puzzle. The Socialist-Poet. The shop-keeper who was willing to
be arrested in his fight against capitalism. The medieval man in the
modern world, with his 'round and genial thirteenth-century face'.[2]
The articles were filled with details of the decoration of Kelmscott
House, as William led his guests from the hall into the dining room,
and then into his study. Often the conversation ended in the garden,
with William offering cigarettes and smoking his own beloved pipe.

Jane stayed out of view when the journalists arrived. But those who knew the family better occasionally saw the quiet companionship between husband and wife. One young friend 'went up to the drawing room to say goodnight'. He interrupted Jane and William 'playing at draughts, with large ivory pieces, red and white. Mrs. M. was dressed in a glorious blue gown, and as she sat on the sofa, she looked like an animated Rossetti picture, or a page from an old MS of a king and queen.'³ So often, visitors were surprised by the strangeness of Jane. Her queenliness seemed somehow at odds with the homely setting.

Most of the writers were struck by the easy way the family lived with beauty. The house was filled with extraordinary sights: the Dürer prints in the entrance hall, the antique rugs on the floors and hanging from the ceiling, room after room decorated with 'more old oak, more quaint china and pottery, more beautiful pictures . . . The art treasures are arranged with a quasi-carelessness.'⁴ One journalist pretended that the dining room looked, at first glance, like a kitchen with a large wooden dresser and a massive scrubbed table. To this observer, it seemed unusually informal. But Jane never hid her great dining table under a cloth; its bare wood was always on show. George Bernard Shaw commented on it when he visited. This was an innovation, copied by William's admirers. The young men of the Century Guild, for example, 'all had their meals together at an ancient oak table, without a cloth of course; in the middle stood a plaster figure and four bowls of bay which . . . were covered in dust.'⁵ This lack of attention to the details, such a failure of basic housekeeping, would never have been allowed by Jane.

William's work room especially fascinated the writers. Here was a man who made a living as a designer of highly patterned textiles, rich stained glass, and yet his own space was almost austere. In his sunny room with a view of the river, 'there was no carpet on the floor, no curtains at the window', just 'an antique carved oak chest, two or three easy chairs, and a large plain deal table'.⁶ And books.

Books everywhere; on the floor-to-ceiling shelves, piled on the tables, and tucked into William's satchel. As Jane explained to a friend, it was hard to find space on the walls to hang another painting, 'books being our chief pictures as you know'.[7]

William's love of books was intense. A visitor could see that the old volumes 'are in daily, hourly use', to be held and studied.[8] He was excited by the physicality of books, the way they felt in the hand. He began putting greater effort into the design of his own writings as they were published. He was very pleased with *The Roots of the Mountains* when it came out in 1889. The publisher used one of William's own chintzes for the binding, and they worked together to get the typography to his liking. The little book made him so happy that 'I am any day to be seen huggling it up'.[9] This is a wonderful image of William, embracing his book. His response is immediate, almost sensual.

*

William's work touches us because it is direct. His writings, his designs, his speeches glow with love for the beauty of the world. He applied the same principles to all works of art, from a single volume of poetry to a row of houses. He was once asked: "Cannot one have a well-designed cheap house?" The answer was clear: "No you cannot, because the essence of good building is that there should be generosity – a superabundance of material. It may be plain, but it must be good, and if you skimp your material, you will ruin your article."[10] Beauty requires generosity, an ability to share and grow.

William did not value ostentation or luxury. But he celebrated the way that living things intertwined, supported each other, created a network of visual pleasure. In his designs, William played with layering: *Rose and Thistle* (1882); *Blackthorn* (1892) for the early spring, woven together with fritillaries, water avens and violets; *Pink and Poppy* (1880); *Jasmine* (1872) for summer with an underpinning of hawthorn leaves and flower clusters. Sometimes the simplest pleasures, as he showed, were the most satisfying. He loved his gardens, and the regular blossoming and fruiting and feasting. Gardens seemed to him to be the ideal of beauty, always renewing, delightful in their colour and movement, their balance of order with wildness, their textures, scents, rustlings and birdsong.

William mourned the loss of the untouched spaces of Nature, as people built indiscriminately. Each new house takes away, as he said, 'a little piece of the flowery green sward, a few yards of the teeming hedgerow'. In its place, we are left with 'arid and pretentious little gardens and cast-iron horrors of railings'.[11] Where houses are needed, then both the buildings and the gardens should be in tune with the land around. Wattle, stone, woven willow or hazel, oak planks and hawthorn hedges: these can be used to create garden structures on a human scale, 'made to look like so many flower-closes in a meadow, or a wood'.[12] And the secret, in his eyes, to lovely garden design is 'to fill up the flower-growing space with things that are free and interesting in their growth, leaving Nature to do the desired complexity, which she will certainly not fail to do'.[13]

William and Jane always took their gardens seriously. They cared for these green spaces, because the gardens fed into their work and brought them great joy, year after year. As May wrote, her father 'noted every turn of a leaf or attachment of a stem . . . nothing in the open air escaped him'.[14] Ever since they built Red House, this had been their way. When Webb had surveyed the site in Kent, he had counted over eighty trees, many of them useful, fruitful: hazel and holly, oak, ash and yew, apples, cherries, pear, plum and quince. He constructed Red House so that the trees would be left standing, to soften the new bricks. Apples would drop through the windows at harvest-time. Now, Jane saw that their concern was necessary, because it was rare. Many of their neighbours gave no thought to the stewardship of their land. For her, 'it is curious to see the want of reverence in so many people about trees'. They mattered to her: 'I almost cry when ever we lose one by age or accident.'[15]

Jane and William planted for beauty and for use. They recognised the importance of traditional varieties of flowers, not just because they were less artificial, but because they fed the bees. As William explained, 'be very shy of double flowers, choose the old columbine' and the single sunflower, with its 'centre clogged with honey and beset with bees and butterflies'.[16] Even at the factory in Merton Abbey, William saw how gardens could make a difference to his employees. The men and women who worked there could take time to tend the flower borders and vegetable patches, to plant and to prune. They produced marvellous asparagus beds, and armfuls of blossom that William would bring back on the train to Hammersmith. He knew that the other commuters thought he looked odd, but he did not mind.

At Kelmscott Manor, their kitchen garden was wonderfully productive and lovely to walk through. William was happy to see 'the raspberry-canes which Giles [the gardener] has trellised up neatly, so that they look like a medieval garden'.[17] They ate their own strawberries and gooseberries, melons and cucumbers. Jane joked with Crom Price that 'we are thinking of trying vegetarianism', adding, 'but not until after your visit.'[18] In the summer, the garden did indeed seem like 'part of the house', as William desired.[19] The doors were open, so friends could wander in and out as they wished. Jane enjoyed her *al fresco* meals in Italy, their sense of informality and warmth. At Kelmscott, she hoped to recreate the same calm, easeful hospitality: 'We have tea out of doors most days,' she told a friend; 'in fact lazyness reigns supreme.'[20]

The birds kept them company as they sat outside. Jane happily wrote about 'the robins singing at my window, they are almost deafening – we feed them and they follow us about the garden and perch on our chairs.'[21] Her husband knew their ways, their calls, and 'watched every bird on the wing with keen alert eye'.[22] He wrote to Jenny about fieldfares and their migrations, the starlings as they gathered at sunset, and the call of the rooks. One summer morning, he tells her 'the garden is full of bullfinches which are pretty fat dears'.[23] He loved the blackbirds especially, even when they woke him at four in the morning. In one letter he described 'the garden, it seems to me its chief fruit is – blackbirds. However they have left us some gooseberries, and I shall set to work this morning to get some before their next sit-down meal'.[24] And William celebrated the bright eyes and mottled plumage of the thrushes in one of his most popular printed cottons, *Strawberry Thief*, drawn in 1883. His designs were alive with birds, and the promise of their movement and song – from the very early stained glass and wallpapers, to the massive tapestries woven by young men sitting three abreast at Merton Abbey.

The call of the cuckoo, heard at breakfast time at Kelmscott, or 'the robins hopping and singing all about the garden' marked the changing seasons for William and Jane.[25] Their letters are full of hope as they describe the richness of the summer trees, or the first signs of spring. When Jenny was poorly, her father would tell her about the transformations he saw on his walks around Kelmscott: 'The fields are all butter-cuppy,' he wrote in the early summer:

> The elms are mostly green up to their tops: the hawthorn not out, but the crabs beautiful, and also that white-beam with the umbelliferous flowers . . . The cherry tree near the arbour opposite my window is a mass of bloom. The heartseases are beautiful.[26]

For Jane, the arrival of warmer weather was even more significant. She was almost housebound in the smoggy London winters, unable to go out in the evenings, and often struggling with rheumatism. She told a friend that 'we hear of little besides influenza and frozen pipes'.[27] That is why she tried to spend the colder months in Italy. She did not mind crisp clear days in London, and wrote with unexpected gusto about striding along the Thames, watching 'the ice floating past' and then returning home 'half frozen to a good fire and thaw myself and become happy for the rest of the day'.[28] But 'the fog and damp are more than I can bear out-of-doors'.[29]

In Italy, Jane was able to relax and see friends. She did not need to worry constantly about Jenny, and so her life there was much more sociable. On her visit to Bordighera in 1892–3, she spent time with George MacDonald and his family, and met 'a good many people in the Hotel of a frivolous and amusing kind'.[30] There was never much time for frivolity with William: his idea of relaxation was just a different sort of work, moving from weaving to writing poetry, or from speech writing to designing a new cotton print. He was often up early. He explained that if he began at four o'clock in the morning, he could 'get half a day's work finished before breakfast'.[31] It could be very wearing to live with someone so obsessively active. In Italy, Jane caught a glimpse of a different sort of life. The people she met had a leisured existence softened by poetry and art. Their world was charming, but not passionate, not driven, not like William with his compulsion to make beauty, to change society, to rise at dawn to tackle the next challenge.

Jane was particularly glad to be introduced to two sisters who were excellent musicians, 'which is an intense pleasure to me'.[32] She was even able to join in with the elaborate *tableaux vivants* orchestrated by the MacDonalds in the Christmas holidays. Her extraordinary looks were an asset again. She was asked to play a man, the 'chief lover as I am so much taller than anybody else'. The girls in the family dressed her in 'a large Italian cloak and sombrero' and asked her to play her mandolin in a 'little love-ditty'. Jane threw herself into her role, despite some trouble with her over-sized hat, and the audience loved it. It made them all laugh, and as she said, 'Laughter does me more good than anything.' She did acknowledge that she felt a long way from home, as if she had stepped into someone else's life, far from Jenny's illness and William's work and May's troubled love affairs. 'It all seems a kind of dream,' she told Blunt, but 'it all helps me to forget myself and forgetfulness is what I need most of all.'[33] However, she could not stay away from home for ever. Spring had arrived at Kelmscott, so it was time to return. 'They tell me that flowers are coming up in the garden and blossom on the fruit trees,' she wrote a little regretfully from San Remo, as she began her journey northwards, 'so I shall not be going back to utter desolation after this land of beauty.'[34]

*

The changing of the seasons, the clothing of the land with gardens and woodlands and little fields: these were simple, satisfying subjects that Jane and William both wrote about regularly. They also formed the backdrop to many of William's stories. They were an additional commentary on his characters and their situations – his imagined terrains could be inhospitable or sustaining, eerily empty or dotted with small homesteads, giving a sense of peace and prosperity.

In his dream-narrative *News from Nowhere*, the transformations in the landscape between London and Oxford reflected the dramatic shifts in society that William envisioned. *News from Nowhere* was first published in the Socialist journal *The Commonweal* from January 1890. It became one of his most successful works, describing the look and feel of England after the Revolution. As the storyteller, known as Guest, travels through London and out into the countryside, he encounters people who reveal to him how the changes came about. They explain how they live convivially in a society without money, formal education, prisons or paid work. These conversations are punctuated with equally telling descriptions of how green and fruitful the land is now. And Guest comments on how his new friends are genuinely interested in 'the sequence of the seasons.'[35] He thinks it strange to constantly talk about something so commonplace. But, as William and Jane showed in their personal letters, the turning of the year could affect their health and happiness. It was worth noticing. They rejoiced in the budding and blooming, the harvesting and resting times.

William's fable is flawed, of course. The sun always shines, the people are impossibly handsome and the food is plentiful. But he has drawn on the best of his own experiences. He writes as a maker, as a man who loves the river and the earth, and as an activist. And *News from Nowhere* offers a hint of what might be, an idealistic encounter with an alternative way of life that lifts the spirits of its readers even now. It is utterly different from the other futuristic fantasies that were causing a stir at the time, like Edward Bellamy's *Looking Backward* (1887). Bellamy saw the twenty-first century as a rigid mechanised society, one against which Morris instinctively rebelled. William's response was typically vigorous: 'If they brigaded him into a regiment of workers,' he said, 'he would just lie on his back and kick.'[36] *News from Nowhere*, by contrast, is a positive, almost pastoral reimagining of places that are familiar, but lovelier now that capitalism and consumerism are no longer the driving forces of society.

As readers, we are entranced by the possibility of London rewilded. Forests stretch from Kensington Gardens northwards through to the marshes of the Lea valley, and children camp out all summer long beneath the great trees. We can imagine the pleasure of seeing a terrace of small, sturdy houses by the Thames, built as if they were 'alive and sympathetic to the life of the dwellers within them'. The homes are of course enhanced by a 'continuous garden in front of them, going down to the water's edge, in which the flowers were now blooming luxuriantly'.[37] The whole scene looks and smells delightful. As Guest journeys further up the river, he notices 'the quiet beauty of the fields . . . planted with trees here and there, often fruit trees'. The fields seemed to be 'treated as a garden made for the pleasure as well as the livelihood of all.'[38] There is no private property, so families move between town and country, from one house to another. Or they set up their 'gaily coloured tents, arranged in orderly lines' in the fields for seasonal work like haymaking.[39] The adults love the informality of camping out just as much as the children. There is almost a festival feel.

In William's new world order, manual work is valued more than book-learning. Students of modern languages and history are humoured. But 'genuinely amusing work, like house-building and street paving and gardening', is regarded as more beneficial and healthy, something that everyone can enjoy.[40] Guest meets a 'weaver from Yorkshire who has rather overdone himself, between his weaving and his mathematics, both indoor work', so he chooses to spend a few weeks as a ferryman on the Thames to restore his mind and body.[41] Those who are good with their hands – in metalwork or sewing or carving – are encouraged, and given the time and materials they need. There is no distinction between useful objects and art. So Guest discovers the potential beauty in all things, from a bunch of roses on the breakfast table, to a loaf of bread, a belt buckle or a tobacco pouch.

He learns more from the old man who lives in the British Museum about how the upheaval came about, through a general strike. But the main message is simple: 'What is the object of Revolution? Surely to make people happy.'[42] Pleasure in work; delight in using your strong, healthy body; care for the living things around you – this is the life that William yearns for, and imagines is possible in after-times. 'The spirit of the new days, of our days', as the old man says, is 'intense and overweening love of the very skin and surface of the earth on which man dwells, such as a lover has in the fair flesh of the woman he loves.'[43]

*

In Nowhere, nothing is done cheaply, scantily. At meals, 'everything was cooked and served with a daintiness which showed that those who had prepared it were interested in it'.[44] William makes a point of celebrating the skills required to run a household. It is worthwhile taking time to source ingredients, cook meals, keep rooms clean and tidy. His descriptions of women's work in *News from Nowhere* show that he acknowledges and values the hidden labour that kept his fellow Victorians comfortable. However, the gendered roles he maps out are too limited, too domestic for many readers now. He argues that 'the women do what they like best, and the men are neither jealous of it or injured by it'. William believes 'that it is a great pleasure to a clever woman to manage a house skilfully'[45] and it is an occupation 'deserving of respect'. But the result is that women, especially older women, are kept busy in the home. They still serve at table and clear the dishes; grandmothers still care for their grandchildren when there are family squabbles; girls still compare each other's looks – who is prettier? who is more tanned?

It might be useful to consider the shifts closer to home in William's own life when he was contemplating Nowhere. What were women doing in the real world around him? Their work was becoming more visible, and their voices stronger. His daughter May, for instance, had been supporting their Socialist friend Walter Crane as he arranged the first Arts and Crafts Exhibition Society display in 1888. The exhibition, held at the New Gallery, showcased many fine works by female designers and makers. In this first display especially, there were obvious limitations, with women mostly exhibiting textiles – a heavily gendered art form. But it was a start.

William had been caught up in political wranglings when the idea of the exhibition was suggested. He thought it was a distraction, and was uncharacteristically harsh in his early comments, arguing that 'the general public don't care one damn about the arts and crafts . . . the rest would tend to be of an amateurish nature . . . I must say I rather dread' the idea of it.[46] Even so, he agreed to give a talk on his own current obsession, tapestry weaving. But William had underestimated the quality of the objects on show – and his own role in nurturing the skill of their creators. As Ned Burne-Jones put it, 'amongst some stuff and nonsense are some beautiful things, delightful to look at, and here for the first time one can measure a bit the change that has happened in the last 20 years'.[47]

There were hugely ambitious objects, like the lavishly decorated grand piano ornamented by Ned and Kate Faulkner. This was made for the drawing room of Alexander Ionides. Kate spent many hours researching gesso decorations on historical instruments in the South Kensington Museum. It was a spectacular object. But there were also personal, hand-held beauties like May's embroidered book cover for her father's copy of *Love is Enough*. Her design of a pomegranate tree and an open rose, surrounded by trailing leaves, was worked in silks and couched gold thread.

Woman after woman, they sent in their contributions. There was an ornamental screen in mother-of-pearl and silk made by Aglaia Coronio; furnishings by cousins Rhoda and Agnes Garrett; dozens of textiles stitched by hopeful needlewomen who finally felt their skills were being recognised beyond the home. The commercial arm of Morris and Company was well represented, by block-printed velvets, silk damasks, carpets and tapestries. May's *Tulip and Pomegranate* screen, worked in floss silk, represented the sort of product on sale in the Oxford Street store. But then there were the more private objects made by other members of the family. Jane and Jenny had stitched an impressive portière together, decorated with honeysuckle and fritillaries; 'one of the finest of all Morris embroideries', according to May.[48] Bessie Burden's skills were also on display. She had completed three of the Chaucer hangings intended for the dining room in Red House, nearly thirty years before. *Penelope*, *Hippolyte* and *Helen of Troy*, embroidered in wool and silk, were shown for the first time in public. Perhaps these works, as much as any of the other exhibits, reminded Ned of how far they had all travelled since the foundation of the Firm.

Two years later, when *News from Nowhere* was being serialised, May Morris and her team of needlewomen demonstrated their growing strength, showing fourteen examples of embroidery at the exhibition: book covers, curtains, workbags and tea cloths. There was also the quilt for a cot decorated with animals, designed by May and stitched by Jane. It was surely meant for the grandchildren who never arrived. This little quilt was a talisman, conjuring up a tranquil home protected by an encircling river. Wild beasts – tigers, elephants, foxes and porcupines – pace around the edges of the design. A lion watches the sun rise. But the house, the orchard and garden are safe. Sadly, May was never able to use the quilt to shelter her own child. Her role as mother, Jane's as a grandmother eluded them. They had to find other ways to construct their lives, to use their skills, to present themselves, beyond the conventional narratives.

William must have been aware of these conversations, these hopes, as he wrote *News from Nowhere*. He did try to incorporate alternative ideas of femininity into his storytelling. What could women do apart from work in the house or the field? William offers his readers the figure of Mistress Philippa, head carver, with her female team. She is an artist and teacher, first seen 'working with a mallet and chisel on the wall near by. She seemed very intent on what she was doing.'[49] Philippa is stern and admirable, but rather stand-offish, especially compared to the other women that Guest meets. She appears almost sexless, unlike Guest's travelling companions Ellen and Clara, or even 'the blue-clad girl' with 'delighted eyes' who works alongside Philippa.

Very often, the women in the novel are described in terms of their dress. William tantalises his readers with images of the girls working in the fields, in light summer robes that skim their bodies, 'most gaily embroidered'. He shows us their well-rounded arms and their bare feet inside their sandals. There is a sensuality in this new age, where women are 'so shapely and well-knit of body' and 'not upholstered like armchairs'.[50] They look at men full in the face; they are not afraid to reach out and touch a friend, or to take a man by the hand. The theoretical reordering of relations between men and women, which was laid out in the Socialist manifestos of the 1880s, is shown in living detail in *News from Nowhere*.

As old Hammond explains, 'We do not deceive ourselves, indeed, or believe that we can get rid of all the trouble that besets the dealings between the sexes.' In this renewed society, there is still unhappiness, but 'we are not so mad as to pile up degradation on that unhappiness'. Personal relationships do not get confused with questions of property. Children are not condemned for being 'the results of love or lust'.[51] And good partnerships do prosper. The old man acknowledges, with some wonder, 'The reasonable longing of a strong and thoughtful man to become the most intimate friend of some beautiful and wise woman, the very type of beauty and glory of the world which we love so well.' He recognises 'all the pleasure and exaltation of spirit which goes with these things'.[52]

Wilfrid Scawen Blunt had declared that William 'did not know . . . the love of women' and 'he had no real experience and remained a child'.[53] However, many of the passages William wrote in *News from Nowhere* suggest a different story: that he was very conscious of the pleasures of intimacy, he cherished the connection between man and woman, but he also understood that things could go amiss. It was also possible, he knew, that a couple could lose each other for a time, and then be reunited. In the tale of Dick and Clara, which plays out during Guest's visit to Nowhere, we see a love rekindled. There are, perhaps, hopeful echoes of his own marriage, or May's complex affairs.

William describes how Dick and Clara have been married and had children. But they separated because Clara wanted to live with someone else. Now, as Guest travels with them, he watches the couple start again, with some shyness, but evident joy and desire. William writes about their physical delight in each other. Clara asks to join Dick's haymaking trip, 'laying her pretty hand on his shoulder'. Dick replies enthusiastically, "'We will manage to send you to bed pretty tired every night; you will look so beautiful with your neck all brown and your hands too, and you under your gown as white as privet" . . . The girl reddened very prettily, and not for shame but for pleasure.'[54] This easy attraction, this lack of primness about the body and its beauty, is refreshing and maybe unexpected. We hear it again in William's writing about Ellen, the young woman who meets Guest in Hammersmith and keeps him company on the journey upriver. There, at the end of the story, she brings him into the shelter of the garden at Kelmscott Manor. This is the homecoming: 'She led me up close to the house, and laid her shapely sun browned hand and arm on the lichened wall as if to embrace it.'[55] We are aware of the textures of skin and stone, warm to the touch, both beloved.

Ellen and Guest explore the house together, 'from the rose-covered porch to the strange and quaint garrets', and talk a little of past and present. But soon enough they are out of doors again, as Ellen murmurs, 'The earth and the growth of it and the life of it! If I could but say or show how I love it!'[56] They part by the garden gate. Guest is invited for a swim in the river, and then a feast in the old church. As he steps inside, he wonders at the loveliness of the scene; the simple little building is dressed 'with festoons of flowers from arch to arch, and great pitchers of flowers standing about on the floor . . . But its best ornament was the crowd of handsome, happy-looking men and women . . . with their bright faces and rich hair.'[57] There the dream ends, as it must, and he watches a 'black cloud rolling along to meet me'. He wakes in 'dingy Hammersmith thinking about it all'.[58] Ellen and the garden and the tents in the meadow are far off.

*

In March 1893, William published a new edition of *News from Nowhere, or An Epoch of Rest*. It included a frontispiece drawn by Charles Gere showing Kelmscott Manor, with its gables and rose garden, a flock of birds overhead. Underneath was printed: 'This is the picture of the old house by the Thames to which the people of this story went.' Kelmscott did not need to be reimagined for the twenty-first century. It was the same as ever, undisturbed by the Revolution.

William named his new venture after Kelmscott. Like the Manor house, his Kelmscott Press was grounded firmly in the old ways, and provided a refuge from the 'shoddy age' in which William found himself.[59] For two guineas, he offered his readers a remarkable, portable work of art: not just the text itself, but the layout, the ink, the paper, the border designs, the very details of the typeface were considered and perfected. William had been collecting early printed books for years, learning how their beauty came from the balance between blank paper and strong black words. He said he wanted the Kelmscott Press to produce books that 'should be easy to read and should not dazzle the eye', that 'were always beautiful by force of the mere typography'.[60] This was the essence of the project.

William decided to develop a fresh font, based on the best examples of fifteenth-century pioneers of printing. He was inspired by a lecture given by his friend Emery Walker as part of the first Arts and Crafts Exhibition in 1888. Walker used magic lantern slides to show enlarged photographs of works by Nicolas Jansen and other master-printers. William was enraptured: 'One after another their splendid pages shone out in the dark room . . . the first and last of the fine printing.'[61] He could see every element of the design, the clarity of each letter, the spacing, the weight of each full stop. Walking home with Emery, he was adamant, they must create their own Press, their own workable typeface. May remembered how she watched 'the very beginnings of this new-old industry taking form and growing more or less under our roof'.[62] Again using photography, William and Emery Walker drew and refined their first fresh type, known as 'Golden'. They enlarged or reduced their drawings until they were happy for the type to be cut by 'the expert and sympathetic hands of Mr Prince'. Then, as May said, 'my father would go about with matchboxes' containing the tiny printed samples 'in his pockets, and sometimes as he sat and talked with us, he would draw one out, and thoughtfully eye the small scraps of paper inside'.[63]

William paid the same attention to the other materials. He sourced his paper from a manufacturer in Kent, and insisted on providing three new watermarks for his stock: 'Flower', 'Perch' and 'Apple'. Good strong ink was eventually tracked down in Germany. He also worked out the best way to balance each page, using the proportions established in 'medieval books, written or printed'. It was simple but very effective: 'Leave the inner margin the narrowest, the top somewhat wider, the outside (fore-edge) wider still, and the bottom widest of all.'[64] This gave plenty of space for decorative borders. William loved designing his own, creating networks of foliage and flowers to gladden the pages. For *News from Nowhere*, for instance, the title page was bordered by a vine and grapes. In *The Story of the Glittering Plain*, published a year later, there were columbines and cornflowers and great scrolling leaves.

William took pleasure in creating these intricate patterns. One of his colleagues, the young architect William Lethaby, described the process:

There were two saucers, one of Indian ink and the other of Chinese white, and two brushes: with one brush he blacked over a length of border, and then with the other began to paint the stems and leafage of his pattern, solving all the problems of the twists and turns as he came to them.[65]

It looked, he said, as if William were stroking a cat. The process was so soothing and supple: 'He used to say that all good designing was felt in the stomach.'[66] William moved on to produce what he called 'blooming letters': a selection of decorative capitals to add even more interest, and punctuate the main text.

William kept a very close eye on every stage of the process. It was all on his doorstep. The first Albion press was set up at 16 Upper Mall, Hammersmith. Within a few months, production had already outgrown this little house. He rented another property at number 14. This had been used as kennels, so Morris called it 'the doggeries'. Here was space for a second press, and more staff. Next door, at number 15, their friend Thomas Cobden-Sanderson set up a workshop for his Doves Bindery. He could provide exquisite vellum-bound copies of some of William's books. Cobden-Sanderson had already proved his worth by rebinding many of William's personal collection, including a very battered copy of *Das Kapital*, which was now splendid in turquoise leather, and finished with gold moons and buds.

It had been Jane's idea that Thomas should begin to train as a bookbinder. He was the husband of her dear companion Anne Cobden. She suggested it to him in 1883, soon after their marriage. Jane said that it 'would add an Art to our little community, and we would work together'. She had told him, 'I should like to do some little embroideries for books, and I would do so for you.'[67] As she envisaged, the Kelmscott Press and its associated workshops did form the heart of a community. It gave William time with his friends again, as they discussed their favourite books, those they had loved long ago, and new-found treasures. There were cheerful evenings in Gatti's restaurant, after the SPAB meetings, where William would pull manuscripts out of his satchel to share with Webb, Walker and Sydney Cockerell, secretary for the Press. Over their 'chops or macaroni' there was 'much merriment and eager talk',[68] washed down with a carafe of wine for some, and hot chocolate for others.

William and Ned Burne-Jones were also able to put their heads together again, as they looked over books to reprint and illustrate. As Ned said plainly, 'The best way of lengthening out the rest of our days, old chap, is to finish off our old things.'[69] Conversation at their Sunday breakfasts now veered away from politics. They went back to their first loves, the writings they had shared as young men: the sacred stories of *The Golden Legend*, Rossetti's poems, Ruskin's *The Nature of Gothic* and Chaucer's tales.

*

The production of *The Works of Geoffrey Chaucer* preoccupied William for the best part of four years. He first started talking about it in the summer of 1891, and the edition was announced at Christmas 1892. All 425 copies were pre-sold almost eighteen months before the printing was complete. It was a joint endeavour with Ned: he provided 87 illustrations, and William did all the rest, including new border patterns and headers, and even a revised typeface, developed from his Gothic 'Troy' font.

Like many of William's friends, Ned recognised that there was something almost Chaucerian about Morris himself – his appearance, his zest for life. As Burne-Jones said, 'Chaucer is very much the same sort of person as Morris; unless he can begin his tale at the beginning and go steadily on to the end, he's bothered.'[70] This perseverance, especially in the face of such a vast project, was one of William's great strengths. Finding the right collaborators was another. He and Ned worked well together. As Burne-Jones said, 'I like a thing perfect, and he likes a thing done.'[71] Their handiwork balanced each other. Ned decided his illustrations 'loved to be snugly cased in borders and buttressed up by the vast initials.'[72]

William's ambitious plans for the Press had an impact on his political and personal life. He was still closely involved with the Socialist movement in London, but increasingly as a spokesman or figurehead rather than a foot-soldier. He stepped away from the weekly grind of writing for *The Commonweal*, and turned his attention instead to his own questing novels and translations: he was tackling *Beowulf*, reading sections of the Anglo-Saxon epic aloud to Ned and Georgie each week. He intended to publish this, along with more than sixty other titles. As he told one journalist: 'Oh it's jolly fun. I like it immensely. There is so much pleasure in seeing a beautiful form given to your favourite writers . . . the books I would like to print are the books I love to read and keep.'[73] And each of the books had its own distinctive form. The *Chaucer* was over 600 pages long. To Ned's eyes, it seemed like a pocket cathedral. 'The dainty, light volume of *Poems by the Way*', by contrast, 'looked like a snowdrop by the side of a gigantic sunflower as it lay on the table' next to a massive fifteenth-century book. But they all had 'the same clear even type, the same mellow tone of the paper, the same deep black ink, and the same innumerable marks of watchful care over all the details'.[74]

While the rest of the family spent most of the warmer months at Kelmscott Manor, William got into the habit of staying in the country every other week, and then going back up to London to attend to the business of the Press. It was still a hectic schedule, but less effortful than his old Socialist preaching days. He longed to find a chance to 'cease being bumbled up and down. I want to work hard at my easy work.'[75] The Press called to him, but so did the old house by the Thames. He wrote about it with love, how it had 'grown up out of the soil and the lives of those who lived in it', how it carried with it 'some thin thread of tradition . . . the delight of meadow and acre and wood and river'.[76] His favourite room, he said, was the original parlour. It almost had 'the look of a particularly pleasant cabin at sea, were it not for the elms and the rooks on the west, and the green garden shrubs and the blackbirds on the east'.[77] He was often woken early by the birdsong.

William's bed at Kelmscott Manor was a work of art in itself. The ancient four-poster stood in the central bedroom for many years before William and Jane ever set eyes on the house. It was constructed out of a jumble of sixteenth- and early seventeenth-century pieces, all reassembled in the 1840s. Despite its untidy origins, William was very fond of it. He wrote a poem for it in 1891. It is not his finest verse. But he wanted to acknowledge the uncomplicated happiness of snuggling under the blankets, thankful for a warm haven on nights when 'the wind's on the wold/ And the night is a-cold/ And the Thames runs chill'. William, as the master of dreamscapes and visionary writing, imagines staying close under the covers, scarcely daring to move, 'lest earth and its love/ Should fade away/ Ere the full of the day'. He writes of the birds singing on a morning in early summer. So, May designed bed curtains for him, with an embroidered rose trellis, and sprinkled with tiny daisies, yellow tulips and blue irises among the fruit trees. Birds perch in the branches. She and her colleagues stitched them in bright wool. They also embroidered the poem onto the deep pelmet that hung over William's head as he slept. He was almost wrapped up in the rich colours, the enchanted garden, the words that sounded like a spell.

The manor house was a place of rest and of quiet productivity. Visitors described how the family and their guests would sit together with their work in their hands. One artist, for example, took up his sketchbook, 'while Mr Morris was designing some cretonnes and Miss Morris knitted; Mrs M joined us during the morning and continued embroidering a book cover'.[78] It was all very sociable. Jane offered hospitality to her own artist friends. She was particularly pleased when Marie Spartali Stillman or her stepdaughter Lisa could visit. They both enjoyed painting the house and garden at Kelmscott. Jenny was also more lively when Lisa visited. Jane said she was 'a wild creature' who encouraged Jenny to join in with the walks and games – her daughter was apt to be too sedentary and placid. We know Lisa made several studies at the Manor over the years, including a picture of Jane in the summerhouse.

Marie Stillman could not visit Kelmscott as often as she liked. Her husband was posted to Italy from 1878, so she was only able to see Jane from time to time. She had known the house from the early days, when she had stayed there as Gabriel's model. As part of the Pre-Raphaelite circle, Marie also modelled for Burne-Jones and was a favourite sitter for Julia Margaret Cameron's photographs. She was visible as a painter too, having studied with Ford Madox Brown. Marie exhibited regularly at the Royal Academy and the Grosvenor Gallery. She was, according to Blunt, 'like a woman in a dream'. He had flirted with her in Rome, feeling 'an electric current' run between them in the Sistine Chapel, and a few months later he 'undid the button of her glove and held her wonderful hand naked in mine'.[79] He declared she was 'the most beautiful woman that ever lived or ever will live in the world'.[80] Jane teased Blunt about his admiration for Marie. But there was no pettiness or jealousy between Jane and her friend. It is a shame that we have to piece together their friendship from the oddments left by Blunt and Rossetti. Although their letters have not survived, it is clear that Jane and Marie kept in touch as they both grew older, and other people slipped away.

We see the manor house briefly through Marie's eyes, in a letter she wrote to her children. In 1885, when the Stillmans were temporarily without a home, William and Jane offered them Kelmscott for a while. Marie's husband was unwell, so they relished the few weeks of calm, gathering forget-me-nots and white moss roses and elderflowers. Marie wrote that it was 'such a treat to have a large roomy house all to oneself and to do as one likes and not to be hurried or flurried and not even to hear a train'.[81]

The Morrises nurtured creativity at Kelmscott, even when, as Jane said, 'we do little here except sit in the garden and walk in the mead-ows'.[82] She was aware that some of her guests were readers rather than makers. She arranged for 'a new bookcase to hold what I call reading books. Several "friends" have complained of the dearth of books in this literary man's house'.[83] This seems surprising, given her frequent references to enjoying her own 'delightful reading time'. She wrote of the charm of starting 'a new book of poems among the June roses'.[84] Jenny, she said, also 'makes herself happy with books and picking flowers'.[85] The love of stories and poems was shared by all the family, enriching their time in the garden. Then they tucked themselves up with books as the days grew colder, 'with everything covered with white frost and . . . blazing fires in every room'. As Jane told Blunt, even on a sharp October day, 'It is so bright here, the birds come to my windows to be fed and I feel well and happy for the moment.'[86]

At Kelmscott, William and Jane could take their time a little. The gardens were generous, and they could find space away from guests. And so we are granted a little glimpse of the couple together. William had slipped away from their friends, 'lounging and larking in the orchard . . . soon afterwards we saw him in a summer bower with his head bowed in his wife's lap, having his head cropped'.[87] Topsy's great mane of hair was being tamed.

*

William needed this place of peace and care. He was often unwell. From the early months of 1890, when William was fifty-five years old, Jane's letters increasingly mention her husband's ailments. In February, it was influenza, and William 'wanted dreadfully to go out-of-doors when he was still feverish'. Jane was looking after him, and May, and a visiting niece, who were all poorly. To make matters harder, 'Jenny was unusually bad with her ordinary illness . . . at the same time.' Jane said wryly, 'I am still alive and uncanonised.'[88] These notes make us reassess the myth of Jane's own bodily frailty. She supported William and the rest of her family, although it made her so tired, she felt she 'could sleep all day as well as all night'.[89]

The following year, they had another testing time. Jenny had meningitis, and her fits became 'so violent that she had to be tied down to the bed'.[90] She needed constant watching. It was very distressing, and Jane and May were both shaken by Jenny's worsening condition. But William could not bear the dreadful changes in his daughter. As Jane explained to Blunt, 'My husband has been very ill, the shock of Jenny's illness was too much for him, and he broke down entirely a few days afterwards . . . I fear it will be a long time before he is anything like his real self.'[91] William acknowledged that he was not well: 'My hand seems like lead and my wrist string.' This weakness was doubly upsetting when he was trying to make progress with establishing the Press. He needed to be able to draw, to write. Thomas Cobden-Sanderson was struck by his appearance. He seemed to have shrunk. William looked 'a little empty, his clothes hanging somewhat looser upon him'.[92] By the summer of 1891, however, he and Jenny were both feeling more buoyant, and they set off for a short holiday in Sussex. Jane created a memorable image of the pair of them, as 'they wander the Downs together like two happy babies'.[93]

And so it went on, with William rallying and then fading a little more. The death of his mother in December 1894 was a blow, as 'although she had been ill so long, she passed away quite suddenly at the last'.[94] Emma Morris had been a seemingly unshakeable figure in William's life, and she had made Jane welcome, too. They had both visited her regularly, and had taken her presence for granted. She was, according to Jane, 'the liveliest old lady possible, she walks and takes drives in an open carriage every day . . . and reads and talks incessantly and is quite happy'.[95] Now, at the age of ninety, she was gone. Philip Webb, ever at William's shoulder, agreed to design her tombstone. As Jane said, 'The saddest part of growing old [is] losing friends or fearing to lose them. I am not sure which is worst.'[96]

William was tiring. On a walk around the lanes of Kelmscott in the autumn of 1894, he sat down heavily on the grass, his legs stretched out. 'I shall sit on the world,' he said.[97] The following year, Georgie Burne-Jones visited the manor house. She joined William on his pilgrimage to the White Horse, the great chalk figure carved into the Downs at Uffington. Georgie thought 'Topsy looks very happy, and is so sweet down here.' She was also delighted by the garden, filled with a mass of flowers. 'The whole place is leafier' than she remembered. And yet, she acknowledged, 'I feel the added years in Janey and Topsy and me, so that it seems like visiting something that is not quite real.'[98] The years seemed heaviest on William. He was barely sixty, but he was sometimes depressed and at a loss: 'Now that I am grown old,' he wrote, 'and see that nothing is to be done, I half wish that I had not been born with a sense of romance and beauty in this accursed age.'[99]

Burne-Jones tried to cheer William, with plans for new works to be illustrated and printed at the Press. After a chat about his own *Sigurd the Volsung*, William told Ned, 'I am afire with the new designs . . . and as to the age, that be blowed.'[100] There had been a moment in 1894 when their friendship had been severely strained, when Ned had accepted the honour of a baronetcy. It was mostly for the sake of his son Philip. But William could hardly bear the idea of his old friends becoming 'Sir Edward and Lady Burne-Jones'. It cut across everything he stood for, politically and socially. Ned and Georgie had not told William in advance – they knew how it would antagonise him – so he only found out when he read it in the newspaper. Jane, too, was aghast, partly at the offer, and partly at the way the Burne-Joneses had handled it. 'It is all too funny and makes one roar with laughing,' she wrote. 'I have got over the sadness of it now – it seemed to me such an insult to offer the same to a man of genius and a successful publican.' Still, as she said, 'A man can be an ass for the sake of his children.'[101] (Unsurprisingly, Ned's son-in-law Mackail did not include these comments in his official biography of William.)

By the early months of 1896, however, their differences were patched up. It was Ned who finally persuaded William to see a doctor. He had refused all Jane's suggestions that he should be concerned about his health. She said they 'had known of this tendency of this illness (diabetes) for many years past'.[102] But after 'a weary dark winter', he was now willing to take it seriously.[103] Early in the new year, William had suddenly seemed more than usually drained. Georgie watched anxiously as 'in the middle of breakfast' he stopped talking and had to lean forward, supporting his head in his hands.[104]

It was his last Sunday morning at The Grange. Ned took him to see Sir William Broadbent, the Prince of Wales's doctor. William described how the doctor was very straightforward: 'He examined me, partly bare, for about 3 quarters of an hour.' Yes, he did have diabetes, but he might 'get rid of it by rigid diet, eggs, milk, puree of meat'.[105]

Jane was less optimistic. Towards the end of March 1896, William was able to work a little at home, but he was still not well enough to go out. Jane told Rosalind Howard, 'I fear there is no chance of his ever regaining any robust health.'[106] As the days lengthened, he wanted to see Kelmscott Manor again. Jane took him there on 22 April, in time for the apple blossom. William was only able to 'walk a very little way outside'.[107] Georgie was extremely concerned about him, so he wrote to reassure her. 'I hope I am no worse,' he said, but he recognised that 'down in this deep quiet, away from the excitements of business and callers and doctors, one is rather apt to brood.' He was not an easy patient. He knew that he had 'made himself disagreeable at times'.[108] Or perhaps that self-criticism was another facet of the depression of his spirit. He returned to London on 6 May. William never saw another spring at Kelmscott.

There were still joyful flashes, reminders of his capacity to take an interest in the things that had always enchanted him. Ned described the fun they had looking over a new manuscript William had bought. His friend's 'heart was aglow', Ned said. William shared it with the Burne-Joneses on the Sunday after he came back from the country. It had cost him £900, a phenomenal sum, but it was a wonderful bestiary. Ned thought how 'happy it must have been for the monks to see. There was a pea-green donkey in it, quite big, standing all by himself'.[109]

*

Jane knew that William was very unwell. She spoke to his doctor, in private, about the long term. Broadbent believed that William was worn out. He told Jane, 'It is a case of overwork for so many years.'

All those early mornings in his study or at his loom, all the long evenings preaching on the platforms of Socialist meeting rooms; they had taken their toll. William's fabled energy was ebbing away: 'The disease was being William Morris and working 18 hours a day.'[110] Jane wrote with the bad news to Georgie. She said the doctor had simply explained that William had 'done more work than most ten men'.[111]

William was losing weight fast. They tried a change of air. Jane and William took rooms in the Norfolk Hotel in Folkestone. As Jane said, 'It is not a lively place [but] we are not lively company just now.'[112] William tried to make the best of it. He liked looking out at the boats, and talked about a sea voyage. Just now, though, it was all he could do to 'toddle about, and sit down, lean over chairs'. He claimed to 'rather enjoy it, especially if there are any craft about'. To William's eyes, 'The Harbour is the only decent place in the town, that and the view of the downs.'[113]

Jane invited old friends to visit them in Folkestone, as William often became melancholy, and it helped him to see Ned or Blunt, or his colleagues from the Press. Georgie, as usual, bustled about. She tried to reorganise William's care. In happier days, Jane would have accepted Georgie's help without fuss. But with the strain of William's illness, these suggestions sounded like criticism of Jane and her ability to manage. Georgie 'gave great offense' by saying William should have a nurse. She also disapproved of his diet. He was supposed to be keeping to his doctor's orders, and Georgie thought his food was 'not always as carefully selected as it ought to be'. But they were staying in a hotel, not a sanatorium, and Jane knew better than anyone that 'no nurse could force him to eat what he refuses to look at'. She was doing her utmost to look after her husband, 'as long as I can keep well'. Jane argued that 'if I break down before he recovers, then will be the time for a nurse.'[114] It was hard for everyone to keep their tempers in the face of the disaster that was clearly unfolding.

There was one highlight of their stay in Folkestone: the arrival of the first copy of the Kelmscott *Chaucer*. William was given it on 24 June. It was a magnificent volume, bound in white leather, decorated with a vine and tiny flowers, and closed by silver clasps. Inside, William's sumptuous borders and lettering were enlivened by Ned's pictures. He and Ned had spent happy hours trying to interpret and recreate the peculiar world of Chaucer's imagination. In response, Ned conjured up a kaleidoscope of off-kilter visions, impossible romances, dancing maidens and enclosed gardens. It was the culmination of a lifetime of thought and love. As Ned said, 'who else could have carried it through, and who else could have designed it' as William had done? Ned wrote to a friend about his delight at seeing it finished. He felt like 'the carver of the images at Amiens'. This great book summarised so much of their time together: 'When Morris and I were little chaps in Oxford, if such a book had come out then we should have just gone off our heads, but we made at the end of our days the very thing we would have made then if we could.'[115]

William was still talking about the possibility of bringing out a companion volume, a glorious Kelmscott edition of Froissart's *Chronicles*. But those who loved him knew that this would never happen. They remembered William's yearnings for emptiness, for a vast clear landscape, to be 'well out of it, and living in a tent in a Persian desert or a turf hut on the Iceland hill side'.[116] Perhaps another voyage Northwards might help? He could reconnect with the landscapes of the sagas, find strength in the sea air. In late July, William sailed from Tilbury, bound for the far shores of Norway. He travelled with a doctor, and an adventurous engineer called John Carruthers. William's heart was not in it. He sat out on deck and watched the dark rocks of the fjords roll past, but he admitted, 'I cannot take an interest in them as I should once have done.'[117] He suffered from bad dreams. On his return, he wrote to Webb, a brief note, ending 'somewhat better, but hated the voyage; so glad to be home'.[118]

William was too unwell to travel again. He was still coughing, and long conversations tired him. His hopes of seeing Jenny at Kelmscott came to nothing. He wrote to his 'Dearest own child, I am so distressed that I cannot get down . . . I long to see you with all my heart.'[119] Jane continued to invite his friends to sit with him for a little. She was finding it hard, telling Crom, 'I can't bear any more griefing [sic] it does not suit me at this age . . . one can't help having misgivings, and then imagination runs wild.'[120] Some days it was difficult to keep her composure. She was exhausted. William's life was getting smaller. The household was turned inwards, focusing on his comfort. He disliked the bother of being ill. When he was told that the door-knocker had been muffled so as not to disturb him, he said that was nonsense: 'Folks would think he was having a baby.'[121]

Jane asked Mary de Morgan to give her some extra practical support. She was 'a great friend' of Jane's and the sister of the ceramicist William de Morgan, who had helped Morris find the 'fictionary' at Merton Abbey.[122] Mary was a regular visitor to Kelmscott, so William was used to her abrupt manner. And she fitted into the new routines at Hammersmith. She was not afraid of sitting up into the small hours with him as he became restless, disconnected.

On a good day, William could enjoy company. In late September, he had a peaceful afternoon with the musician Arnold Dolmetsch who was reviving old musical instruments in the same way that William had researched and revived lost dyes and damasks. Dolmetsch had made his first lute in 1893. William encouraged him to resurrect the harpsichord, so that domestic music from the world of Shakespeare and Spenser could be played again in homes, shared with friends. They sat together after tea, talking about the beautiful pair of virginals that Dolmetsch had made. And William heard the sounds of long ago, tunes by Byrd and other Elizabethans. He asked Dolmetsch to play Byrd's pavane and galliard one more time, and he wept. It was too much.

This was a time of winding down. Sydney Cockerell came to talk to William about the future of the Press. Very sadly they agreed that it would not outlive him. It was better not to make compromises, not to submit to someone else's direction. The *Chaucer* would have to be enough. It was a fitting final act.

William was surrounded by familiar faces as he lay in bed. On warm mornings, friends wheeled him out into the gentle sunshine. Jane and May were close at hand. Cockerell slept on a sofa in the study, in case William called out in the night. His sister Isabella visited, and so did Philip Webb. Georgie and Ned saw him most days, separately. He began to drift. It was the beginning of October. Darkness and death were closing in. All his bright colours, his fierce words, his love of living things could not hold them at bay. Thomas Cobden-Sanderson described the eeriness as William faced the end of his life:

> Morris is dying, slowly. It is an astonishing spectacle . . . It comes nearer and nearer. He waits. Soon it will envelop all the familiar scene, the sweet river, England green and grey, Kelmscott, Kelmscott House, the trees which tremble with little noises in their leaves, the Press, the passage, the Bindery, the light coming in through the windows, the green paint within, the old books on the shelves, the dining-room, the long table, the big chair at the head, the long garden, all, all, all.[123]

Jane and May were with William when he died, on Saturday morning, 3 October 1896. Georgie was close beside his bed, too. She said he slipped away without a struggle. William left at the turn of the seasons, at a time when he knew that 'the year is beginning to fail'. In the closing passages of *News from Nowhere*, he had written 'of the coming of the dark days, and the shorn fields and empty gardens . . . It is, then, in the autumn, when one almost believes in death.'[124]

Chapter 14

Wanderings, 1897–1914

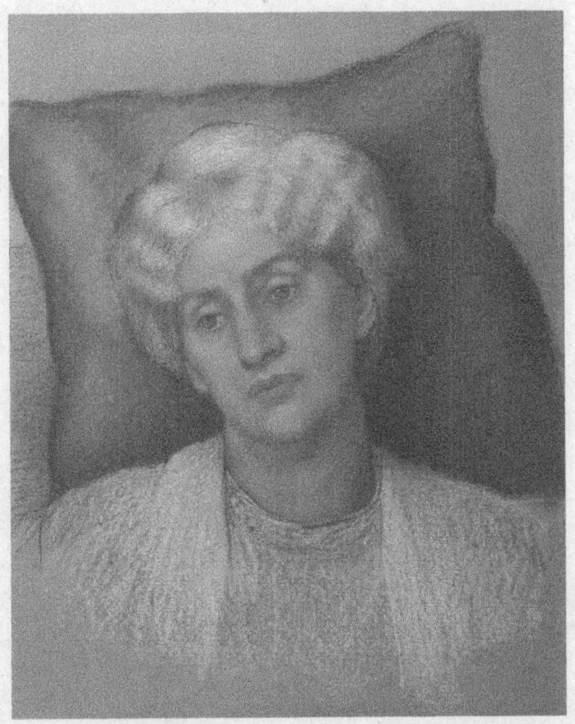

Evelyn de Morgan, *Study for 'The Hour Glass'*,
(portrait of Jane Morris), 1904–5, chalk, De Morgan Collection

Jane lay awake in the dark, listening to the unfamiliar scuttlings and rustlings, breathing in the strange scents: jessamine, apricot and orange blossom and unidentifiable things in the night air. She could hear May stirring in the next room. Her back ached after the long journey. She had wanted to get away from the cold and the fog, and the loneliness of London. So, Jane had travelled to the edge of the desert. She would see Egypt at last.

In the whirling days after William's death, Blunt had offered her refuge. He had suggested Jane come to join him at his house, just outside the ancient city of Heliopolis. His wife Anne and daughter Judith would be there too, so this was a kindly gesture, nothing more. Jane would find warmth, far away from the forlorn business of Hammersmith. She could leave behind, for a while, the constant questions about what happens next with the Press, the Firm, the houses, the staff. Jane and May spent Christmas 1896 at Sheyk Obeyd. They stayed in the guest house, El Kheysheh, tucked inside the walled gardens. For many years after, Jane looked back thankfully to this 'dear little pink house'; she said it 'has become part of myself'.[1]

When Blunt had bought the land in 1882, it was almost ruinous, with only a small gardener's house on the site, and a white-domed tomb. This was the shrine of the holy man who gave his name to the place. Blunt and Anne had camped in the garden, and begun to replant, starting with citrus trees and acacias. They had established their stables here, filled with fine Arab horses. While the gardens were glorious, with olives and roses and a giant lebbek tree, the house was deliberately empty. Judith Blunt complained that there was hardly any furniture, and she got tired sitting cross-legged on the carpets. The family wore Arab dress and offered camel's milk and dates to their guests.

For Jane and May, the whole experience was extraordinary. They felt a very long way from home. As Jane said, their 'life in Egypt seems like a brilliant dream'.[2] She was grateful that 'the conditions of life here are so simple and soothing'.[3] In Hammersmith, she was surrounded by things, old and new, that pulled her back constantly to William. Here, for a time, she was free of the piles of books, the wall-hangings cocooning the rooms, the heavy tables, the pictures of her own young face. William had found peace in the rocks and rivers of Iceland. Jane found it in the sunlight and white sanded floors of Sheyk Obeyd. It was a bold decision to go. In accepting this chance to travel, Jane showed that she was willing to carry on living, on her own terms. William would never have taken her to Egypt. But now, it was her choice, her way of resolving her loss.

It was not an easy stay, of course. Jane and May were both in profound grief. Jane said her daughter 'does her best, we never speak of what we are both thinking of incessantly'.[4] Blunt found their company tedious much of the time: he described May as 'a most obstinately silent woman'.[5] For him, the visit 'has been rather a disappointment'. He had built the little guest house for intimacy and seduction and 'I am at my wits end how to amuse them, for I cannot make love to either of them, and what else is there to be done.'[6] But for the two mourning women, there was a sense of release. Jane had endured years of nursing and anxiety. As the widow of a celebrity, she would have been looked at in London, expected to conform to the role, limited in her movements. In Egypt, she could remain quiet, if she wished, or explore this new world. May was taken to see the pyramids, she learnt a little Arabic and made some sketches of flowers in the enclosed garden. They both ventured out into the desert on horseback, with Jane's horse being led softly across the deep sand. Jane told a friend she had not mounted a camel, yet. But it seemed 'the pace is not unpleasant when you get used to being so high up'.[7] Most days, Jane simply sat in the scented shade, listening to the ripples of water along the edges of the paths. She could think about what she had left behind.

Blunt had visited Jane in Hammersmith on the day before William's funeral. She was lying on the sofa in the drawing room, wearing her usual blue shawl, comforting and familiar. She had not changed into her formal widow's black. She was not yet ready. Her hair was all white, her thick curls ghostly. Blunt could not resist making a little tender scene of their meeting, an emotional drama with himself at the centre of it all. 'I kissed her,' he wrote, 'which I had not done for long.' He recorded that Jane had confided in him, 'I am not unhappy . . . though it is a terrible thing, for I have been with him since I first knew anything. I was 18 when I married but I never loved him.'[8]

How should we read these words now? Was Jane really unmoved, or is it more likely that she was in shock, coming to terms with the end of her shared life with William? Can we believe Blunt's account? Her affection for William might not have had the emotional intensity of her relationships with Gabriel or Blunt, even in the early days. They both knew it would have been unthinkable for Jane to say no to his offer of marriage. She had been clearsighted in her decision to become William's wife; it was a practical rather than a passionate engagement. But their life together had been filled with other good things: tenderness, encouragement, freedom to grow, constant care for their daughters and attachment to the homes they made together.

This is also love. But perhaps Blunt could not recognise something so gentle, so unromantic.

*

Jane travelled with William as he made his last journey to Kelmscott. He was buried in the shadow of the little Norman church dedicated to St George. That was his wish.

On the day he died, as the room began to darken, Charles Fairfax Murray had drawn his portrait, his face uncanny in its stillness. William's friends had rarely seen him at rest. By morning he was lying in his 'very plain box'. There was a small wreath on the lid, woven from 'leaves and sad-coloured flowers', and the coffin was draped with a favourite piece of Turkish brocade.[9] On 6 October, as the rain fell, he was carried to Paddington station. The funeral train passed through Oxford, and on to Lechlade. The drizzle became a downpour. William was carefully lifted onto a harvest cart for the final few miles, a yellow wagon with red wheels, dressed in willow and vine and with a cushion of moss for the coffin. The mourners came behind: Jane, May and Jenny; Ned Burne-Jones and Crom Price, his oldest friends; William's sisters and brothers; neighbours and colleagues from London; Bessie Burden, always there in the background. As they drove slowly to the village, 'the noise of waters was everywhere'.[10]

Inside the church, all was red and gold and ready for the harvest thanksgiving service. The font and the pillars were decorated with shiny bunches of autumn leaves. Ripe fruit and sheaves of corn had been brought in from the fields and gardens. William's friends gathered for the simplest possible service. He had explained, only last spring, that he did not believe 'in any God the Creator of the World, or any Providence, or, I think, any future life'.[11] And so he was laid to rest in his coffin of unpolished oak. Ned and Jane stood at his graveside. To the onlookers, she seemed transformed, an artefact rather than a living person. Jane looked 'like the photograph of her as a very young woman, with the same sway in the folds of her cloak from the neck to the ground'.[12] Then she and her daughters had to walk away from William and return to Kelmscott Manor. There were roses lingering in the garden, and the last sweet peas and mignonette. The grass of the orchard was strewn with fallen apples. The rooks were silent.

In the aftermath of William's death, Jane turned to Sydney Cockerell, his secretary at the Press. Cockerell supported her as she dealt with the paperwork and decision-making that inevitably followed. Their correspondence shows how, together, they managed the practical and emotional process of leaving Hammersmith, winding up the Press, making provision for Jenny.

William's estate was valued at £55,000 (equivalent to around £4.3 million in 2020). This included his portions of the Press and the Firm, and his valuable collections of art and manuscripts. But Jane did not inherit any of this outright. William had left his wealth in trust for his wife and their daughters – mostly as a safety net for Jenny, in case Jane became ill or died. Or, perhaps, remarried. Jane was consulted by the trustees, but was reliant on their regular cheques to pay her own expenses, to support Jenny and to manage her taxes. She had an income in this way of around £1,000 a year, a handsome amount, although, as she said, Jenny's epilepsy and her own uncertain health 'renders many expenses more or less necessary to us'.[13] May received a yearly allowance of £250, and William's estate continued to send small regular payments to Bessie Burden. The trustees were men who Jane knew well, and could work with: Cockerell, F. S. Ellis – William's publisher – and Emery Walker – a neighbour and SPAB friend. She had little experience of dealing with business matters, so it was a reasonable arrangement. Jane had people she could rely on. They would understand when she wrote, on the second anniversary of William's death, 'I perceive that I am really rich, but feel inexpressibly poor today'.[14]

The Firm continued in the Morris name, and was run by the managers of the Oxford Street store, Frank and Robert Smith. They had become his partners in 1890 and bought out William's share of the business when he died. But they kept on many of the key staff, including Henry Dearle, who had been designing patterns for textiles and ceramics since the 1870s. So, the distinctive 'Morris' look continued well into the new century. May stepped down from her formal role as head of the embroidery studio, and became a freelance maker and design consultant. She was a successful lecturer, like William, and travelled to North America to promote her ideas and craft. She also developed her skills in directions that her father had never attempted, making experimental jewellery, working with silver and semi-precious stones. May kept her house by the river at Hammersmith Terrace.

This helped Jane with another difficult choice. If May had a room for her, when she was in London, Jane could give up Kelmscott House. She no longer needed a large residence in town, as a showcase for William's work or a meeting place for his comrades. By August 1897, she tells a friend that she has found a new tenant; 'The workmen are already in the house – so I will get out of it as soon as possible.'[15] In many of her letters, she seems relieved to be letting go. Object by object, she clears more space, finds new owners for the beautiful things she has lived with, disentangles herself from the weight of it all. She has boxes of books that she wants to be rid of. She asks Cockerell for suggestions – who might like a copy of a Chiswick Press edition of *Gunnlaug the Worm Tongue*? She gives away Kelmscott Press volumes as wedding presents and samples of William's calligraphy experiments as tokens of remembrance. Cockerell borrows a bookcase. Some of the green glasses from Red House are sent down to Kelmscott Manor, but she cannot find houseroom for the huge dining table. She offers it to Blunt, and so it is still there, at Newbuildings, his home in Sussex.

Jane also faced the prospect of substantial death duties. She agreed with the trustees that she could offset these taxes by donating some pictures and furniture to Oxford University. What should go? She had already lent out several of the more valuable works of art to exhibitions, as part of the commemorations of William's life. Four of Gabriel's large portrait drawings were on display in the South London Gallery, in Camberwell, and so was her wedding present from Ned Burne-Jones, the *Prioress's Tale Cabinet*. Jane's face was being inspected by the working men and women of Camberwell; her most personal objects were now on public view. She had already let them go. She now offered them permanently to the Keeper of the University Galleries in Oxford, in recognition of William's enduring affection for the city. Her pictures were repacked and transferred into his care. Her old life as *Proserpine*, her patience as she posed for *Reverie*, her days sitting quietly under Gabriel's gaze – this was all handed over. She kept the large oil painting, wearing the *Blue Silk Dress* that she had spent so long stitching. But she could not hold on to them all.

There were some very difficult choices. It was hardest to say goodbye to the things that had been loved by William, like 'the big old backgammon board . . . I could never play on it more, and I think none of us could'. What should she do with it?[16] The red and white pieces remained untouched in the evening, since he was gone.

*

While she was clearing the big house in Hammersmith, Jane was also considering her long-term future at Kelmscott Manor. This would be home from now on. Jane understood the importance of maintaining William's legacy, not just as a writer and designer, but as a social reformer. She chose to continue his work in her own way, with local, useful projects. Jane began talking to Robert Hobbs, the owner of the Manor and the estate, about ways to improve conditions for her village neighbours. She had the idea of opening a Reading Room, as a communal social space, where people could gather and learn. She hoped to move the piano from the coach house in London, and perhaps some of the simple chairs, too. May's Socialist choir was no longer meeting in Hammersmith every week. Therefore this was an opportunity to donate the piano and furniture to working people who might value them. But in the end, the scheme was shelved for many years. She managed to establish 'a little Reading Room' in a cottage in 1904, which she said was 'A great success. The men come instead of going to the public house.'[17] But it was not until 1934, the centenary of William's birth, that a Memorial Hall was opened in the village.

However, Jane did see another plan come to fruition, with the help of Philip Webb. She hoped to build some cottages in William's memory. She thought this might encourage a new teacher to join the school perhaps, and offer affordable, good-quality housing to one of the village families. Webb had already agreed to design William's gravestone. He had created William's first home at Red House, and now carefully crafted his last. Webb imagined a very restrained 'remembrance-stone': he said he wanted it to 'look like a shield or roof over the grave' and without a railing. He did not want his friend to look isolated 'in God's acre – a common ground for all'.[18]

With Webb's sensitivity to the place, and to her project, it was right that Jane turned to him for help with the new buildings. They began discussing 'the cottage and the land, and the ways and means' in August 1898. Webb wrote to Jane about what she thought was essential for these workers' homes. He suggested a pair of cottages, semi-detached, without the 'fashionable and useless parlour'. He said, 'I believe in a good sized sitting room, and a decent wash house. I suppose there must be 3 bedrooms to each cot?'[19]

The following summer he visited Kelmscott and walked the half-acre of field that had been set aside for the new buildings. Webb drew up his first sketch, showing the 'two simple gabled roofs'. He also took into account Jane's own view 'from the Manor house, if the trees would let you see it'. He had thought through the needs of the families who would live there, especially the woman's work of cooking and cleaning. (Despite his longstanding Socialist commitment, he still held firm to the convention that women and girls would be responsible for these heavy household tasks.) Webb planned a long 'keeping room' or 'chief living-room', with plenty of light and 'a work table being in the recessed part, away from the fireplace'. He hoped this would mean 'that the members of the family need not tumble over each other'. They would have 'breathing space'. There was a 'little yard with its covered sheds' where 'the mother of the family can do a good deal of wet work out of doors, and partly under the pent house roof, where she can air her pots and pans as well as her children'. There would be a well in the front garden, three bedrooms and 'a good corner for the little pantry'.[20] For Jane, these arrangements must have brought back memories of her own upbringing in a crowded, damp cottage, with no garden, no convenient space to wash up, nowhere to 'air' the children. Her desire to provide decent housing surely reflects Jane's personal experience, as much as William's influence.

The building of the cottages was delayed until Webb had formally retired. He was concerned that the quotations coming in for labour and materials were over-priced, and advised Jane to wait. Together they continued to talk through the look and feel of the houses, inside and out. They deliberately did not put a window in the attic; they wanted to avoid it being used as a cramped extra bedroom. And they made the downstairs more robust, deciding that 'the lower part of the kitchen walls is cemented, so that chairs and children should not dint it.'[21]

Jane was there in 1902 when they finally broke ground for this simple, sensible monument to her husband. She and Webb were creating a fitting tribute to William and his work. But others around Jane had already presented their own memories, their own versions of his life to public scrutiny. There were the many obituaries, which largely concentrated on William's career as a poet or interior designer.

The *Daily Telegraph* briefly referred to the more robust parts of his character, calling him 'a difficult man to tackle'.[22] For *The Times*, his political digressions were 'the results of a warm heart and a mistaken enthusiasm'.[23] They did not take his Socialism seriously. However, his comrades felt his loss keenly. The editor of one radical newspaper wrote: 'It does not matter what goes into the *Clarion* this week, because William Morris is dead . . . he was our best man, and he is dead.'[24] This tussle over his reputation, the need to define the 'real' William Morris, meant that there was a very swift attempt to publish an authorised 'Life'. Ned and Georgie Burne-Jones took the lead in this, sidestepping Jane and May.

William's written memorial was taken out of Jane's hands and given to Ned's son-in-law, J.W. Mackail, for safekeeping. On the very last page of his *Life*, William was described by Burne-Jones, 'his most intimate friend': 'He lives absolutely without the need of man or woman. He is really a sort of Viking, set down here, and making art because there is nothing else to do.'[25] Statements like this seemed to downplay his relationship with his wife and children.

Webb was not enthusiastic about the Mackail biography. He told Cockerell he was 'just a trifle upset by this "memoir" business – bother all biographies'. He remembered the unpleasantness caused by William Michael Rossetti, 'who stirred up his brother's quietly decomposing bones to stink-pot pitch'.[26] (No doubt there were deliberate echoes, in this troubling image, of Lizzie Siddall's exhumation, and fears that Jane's intimacy with Gabriel might be brought to light.) Webb imagined William himself reading Mackail's version of his life, the 'muttered thunder from the belly, ending with the penetrating punctuation of the "damn"'.[27]

There were difficulties about what to include, what to leave out. Mackail removed any mention of Jenny's epilepsy from the text and left her indisposition deliberately vague. Caring for Jenny was a central part of William and Jane's life. But instead Mackail's focus was turned on Jane, and her occasional melancholy, her weariness and bodily distress. Readers could not understand Jane's actions and appearance, if they did not know about the difficulties at home. The silence about Jenny created gaps in the narrative, uncomfortable moments that implied that Jane was self-absorbed, unnaturally aloof.

Mackail also made things awkward for Jane when he failed to fathom her reticence about her own upbringing. She was reluctant to allow him to print an image of her childhood home. She did not want to be reminded of the shabby passages off Holywell Street where she grew up. Mackail was not sympathetic to Jane's point of view. He found it 'unintelligible' that 'Mrs Morris feels ashamed of having lived in a little house among surroundings of extreme beauty before she married'. He implied that she was being unreasonable. Mackail hoped to emphasise William's honourable, almost heroic decision to become engaged to a working-class woman, as if he were a figure from a courtly love romance. Mackail wrote to Cockerell, hoping that he would persuade Jane to change her mind: 'I feel that it does fair injustice to Morris himself to gloss over the fact that he married "beneath him" and did so with perfect simplicity & as a thing which *he* had no reason to feel ashamed of in anyway. I have been obliged in some way to slur it over.'[28]

By pointing out the differences in background so bluntly, Mackail seems oblivious to his own insensitivity towards Jane's feelings. It is rare to find any of her circle referring to her humble origins, or showing any class prejudice towards her. Rosalind and George Howard did not do it. Neither did Lady Anne Blunt. But Mackail implies that Jane, as the working-class bride, matters less than her late husband. Mackail calls on Burne-Jones and Webb too, in his attempts to push her towards accepting his reading of her story.

It is Webb who listens to Jane. At first he tries to make a joke of her reluctance. We do not have her reply, but clearly she felt wounded, as he answers immediately, 'My dear Janey, O, dear me, what have I said? . . . I hope there was nothing in my letter which hurt you.'[29] And then, in response to her next letter, he writes more fully:

> My dear Janey,
> Your tenderly kind letter is very comforting to me, and I am almost glad I unwittingly gave you some pain . . . now that you have opened to me your real reason for objecting to its use there . . . I have always felt that your having been born in Oxford was a kindly tie between us, and I feel it even more now that both of our families had their rather sad lives there.[30]

It was not shame that Jane wanted to forget, but sadness. We do not know what she told Webb about her girlhood, what revelations she made about her family. But he immediately took her part in the disagreement with Mackail. He recognised that it would be doing Jane an 'injustice', to use Mackail's word, if her oldest friends tried to compel her to revisit the unhappiness of her early years in Oxford. None of them could fully know what she had escaped by marrying William. Only Bessie, who visited Jane more frequently in the years after William's death, understood the difficulties of their background, the grim realities of dirt and drunkenness and early death that the sisters had witnessed.

Webb made sure that Jane knew he was on her side. He wrote to her often, thanking her for sending gifts of flowers when he was sick. She posted some fritillaries to him in April 1903. 'They travelled beautifully,' he said and 'are hearty flowers, and to my child's eye are Maudlin water walks all over'.[31] This was, he hoped, a shared and cheerful memory of their growing up close to the meadows that still skirted Oxford in the 1840s. He also reminded her of the things that William had taught them together, the tales he had woven for his friends. 'You remember', Webb wrote shakily in pencil, 'in the Icelandic Edda, tis said "those I loved most I treated worst" – or to that effect . . . Well I could not lift myself to return the good wishes of your last letter, for the whole body of me was against doing anything, & I could not even read.'[32] These ancient stories had become part of themselves, their way of framing the world.

Webb tried to keep in touch with May too, especially when Jane was busy with Jenny. As he never married, the Morris girls were almost like family to him. He wanted to be a sympathetic friend to May, as he tried to be for her mother. Webb saw her around the time that May's divorce from Sparling was made absolute. He wanted to encourage her, but he said he feared 'hurting her feeling in any way, and you know I am apt to be too frank . . . I think too she has some of her father's shyness.' It was hard to watch May's misery. 'I am saddened', he said, 'when I see her sitting as the pain-touched woman in a dark dress.'[33] May was even more upset by Mackail's biography than her mother. She had wanted William's life to be celebrated by someone who knew 'at first hand, not by hearsay and scholarly learning'. She complained to Anne Cobden-Sanderson about her 'dislike of his handling this subject', saying 'I wish I were able to keep my opinions more closely bottled. For Heaven's sake, don't give me away.'[34] She did not want to cause a permanent rift with the Burne-Joneses.

May was able to transform her discontent into something more positive, when she took on responsibility for editing her father's writings. She could now redress the balance of the Mackail biography by publishing her own memories and readings of William's lectures, stories and poems in the *Introductions to the Collected Works*. The twenty-four volumes came out steadily from 1910 to 1915. Jane was closely involved with the process. Not only did she provide her daughter with information about the early days of Red House and the beginnings of the Firm; she also took great care to look through many of the manuscripts as they were being edited. This was a joint effort by mother and daughter. It was a scholarly edition, but with the added pleasure of May's personal prefaces. The family tales, the 'few fragments of "Arthurian" verses' from the 1850s, the sympathetic accounts of William's travels and political convictions all made these volumes more intimate. Even now, as we read them, we seem to stand closer to William and his work, to walk with him in the gardens at Merton Abbey, to feel his excitement at a new pattern, a new dye. May ended the last introduction by William's graveside: 'A bay-tree stands at the head . . . An Oak branch on one side of the grey stone, a Vine on the other.' Jane did not live to see the final volumes printed. And so May reminds her readers of her mother's part in the story she has been telling. She says that 'now, beside the letters into which the little mosses have clustered, another name is being cut.'[35]

*

William's family had to find new ways of living after his death. As Jane said, 'I found it very difficult to mix with humankind, and I am not unhappy in this seclusion.'[36] She developed a new rhythm to her year. Most of the time Jane saw 'a few intimate friends only'.[37] During the winter months, she moved from place to place, staying in hotels or rented rooms, returning to London occasionally. She developed a close network of female friends. With some, she could share the experience of growing old together. Others were younger, often artists or writers, like the bookbinder Katharine Adams, who exchanged cheerful letters with Jane. In the winter of 1899–1900, and again the following year, Jane tried taking a house with Crom's sister, Marion Price Grove. They leased 22 St Mary Abbots Terrace, a townhouse very close to the home of Frederic Leighton, at the far end of Kensington High Street. Jane stayed there for a few days in early October to help Marion Grove settle in. She had the chance to see the Arts and Crafts exhibition which included a large memorial display of William's work. 'I think our things look extremely well,' she told Cockerell. 'I was greatly pleased and told everybody so. Some of the designs I had not seen since the day they were finished.'[38] In this letter, Jane sounds optimistic, glad that the objects she and William had cherished were valued by others, too. However, after two winters in town, she did not repeat the experiment. She spent too many weeks away to make it worthwhile, in Bognor, and then in Falmouth and Torquay.

Jane wrote to Crom that it was 'curious to see how very soon one sinks away from things' although 'not out of remembrance of a few faithful souls.'[39] She tried Lyme Regis several times, where she found 'a comfortable lodging with our servants'. She could 'get to the beach in two minutes – I walk there every morning and watch the gulls either soaring overhead or drifting on the waves – a most beautiful sight.'[40] The following year, staying in the same house, she found the early spring weather 'now perfect'. She told Cockerell, 'I noticed a frisky air on all faces this morning.'[41]

Jane was not especially lonely. At least in the years immediately after William's death, friends made an effort to visit. Mary de Morgan, who had helped nurse William in his last days, stayed in Lyme for the Easter holidays in 1898. Jane said, 'She seemed to like roving about the shore.' Lucy Faulkner, now Mrs Orrin-Smith, her old neighbour from Queen Square days, was also close at hand. She had taken lodgings next door. Jane said 'We often meet on our morning rambles.' It was a reason for Jane to get up and out, to walk a little way along the seafront, talking about friends near and far. Lucy's sister Kate was very poorly with tuberculosis. And her brother Charley had died in 1892, three years after suffering a stroke. Philip Webb was close to all the Faulkners. He had spent long evenings with his bed-ridden friend, and supported his sisters when they were in London. Ned Burne-Jones blamed Charley's illness on his Socialist agitation – 'It killed him by the most painful of deaths,' Ned said, 'a terrible one lasting for years.'[42]

Ned also died too soon. He never fully recovered from losing

William; Ned said it felt like the halving of his life. His death, on 16 June 1898, was a 'bitter sorrow' to Jane, 'a frightful time'.[43] She did her best to console Georgie, and visited her in the Burne-Joneses' country house at Rottingdean. Like Jane, Georgie had to empty the big family home. She cleared Ned's vast studio, filled with half-finished canvases, and beloved works that he had kept for sentiment's sake. There was a sale at Christie's barely a month after his death. As Jane well knew, 'winding up a household is so costly'.[44] She managed to see the retrospective show of Ned's work at the New Gallery, which closed in April 1899. Webb had visited some weeks earlier, and wrote to her with great affection for the 'fabulous pictures . . . of sailed-away Ned's'. He said he was left feeling 'sadly-serious, with a lurking joy at the bottom, that I had been allied for those 40 years with the two men we knew – enough'.[45]

Georgie and Jane became more companionable as widows. They recovered some of the early intimacy they had enjoyed as young wives, before politics and careers and ill-health intervened. Jane continued to write to her daughters about her visits to 'Aunt Georgie' well into the twentieth century. We know that they had a 'delightful week' together in July 1913, 'talking of old times'. 'She is not very strong,' Jane told Cockerell, 'but better than I expected to find her.'[46]

Jane was staying 'at Rottingdean very happily' shortly after Georgie's biography of her own husband was published.[47] *Memorials of Edward Burne-Jones* was a remarkable record of his thoughts, his work and his friendships. By taking matters into her own hands, Georgie was also able to avoid any revelations about Ned's chaotic and long-standing affair with Maria Zambaco. She simply skipped over the whole dreadful year of 1869. The only hint she gave was in the opening line of her second volume: 'Heart, thou and I are here, sad and alone.'[48] Georgie's meticulous research makes *Memorials* an essential resource for understanding Ned, William and their circle. And her warm style, her appreciation of their delight in the Gothic world, their desire to make something fresh and beautiful, these are the qualities that make Georgie's writing so precious. Undoubtedly, she wanted to safeguard her husband's reputation. But she still created a joyful book about an extraordinary group of men. Jane was delighted that Georgie's book 'has been well received, as it deserves to be'. Blunt evidently thought that Jane herself should have been more visible in Georgie's account. But Jane replied, 'Why should there be any special record of me when I have never done any special work?'[49]

This is a good question. Jane had rarely sought attention and especially since William's death, she led 'a curious isolated life ... almost that of a hermit, and somehow it suits me'.[50] She was still stitching, when she was strong enough and the light was good, but no longer producing the big embroidery projects that had brightened the homes of her husband's clients. Jane had become famous as a model. And she was admired and reviled in equal measure as a pioneer of 'Artistic' dress. She had created a welcoming space for painters, poets and activists in her homes. In her own mind, though, she had done nothing special. Old friends still valued her company, however, and younger people sought her out. She nurtured their talent, sometimes by offering them small commissions, and sometimes by inviting them to Kelmscott Manor, to paint or think or simply look around.

Jane still had the quiet presence of a great model. Mary de Morgan's sister-in-law, Evelyn, was an established painter working in the Pre-Raphaelite tradition. She wanted to make an image of Jane in her splendid sixties. In 1904, she sat for the stately figure in Evelyn's allegory *The Hour Glass*. Evelyn drew a pastel portrait of Jane, her white hair framed by a deep blue cushion, her head slightly tilted, her eyes lowered, thoughtful.

The queenliness that other artists had seen in Jane was also revealed in this work. Evelyn de Morgan created a large oil painting based on her study. In the final image, the woman's hair is dark again, and her cheeks are slightly smoother. But it is Jane, the survivor, in a gorgeous robe decorated with seed pearls. She holds an hourglass, watching the sand flow out, like an ancient figure of time passing. The painting is perhaps overladen with decorative details, too rich in esoteric symbolism: we see the angelic musician in the doorway, the procession of lovers in the tapestry behind the throne. But Jane holds our attention as we imagine her train of thought. As she wrote to Blunt, a few years later, 'I know too well these windings up of life are not very cheerful, if one could just drop off quietly like Autumn leaves, it would be so pleasant for everybody.'[51]

*

Jane's closest friend in these later years was Marie Spartali Stillman, now returned from Italy. She visited Marie 'in her new house among the woods' in Surrey, and also enjoyed spending time with her on the Isle of Wight.[52] They travelled there together in late December 1902, but Marie had to visit her parents for Christmas. So Jane told Crom, 'I passed my Xmas Day in the company of total strangers.' She was looking forward to the arrival of Olive Cockerell, Sydney's sister and a professional illustrator. Olive was 'an excellent walker too', so they could enjoy the views around Ventnor.[53] As so often, reading Jane's surviving letters, we see this creative woman in passing. She is mentioned briefly as a companionable, energetic friend, and then she disappears from view. Olive is another of the many skilled women in Jane's circle who left no 'special record', and who died too young. She was lost to cancer at forty-two.

Still, Jane kept welcoming friends like Olive and Marie to join her at Kelmscott, as she returned home, season by season, to the old house. In springtime, she said she liked to 'be in my own den once more . . . watching things get greener every day'.[54] As she grew older, she worried about what would happen to her girls when she was gone. In 1904, she started discussing the possibility of buying the Kelmscott Manor outright – she was still leasing it from Hobbs. She did not complete the purchase until the very end of 1913, when she said, finally, 'I am to be the proud possessor of this place soon, it makes May very happy.'[55] It was, indeed, a good home for May in the long run. As Jane had hoped, May settled there, finding companionship and affection with a Cornishwoman, Mary Lobb. Miss Lobb, a land girl in the Great War, was devoted to May, and together they retraced William's journeys through Iceland. They both cared for Kelmscott Manor and its remarkable contents, ensuring that the stories of the place and the people who loved it would not be lost.

*

The garden at Kelmscott Manor, the way it sat in the landscape, was always as important as the things inside the house. To the end of her life, Jane still paid close attention to the small, hopeful changes outside. She noticed, one April, how 'The garden is beginning to grow at last, we shall have blossom (apple) out in a day or two and then I always feel good and grateful to the powers that be.'[56] She liked to be in the open air whenever she could. Jane told May of the lovely sight she found on one of her last visits to Kelmscott. She 'was tempted to go out after tea and saw such a sunset with the harvest moon rising . . . the men working in the cornfields, many of them on the wains showing clear against the sky'.[57] Mixed in with this beauty was the memory, too, of the wagon that had carried William to the churchyard, back in the last century.

There was a sense of closeness to the soil here, of being exposed to the elements. Even in the early summer, Jane and her guests could be surprised by the wildness. She wrote to Cockerell in May 1898 how she 'almost cried with the cold yesterday afternoon in the meadows where we had gone to look for fritillaries, the wind nearly blew us into the river'.[58] Despite this, she stayed in the old house as much as possible, largely for Jenny's sake. When her daughter was really struggling – sometimes Jenny had seizures every day – Jane had to arrange for her to be looked after away from home. They found some rooms in Burford, where Jenny could recover and Jane could visit. But with the help of live-in nurses, they tried to make themselves comfortable at Kelmscott.

There was always the risk of the water rising, and flooding the fields around. Occasionally the floods were more serious. Even in the summer the house was sometimes not safe. In June 1903, Jane reported that they were 'surrounded by water and cut off from the world . . . Though we blocked up the doors cleverly, it was too strong for us and by midday we had 6 or 7 inches of water in the house.' With the help of the housekeeper and gardener, they were able to lift the furniture and fabrics. 'The newly hatched chicks are in the attic above my head,' she wrote, and the other poultry were scooped up and 'hastily pushed into the brewhouse', tucked into packing crates. Most of the villagers had their own little boats, and Jane kept one in her boathouse, so they managed for several days. When the baker came across from Lechlade, it was a relief to everyone.[59] The villagers relied on him for their daily bread. Jane's description of this inundation suggests that she rather enjoyed the excitement, once she knew that everyone was safe, chickens and people alike.

Even without the flooding, Kelmscott still felt remote. When Marie Stillman visited in the early autumn of 1901, she was pleased that the house had retained the out-of-the-way atmosphere that she remembered. She wrote to a friend:

> I stayed at Kelmscott . . . for ten days & felt quite shut out of the busy world in that beautiful walled garden. I made two watercolours of the house and garden. One cannot imagine any place as quiet . . . Things have been at a standstill for 300 years probably.[60]

The twentieth century did reach Jane, little by little. She was still sitting in the orchard at the manor house ten years later, when some

American guests 'motored here from Broadway'. Jane said, 'I gave them tea in the garden on a Persian rug'. She showed them around the grounds but was too tired to give them a tour of the attics. Her visitors were charmed. Kelmscott was everything they had imagined. They found Jane 'all in white, sitting under a cherry tree in full bloom'. It was an image to treasure.

Other guests became flustered when they met Jane in real life, having known her only from Gabriel's idealised pictures and sensual verses. The poet Richard Le Gallienne, an admirer of Oscar Wilde, was also treated to tea in the orchard. When he said how much he liked the quince jam, Jane was delighted, telling him she had made it herself. She gave him a jar to take home. 'A jar of quince jam', he wrote, 'made by the beautiful lady whom Morris had loved and Rossetti had painted! It was like receiving it at the hands of Helen of Troy'.[61] Jane's gift troubled him. Le Gallienne found it hard to treat her like a real woman, competent in the kitchen, transforming the fruits of her garden into this golden preserve. He wanted her to retain the two-dimensionality of the poems and pictures created thirty years ago. To him, Jane's character did not match her appearance. He imagined her as extraordinary, mythical, unnervingly beautiful. Jane had always found it rather amusing that people would seek her out, just to look at her, as if she were indeed a work of art left over from another age. But those who knew her understood that Jane had always been more than just a face, a pose. She was caring, practical, shyly humorous, and skilled.

From 1910, Jane was finishing a last embroidery: it now covers William's beautiful bed, although he never lived to see it. She completed May's pattern of knots and flowers, in wool and silk on linen. There are tulips and violets, poppies, daisies and a single clump of violets. A tiny stream runs along the edge, with an even tinier image of Kelmscott Manor, its rose bushes and its birds. Jane carefully stitched a verse from one of William's poems across the top:

> I know a little garden close
> Set thick with lily and red rose
> Where I would wander if I might
> From dewy dawn to dewy night
> And have one with me wandering.

When it was done, Jane was pleased with her work. She took her needle and stitched her signature on the corner of the fabric, claiming this as her own. At last, after a lifetime of making, she felt able to put her name to one of her creations. This was Jane's final act, perhaps, in her long career of self-fashioning. She could now see herself as an artist, too.

Jane knew she was growing old. At New Year 1914, she was in Bath, having striven against depression, colds, and 'my battered heart'.[62] She was taking the advice of a new doctor, although she recognised that there was little he could reasonably suggest: 'Of course, he can't cure me of being 74'. But she added, 'I am looking forward hopefully to the glorious spring-time once more.'[63] She did not live to see the apple blossom. Jane died on 26 January 1914, suffering from heart disease and diabetes. She had 'wanted to live on for Jenny's sake, because she felt how Jenny would miss her'.[64] But she had to trust that May and her old friends would now care for her daughter.

Jane was buried beside William. Her death was noticed by *The Times*, which printed a sympathetic obituary, recognising her skills as 'an exquisite embroideress'. The article began by offering Jane as an image to be looked at and admired, a catalogue of parts, public property: 'All the world knows the masses of dark hair, the ivory complexion and exquisite features, the beautiful hands and the great grey eyes'. But then the writer went on, questioning this view of Jane as surface, and showing her depths: 'Only her intimate friends knew the kindliness, the good sense and the girlish love of fun, which remained until the end of her life.'[65]

It seems right to leave the last word to Jane herself. She was silenced for so long. It is good to hear her own voice, to think of her sitting in the garden in the spring of 1912, a little frail but warm, content. She tells her daughter, 'I am basking in the sunshine today like a pussy.'[66]

Recipes from Kelmscott

When Jane moved to Kelmscott Manor after William's death, she brought with her a small collection of recipes. She kept it in a blue leather folder, tied with ribbon, and embossed with the Kelmscott Press emblem. It was evidently a well-loved thing. Jane and May added more recipes year by year. Some they wrote out carefully, others were hurried notes. Several were given to them by friends. Many were imaginative ways to use up a glut of ingredients; apples, tomatoes or elderberries from their garden. One, a dish of chicken and rice, was adapted from a recipe by the famous chef Charles Francatelli (1805-1876). A selection of these recipes are transcribed and reprinted here in their original forms for the first time, from the stockpot left to simmer for two days, to the salt cod cooked in white wine and cinnamon. They have not been tested in a 21st century kitchen or with 21st century methods, and are presented in their original formats and with traditional measurements, in exactly the way that Jane wrote them down.

There are recipes that reminded Jane and May of their travels. We find instructions for gnocchi with parmesan, written in pencil by Jane, perhaps when she was staying in Italy. There is also a recipe for sweet Icelandic waffles, typed out by a friend from Reykjavik.

Seasonings are often as important as the main ingredients. The dishes are flavoured with onions, cayenne, tamarinds, chillies, and sultanas for sweetness.

These are records of Jane's home life, her family and her friendships. The quantities show that she was rarely catering for large numbers. These are mostly recipes for small dinners or tea parties, not formal entertainments. She includes some traditional local favourites, like her Dough Cake, a version of the Oxfordshire lardy cake. Occasionally we find something unexpected. Jane's Cornish pasties are filled with pork, not beef. Her 'Eggs in Snow' resemble a soufflé, but are unsweetened and flavoured simply with vanilla. Perhaps her 'Soho Cod' was named after a memorable dinner out with friends.

Most of the pages come down to us without context. We do not know, for example, who Ada was – but she passed on at least two recipes to the Morris family. It is not even clear why these particular recipes were so carefully preserved. After all, the family employed a cook, even when Jane was first married, so she did not have to work in the kitchen herself. Do the recipes reflect their favourite dishes, or special memories of meals at home, or cherished times with friends? They certainly open up another unacknowledged aspect of Jane's practical skills as a homemaker. Most of the recipes assume that the reader is reasonably experienced, that she knows how to manage a slow or brisk fire, how to mix or whisk, how to bottle or broil. The range of recipes suggests that Jane was familiar with the workings of her kitchen. It was not enough for her to plan menus with her cook, and then return to the drawing room. She was handy here by the stove, and enjoyed preparing fruit for jams, or stirring a cake batter.

We know that May spent a few weeks at Kelmscott Manor before her wedding, learning to cook and keep house. It seems likely that Jane wrote down some of these recipes at that time. She wanted to prepare her daughter: May and her fiancé were starting married life on a limited income. So Jane shared her method for making bread.

As we read it, we see how Jane took pleasure in the process. This most homely food is described carefully. It is a tactile experience, requiring patience. Jane shows her daughter how to work the dough with her hands, when she should pick up a wooden spoon, or shake a little flour onto her board. She explains how to make something simple but lovely to look at and touch and smell. Jane ends with a note of satisfaction: 'it needs some practice to make the loaves round and shapely'.

BREAD

To make bread

Flour, 1 peck
Water, 1 quart (tepid)
Salt, 3 oz
Yeast, very small teacupful (brewer's)

Put the flour in a large pan, mix in the salt well with the hands, then take a wooden spoon and make a hole in the middle of the flour, then pour in it the water mixing therein a very little of the flour, add the yeast, then sprinkle a little flour on the top, cover the pan with a cloth and set before the fire for an hour. (This is called setting the sponge).

Next take 3 pints of water (tepid, have ready another pint) and pour into the pan, then knead all together for a few minutes, if then you find any flour dry, add a little more water, go on kneading for about a quarter of an hour, then set the pan before the fire again for about 2 hours, the dough will then have risen, you then divide the mass in 5 or 6 pieces, and knead them on the pastry slab, shaking a little flour at intervals, put each loaf in the oven when you have kneaded it, and be careful not to place them too near each other. 2 or 3 inches spaces should be left for the rising- (it needs some practice to make the loaves round and shapely).

CAKES

Swedish apple cake (from 19 Kensington Park Gardens, W11)

The eggs are mixed in with the butter, sugar, cornflour & ground sweet almonds.

Apples, almonds, cornflour, sugar, 4 eggs, candied peel, cream

Core and stew 2 lbs apples, which have been cut into quarters. Butter a baking dish & put the apples at the bottom. Then make a paste of the following:

½ lb butter, 3 tablespoons cornflour, ½ lb caster sugar, ½ lb ground sweet almonds, a handful of chopped peel. Cream the butter and add it, make all into a paste and spread a layer over the apples; then another layer of apples, and finish with a layer of the almond paste atop. Sprinkle the top with chopped almonds and bake

Dough Cake

2 lbs dough, 6 ozs lard or nice fresh dripping, 6 ozs sugar, 6 ozs currants, a little peel & spice if liked

Roll out the dough, spread on it a third of the lard, sugar & currants, fold over – and repeat twice. Bake on a tin.

Recipe for waffles

1 pint wheat flour

1 pint sweet milk

1 heaping spoonful butter

2 eggs

1 heaping spoonful baking powder (Royal baking powder is best)

½ teaspoon salt

Stir baking powder and salt into the dry flour. Beat eggs and butter together until light. Sift flour into butter and eggs, a little at a time, and add milk alternately with flour, until you have a batter of the consistency of thick custard.

The waffle-iron must be *very* hot, and well greased. In irons of ordinary size put about 3 tablespoons full of batter; shut quickly, and bake to a rich brown. The irons should be greased only enough to keep the batter from sticking.

(Reykjavik)

Orange cake

The syrup: 30 lumps of sugar; 4 oranges; 1 lemon

Rub the sugar on the rind of the lemon and of three oranges: put this sugar in a saucepan with the juice and boil it until it is syrupy

The cake: weight of 5 eggs in sugar, 3 in self-raising flour, whisk the whites and yolks separately then together – Dribble in the mixed flour and sugar, beating with a fork. A tablespoon of boiling water just before putting in oven in a flat tin.

The cake is sliced in two horizontally, the syrup laid on the lower half to soak in well; the upper half laid on, and then all cut in oblongs.

Cake (Ada 1911)

¾ lb Flour

½ lb currants

¼ lb sultanas

6 oz butter

6 oz castor sugar

3 eggs

A little lemon peel finely grated

A little lemon juice

Bake in a good oven

Gingerbread cake

8oz Pastry flour

4oz butter (salt is preferable)

4 oz syrup

4 oz demerara sugar

6 oz sultana raisins

4 oz china ginger sliced fine

3 oz ground almonds

2 eggs

1½ teaspoons mixed spice

1 teaspoon ground dried ginger

½ oz carbonate of soda

Mix the dry ingredients together

Boil the butter, sugar & syrup together. Draw off & allow to cool a little, stirring occasionally.

Whip the eggs alone and then beat them into the syrup mixture when it is cooled enough not to crack them.

Make a hole in the centre of the dry ingredients & pour in the syrup mixture, thoroughly stirring till the ingredients are perfectly blended.

Bake in a *slow* oven. It is very important that it should not be overbaked, but taken out as soon as the testing needle comes out clean. Lay a sheet of paper over the top.

Time to bake: about 3 hours. Keeps 6 months in a biscuit tin.

EGGS & DAIRY

Eggs in snow

Take 3 eggs, beat them up well, then take three quarters of a pint of milk and a bit of vanilla, put in a round dish, and place on the top of a sauce-pan of boiling water, leave it till the milk boils gently, then pour the beaten eggs in and set the dish in the oven to bake lightly.

Cheese Balls

Beat the whites of two eggs to a stiff froth. Stir in two ounces of grated Parmesan cheese, salt and cayenne to taste; shape the mixture into balls the size of marbles, and drop them into boiling fat. Fry them for five minutes till of a golden brown, drain well and sprinkle cheese over them.

Gnocchi di Semolina

Into boiling milk drop semolina, enough to make a stiff porridge when cooked. Boil thoroughly with some salt, & pour it out onto a pastry-board. Smooth out with a knife till it is 1/3 inch thick. Let it get quite cold.

Cut into rounds with a small wine-glass or pastry cutter, & arrange in an earthenware baking dish with grated parmesan & dabs of butter. Bake in a quick oven until brown.

SOUP

Haricot bean soup

½ pint beans, soak all night, strain and put in boiling water with 3 large onions, a little salt, boil 1 hour. Strain, put back in saucepan with pint of cold milk, boil until tender, rub through hair sieve, season.

Stockpot (no salt)

Wash the bones, lots of onions cut in halves without peeling, scrub the carrots cut in halves – bacon bones, rinds, any odds and ends, herbs many – boil for 2 days.

FISH

Soho Cod

Take a piece of cod, sprinkle over with chopped onions, a little parsley, peper [sic] & a little lemon juice; cover it over with water, and braise it till half the water is gone; then with the remainder of the water mix a little butter & flour, & cover the fish with this sauce. If cod is used in place of meat, serve with boiled rice.

Broiled Brill

Wash and trim the fish, dry it well with a cloth.

Put in a deep plate 3 tablespoonsful of salad-oil, pepper & salt & cayenne & juice of ½ a lemon.

Dip fish in the marinade & grill it over a clear fire for 8 or 10 minutes, brush the grill with some of the mixture, turn it over and cook for 25 minutes. Can be served with any kind of sauce.

Stewed salt cod

Take 3 lbs of cod, wash it and dry in cloth. Cut in small pieces and dip in oatmeal flour. Fry 2 oz fine chopped onion with 2oz butter & 2 tablespoonfuls of oil. Fry onion to a light brown, add the cod, cook for 7 or 8 minutes, stirring gently, and now a gill of warm broth by degrees & 1 wineglassful of white wine; season with pepper & a pinch of cinnamon. Stew slowly for 25 minutes in saucepan partly covered with its lid.

VEGETABLES

Cabbage with cheese

Boil large cabbage till tender with salt, drain thoroughly, chop fine – butter a pie-dish, put in alternate layers of cabbage and grated cheese (finishing with cheese), place little lumps of butter on the top and bake till brown (about 1 hour).

MEAT

Cornish Pasties – sufficient for four good sized

Ingredients:

1 lb pork

4 potatoes

2 onions

Little sage, pepper and salt to taste

Cut the pork up into dice, chop the onions, & slice potatoes very thin, add seasonings etc, mix all together & damp slightly.

Pastry

1 ½ lbs flour

6 oz lard

Pinch salt

Mix with water roll out and divide into four

Place the meat etc on to a piece of pastry, one half of it, and fold the other half over, turn up the edge all round & crinkle with the thumb and finger.

Bake in a moderate over for 1 ½ hrs or till it smells which is a sign it is cooked in hottest place.

Quick oven for 10 min: to set the edges, then on the bottom shelf – shd [sic] done in an hour

Chicken and rice

Truss the chicken for boiling and put in the pot with half a pound of rice, 1 oz butter, a few peppercorns and a little salt; just cover the fowl with water. Put in onions and carrots sliced small, a bunch of mixed herbs and a bay leaf. Set the whole to simmer very gently indeed over a slow fire for 4 hours. Serve in the broth, with the vegetables and rice arranged round neatly.

Francatelli (modified)

Note: it is better to put the carrots in with the fowl, and the rice and other vegetables 2 hours later

DRINKS

Barley Water

3 tablespoons pearl barley

Washed several times. Then put it in a fresh quart of water. Bring to the boil, simmer 10 min. Strain, add sugar & lemon to taste.

Sloe Gin

Equal amounts of sloes and white sugar. Prick the sloes & half fill the bottles with the sugared fruit, & fill up with gin.

Hot orangeade

Peel of an orange cut very thin and put in a glass with honey or sugar, boiling water poured on this, then the juice of the orange squeezed in.

Elderflower Wine

6 gallons water

18 lbs sugar (loaf)

2 quarts flowers

Juice and rind of 6 lemons

6lbs raisins chopped

Put all into a barrel – work with a little yeast. Stir it every day for a week then fasten down. It will be ready to bottle in 6 months.

PRESERVES

English tomato Chutnee (ripe)

3 lbs: Tomatoes (scald and skin)

1 lb onions shred

1 lb apples

½ lb tamarinds

¾ lb brown sugar

¾ pint dark vinegar

14 pickled chilies

1½ oz whole ginger (bruised)

½ oz whole pepper

½ oz all spice (these put in muslin bags)

½ lb sultana raisins

A few [illegible] seeds

Boil all together for 1½ hours

To stew pears (Ada 1910)

Pare, place in saucepan, cover with water, boil fast for 2 hours (put a few bits of peel in a bag), they will then be a nice pink colour, then add sugar, boil quickly for half an hour, they come out in a clear syrup.

Elderberry syrup

1 lb berries 1 lb sugar 1 pint water, juice of a lemon, a tiny bit of the peel, a shredded almond

Boil about ¾ hour, strain and bottle when cold.

Orange Marmalade

Feb 1908

12 Seville Oranges

6 Sweet Oranges

3 Lemons

A pint of water & 1 lb sugar to each orange-

Peel the oranges very thin, cut up fine both oranges and peel, taking out all pips, peel the lemons and cut up fine the peel only – Put all in a large basin, leave to stand all night in the water – Next day put all in a preserving-pan and boil for two hours, then add the sugar & boil again for one hour.

Squeeze the lemons, add the juice and boil for another ten minutes.

Tomato chutnee

Take 8 lbs: of Tomatoes, cut in thick slices, sprinkle 1/4lb salt over them, let them stand all night. Next morning boil the tomatoes with 4 large onions cut in slices for 2 hours, strain through a coarse sieve. Then add

4 large apples

1 lb brown sugar

1 lb sultanas & chillies

1 oz black pepper

Tamarinds

Crushed ginger

½ oz powdered cloves

Salt spoonful cayenne

Same of allspice

1 pint vinegar

Boil again for 2 or 3 hours till quite thick. Put into bottles well corked.

Acknowledgements

This book could not have been written without the encouragement of Dr Jan Marsh. Her scholarship has transformed our understanding of the 19th century art world. She has led the way in telling the stories of the women of the Pre-Raphaelite movement, in pioneering biographies and exhibitions. I am especially grateful for her work with Frank C. Sharp, in rediscovering and editing Jane Morris's letters. These have formed the backbone of my rewriting of Jane's life here. She has kindly discussed this project from the beginning and dealt patiently with my questions over many years.

I would also like to thank the convenors, speakers and participants at the 'Pre-Raphaelite Sisters' Conference, held at the University of York, December 2019, to coincide with the National Portrait Gallery exhibition. Both the exhibition and conference demonstrated the wealth of new work on Victorian women. I enjoyed talking to Robyne Calvert, for her knowledge of Artistic Dress, among many other things, and I have also benefited from the wisdom of Katie Faulkner. Melissa Gustin, Rhian Addison Mc Creanor and Caroline Dakers have responded thoughtfully to my questions about Sara Prinsep and her circle.

Nerissa Taysom and her colleagues at the Watts Gallery, and Cathy

De'Freitas and her colleagues at the William Morris Society have generously given me the chance to share early versions of my research.

I have relied on the help of many archivists and curators, as I have tried to look afresh at the manuscript letters and notes. Thanks go to the staff at the British Library who made it possible for me to see Jane's little keepsake books, and her correspondence with Gabriel Rossetti. I am grateful to Ainsley Vinall and his colleagues at the William Morris Gallery for access to the archives, and help with numerous questions.

I am also thankful to Rupert Maas for showing me a pastel portrait of Jane by Gabriel Rossetti, and offering access to his extensive library and archive; to Richard Bucht at Hatchards; and Hon. Philip Howard and the Estate Office at Naworth Castle.

Special thanks go to the Fellows and staff of the Society of Antiquaries, for information and access to Kelmscott Manor and its collections, especially Peter Cormack, Dominic Walsh and Kathy Haslam. This has been a time of transformation at Kelmscott, and their knowledge of the house and its history has been invaluable. It is reassuring to know that this remarkable place will continue to be preserved and loved, as a place of renewal, creativity and good fellowship. I am especially grateful to be granted permission to transcribe and publish the file of recipes from Kelmscott Manor, collected by Jane and May Morris.

The team at Quercus have been a constant support. I am so glad that we have been able to create this beautiful book together. My editor, Ben Brock, has been enthusiastic about Jane and William's story from the outset. Ana Sampson McLaughlin, Elizabeth Masters, and Ellie Nightingale have responded imaginatively, helping to bring this work to a wider audience. I am grateful to them and all their colleagues, especially Alison MacDonald, Georgina Difford, Andrew Smith, John English and Robert Davies. My agent Jonathan Conway has been there, at every stage, to give me words of encouragement.

This book has been written in difficult circumstances. It has been a time of lockdown, loss and separation. We have all been working in the shadow of illness. At every stage, I have been encouraged by my dear friends. They have never failed to lift me up, even though they too have faced upheavals and sadness. I will always be thankful for the constant friendship of Julia, Elizabeth and Heather; for my own History Girls, Susan and Clare; and for Melissa and Angela, unfailingly funny, wise and caring.

While I have been writing about Jane and William and their family, I have inevitably been aware that this too has been a family project. John has listened to my tales of Kelmscott and Red House for more than twenty years. My parents have given practical and loving support. Without them, this book would have been very hard to write. Thank you for your abiding faith in my work. Jonathan has been splendid and kind as ever. My girls, Rosalind and Beatrice, have shown me joy and wisdom beyond words. You are the best of me. You have helped me to 'Keep Writing. Keep Going'.

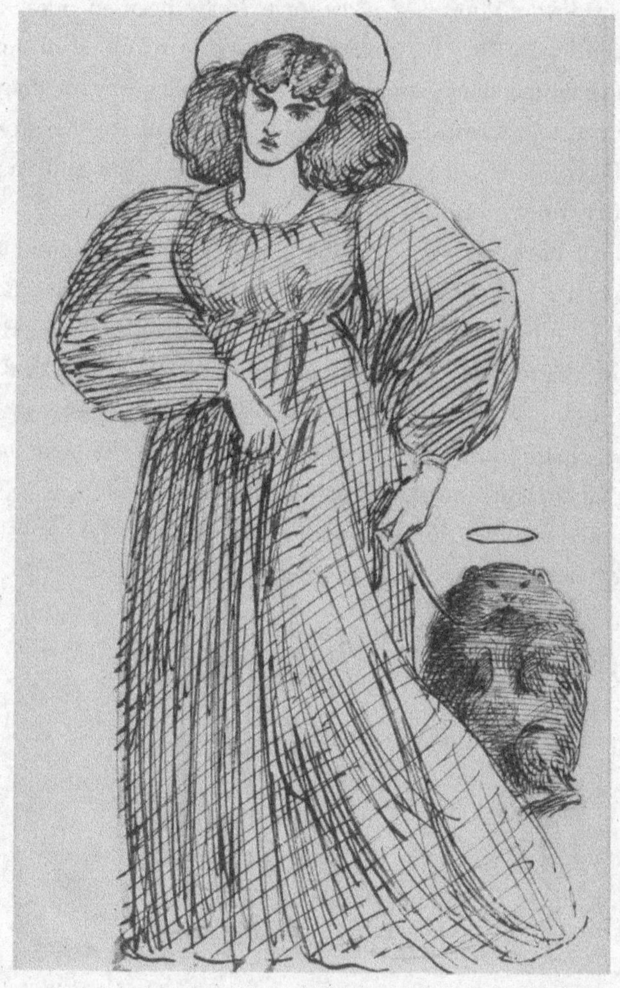

Dante Gabriel Rossetti, *Janey and the Wombat*, pen and ink, 1869,
British Museum

Notes

Preface: How We Might Live

1   William Morris, 'The Prospects of Architecture in Civilization' (1881), *The Collected Works of William Morris, with Introductions by his Daughter May Morris* (1913), reprinted New York: Russell & Russell, 1966, vol. 22, p. 150.

2   W. B. Yeats, recollected in *Fortnightly Review*, March 1903, quoted E. P. Thompson, *William Morris: Romantic to Revolutionary* (London: Lawrence & Wishart, 1955), reprinted London: Merlin Press, 1976, p. 251.

3   J. W. Mackail, *The Life of William Morris*, London, New York and Bombay: Longmans, Green and Co., 1901, vol. 2, p. 349.

4   Charles Rowley, quoted Frank C. Sharp and Jan Marsh (eds), *The Collected Letters of Jane Morris*, Woodbridge: The Boydell Press, 2012, p. 14.

5   Jane Morris to Wilfrid Scawen Blunt, March 1893, ibid., p. 16.

6   William Morris, 'The Aims of Art' (1886), *Collected Works*, vol. 23, p. 94.

7   William Morris, 'How we live & How we might live', 1885, *Collected Works*, vol. 23, p. 21.

8   Edward Burne-Jones, quoted J. W. Mackail, manuscript notebooks, William Morris Gallery, vol. 2, p. 85.

Chapter 1: Epping Forest, 1834–1852

1 Mackail, *Life of William Morris*, vol. 1, pp. 19–20.

2 Ibid., p. 8.

3 Ibid., p. 5.

4 Morris's comment was recalled by Wilfrid Scawen Blunt in his diary, 31 May 1896. See Fiona MacCarthy, *William Morris: A Life for Our Time*, London: Faber and Faber, 1994, p. 18.

5 Mackail, *Life of William Morris*, vol. 1, p. 10.

6 William Morris to William Sharman, April 1886, quoted MacCarthy, *William Morris: A Life*, p. 21.

7 Mackail, *Life of William Morris*, vol. 1, p. 10.

8 William Morris , *The Novel on Blue Paper* (1872), ed. Penelope Fitzgerald, London and West Nyack: The Journeyman Press, 1982, p. 22.

9 Ibid., p. 26.

10 William Morris, 'News from Nowhere' (1890), *Collected Works*, vol. 16, p. 60.

11 MacCarthy, *William Morris: A Life*, p. 7.

12 William Morris, 1895, quoted MacCarthy, *William Morris: A Life*, p. 15.

13 Charles Manby Smith, 'Unfashionable Clubs', *Curiosities of London Life* (1853), quoted by Lee Jackson in The Dictionary of Victorian London website: https://www.victorianlondon.org/.

14 Ibid.

15 William Morris, 1895, quoted MacCarthy, *William Morris: A Life*, p. 15; Aymer Vallance, *William Morris: His Art, his Writings and his Public Life* (1897), London: Studio Editions, 1995, p. 3.

16 William Morris, 'The Lesser Arts of Life' (1882), *Collected Works*, vol. 22, p. 254.

17 William Morris to William Sharman, April 1886, quoted MacCarthy, *William Morris: A Life*, p. 21.

18 It is not clear why William Morris Senior died so suddenly. His death

certificate does not seem to be accessible. The only 'William Morris' whose death was registered in Epping in September 1847 was the infant son of a bricklayer, who died of inflammation of the throat.

19 William Morris to Andreas Scheu, 15 September 1883, Norman Kelvin (ed.), *The Collected Letters of William Morris*, Princeton, New Jersey and Guildford: Princeton University Press, 1984, vol. 2, p. 228.

20 Ibid., p. 227.

21 MacCarthy, *William Morris: A Life*, p. 31.

22 William Morris to Philip Burne-Jones, December 1874, Kelvin (ed.), *Collected Letters*, vol. 1, p. 241.

23 MacCarthy, *William Morris: A Life*, p. 42.

24 William Morris to Andreas Scheu, 15 September 1883, Kelvin (ed.), *Collected Letters*, vol. 2, p. 228.

25 William Morris to Emma Morris, 13 April 1849, Kelvin (ed.), *Collected Letters*, vol.1, p. 7.

26 Ibid.

27 Ibid.

28 Ibid., p. 8.

29 Ibid., p. 7.

30 William Morris to Emma Morris, 1 November 1848, Kelvin (ed.), *Collected Letters*, vol. 1, p. 3.

31 Ibid.

32 Edward Lockwood, quoted MacCarthy, *William Morris: A Life*, pp. 46–7.

33 William Morris to Rosalind Howard, 28 November 1881, Kelvin (ed.), *Collected Letters*, vol. 2, p. 83.

34 MacCarthy, *William Morris: A Life*, p. 29.

35 William Morris, 'News from Nowhere', *Collected Works*, vol. 16, p. 104.

36 MacCarthy, *William Morris: A Life*, p. 47.

37 William Morris to Emma Morris, 13 April 1849, Kelvin (ed.), *Collected Letters*, vol. 1, p. 6.

38 William Morris, 'The Dream of John Ball' (1888), *Collected Works*, vol. 16, p. 223.

Chapter 2: Oxford, 1853–1856

1   Edward Burne-Jones, 1 May 1853, quoted Mackail, *Life of William Morris*, vol. 1, p. 63.

2   Edward Burne-Jones, 16 October 1854, quoted ibid., p. 64.

3   Gardner's Directory of Oxfordshire, 1852, accessed via http://www.oxfordhistory.org.uk/

4   Edward Burne-Jones, quoted Mackail, *Life of William Morris*, vol. 1, pp. 29–30.

5   Edward Burne-Jones, quoted ibid., p. 51.

6   Ibid.

7   Ibid.

8   Edward Burne-Jones, quoted ibid., p. 35.

9   Ibid.

10 Georgiana Burne-Jones, *Memorials of Edward Burne-Jones* (1904), London: Macmillan and Co., reprinted London: Lund Humphries, 1993, vol. 1, p. 74.

11 W. G. Barr, www.exeter.ox.ac.uk/inc/uploads/2017/04/college_history.pdf, p. 17.

12 Mackail, *Life of William Morris*, vol. 1, p. 43.

13 Ibid., p. 44.

14 Burne-Jones, *Memorials*, vol. 1, p. 77.

15 Burne-Jones to Cormell Price, 1853, quoted MacCarthy, *William Morris: A Life*, p. 59.

16 Mackail, *Life of William Morris*, vol. 1, p. 43.

17 Burne-Jones to Frances Horner, quoted MacCarthy, *William Morris: A Life*, p. 57.

18 Cambridge undergraduate, George Nugent-Banks, 1881, quoted Serena Dyer, 'Masculinities, Wallpaper, and Crafting Domestic Space within the University, 1795–1914', in Freya Gowrley and Katie Faulkner (eds), 'Special Issue: Making Masculinity: Craft, Gender and Material Production in the Long Nineteenth Century', *Nineteenth Century Gender Studies*, 14.2, Summer 2018, p. 15.

19 Cuthbert Bede, *The Adventures of Mr Verdant Green, an Oxford Freshman*, London: Nathaniel Cooke, 1853, chapter 4.

20 Ibid., chapter 3.

21 Ibid., chapter 7.

22 Mackail, *Life of William Morris*, vol. 1, p. 47.

23 Ibid., p. 40.

24 Ibid.

25 William Morris to Cormell Price, 6 July 1855, Kelvin (ed.), *Collected Letters*, vol. 1, pp. 14–15.

26 Burne-Jones, *Memorials*, vol. 1, p. 110.

27 Ibid.

28 May Morris, *The Introductions to the Collected Works of William Morris*, New York: Oriole Editions by arrangement with the Society of Antiquaries, 1973, vol. 1, p. 5.

29 Mackail, *Life of William Morris*, vol. 1, p. 52.

30 William Morris to Cormell Price, 3 April 1855, Kelvin (ed.), *Collected Letters*, vol. 1, p. 10.

31 Ibid.

32 William Morris to Cormell Price, 6 July 1855, ibid., p. 13.

33 Mackail, *Life of William Morris*, vol. 1, p. 72.

34 William Morris to Cormell Price, 10 August 1855, Kelvin (ed.), *Collected Letters*, vol. 1, p. 19.

35 William Morris to Emma Morris, 20 July 1855, ibid., p. 15.

36 William Morris to Emma Morris, 29 July 1855, ibid., p. 17.

37 William Morris to Cormell Price, 10 August 1855, ibid., p. 20.

38 Ibid., p. 21.

39 Burne-Jones, *Memorials*, vol. 1, pp. 113–14.

40 Ibid, p. 113.

41 William Morris to Cormell Price, 10 August 1855, Kelvin (ed.), *Collected Letters*, vol. 1, p. 21.

42 Ibid., p. 20.

43 Burne-Jones, *Memorials*, vol. 1, p. 114.

44 Ibid.

45 Mackail, *Life of William Morris*, vol. 1, p. 72.

46   John Ruskin, 'Pre-Raphaelitism', in E. T. Cook and Alexander Wedderburn (eds), *The Complete Works of John Ruskin*, London: George Allen, 1904, vol. 12, p. 358n.

47   Mackail, *Life of William Morris*, vol. 1, p. 35.

48   Burne-Jones, *Memorials*, vol. 1, p. 108.

49   Ibid., pp. 114-15.

50   William Morris to Emma Morris, 11 November 1855, Kelvin (ed.), *Collected Letters*, vol. 1, pp. 25–6.

51   Philip Webb to Giacomo Boni, 16 September 1889, John Aplin (ed.), *The Letters of Philip Webb*, vol. 2: 1888–1898, London: Routledge, 2015, letter 353.

52   John Aplin (ed.), *The Letters of Philip Webb*, vol. 1: 1864–1887, p. xxii.

53   G. E. Street, 'On the revival of the ancient style of domestic architecture', a paper read before the Oxford Architectural Society on February 16th 1853, *The Ecclesiologist*, Ecclesiological Late Cambridge Camden Society, London, 1853, vol. 14, p. 75.

54   Mackail, *Life of William Morris*, vol. 1, p. 78.

Chapter 3: Red Lion Square, 1856–1859

1   Burne-Jones, *Memorials*, vol. 1, p. 151.

2   Mackail, *Life of William Morris*, vol. 1, p. 121.

3   Ibid., p. 96.

4   'The Hollow Land', *The Oxford and Cambridge Magazine*, September 1856, pp. 567–8.

5   Ibid., p. 575.

6   Ibid., October 1856, p. 635.

7   Ibid.

8   Ibid., p. 632.

9   Ibid., September 1856, p. 570.

10   Ibid., October 1856, pp. 637–8.

11   Ibid., pp. 639–41.

12   Ibid., p. 640.

13   Ibid., September 1856, p. 565.

14 William Morris, *Collected Works*, vol. 16, p. xxi.

15 William Morris to Cormell Price, July 1856, Kelvin (ed.), *Collected Letters*, vol. 1, p. 28.

16 Ibid.

17 Edward Burne-Jones, quoted MacCarthy, *William Morris: A Life*, p. 110.

18 William Morris to Edward Burne-Jones, 17 May 1856, quoted Burne-Jones, *Memorials*, vol. 1, p. 132.

19 John Ruskin, *Academy Notes*, quoted Ray Watkinson in Linda Parry (ed.), *William Morris*, London: V&A Museum, 1996, p. 25.

20 William Morris to Cormell Price, July 1856, Kelvin (ed.), *Collected Letters*, vol. 1, p. 28.

21 Burne-Jones, *Memorials*, vol. 1, p. 149.

22 Ibid., pp. 145–50.

23 Dante Gabriel Rossetti to William Allingham, 18 December 1856, quoted MacCarthy, *William Morris: A Life*, p. 123.

24 Ford Madox Brown, diary Sunday 24 August 1856, quoted Mary Bennett in Parry (ed.), *William Morris*, p. 24.

25 A few months later William also acquired a complex work that had belonged to Ruskin, *Francesca da Rimini*, showing Dante's encounter with Francesca and her lover Paolo in Hell.

26 William Morris, 'The Tune of Seven Towers', in *The Defence of Guenevere, and Other Poems* (1858), reprinted in William Morris, *Prose and Poetry (1856–1870)*, Oxford: Oxford University Press, 1920, p. 285.

27 William Morris, 'The Blue Closet', in ibid., p. 284.

28 Ibid.

29 William Morris, 'The Tune of Seven Towers', in ibid., p. 286.

30 John Ruskin, 'The Nature of Gothic', *The Stones of Venice*, in Cook and Wedderburn (eds), *Complete Works of John Ruskin*, vol. 10, p. 206.

31 William Morris to Cormell Price, July 1856, Philip Henderson (ed.), *The Letters of William Morris to his Family and Friends*, London: Longmans, Green and Co., 1950, pp. 17-18.

32 May Morris, *The Introductions to the Collected Works of William Morris*, vol. 1, p. 7.

33   Edward Burne-Jones, quoted MacCarthy, *William Morris: A Life*, p. 117.

34   Dante Gabriel Rossetti to William Allingham, 18 December 1856, quoted ibid., p. 118.

35   Burne-Jones, *Memorials*, vol. 1, p. 146.

36   Dante Gabriel Rossetti, quoted in Mackail, *Life of William Morris*, vol. 1, p. 113.

37   Burne-Jones, *Memorials*, vol. 1, p. 147.

38   Henry Price, quoted Frances Collard in Parry (ed.), *William Morris*, V&A, 1996, p. 156.

39   William Morris, 'The Lesser Arts of Life', quoted Frances Collard in ibid., p. 155.

40   Burne-Jones, *Memorials*, vol. 1, p. 113

41   Mackail, *Life of William Morris*, vol. 1, p. 114.

42   Fiona MacCarthy, *The Last Pre-Raphaelite: Edward Burne-Jones and the Victorian Imagination*, London: Faber and Faber, 2011, p. 70.

43   Burne-Jones, *Memorials*, vol. 1, p. 170.

44   Ibid., p. 169.

45   Ibid., p. 171.

46   Ibid.

47   Ibid.

48   Edward Burne-Jones, quoted MacCarthy, *William Morris: A Life*, p. 126.

49   William Morris, 'The Defence of Guenevere' (1858), in *The Defence of Guenevere, and Other Poems*, p. 191.

50   Edward Burne-Jones, quoted MacCarthy, *William Morris: A Life*, p. 126.

51   Edward Burne-Jones, quoted MacCarthy, *The Last Pre-Raphaelite*, p. 70.

52   Burne-Jones, *Memorials*, vol. 1, p. 171.

53   Mackail, *Life of William Morris*, vol. 1, p. 111.

54   William Morris to Cormell Price, July 1856, Kelvin (ed.), *Collected Letters*, vol. 1, p. 28.

55   Dante Gabriel Rossetti to William Bell Scott, February 1857, quoted

Mackail, *Life of William Morris*, vol. 1, p. 110.

56   William Morris quoted ibid., p. 111.

57   Ibid., p. 110.

58   Edward Burne-Jones to Cormell Price, quoted Burne-Jones, *Memorials*, vol. 1, p. 127.

59   William Morris, 'Preface' to Kelmscott Press edition of *On the Nature of Gothic*, 1892.

60   John Ruskin, *On the Nature of Gothic*, London: Kelmscott Press, 1892, pp. 17–18.

61   Ibid., p. 23.

62   Ibid., pp. 77–8.

63   William Morris, 'How I Became a Socialist', *Collected Works*, vol. 23, p. 279.

64   Ruskin, *On the Nature of Gothic*, p. 23.

65   Burne-Jones, *Memorials*, vol. 1, p. 147.

66   Mackail, *Life of William Morris*, vol. 1, p. 108.

67   Burne-Jones, *Memorials*, vol. 1, p. 139.

68   D. G. Rossetti to Christina Rossetti, 8 November 1853, William Michael Rossetti (ed.), *Dante Gabriel Rossetti: His Family-Letters*, London: Willis, 1895, vol. 2, p. 120.

69   Valentine Prinsep, quoted MacCarthy, *William Morris: A Life*, p. 134.

70   Edward Burne-Jones, quoted ibid.

71   William Morris to James Richard Thursfield, Kelvin (ed.), *Collected Letters*, vol. 1, p. 105.

72   Coventry Patmore, *Saturday Review*, 26 December 1857, quoted Mackail, *Life of William Morris*, vol. 1, p. 126.

73   Burne-Jones, *Memorials*, vol. 1, pp. 161–2.

74   Mackail, *Life of William Morris*, vol. 1, p. 118.

75   Dante Gabriel Rossetti, quoted Suzanne Fagence Cooper, 'John Hungerford Pollen (1820–1902), decorative artist and Roman Catholic convert', in *Oxford Dictionary of National Biography*, Oxford University Press, 2004.

76   Mackail, *Life of William Morris*, vol. 1, p. 121.

77   Burne-Jones, *Memorials*, vol. 1, p. 163.

78 Geoffrey Tillotson and Kathleen Tillotson, *Mid-Victorian Studies* (1965), new edition, London: Bloomsbury, 2013, p. 214.

79 Burne-Jones, *Memorials*, vol. 1, p. 165.

80 Valentine Prinsep, quoted MacCarthy, *William Morris: A Life*, p. 132.

81 Burne-Jones, *Memorials*, vol. 1, p. 165.

Chapter 4: Oxford, 1857–1859

1 Fiona MacCarthy states that Jane was attending a performance of the popular drama *Ben Bolt* in a temporary theatre set up in Russell's Indoor Tennis Court on Oriel Lane. It is possible that they saw a play at the New Theatre between George Street and Magdalen Street instead. See MacCarthy, *The Last Pre-Raphaelite*, p. 83.

2 There was a school attached to St Peter-in-the-East from at least 1863; there are logbooks in the Oxfordshire Record Office dating from this year. There are also records of a mixed school at Holywell from 1872–1938.

3 Burne-Jones, *Memorials*, vol. 1, p. 168.

4 For details of census records and building use, see www.oxfordhistory. org.uk/holywell.

5 MacCarthy, *William Morris: A Life*, p. 136.

6 Planning applications for Bath Place, quoted in www.oxfordhistory. org.uk.

7 *Map of Oxford to illustrate Dr. Acland's Memoir on cholera in Oxford in 1854 . . .*, London: J. Churchill, and Oxford: J. H. and J. Parker, 1856.

8 *Illustrated London News*, 18 July 1857, p. 77.

9 See Sharp and Marsh (eds), *Collected Letters of Jane Morris*, p. 2.

10 Jane Morris to Dante Gabriel Rossetti, September 1878, ibid., p. 77.

11 Jane Morris to Cormell Price, 29 August 1879, ibid., p. 92.

12 Burne-Jones, *Memorials*, vol. 1, p. 133.

13 Ibid., p. 156.

14 January 1858, *The Diary of Ford Madox Brown*, quoted MacCarthy, *William Morris: A Life*, p. 151.

15 Mackail, *Life of William Morris*, vol. 1, p. 129.

16   Cormell Price to his father, 10 December 1857, quoted MacCarthy, *William Morris: A Life*, p. 135.

17   Algernon Charles Swinburne to Edwin Hatch, 26 April 1858, quoted ibid.

18   Mackail, *Life of William Morris*, vol. 1, p. 129.

19   Algernon Swinburne to Edwin Hatch, 17 February 1859, quoted ibid., p. 140.

20   In his diary, Wilfrid Scawen Blunt wrote about William and Jane: 'As a young man he had married for love, and his wife had never loved him. He had a strong and affectionate heart.' These notes were made in the late 1880s, while Blunt was Jane's lover, so we might question both Jane's description of her marriage, and Blunt's reading of her meaning. See Peter Faulkner (ed.), *Jane Morris to Wilfrid Scawen Blunt*, Exeter: University of Exeter Press, 1986, p. 30.

21   Dr Henry Acland, quoted Jan Marsh, *The Legend of Elizabeth Siddall*, London: Quartet, 1989, p. 62, and John Ruskin to Dante Gabriel Rossetti, 12 May 1855, quoted ibid., p. 209.

22   John Ruskin, quoted Tim Hilton, *John Ruskin: the Early Years 1819–1859* (1985), new edition, New Haven and London: Yale University Press, 2000, p. 221.

23   John Ruskin, quoted Marsh, *Legend of Elizabeth Siddall*, p. 60.

24   Mackail, Manuscript notebooks, vol. 1, p. 22.

25   Dante Gabriel Rossetti to his mother, 1 July 1855, quoted Hilton, *Ruskin: The Early Years*, p. 221.

26   Details of the household based on 1861 census.

27   *The Englishwoman's Domestic Magazine*, London, 1858, vol. 6, p. 64.

28   Ibid., p. vii.

29   MacCarthy, *William Morris: A Life*, p. 149.

30   May Morris, *Introductions*, vol. 1, p. 16.

31   William Morris, 'The Defence of Guenevere', *Prose and Poetry (1856–1870)*, p. 187.

32   Ibid., pp. 193–4.

33   William Morris, 'Praise of my Lady' (1858), ibid., p. 307.

34   William Morris, 'The Aims of Art' (1887), *Collected Works*, pp. 83, 94.

35   Ibid., p. 85.

36   Ibid., p. 92.

37   Ibid., p. 81.

38   William Morris, 'The Hollow Land' (1856), *Prose and Poetry (1856–1870)*, p. 165.

Chapter 5: Red House, 1860

1   Burne-Jones, *Memorials*, vol. 1, p. 208.

2   Quoted Mackail, *Life of William Morris*, vol. 1, p. 160.

3   Ibid., p. 165.

4   Philip Webb to Jane Morris, 30 January 1903, John Aplin (ed.), *The Letters of Philip Webb*, vol. 4: 1903–1914, London: Routledge, 2015, letter 864.

5   Philip Webb to Jane Morris, August 1897, *The Letters of Philip Webb*, vol. 2, letter 558.

6   Advertisement to let 'Red House', Mr Marsh, Auctioneer, Surveyor and Land Agent, June 1866, illustrated in Kelvin (ed.), *Collected Letters*, vol. 1, p. 43.

7   D. G. Rossetti to Ford Madox Brown, 23 May 1860, quoted MacCarthy, *William Morris: A Life*, p. 154.

8   Ford Madox Brown, quoted Angela Thirlwell, *Into the Frame: The Four Loves of Ford Madox Brown*, London: Chatto and Windus, 2010, p. 71.

9   William Morris, 'The Defence of Guenevere', in *The Defence of Guenevere, and Other Poems* (1858), new edition, London: Longmans, Green & Co., 1908, p. 14.

10   Letitia Bell-Scott, quoted MacCarthy, *William Morris: A Life*, p. 157.

11   Laura Jane Friswell, 1898, quoted Tessa Wild, *William Morris and his Palace of Art*, London: Philip Wilson, 2018, p. 142.

12   Mackail, *Life of William Morris*, vol. 1, p. 142.

13   Burne-Jones, *Memorials*, vol. 1, p. 208.

14   Wild, *William Morris and his Palace of Art*, p. 203.

15   William Morris, 'Making the Best of It', lecture (1879), quoted in ibid., p. 210.

16   Mackail, *Life of William Morris*, vol. 1, p. 143.

17   Jane Morris to Wilfrid Scawen Blunt, 25 February 1903, *Collected Letters of Jane Morris*, p. 362.

18   Burne-Jones, *Memorials*, vol. 1, p. 211.

19   John Ruskin, 'The Nature of Gothic', *The Stones of Venice*, in Cook and Wedderburn (eds), *Complete Works of John Ruskin*, vol. 10, p. 236.

20   Ibid., pp. 206, 212.

21   Jane Morris to her daughter May, letter 495, *Collected Letters of Jane Morris*, p. 422.

22   May Morris, quoted Wild, *William Morris and his Palace of Art*, p. 174.

23   'The Legend of Good Women', *The Riverside Chaucer*, Oxford: Oxford University Press, 1987, new edition, 1991, pp. 589–90.

24   Burne-Jones, *Memorials*, vol. 1, p. 212.

25   Jane Morris to May Morris, c.1909, *Collected Letters of Jane Morris*, p. 422. The panels are now kept at Kelmscott Manor and Castle Howard. After the Morrises left Red House, the series was split. At least one, 'St Catherine', was used as a portière in the Burne-Joneses' dining room at The Grange. Jane refers to them as tapestries because they were intended to line the walls, as traditional woven tapestries would have done, rather than, more correctly, embroideries.

26   Ibid.

27   May Morris, quoted Wild, *William Morris and his Palace of Art*, p. 87.

28   William Morris, 'The Lesser Arts', lecture, 1882, quoted ibid., p. 86.

29   Burne-Jones, *Memorials*, vol. 1, p. 210.

30   Ibid., p. 213.

31   Ibid., p. 212.

32   Ibid., p. 177.

33   Letter from Warrington Taylor to Philip Webb, 1866, quoted Wild, *William Morris and his Palace of Art*, p. 76.

34   Quoted Wild, ibid., p. 146.

35   I am grateful to the research of Tessa Wild and her colleagues, including John Tredinnick, at the National Trust for the reconstruction of the Red House drawing room illustrated in *William Morris and his Palace of Art*, pp. 122–3.

36 Rossetti to Ford Madox Brown, 22 June 1859, quoted Wild, *William Morris and his Palace of Art*, p. 149.

37 See letter from Jane Morris to D. G. Rossetti, September 1878, *Collected Letters of Jane Morris*, p. 77.

38 Dante, *La Vita Nuova*, translated by D. G. Rossetti, in *The Early Italian Poets From Ciullo D'Alcamo to Dante Alighieri*, London: Smith, Elder & Co., 1861, pp. 225, 226, 230.

39 Dr John Simon, quoted Judith Flanders, *The Victorian Home*, London: HarperCollins, 2003, p. 70.

40 Mrs Panton, *From Kitchen to Garret*, 1888, quoted Flanders, ibid., p. 10.

41 Mackail, *Life of William Morris*, vol. 1, p. 160.

42 Thirlwell, *Into the Frame*, pp. 88–9.

43 Ibid., p. 73.

44 Ibid., pp. 90–1.

45 Burne-Jones, *Memorials*, vol. 1, p. 179–80.

46 Thirwell, *Into the Frame*, p. 75.

47 Ibid., p. 74.

48 Pye Henry Chavasse, *Advice to a wife on the management of her own health and on the treatment of some of the complaints incidental to pregnancy, labour and suckling* (1839), 10th edition, London: J. & A. Churchill, 1873, p. 109.

49 Wild, *William Morris and his Palace of Art*, p. 157.

50 Elizabeth Siddall, quoted Wild, ibid., p. 163.

51 William Morris to Ford Madox Brown, 18 January 1861, Philip Henderson (ed.), *The Letters of William Morris to his Family and Friends*, London: Longmans, Green and Co., 1950, p. 21.

52 Chavasse, *Advice to a Wife*, p. 192.

53 Ibid., p. 202.

54 Edward Burne-Jones to Cormell Price, 23 February 1862, quoted Judith Flanders, *A Circle of Sisters: Alice Kipling, Georgiana Burne-Jones, Agnes Poynter and Louisa Baldwin*, London: Viking, 2001, p. 82. Emma Brown relied on breastfeeding as a form of contraception. Jane probably only breastfed Jenny for the first few months, as she was pregnant again by the end of June 1861.

55   MacCarthy, *William Morris: A Life*, p. 186.

56   Georgiana Burne-Jones, quoted MacCarthy, ibid., p. 186.

57   Burne-Jones, *Memorials*, vol. 1, p. 223.

58   Ibid., p. 208.

59   16 March 1857, Virginia Surtees (ed.), *The Diary of Ford Madox Brown*, New Haven and London: Yale University Press, 1981, p. 195.

60   Burne-Jones, *Memorials*, vol. 1, p. 219.

61   Ibid., p. 213.

62   Mackail, *Life of William Morris*, vol. 1, p. 139.

63   William Morris to the Rev. F. G. Guy, 19 April 1861, Henderson (ed.), *Letters of William Morris to his Family and Friends*, p. 21.

64   Linda Parry, 'Textiles', in Parry (ed.), *William Morris*, V&A, 1996, p. 226.

65   Burne-Jones, *Memorials*, vol. 1, pp. 235–6.

Chapter 6: Red House 2, 1861–1865

1   Dante Gabriel Rossetti to William Allingham, c.20 January 1861, quoted MacCarthy, *The Last Pre-Raphaelite*, p. 130.

2   Burne-Jones, *Memorials*, vol. 1, p. 202.

3   Mackail, *Life of William Morris*, p. 143.

4   See Parry (ed.), *William Morris*, V&A, 1996, p. 50.

5   G. E. Street, 1853, quoted Clive Wainwright, 'Morris in Context', in ibid., p. 355.

6   Mackail, *Life of William Morris*, vol. 1, p. 113.

7   Philip Webb to Sydney Cockerell, 1898, quoted Wild, *William Morris and his Palace of Art*, p. 79.

8   Charles Knight, 'Ragged and Industrial Schools: Refuges for Destitute Children', *English Cyclopaedia*, London, 1862.

9   Major Gillum commissioned furniture, stained-glass designs and paintings from Ford Madox Brown and his friends. In the early 1860s, Gillum asked Webb to design a row of shops and houses in Shoreditch, and then a larger property in East Barnet. Gillum wanted to move closer to the Boys' Farm Home which he set up in the countryside

outside London. This Farm Home was a precursor of the 'Back to the Land' culture which grew up around many Arts and Crafts studios.

10 Circular issued by Morris, Marshall, Faulkner and Co., Fine Art Workmen, 11 April 1861, quoted May Morris, *Introductions*, vol. 1, pp. 37–8.

11 Charles Lock Eastlake, August 1862, quoted Clive Wainwright in Parry (ed.), *William Morris*, V&A, 1996, p. 358.

12 Circular, April 1861, p. 38.

13 William Morris to the Rev. F. G. Guy, 19 April 1861, Henderson (ed.), *Letters of William Morris to his Family and Friends*, p. 21.

14 For these images and more detailed analysis, see Max Donnelly, '"Rapture and Ridicule": Furniture in the 1862 Medieval Court', in special issue 'Almost Forgotten: The International Exhibition of 1862', *The Journal of the Decorative Arts Society 1850–the Present*, No. 38, 2014, pp. 106–31.

15 *Civil Engineer and Architect's Journal*, 1 November 1862, p. 356, quoted Donnelly, ibid., p. 110.

16 *Building News*, 8 August 1862, quoted Donnelly, ibid., p. 121.

17 Ibid.

18 Parry (ed.), *William Morris*, V&A, 1996, p. 170.

19 Circular issued by Morris, Marshall, Faulkner and Co., Fine Art Workmen, 11 April 1861, quoted May Morris, *Introductions*, vol. 1, pp. 37–8.

20 Parry (ed.), *William Morris*, V&A, 1996, p. 140.

21 John Ruskin to Lady Trevelyan, 20 July 1862, in Cook and Wedderburn (eds), *Complete Works of John Ruskin*, vol. 36, p. 414.

22 Edward Burne-Jones to Helen Mary Gaskell, quoted MacCarthy, *The Last Pre-Raphaelite*, p. 150.

23 Thirlwell, *Into the Frame*, p. 92.

24 Ford Madox Brown, October 1854, quoted Marsh, *The Legend of Elizabeth Siddall*, p. 59.

25 Dante Gabriel Rossetti to William Michael Rossetti, 17 April 1860, quoted Marsh, ibid., pp. 62–3.

26 Burne-Jones, *Memorials*, vol. 1, pp. 220, 223.

27   Elizabeth Siddall Rossetti to Dante Gabriel Rossetti, quoted MacCarthy, *The Last Pre-Raphaelite*, pp. 133–4.

28   Burne-Jones, *Memorials*, vol. 1, p. 222.

29   Ibid.

30   Dante Gabriel Rossetti to Georgiana Burne-Jones, June/July 1861, quoted MacCarthy, *The Last Pre-Raphaelite*, p. 134.

31   Burne-Jones, *Memorials*, vol. 1, pp. 237–8.

32   Edward Burne-Jones, quoted Mackail, *Life of William Morris*, vol. 1, p. 159.

33   May Morris, *Introductions*, vol. 1, pp. 8–9.

34   John Ruskin to Georgiana Burne-Jones, Burne-Jones, *Memorials*, vol. 1, pp. 235–6.

35   John Ruskin to Mrs Acland, 10 July 1855, in Cook and Wedderburn (eds), *Complete Works of John Ruskin*, vol. 36, p. 217.

36   John Ruskin to Dante Gabriel Rossetti, 1860, ibid., p. 343.

37   Burne-Jones, *Memorials*, vol. 1, p. 277.

38   Wild, *William Morris and his Palace of Art*, pp. 236–8.

39   Burne-Jones, *Memorials*, vol. 1, p. 277.

40   Ibid., pp. 278–9.

41   Georgiana Burne-Jones to Rosalind Howard, 11 February 1892, quoted MacCarthy, *The Last Pre-Raphaelite*, p. 172.

42   Burne-Jones, *Memorials*, vol. 1, p. 284.

43   Ibid.

44   Charles Faulkner, quoted Wild, *William Morris and his Palace of Art*, p. 227.

45   Burne-Jones, *Memorials*, vol. 1, p. 294.

46   Marion Heathcote, quoted Wild, *William Morris and his Palace of Art*, p. 245.

47   Mackail, *Life of William Morris*, vol. 1, p. 165.

48   Burne-Jones, *Memorials*, vol. 1, p. 294.

49   Ibid., vol. 2, p. 310.

Chapter 7: Queen Square, 1865–1871

1   The photograph album, also containing earlier images of Jane Morris, is now in the collection of the Victoria and Albert Museum, catalogue number X610A.

2   William Michael Rossetti (ed.), *Rossetti, His Family-Letters*, vol. 1, pp. 251–2.

3   Ibid., p. 254.

4   May Morris, *Introductions*, vol. 1, p. 78.

5   Ibid., p. 79

6   Wild, *William Morris and his Palace of Art*, p. 176.

7   William Morris, 'Making the Best of It' (1879), *The Collected Works of William Morris*, vol. 22, p. 113, quoted Emma Ferry, 'The Other Miss Faulkner: Lucy Orrinsmith and the "Art at Home Series"', *The Journal of William Morris Studies*, Summer 2011, p. 60.

8   May Morris, *Introductions*, vol. 1, pp. 79–80.

9   May Morris, *Introductions*, vol. 1, p. 80.

10   *The Times*, London, 18 June 1862, quoted by https://www.ucl.ac.uk/bloomsbury-project/institutions/female_school_of_art.htm, accessed 16/10/2020.

11   May Morris, *Introductions*, vol. 1, p. 79.

12   Mrs Richmond Ritchie, quoted MacCarthy, *William Morris: A Life*, p. 184.

13   May Morris, *Introductions*, vol. 1, p. 79.

14   Ibid., p. 78

15   Burne-Jones, *Memorials*, vol. 2, p. 6.

16   Edward Burne-Jones, quoted in Parry (ed.), *William Morris*, V&A, 1996, p. 134.

17   John Press and Charles Harvey, 'William Morris, Warington Taylor and the firm, 1865–75', *Journal of the William Morris Society*, Autumn 1986, p. 43.

18   Warington Taylor to Edward Robert Robson, 1865, quoted MacCarthy, *William Morris: A Life*, p. 209.

19   Philip Webb, quoted Parry (ed.), *William Morris*, V&A, 1996, p. 140.

20   Georgina Cowper, Lady Mount-Temple, quoted MacCarthy, *William Morris: A Life*, pp. 211–12.

21   Ibid., p. 211.

22   Burne-Jones, *Memorials*, vol. 1, p. 299.

23   May Morris, *Introductions*, vol. 1, p. 79.

24   Ibid., p. 43.

25   John Ruskin, quoted, ibid., p. 45.

26   Burne-Jones, *Memorials*, vol. 1, p. 297.

27   Warington Taylor to Dante Gabriel Rossetti, 1867, quoted MacCarthy, *William Morris: A Life*, p. 210.

28   May Morris, *Introductions*, vol. 1, p. 69.

29   Ibid., p. 81.

30   H. Allingham and D. Radford (eds), *William Allingham: A Diary, 1824–1889* (1907), revised edition, Harmondsworth, Middlesex: Penguin, 1985, p. 181.

31   May Morris, *Introductions*, vol. 1, p. 81.

32   Ibid., p. 67.

33   Dante Gabriel Rossetti to Jane Morris, 30 August 1869, John Bryson and Janet Camp Troxell (eds), *Dante Gabriel Rossetti and Jane Morris: Their Correspondence*, Oxford: Clarendon Press, 1976, pp. 26–7.

34   Dante Gabriel Rossetti to Jane Morris, 6 March 1868, ibid., p. 1.

35   Dante Gabriel Rossetti to Jane Morris, 5 May 1868, ibid., p. 2.

36   Dante Gabriel Rossetti to Jane Morris, 5 May 1868, ibid., p. 4.

37   May Morris, quoted Wendy Parkins, *Jane Morris: The Burden of History*, Edinburgh: Edinburgh University Press, 2013, p. 131.

38   See Robyne Erica Calvert, *Fashioning the artist: artistic dress in Victorian Britain 1848–1900*, PhD thesis, University of Glasgow, 2012, for a survey of literature and exhibitions on this subject.

39   George du Maurier, quoted, ibid., pp. 78–9.

40   Anne Thackeray Ritchie, quoted, ibid., p. 78.

41   Henry James to Alice James, 10 March 1869, quoted Sharp and Marsh (eds), *Collected Letters of Jane Morris*, p. 34.

42   Henry James to Alice James, quoted MacCarthy, *William Morris: A Life*, p. 230.

43 Dante Gabriel Rossetti to Ford Madox Brown, 23 January 1869, quoted, ibid., p. 228.

44 Judith Flanders, *Circle of Sisters*, p. 122.

45 William Morris to Edward Burne-Jones, 25 May 1869, Kelvin (ed.), *Collected Letters*, vol. 1, p. 76.

46 Dante Gabriel Rossetti to Miss Losh, 9 November 1868, quoted MacCarthy, *William Morris: A Life*, p. 224.

47 William Bell Scott to Alice Boyd, 9 November 1868, quoted MacCarthy, *William Morris: A Life*, pp. 224–5.

48 Anecdote attributed to a relative of William de Morgan, quoted Parkins, *Jane Morris: the Burden of History*, p. 7.

49 Burne-Jones, *Memorials*, vol. 1, p. 299.

50 Jane Morris to Susan Sedgwick Norton, 13 July 1869, *Collected Letters of Jane Morris*, p. 35.

51 May Morris, *Introductions*, vol. 1, p. 112.

52 Flanders, *Circle of Sisters*, p. 59.

53 MacCarthy, *William Morris: A Life*, p. 233.

54 William Morris to Philip Webb, quoted May Morris, *Introductions*, vol. 1, pp. 116–21.

55 William Morris to Philip Webb, 22 July 1869, Kelvin (ed.), *Collected Letters*, vol. 1, p. 78.

56 William Morris to Philip Webb, 29 August 1869, quoted MacCarthy, *William Morris: A Life*, p. 246.

57 William Morris to Philip Webb, 20 August 1869, quoted May Morris, *Introductions*, vol. 1, p. 117.

58 MacCarthy, *William Morris: A Life*, p. 242.

59 William Morris to Philip Webb, quoted May Morris, *Introductions*, vol. 1, p. 116.

60 William Morris to Philip Webb, 27 August 1869, quoted May Morris, *Introductions*, vol. 1, p. 118.

61 Gabriel Rossetti to Jane Morris, 21 July 1869, *Dante Gabriel Rossetti and Jane Morris: Their Correspondence*, p. 5.

62 William Morris quoted MacCarthy, *William Morris: A Life*, p. 223.

63 Henry James to Alice James, 10 March 1869, quoted Sharp and Marsh (eds), *Collected Letters of Jane Morris*, p. 34.

64 Dante Gabriel Rossetti to Jane Morris, 30 July 1869, *Dante Gabriel Rossetti and Jane Morris: Their Correspondence*, pp. 10–14.

65 Dante Gabriel Rossetti to Jane Morris, 23 August 1869, ibid., p. 24.

66 Dante Gabriel Rossetti to Jane Morris, 30 July 1869, ibid., p. 25.

67 Dante Gabriel Rossetti to Jane Morris, 30 August 1869, ibid., p. 28.

68 Dante Gabriel Rossetti to Jane Morris, 11 September 1869, ibid., p. 31.

69 Jane Morris to Susan Sidgwick Norton, 21 December 1869, *Collected Letters of Jane Morris*, p. 37.

70 Jane Morris does refer, in passing, to one of Lizzie Siddall's drawings that Gabriel Rossetti had recovered from the American collector and critic Charles Eliot Norton. Norton returned *Clerk Saunders* and received one of Rossetti's watercolours in exchange. Jane Morris to Susan Sidgwick Norton, 21 December 1869, *Collected Letters of Jane Morris*, pp. 36n, 37.

71 'I have told Janey and Scott and Dunn. It has become known to Morris, Jones, and Watts through Howell'. Dante Gabriel Rossetti to William Michael Rossetti, 14 October 1869, William E. Fredeman (ed.), *The Correspondence of Dante Gabriel Rossetti Vol. 4: The Chelsea Years 1863–1872 (Part II: 1868–1870)*, Cambridge: D. S. Brewer, 2004, p. 303.

72 Dante Gabriel Rossetti to Algernon Swinburne, 26 October 1869, ibid., p. 312.

73 Dante Gabriel Rossetti to William Michael Rossetti, 14 October 1869, ibid., p. 303.

74 Dante Gabriel Rossetti to William Michael Rossetti, 15 October 1869, ibid., p. 305.

75 Dante Gabriel Rossetti to William Michael Rossetti, 14 October 1869, ibid., p. 303.

76 Jane Morris to Susan Sedgwick Norton, 21 December 1869, *Collected Letters of Jane Morris*, p. 37.

77 Dante Gabriel Rossetti to Jane Morris, 30 January 1870, *Dante Gabriel Rossetti and Jane Morris: Their Correspondence*, p. 33.

78 Dante Gabriel Rossetti to Jane Morris, 4 February 1870, *Dante Gabriel Rossetti and Jane Morris: Their Correspondence*, p. 34.

79   William Bell Scott to Alice Boyd, 4 November 1868, quoted Parkins, *Jane Morris: The Burden of History*, p. 30.

80   William Bell Scott to Alice Boyd, 24 May 1869, quoted, ibid., p. 31.

81   Ibid., p. 30.

82   Philip Webb to William and Jane Morris, 23 July 1869, *The Letters of Philip Webb*, vol. 1: 1864–1887, letter 25.

83   Dante Gabriel Rossetti to Jane Morris, 4 March 1870, *Dante Gabriel Rossetti and Jane Morris: Their Correspondence*, p. 36. Gabriel Rossetti had visited Barbara Bodichon (née Barbara Leigh-Smith) with Lizzie Siddall at Scalands in 1854. Barbara Bodichon was a campaigner for female education and suffrage, as well as a landscape painter who worked in Cornwall, France and North Africa.

84   William Morris to Charles Eliot Norton, 21 December 1869, Kelvin (ed.), *Collected Letters*, vol. 1, p. 99.

85   Jane Morris to Susan Sedgwick Norton, 21 December 1869, *Collected Letters of Jane Morris*, p. 37.

86   William Morris to Jane Morris, 25 November 1870, Kelvin (ed.), *Collected Letters*, vol. 1, p. 126.

87   May Morris, *Introductions*, vol. 1, p. 99.

88   May Morris, *Journal of my visit to Naworth Castle*, MS J2416, William Morris Gallery, 1870.

89   Ibid.

90   Jane Morris to Rosalind Howard, 30 June 1870, *Collected Letters of Jane Morris*, p. 41.

91   Dorothy Henley, *Rosalind Howard, Countess of Carlisle*, London: The Hogarth Press, 1958, pp. 26–7.

92   Jane Morris to Rosalind Howard, late summer 1870, *The Collected Letters of Jane Morris*, p. 42.

93   Jane Morris to Rosalind Howard, 6 July 1870, ibid., p. 42.

94   Georgiana Burne-Jones to Rosalind Howard, January 1869, quoted MacCarthy, *The Last Pre-Raphaelite*, p. 213.

95   William Morris to Charles Faulkner, 16 October 1886, quoted MacCarthy, *William Morris: A Life*, p. 227.

96   Georgiana Burne-Jones to Rosalind Howard, 18 February 1869, quoted MacCarthy, *The Last Pre-Raphaelite*, p. 214.

97   William Morris to Jane Morris, 5 December 1870, Kelvin (ed.), *Collected Letters*, vol. 1, p. 129.

98   Jane was staying in Torquay with Mrs Emma Morris and her daughter Henrietta. William Morris to Jane Morris, 3 December 1870, ibid., p. 128.

Chapter 8: Iceland, 1871

1   William Morris, 17 July 171871, Lavinia Greenlaw (ed.), *Questions of Travel: William Morris in Iceland*, Kendal: Notting Hill Editions, 2011, p. 39.

2   William Morris, 13 July 1871, 'Journal of Travels in Iceland', *Collected Works*, vol. 8, p. 20.

3   William Morris, 18 July 181871, Greenlaw (ed.), *Questions of Travel*, p. 41.

4   William Morris, 20 July 1871, 'Journal of Travels in Iceland', *Collected Works*, vol. 8, p. 42.

5   William Morris, 14 July 1871, ibid., p. 23.

6   Undated manuscript, British Library, quoted MacCarthy, *William Morris: A Life*, p. 303.

7   William Morris, 'Journals of Travel in Iceland', *Collected Works*, vol. 8, p. 85.

8   Ibid., p. xix. Eirikur Magnusson was an Icelandic scholar who later became deputy librarian at the University Library in Cambridge. He was William's travelling companion, along with Charley Faulkner and W. H. Evans, an officer in the Dorset Yeomanry. Morris did not know him before their voyage, but on first meeting Evans, he decided he was 'a quiet well conducted chap and not stupid'. He also had 'the advantage of being used to wild travel'. William Morris to Charley Faulkner, 12 June 1871, quoted MacCarthy, *William Morris: A Life*, p. 280

9   May Morris, *Introductions*, vol. 1, p. 224.

10   William Morris, 18 August 1871, 'Journals of Travel in Iceland', *Collected Works*, vol. 8, p. 124.

11   William Morris, 12 August 1871, ibid.

12   William Morris, 13 July 1871, ibid., p. 20.

13   Ibid.

14   William Morris to Jane Morris, 11 August 1871, ibid., p. xxiii.

15   Ibid., p. xxiv.

16   William Morris to Aglaia Coronio, autumn 1872, Kelvin (ed.), *Collected Letters*, vol. 1, p. 173.

17   William Morris, 'The Lovers of Gudrun', *Collected Works*, vol. 5, p. 395.

18   William Morris to Jane Morris, 11 August 1871, Kelvin (ed.), *Collected Letters*, vol. 1, p. 146.

19   William Morris to Charles Faulkner, 17 May 1871, ibid., p. 133.

20   Jane Morris to Philip Webb, [June–early July 1871], *Collected Letters of Jane Morris*, p. 44.

21   Jane Morris to Philip Webb, 4 August 1871, ibid., p. 47.

22   Jane Morris to Philip Webb, 10 August 1871, ibid., p. 48.

23   Jane Morris to Philip Webb, 25 July 1871, ibid., p. 47.

24   May Morris, *Introductions*, vol. 1, p. 233.

25   William Morris to Charles Eliot Norton, 19 October 1871, Kelvin (ed.), *Collected Letters*, vol. 1, p. 153.

26   William Morris to Charles Faulkner, 17 May 1871, ibid., letter 134, p. 133.

27   May Morris, *Introductions*, vol. 1, p. 234.

28   John Bruce Glasier, quoted *Collected Letters of Jane Morris*, p. 12.

29   William Morris to Charles Faulkner, 17 May 1871, Kelvin (ed.), *Collected Letters*, vol. 1, p. 133.

30   Jane Morris to Philip Webb, [June–early July 1871], *Collected Letters of Jane Morris*, p. 44.

31   William Morris, 'News from Nowhere', *Collected Works*, vol. 16, p. 202.

32   William Morris, quoted Mackail, *Life of William Morris*, vol. 1, p. 229.

33   John Maddison and Merlin Waterson (ed.), *Kelmscott Manor & Estate Conservation Management Plan*, London: Society of Antiquaries, November 2013, pp. 23, 30–1.

34   Ibid., p. 79.

35   Ibid., p. 94.

36   May Morris, *Introductions*, vol. 1, p. 233.

37 Maddison and Waterson, *Kelmscott Manor & Estate*, p. 97.

38 May Morris, *Introductions*, vol. 1, p. 233.

39 Henry James to John La Farge, 20 June 1869, quoted *Collected Letters of Jane Morris*, p. 33.

40 Walford Graham Robertson, *Time Was*, 1931, quoted ibid., p. 13.

41 Jane Morris to Gabriel Rossetti, 9 February 1879, ibid., p. 82.

42 William Morris to Charles Eliot Norton, 19 October 1871, Kelvin (ed.), *Collected Letters*, vol. 1, p. 153.

43 Gabriel Rossetti to his mother, 17 July 1871, quoted MacCarthy, *William Morris: A Life*, p. 316.

44 Gabriel Rossetti, quoted Maddison and Waterson, *Kelmscott Manor & Estate*, p. 40.

45 'Between Kisses' was published in an amended version in 1881, as 'Mid-Rapture'. This poem, with 'Down Stream' and other verses, was a transcribed by Gabriel Rossetti in 1874 and given to Jane Morris. This handwritten copy is now in the Bodleian Library, Oxford.

46 'Silent Noon', sonnet by Gabriel Rossetti, written in 1871, and published in *Ballads and Sonnets*, 1881.

47 Jane Morris to Philip Webb, 25 July 1871, *Collected Letters of Jane Morris*, p. 47.

48 Edward Burne-Jones to George Howard, July 1871, quoted MacCarthy, *The Last Pre-Raphaelite*, p. 240.

49 Edward Burne-Jones to Thomas Rooke, Mary Lago (ed.), *Burne-Jones Talking: His Conversations, 1895–98, Preserved by His Studio Assistant Thomas Rooke*, London: John Murray, 1982, p. 49.

50 Jane Morris to Gabriel Rossetti, 7 December 1878, *Collected Letters of Jane Morris*, p. 80.

51 Jane Morris to Gabriel Rossetti, Tuesday [September 1878], ibid., p. 77.

52 William Morris, 9 July 1871, 'Journals of Travel in Iceland', *Collected Works*, vol. 8, p. 9.

53 William Morris, 11 July 1871, ibid., pp. 11, 15.

54 William Morris, 15 July 1871, ibid., pp. 25, 93.

55 William Morris, 6 August 1871, Greenlaw (ed.), *Questions of Travel*, p. 117.

56 William Morris lifted this phrase from Matthew Arnold's poem 'The Scholar-Gipsy', 1853.

57 William Morris, 2 August 1871, 'Journals of Travel in Iceland', *Collected Works*, vol. 8, p. 90.

58 William Morris, ibid., p. 135.

59 William Morris, 'News from Nowhere', *Collected Works*, vol. 16, p. 27.

60 William Morris, 17 July 1871, 'Journals of Travel in Iceland', *Collected Works*, vol. 8, p. 28.

61 William Morris, 16 August 1871, Greenlaw (ed.) *Questions of Travel*, p. 139.

62 William Morris, 20 July 1871, 'Journals of Travel in Iceland', *Collected Works*, vol. 8, p. 42.

63 William Morris, 29 August 1871, *Questions of Travel*, p. 181.

Chapter 9: Turnham Green, 1872–1878

1 Jane Morris to Cormell Price, February, July & August 1877, *Collected Letters of Jane Morris*, pp. 62–5.

2 Jane Morris to Cormell Price, [Summer 1877], ibid., p. 64.

3 May Morris, quoted Jan Marsh, *Jane and May Morris: A Biographical Story 1839–1938*, London and New York: Pandora, 1986, p. 146.

4 Jane Morris to Cormell Price, Wednesday, [August 1877], *Collected Letters of Jane Morris*, p. 65.

5 Jane Morris to Cormell Price, [Summer 1877], ibid., p. 64.

6 Jane Morris to Cormell Price, Wednesday [August 1877], ibid., pp. 65–6.

7 Edward Burne-Jones to Charles Eliot Norton, quoted *Memorials*, vol. 2, p. 23.

8 Edward Burne-Jones to Charles Eliot Norton, quoted ibid.

9 May Morris, *Introductions*, vol. 1, p. 247.

10 Jane Morris, quoted Mackail, *Life of William Morris*, vol. 1, p. 289.

11 May Morris, *Introductions*, vol. 1, p. 247.

12 William Morris to Aglaia Coronio, 11 February 1873, Kelvin (ed.), *Collected Letters*, vol. 1, p. 177.

13 May Morris, *Introductions*, vol. 1, p. 249

14   William Morris to Aglaia Coronio, 6 April 1874, Kelvin (ed.), *Collected Letters*, vol. 1, p. 221.

15   Margaret Burne-Jones, quoted MacCarthy, *William Morris: A Life*, p. 326.

16   Jane Morris to Cormell Price, 3 February 1878, *Collected Letters of Jane Morris*, p. 69.

17   May Morris, *Introductions*, quoted MacCarthy, *William Morris: A Life.*, p. 335.

18   May Morris, *Introductions*, vol. 1, p. 248.

19   Mackail, *Life of William Morris*, vol. 1, p. 289.

20   May Morris, *Introductions*, vol. 1, p. 247.

21   William Morris to Aglaia Coronio, Monday 3 o'clock, [6 April 1874], Kelvin (ed.), *Collected Letters*, vol. 1, p. 221.

22   William Morris to Aglaia Coronio, 11 February 1873, ibid., vol. 1, p. 178.

23   Edward Burne-Jones, quoted May Morris, *Introductions*, vol. 1, p. 248.

24   William Morris to Aglaia Coronio, 23 January 1873, Kelvin (ed.), *Collected Letters*, vol. 1, p. 176.

25   'Thomas Maitland' [Robert Buchanan], 'The Fleshly School of Poetry: Mr D G Rossetti', *The Contemporary Review*, October 1871, p. 337.

26   Ibid., p. 343.

27   Ibid., p. 338.

28   'Mr Buchanan and the Fleshly Poets', 1 June 1872, *Saturday Review*, quoted Christopher D. Murray, 'D. G. Rossetti, A. C. Swinburne and R. W. Buchanan: The Fleshly School Revisited', *Bulletin of the John Rylands University Library of Manchester*, vol. 65, No. 2, Spring 1983, p. 198.

29   Dante Gabriel Rossetti to William Michael Rossetti, 14 October 1869, *Correspondence of Dante Gabriel Rossetti: The Chelsea Years 1863–1872*, p. 303.

30   William Bell Scott to Alice Boyd, quoted ibid., p. 426.

31   Henry Treffry Dunn to William Michael Rossetti, 22 July 1872, quoted Murray, 'D. G. Rossetti, A. C. Swinburne and R. W. Buchanan: The Fleshly School Revisited', p. 200.

32   William Bell Scott to Alice Boyd, quoted *Correspondence of Dante Gabriel Rossetti: The Chelsea Years 1863–1872*, p. 426.

33   Ibid., p. 427.

34   William Bell Scott to Alice Boyd, 17 June 1872, quoted ibid., p. 429.

35   *Collected Letters of Jane Morris*, p. 54, n. 1.

36   William Bell Scott to Alice Boyd, 17 June 1872, quoted *Correspondence of Dante Gabriel Rossetti: The Chelsea Years 1863–1872*, p. 429.

37   Ibid.

38   Jane Morris to Dr Thomas Gordon Hake, 13 September 1872, *Collected Letters of Jane Morris*, p. 53.

39   Jane Morris to William Bell Scott, 9 July 1872, ibid., p. 49.

40   Jane Morris to Ford Madox Brown, Thursday [July 1872], ibid., p. 51.

41   Jane Morris to Emma Madox Brown, Friday [late August 1872], ibid., p. 53.

42   Jane Morris to William Bell Scott, 15 July 1872, *Collected Letters of Jane Morris*, p. 50.

43   William Morris to Aglaia Coronio, 25 November 1872, Kelvin (ed.), *Collected Letters*, vol. 1, p. 171.

44   Jane Morris to Lucy Madox Brown, March 1874, *Collected Letters of Jane Morris*, p. 56.

45   William Morris to Emma Morris, 25 May 1874, Kelvin (ed.), *Collected Letters*, vol. 1, p. 223.

46   Dante Gabriel Rossetti to Theodore Watts Dunton, 9 March 1874, *Collected Letters of Jane Morris*, p. 58, n. 2.

47   Jane Morris to Lucy Madox Brown Rossetti, 24 June 1874, ibid., p. 57. Ford Madox Brown's daughter, Lucy, married William Michael Rossetti on 31 March 1874.

48   Dante Gabriel Rossetti, 'Proserpine (For a Picture)', 1877, manuscript, Harry Ransom Humanities Center, the University of Texas at Austin.

49   William Morris to Aglaia Coronio, 25 November 1872, Kelvin (ed.), *Collected Letters*, vol. 1, p. 172.

50   Ibid., p. 173.

51   William Morris to Philip Webb, 10 April 1873, ibid., p. 185.

52   William Morris to Emma Morris, 9 April 1873, ibid., pp. 184–5.

53 William Morris to Jane Morris, 6 April 1873, ibid., p. 183.

54 William Morris to Philip Webb, 10 April 1873, ibid., p. 185.

55 Ibid., p. 186.

56 William Morris to Philip Webb, 11 July 1873, ibid., p. 195.

57 William Morris to Jane Morris, 18 July 1873, ibid., p. 196.

58 Ibid.

59 Ibid.

60 William Morris, 'A Diary of Travel in Iceland 1873', *Collected Works*, vol. 8, p. 188.

61 Ibid., p. 214.

62 Ibid., p. 189.

63 Ibid., p. 190.

64 Ibid., p. 194.

65 Ibid., p. 228.

66 Ibid., p. 236.

67 Ibid., p. 192.

68 William Morris to Aglaia Coronio, 14 September 1873, Kelvin (ed.), *Collected Letters*, vol. 1, p. 198.

69 William Morris to Aglaia Coronio, 14 September 1873, ibid. Charles' Wain or *carles wæn* (Old English) is another name for the Plough constellation.

70 William Morris to Louisa Macdonald Baldwin, 26 March 1874, ibid., p. 218.

71 Mackail, *Life of William Morris*, vol. 1, p. 12.

72 Ibid., p. 13.

73 William Morris, 'Making the Best of It', *Hopes and Fears for Art*, vol. 22, 1879, p. 82.

74 Walt Whitman's *Leaves of Grass* had been edited and published in 1868 by William Michael Rossetti, so his work was known among Morris's circle.

75 Edward Carpenter, 'William Morris: Obituary', reprinted in *Labour Leader*, 19 December 1896.

76 Moncure Conway, quoted Charles Harvey & Jon Press, *William Morris: Design and Enterprise in Victorian Britain*, Manchester and New York: Manchester University Press, 1991, p. 120.

77	Henry James, quoted Lesley Hopkins, 'Wallpaper', in Parry (ed.), *William Morris*, V&A, 1996, p. 198.

78	William Morris notes and wallpaper sample, *Lily*, illustrated Hopkins, ibid., p. 211.

79	Hopkins, 'Wallpaper', in ibid., p. 209.

80	William Morris, 'Making the Best of It' (1879), and brochure for the Foreign Fair display, Boston, 1883, quoted in ibid., p. 204.

81	William Morris, 'Making the Best of It' (1879), *Collected Works*, vol. 22, p. 96.

82	Dante Gabriel Rossetti to William Morris, 25 October 1874, quoted in Kelvin (ed.), *Collected Letters*, vol. 1, p. 237, n. 2.

83	William Morris to Aglaia Coronio, 11 February 1873, Kelvin (ed.), *Collected Letters*, vol. 1, p. 177.

84	Carpenter, 'William Morris: Obituary', *Labour Leader*, 19 December 1896.

85	William Morris to Eiríkr Magnusson, 18 March 1873, Kelvin (ed.), *Collected Letters*, vol. 1, p. 180.

86	William Morris to Theodore Watts-Dunton, 28 August 1874, ibid., p. 230.

87	Jane Morris to Ford Madox Brown, September 1874, *Collected Letters of Jane Morris*, p. 60.

88	Dante Gabriel Rossetti to Theodore Watts Dunton, 1 April 1875, William E. Fredeman (ed.), *The Correspondence of Dante Gabriel Rossetti vol. 7: The Last Decade 1873–1882 (Part II: 1875–1877)*, Cambridge: D. S. Brewer, 2008, p. 27.

89	Theodore Watts-Dunton, 'Dante Gabriel Rossetti', *The Nineteenth Century*, March 1883, pp. 412–13.

90	Jane E. Sayers, 'Jones, Harriet Morant (1833–1917), headmistress' in *Oxford Dictionary of National Biography*.

91	William Morris to Jane Morris, 9 November 1875, Kelvin (ed.), *Collected Letters*, vol. 1, p. 276.

92	William Morris to Jane Morris, 26 January 1876, ibid., pp. 286–7.

93	William Morris to Thomas Wardle, 16 November 1875, ibid., p. 278.

94	William Morris to Thomas Wardle, August 1875, ibid., p. 265.

95   William Morris to Georgiana Burne-Jones, 26 March 1876, ibid., p. 292.

96   Jane Morris to Theodore Watts-Dunton, 26 April 1888, *Collected Letters of Jane Morris*, p. 166.

97   William Michael Rossetti, *Correspondence of Dante Gabriel Rossetti: 1875–1877*, p. 291, n. 1.

98   William Michael Rossetti, ibid., p. 308, n. 1.

99   Wilfrid Scawen Blunt, 5 May 1892, 'My Diaries', in Faulkner (ed.), *Jane Morris to Wilfrid Scawen Blunt*, p. 66.

100 Dante Gabriel Rossetti to Jane Morris, 31 May 1878, *Dante Gabriel Rossetti and Jane Morris: Their Correspondence*, p. 68.

101 Dante Gabriel Rossetti to Jane Morris, August 1878, ibid., p. 76

102 Dante Gabriel Rossetti to Jane Morris, September 1878, ibid., p. 81

103 Georgiana Burne-Jones, quoted MacCarthy, *William Morris: A Life*, p. 368.

104 Richard Watson Dixon, in Mackail, Manuscript notebooks, quoted ibid., p. 78.

105 Mackail, *Life of William Morris*, vol. 1, p. 328.

106 Ibid.

107 Jane Morris to Wilfrid Scawen Blunt, 9 August 1888, *Jane Morris to Wilfrid Scawen Blunt*, p. 19.

108 Jane Morris to Wilfrid Scawen Blunt, 3 October 1888, ibid.

109 Jane Morris to Wilfrid Scawen Blunt, 9 August 1888, ibid.

110 Ibid.

111 Georgiana Burne-Jones, quoted Marsh, *Jane and May Morris: A Biographical Story*, p. 268.

112 May Morris, quoted Marsh, ibid., p. 146.

Chapter 10: Italy, 1877–1878

1   Jane Morris to Cormell Price, 3 February 1878, *Collected Letters of Jane Morris*, p. 69.

2   Jane Morris to Rosalind Howard, 6 September 1877, ibid., p. 67.

3   May Morris, quoted Marsh, *Jane and May Morris: A Biographical Story*, p. 136.

4   Jane Morris to Rosalind Howard, 6 September 1877, *Collected Letters of Jane Morris*, p. 67.

5   Marsh, *Jane and May Morris: A Biographical Story*, p. 149.

6   Jane Morris to Rosalind Howard, 23 August 1877, *Collected Letters of Jane Morris*, p. 66.

7   Jane Morris to Rosalind Howard, 6 September 1877, ibid., p. 67.

8   Jane Morris to Cormell Price, 3 February 1878, ibid., p. 68.

9   Ibid., p. 67.

10   Ibid., p. 69.

11   Ibid., p. 68.

12   Ibid.

13   Ibid., p. 69.

14   Ibid.

15   Marsh, *Jane and May Morris: A Biographical Story*, p. 149.

16   Notes taken by Sydney Cockerell, 1892, in Mackail, Manuscript notebooks, vol. 2, p. 100.

17   William Morris to the editor of *The Times*, 4 June 1877, Kelvin (ed.), *Collected Letters*, vol. 1, p. 374.

18   William Morris to the editor of *The Times*, 7 June 1877, ibid., p. 376.

19   Quoted MacCarthy, *William Morris: A Life*, p. 376.

20   William Morris to John Ruskin, 10 July 1877, Kelvin (ed.), *Collected Letters*, vol. 1, p. 383.

21   Society for the Protection of Ancient Buildings, Annual Report, 1880, p. 35, quoted Robert Hewison, *Ruskin on Venice*, New Haven and London: Yale University Press, 2009, p. 378.

22   Manifesto for the Society for the Protection of Ancient Buildings, 1877, www.spab.org.uk/about-us/spab-manifesto.

23   William Morris to the editor of the *Daily News*, 24 October 1876, Kelvin (ed.), *Collected Letters*, vol. 1, p. 324.

24   William Morris, 11 May 1877, quoted MacCarthy, *William Morris: A Life*, p. 382.

25   William Morris to Jane Morris, 2 May 1877, Kelvin (ed.), *Collected Letters*, vol. 1, p. 370.

26   William Morris, 'Wake! London Lads' (1878), quoted ibid., p. 436 n. 8.

27 Henry Broadhurst, quoted MacCarthy, *William Morris: A Life*, p. 384.

28 William Morris to Jenny and May Morris, 25 December 1877, Kelvin (ed.), *Collected Letters*, vol. 1, p. 423.

29 William Morris to May Morris, 26 January 1878, ibid., p. 439.

30 William Morris to Jane Morris, 28 December 1877, ibid., p. 428.

31 William Morris to Jane Morris, 29 November 1877, ibid., p. 414.

32 William Morris to Jane Morris, 12 March 1878, ibid., p. 457.

33 William Morris to Jane Morris, 18 March 1878, ibid., p. 459.

34 Ibid.

35 William Morris, quoted ibid., p. 458, n. 4.

36 William Morris to Jane Morris, 12 March 1878, ibid., p. 457.

37 Dante Gabriel Rossetti to Jane Morris, 1 April 1878, *Dante Gabriel Rossetti and Jane Morris: Their Correspondence*, pp. 61–2.

38 Dante Gabriel Rossetti to Jane Morris, 24 January 1878, ibid., p. 49.

39 Dante Gabriel Rossetti to Jane Morris, 27 February 1878, ibid., p. 53.

40 Dante Gabriel Rossetti to Jane Morris, 18 March 1878, ibid., p. 59.

41 Dante Gabriel Rossetti to Jane Morris, 2 December 1877, ibid., p. 42.

42 Dante Gabriel Rossetti to Jane Morris, 19 December 1877, ibid., p. 45.

43 Dante Gabriel Rossetti to Jane Morris, August 1878, ibid., p. 75.

44 Dante Gabriel Rossetti, translation from Dante's *Vita Nuova*, Dante Gabriel Rossetti to Jane Morris, August 1878, ibid., p. 75.

45 Dante Gabriel Rossetti to Jane Morris, 27 February 1878, ibid., p. 54.

46 Dante Gabriel Rossetti to Jane Morris, 3 March 1878, ibid., p. 90.

47 William Morris, Mackail, *Life of William Morris*, vol. 1, p. 368.

48 Ibid., p. 367.

49 May Morris, *Introductions*, vol. 1, p. 338.

50 William Morris, Mackail, *Life of William Morris*, vol. 1, p. 370.

51 William Morris to Georgiana Burne-Jones, 15 May 1878, Kelvin (ed.), *Collected Letters*, vol. 1, p. 486.

52 William Morris to George Howard, 18 May 1878, ibid., p. 487.

53 William Morris to Georgiana Burne-Jones, May 1878, ibid., p. 484.

54 William Morris to Charles Fairfax Murray, 29 April 1878, ibid., p. 483.

55 William Morris to George Howard, 18 May 1878, ibid., p. 487.

56 Jane Morris to Rosalind Howard, June 1878, *Collected Letters of Jane Morris*, p. 73.

57 Jane Morris to Rosalind Howard, June 1878, ibid., pp. 72–3.

58 Ibid.

59 William Morris to Jane Morris, 2 April 1878, Kelvin (ed.), *Collected Letters*, vol. 1, p. 469.

60 Dante Gabriel Rossetti to Jane Morris, 2 September 1878, *Dante Gabriel Rossetti and Jane Morris: Their Correspondence*, p. 78.

61 Dante Gabriel Rossetti to Jane Morris, 1 April 1878, ibid., p. 63.

62 Jane Morris to Dante Gabriel Rossetti, 31 May 1878, ibid., p. 68.

63 Jane Morris to Rosalind Howard, 26 May 1878, *Collected Letters of Jane Morris*, p. 71.

Chapter 11: Hammersmith, 1878–1883

1 Jane Morris to Cormell Price, June 1878, *Collected Letters of Jane Morris*, p. 75.

2 Ibid.

3 Dante Gabriel Rossetti to Jane Morris, 3 September 1880, *Dante Gabriel Rossetti and Jane Morris: Their Correspondence*, p. 159.

4 Dante Gabriel Rossetti to Jane Morris, 26 February 1880, ibid., p. 141.

5 Dante Gabriel Rossetti to Jane Morris, 3 September 1880, ibid., p. 159.

6 Jane Morris to Dante Gabriel Rossetti, August 1879, ibid., p. 115.

7 Ibid.

8 Jane Morris to Dante Gabriel Rossetti, 1879, ibid., p. 100 and Dante Gabriel Rossetti to Jane Morris, July 1879, ibid., p. 97.

9 Dante Gabriel Rossetti to Jane Morris, August 1879, ibid., p. 111.

10 Jane Morris to Cormell Price, June 1878, *Collected Letters of Jane Morris*, p. 75.

11 Ibid.

12 Ibid.

13 William Morris to Jane Morris, 18 March 1878, Kelvin (ed.), *Collected Letters*, vol. 1, p. 459.

14 Dante Gabriel Rossetti to Jane Morris, August 1879, *Dante Gabriel Rossetti and Jane Morris: Their Correspondence*, p. 109.

15 Jane Morris to Dante Gabriel Rossetti, September 1878, ibid., p. 80.

16 William Morris to Jane Morris, before 28 March 1878, Kelvin (ed.), *Collected Letters*, vol. 1, p. 462.

17 William Morris to Jane Morris, 26 March 1878, ibid., p. 466.

18 William Morris to Jane Morris, 26 March 1878, ibid.

19 William Morris to Jane Morris, before 28 March 1878, ibid., pp. 460–1.

20 Edward Burne-Jones, in Mackail, Manuscript notebooks, vol. 2, p. 85.

21 William Morris to Jane Morris, before 28 March 1878, Kelvin (ed.), *Collected Letters*, pp. 460–1.

22 William Morris to Jane Morris, 18 March 1878, ibid., p. 458.

23 William Morris to Jane Morris, before 28 March 1878, ibid., p. 461.

24 William Morris to Jane Morris, 18 March 1878, ibid., p. 458.

25 Ibid.

26 Mackail, Manuscript notebooks, February 1879, vol. 2, p. 47.

27 Jane Morris to Cormell Price, 15 July 1880, *Collected Letters of Jane Morris*, p. 111.

28 William Morris, quoted Linda Parry, in Parry (ed.), *William Morris*, V&A, 1996, pp. 270–1.

29 May Morris, *Introductions*, vol. 2, p. 340.

30 May Morris, quoted Design Council exhibition catalogue, *William Morris & Kelmscott*, London: Design Council, 1981, p. 163.

31 Mackail, *Life of William Morris*, vol. 2, p. 92.

32 William Morris to May Morris, 21 March 1878, Kelvin (ed.), *Collected Letters*, vol. 1, p. 464.

33 May Morris, quoted MacCarthy, *William Morris: A Life*, p. 397.

34 William Morris, 'Textile Fabrics: a lecture delivered in the Lecture Room of the Exhibition' (1884), quoted Studio Carrom & William Morris Gallery, *A Distant Fellowship: William Morris and South East Asia*, London: William Morris Gallery, 2021, p. 63.

35 May Morris, *Introductions*, vol. 1, p. 371.

36 Georgiana Burne-Jones to Rosalind Howard, 6 October 1877, and

Rosalind Howard to Georgiana Burne-Jones, 26 March 1876, quoted MacCarthy, *William Morris: A Life*, p. 353.

37 William Morris to Jane Morris, 23 February 1881, Kelvin (ed.), *Collected Letters*, vol. 2, p. 24.

38 Ibid., p. 24, n. 3.

39 William Morris to Jane Morris, 17 March 1881, ibid., p. 32.

40 Jane Morris to Cormell Price, 15 July 1880, *Collected Letters of Jane Morris*, p. 111.

41 May Morris, quoted MacCarthy, *William Morris: A Life*, p. 424, and William Morris to Georgiana Burne-Jones, 10 August 1880, Kelvin (ed.), *Collected Letters*, vol. 1, p. 578.

42 William Morris to Georgiana Burne-Jones, 19 August 1880, ibid., p. 581.

43 Jenny Morris, quoted Marsh, *Jane and May Morris: A Biographical Story*, p. 158.

44 William Morris to Georgiana Burne-Jones, 10 August 1880, Kelvin (ed.), *Collected Letters*, vol. 1, p. 578, and William Morris to Georgiana Burne-Jones, 19 August 1880, ibid., p. 581.

45 William Morris to Georgiana Burne-Jones, 10 August 1880, ibid., pp. 578–9.

46 William Morris to Georgiana Burne-Jones, 19 August 1880, ibid., pp. 582–3.

47 Ibid., p. 583.

48 Jane Morris to Cormell Price, 11 February 1880, *Collected Letters of Jane Morris*, p. 107.

49 Jane Morris to Dante Gabriel Rossetti, January 1880, ibid., p. 105.

50 William Morris to Georgiana Burne-Jones, 19 August 1880, Kelvin (ed.), *Collected Letters*, vol. 1, p. 583.

51 May Morris, *Introductions*, vol. 1, p. 333.

52 Letitia Bell Scott, in Mackail, Manuscript notebooks, vol. 1, p. 33.

53 Jane Morris to Theodore Watts Dunton, 28 December 1882, *Collected Letters of Jane Morris*, p. 124.

54 Helena Sickert, quoted ibid., p. 103.

55 Jane Morris to Dante Gabriel Rossetti, July 1880, ibid., p. 110.

56 William Morris to Catherine Holiday, 9 March 1878, Kelvin (ed.), *Collected Letters*, vol. 1, p. 455.

57 Jane Morris to Sara Sedgwick Darwin, 28 March 1880, *Correspondence of Jane Morris*, pp. 109–10. George Wardle was business manager at Morris & Co. He had worked with William since 1866, and was brother-in-law of Thomas Wardle, the textile manufacturer.

58 Jane Morris to Dante Gabriel Rossetti, 2 February 1881, *Correspondence of Jane Morris*, p. 116, and Jane Morris to Dante Gabriel Rossetti, January 1881, ibid., p. 115.

59 Jane Morris to Dante Gabriel Rossetti, 2 February 1881, ibid., p. 116.

60 Jane Morris to Louisa Powell Macdonald, 3 March 1881, ibid., p. 121.

61 Jane Morris to Moncure Daniel Conway, 20 May 1880, ibid., p. 110.

62 Henry James, 24 March 1881, quoted *Correspondence of Jane Morris*, pp. 118–19, n. 5, and Moncure Daniel Conway, quoted ibid., p. 94, n. 1.

63 Jane Morris to Moncure Daniel Conway, 24 August 1882, ibid., p. 123.

64 William Morris to Georgiana Burne-Jones, late autumn 1879, Kelvin (ed.), *Collected Letters*, p. 525.

65 William Morris, 'The Art of the People', *Collected Works*, vol. 22, p. 47.

66 John Ruskin, 'Traffic', *The Crown of Wild Olive*, in Cook and Wedderburn (eds), *Complete Works of John Ruskin*, vol. 18, pp. 434–5.

67 John Ruskin, 12 February 1878, Helen Viljoen (ed.), *The Brantwood Diary*, New Haven and London: Yale University Press, 1971, p. 63.

68 William Morris, 'The Art of the People', *Collected Works*, vol. 22, p. 42.

69 Ibid., p. 47.

70 Ibid., p. 48.

71 Ibid.

72 Ibid.

73 Ibid.

74 Ibid., p. 44.

75 Ibid., p. 45.

76 Ibid., p. 31.

77 Ibid., p. 42.

78 Ibid., p. 36.

79   Ibid., p. 37.

80   Ibid., p. 33.

81   Ibid., p. 38.

82   Ibid.

83   Ibid., pp. 30–1.

84   Ibid., p. 30.

85   Ibid, p. 39.

86   Ibid.

87   Ibid., p. 50.

88   James Whistler, ed. Sheridan Ford, *The Gentle Art of Making Enemies*, New York: Frederick Stoke & Brother, 1890, p. 46.

89   James Whistler, *Mr Whistler's Ten O'Clock*, delivered in London, 20 February 1885, London: Chatto and Windus, 1888, p. 11.

90   F. S. Ellis, in Mackail, Manuscript notebooks, vol. 1, p. 9.

91   *The Diary of Lady Frederick Cavendish*, quoted *Collected Letters of Jane Morris*, p. 13.

92   George du Maurier, quoted ibid., p. 13.

93   *The Times*, 12 April 1882, quoted ibid., p. 123.

94   Jane Morris to Cormell Price, 28 April 1882, ibid., p. 122.

95   Jane Morris to Dante Gabriel Rossetti, 5 November 1878, ibid., p. 79.

96   Jane Morris to Dante Gabriel Rossetti, December 1880, ibid., p. 113.

97   Jane Morris to Gabriel Rossetti, March 1879, ibid., p. 86.

98   Dante Gabriel Rossetti to Jane Morris, July 1879, *Dante Gabriel Rossetti and Jane Morris: Their Correspondence*, p. 97.

99   Jane Morris to Dante Gabriel Rossetti, August 1879, *The Collected Letters of Jane Morris*, p. 89.

100 Jane Morris to Dante Gabriel Rossetti, July 1879, ibid., p. 88.

101 Dante Gabriel Rossetti to Jane Morris, 7 January 1880, *Dante Gabriel Rossetti and Jane Morris: Their Correspondence*, p. 130.

102 Dante Gabriel Rossetti to Jane Morris, 26 November 1880, ibid., pp. 165–6.

103 Dante Gabriel Rossetti to Jane Morris, 25 July 1879, ibid., p. 103.

104 William Morris to William Bell Scott, 27 April 1882, Kelvin (ed.), *Collected Letters*, vol. 2, p. 109.

105 Ibid.

106 Burne-Jones, *Memorials*, vol. 2, p. 133.

107 William Morris to William Bell Scott, 27 April 1882, Kelvin (ed.), *Collected Letters*, vol. 2, p. 109.

108 Jane Morris to Cormell Price, 28 April 1882, *Collected Letters of Jane Morris*, p. 122.

109 Burne-Jones, *Memorials*, vol. 2, p. 133.

110 Jane Morris to Theodore Watts Dunton, March 1883, *Collected Letters of Jane Morris*, p. 127.

111 William Morris to Algernon Charles Swinburne, 22 July 1882, Kelvin (ed.), *Collected Letters*, vol. 2, p. 115.

112 Jane Morris to Theodore Watts Dunton, 28 December 1882, *Collected Letters of Jane Morris*, p. 124.

113 Harry Quilter, 'The Art of Rossetti', *Contemporary Review*, February 1883, quoted ibid., p. 127, n. 4.

114 Sidney Colvin, 'Rossetti as Painter', *The Magazine of Art*, January 1883, quoted ibid., p. 128, n. 5.

115 Marsh, *Jane and May Morris: A Biographical Story*, p. 172.

116 Jane Morris to Theodore Watts Dunton, March 1883, *Collected Letters of Jane Morris*, p. 127.

117 Ibid., p. 126.

118 Ibid., p. 127.

119 Dante Gabriel Rossetti to Jane Morris, July 1879, *Dante Gabriel Rossetti and Jane Morris: Their Correspondence*, p. 97.

120 *Collected Letters of Jane Morris*, p. 126, n. 3. Jane, in turn, left these drawings to the Ashmolean Museum, and her correspondence with Gabriel she bequeathed to May.

121 Emma Lazarus, 4 July 1883, quoted *Collected Letters of Jane Morris*, p. 99.

122 John Bruce Glasier, quoted ibid., p. 101.

123 Ernest Rhys, 1887, quoted ibid.

124 Jane Morris, recorded by Wilfrid Scawen Blunt, diary entry, 13 May 1890, in Faulkner (ed.), *Jane Morris to Wilfrid Scawen Blunt*, p. 43.

Chapter 12: The Coach House, 1883–1890

1   Florence Boos (ed.), *William Morris's Socialist Diary*, London and New York: Journeyman/London History Workshop Centre, 1982, reprinted 1985, p. 50, and William Morris to Jenny Morris, 23 April 1887, Henderson (ed.), *Letters of William Morris to his Family and Friends*, p. 272.

2   Boos (ed.), *William Morris's Socialist Diary*, p. 53.

3   William Morris, *Newcastle Chronicle*, 12 April 1887, quoted MacCarthy, *William Morris: A Life*, p. 561.

4   William Morris to Georgiana Burne-Jones, May 1886, quoted MacCarthy, *William Morris: A Life*, p. 532.

5   William Morris to Georgiana Burne-Jones, September 1883, Mackail, *Life of William Morris*, vol. 2, p. 113.

6   William Morris, 14 March 1883, *Manchester Examiner*, quoted MacCarthy, *William Morris: A Life*, p. 476.

7   William Morris to C. E. Maurice, 22 June 1883, Mackail, *Life of William Morris*, vol. 2, pp. 106–8.

8   William Morris to Georgiana Burne-Jones, August 1883, ibid., p. 111.

9   William Morris to C. E. Maurice, 22 June 1883, ibid., p. 103.

10   Charles Mowbray, quoted MacCarthy, *William Morris: A Life*, p. 583.

11   30 March 1887, *William Morris's Socialist Diary*, p. 45.

12   23 February 1887, ibid., p. 33.

13   *The Times*, 14 November 1887, quoted Fiona MacCarthy, *William Morris: A Life*, p. 568.

14   William Morris, *The Commonweal*, 19 November 1887, quoted MacCarthy, *William Morris: A Life*, p. 568.

15   William Morris, *The Commonweal*, 24 December 1887, quoted ibid., p. 572.

16   H. A. Barker, quoted MacCarthy, *William Morris: A Life*, p. 573.

17   William Morris to Jenny Morris, 26 October 1885, Henderson (ed.), *The Letters of William Morris to his Family and Friends*, p. 240.

18   William Morris to Georgiana Burne-Jones, 31 October 1885, ibid., p. 241.

19   William Morris to Georgiana Burne-Jones, 24 December 1884, ibid., p. 223.

20   Ibid.

21   William Morris to Georgiana Burne-Jones, 31 October 1885, ibid., p. 241.

22   William Morris to Charles Faulkner, 23 October 1883, ibid., p. 188.

23   William Morris, 'Art and Democracy' (1883; published as *Art and Plutocracy*), quoted MacCarthy, *William Morris: A Life*, p. 477.

24   Ibid.

25   Ibid., p. 478.

26   Ibid.

27   William Morris, Letter to the Editor of *The Standard*, 21 November 1883, quoted MacCarthy, *William Morris: A Life*, p. 479.

28   Owen Carroll, *William Morris among the Reds*, 23 September 1933, quoted MacCarthy, *William Morris: A Life*, p. 542.

29   William Morris to Georgiana Burne-Jones, 1 June 1884, Henderson (ed.), *The Letters of William Morris to his Family and Friends*, p. 197.

30   William Morris to Thomas Cobden-Sanderson, 16 January 1884, quoted MacCarthy, *William Morris: A Life*, p. 457.

31   William Morris recollected by W. B. Yeats, quoted, ibid., p. 523.

32   W. B. Yeats, quoted, ibid.

33   H. G. Wells, quoted, ibid., p. 522.

34   William Morris to Jane Morris, 31 March 1881, Henderson(ed.), *The Letters of William Morris to his Family and Friends*, p. 148.

35   Oscar Wilde, *The Soul of Man Under Socialism* (1891), reprinted London: Arthur L. Humphreys, 1909, p. 3.

36   Ibid., pp. 10–11.

37   Harold Laski, quoted MacCarthy, *William Morris: A Life*, p. 548.

38   William Morris, *A Dream of John Ball* (1888), reprinted London: Reeves and Turner, 1895, p. 75.

39   Ibid., pp. 77–8.

40   Ibid., p. 80.

41   Ibid.

42   Jane Morris to Wilfrid Scawen Blunt, 20 March 1885, *Collected Letters of Jane Morris*, p. 137.

43   Isabel Meredith (pseudonym of William Michael Rossetti's daughters, Helen and Olivia), *A Girl among the Anarchists*, quoted MacCarthy, *William Morris: A Life*, pp. 470–1.

44   Jane Morris to Wilfrid Scawen Blunt, 16 January 1889, *Collected Letters of Jane Morris*, p. 178.

45   Bruce Glasier, quoted MacCarthy, *William Morris: A Life*, p. 498.

46   Rachel Holmes, *Eleanor Marx: A Life*, London: Bloomsbury, 2014, p. 317.

47   Ibid., pp. 232–3.

48   Edward Aveling, *The Commonweal*, October 1885, quoted MacCarthy, *William Morris: A Life*, p. 527.

49   *Daily News*, 22 September 1885, quoted MacCarthy, ibid., pp. 527–8.

50   William Morris to Jane Morris, 22 September 1885, Henderson (ed.), *The Letters of William Morris to his Family and Friends*, p. 239.

51   Jane Morris to Wilfrid Scawen Blunt, *Collected Letters of Jane Morris*, p. 159.

52   Eleanor Marx to Wilhelm Liebknecht, 1 January 1885, quoted Holmes, *Eleanor Marx: A Life*, p. 233.

53   William Morris to Andreas Scheu, 28 December 1884, Kelvin (ed.), *Collected Letters*, vol. 2, p. 360.

54   Ibid.

55   Friedrich Engels to Bernstein, 29 December 1884, quoted Holmes, *Eleanor Marx: A Life*, p. 233.

56   Eleanor Marx to Paul Lafargue, 12 April 1885, quoted Holmes, ibid., p. 235.

57   May Morris, quoted MacCarthy, *William Morris: A Life*, p. 508.

58   Socialist League Manifesto, quoted MacCarthy, *William Morris: A Life*, p. 508.

59   May Morris, quoted MacCarthy, ibid.

60   Gertrude Gentry to Edith Lanchester, 1 May 1898, quoted Holmes, *Eleanor Marx: A Life*, p. 441.

61   Jane Morris to Cormell Price, June 1878, *Collected Letters of Jane Morris*, p. 75.

62   May Morris to George Bernard Shaw, 5 May 1936, quoted in Jenny

Lister, Jan Marsh and Anna Mason (eds), *May Morris: Arts and Crafts Designer*, London: Thames & Hudson, V&A Museum, William Morris Gallery, 2017, p. 29.

63 H. G. Wells, quoted MacCarthy, *William Morris: A Life*, p. 522.

64 George Gissing, 1886, quoted, ibid., p. 519.

65 George Bernard Shaw, 'Morris as I knew him', in May Morris (ed.), *William Morris: Artist, Writer, Socialist*, vol. 2, Oxford: Basil Blackwell, 1936, reprinted Cambridge: Cambridge University Press, 2012, pp. xxvii–xviii.

66 May Morris to George Bernard Shaw, 8 November 1885, quoted Marsh, *Jane and May Morris: A Biographical Story*, p. 205.

67 George Bernard Shaw, quoted Marsh, ibid., p. 210.

68 Jane Morris to Rosalind Howard, 3 June 1887, *Collected Letters of Jane Morris*, p. 153.

69 Wilfrid Scawen Blunt, quoted ibid., p. 154.

70 Jane Morris to Rosalind Howard, 23 August 1887, ibid.

71 Jane Morris to Wilfrid Scawen Blunt, 12 February 1889, ibid., p. 179.

72 Jane Morris to Wilfrid Scawen Blunt, 13 June 1890, ibid., p. 207.

73 George Bernard Shaw, 'Morris as I knew him', p. xxx.

74 Jane Morris to Wilfrid Scawen Blunt, 26 May 1894, *Collected Letters of Jane Morris*, p. 253.

75 Jane Morris to Wilfrid Scawen Blunt, 24 May 1894, ibid., p. 252.

76 Lucy Carr Shaw, quoted Marsh, *Jane and May Morris: A Biographical Story*, pp. 237–8.

77 George Bernard Shaw, 'Morris as I knew him', p. xxiv.

78 Ibid.

79 Ibid., p. xxv.

80 Jane Morris to Mary Howard, 19 August 1885, *Collected Letters of Jane Morris*, p. 141.

81 May Morris, *Introductions*, vol. 1, pp. 377–8.

82 Jane Morris to Wilfrid Scawen Blunt, 11 July 1888, *Collected Letters of Jane Morris*, p. 168.

83 Jane Morris to Cormell Price, 13 January 1886, ibid., p. 144.

84 George Bernard Shaw, 'Morris as I knew him', p. xxiv.

85   Jane Morris to Cormell Price, 13 January 1886, *Collected Letters of Jane Morris*, p. 144.

86   Jane Morris to Wilfrid Scawen Blunt, 26 July 1884, ibid., p. 132.

87   Wilfrid Scawen Blunt, quoted Elizabeth Longford, *A Pilgrimage of Passion: The Life of Wilfrid Scawen Blunt*, New York: Alfred Knopf, 1980, p. 87.

88   Wilfrid Scawen Blunt, diary entry, 29 January 1885, in Faulkner (ed.), *Jane Morris to Wilfrid Scawen Blunt*, p. 4.

89   Wilfrid Scawen Blunt, diary entry, 7 May 1891, ibid., p. 53.

90   Jane Morris to Wilfrid Scawen Blunt, 31 October 1889, *Collected Letters of Jane Morris*, p. 189.

91   Jane Morris to Cormell Price, 10 September 1883, ibid., p. 129.

92   Wilfrid Scawen Blunt, quoted ibid., p. 129n.

93   Wilfrid Scawen Blunt, diary entry, 29 July 1884, in Faulkner (ed.), *Jane Morris to Wilfrid Scawen Blunt*, p. 3.

94   Jane Morris to Wilfrid Scawen Blunt, 6 August 1884, *Collected Letters of Jane Morris*, pp. 132–3.

95   Jane Morris to Wilfrid Scawen Blunt, 12 February 1885, and 20 March 1885, ibid., pp. 135, 137.

96   Jane Morris to Wilfrid Scawen Blunt, 4 March 1885, and 14 June 1885, ibid., pp. 136, 139.

97   Jane Morris to Wilfrid Scawen Blunt, 11 August 1885, ibid., p. 141.

98   Jane Morris to Jane Cobden, 14 January 1888, ibid., p. 163.

99   Jane Morris to William Scawen Blunt, 13 December 1888, ibid., p. 173.

100 Jane Morris to Wilfrid Scawen Blunt, 8 November 1888, ibid., p. 172.

101 Jane Morris to Wilfrid Scawen Blunt, 11 August 1889, and 21 August 1889, ibid., p. 186.

102 Jane Morris to Wilfrid Scawen Blunt, 9 August 1888, ibid., p. 169.

103 Wilfrid Scawen Blunt, diary entry, quoted in Faulkner (ed.), *Jane Morris to Wilfrid Scawen Blunt*, p. 29.

104 Ibid., p. 30.

105 Ibid.

106 Ibid.

107 Ibid., p. 31.

108 Ibid., pp. 30–1.

109 Ibid., p. 31.

110 Wilfrid Scawen Blunt, diary entry, 9 June 1893, ibid., p. 80.

111 Wilfrid Scawen Blunt, diary entry, quoted ibid., p. 31.

112 Wilfrid Scawen Blunt, diary entry, 5 May 1892, ibid., p. 66.

113 Wilfrid Scawen Blunt, diary entry, 11 August 1892, ibid., p. 69.

114 Ibid.

115 Wilfrid Scawen Blunt, diary entry, 18 October 1890, ibid., p. 47.

116 Wilfrid Scawen Blunt, diary entry, 20 October 1892, ibid., p. 71.

117 Jane Morris to Wilfrid Scawen Blunt, 28 December 1892, *Collected Letters of Jane Morris*, p. 239.

118 Jane Morris to Wilfrid Scawen Blunt, 26 October 1895, ibid., p. 261.

119 Jane Morris to Wilfrid Scawen Blunt, 28 December 1888, ibid., p. 174.

120 Moncure Daniel Conway, quoted ibid., p. 94n.

121 May Morris, *Introductions*, vol. 1, p. 362.

122 William Morris, quoted by MacCarthy, *William Morris: A Life*, p. 559.

123 Jane Morris to Jane Cobden, 1 January 1889, *Collected Letters of Jane Morris*, p. 175.

124 William Morris to Jenny Morris, 21 January 1889, Kelvin (ed.), *Collected Letters*, vol. 3, p. 18.

125 Jane Morris to Cormell Price, 26 February 1907, *Collected Letters of Jane Morris*, p. 401.

126 Ibid.

127 William Morris, 'A Talk with William Morris on Socialism', 8 January 1883, *Daily News*, in Tony Pinkney (ed.), *We Met Morris: Interviews with William Morris 1885–96*, Reading: Spire Books and William Morris Society, 2005, pp. 24–5.

128 Eleanor Marx and Edward Aveling, 'The Woman Question' (1886), quoted Holmes, *Eleanor Marx: A Life*, p. 263.

129 Ibid., p. 264.

130 Jane Morris to Cormell Price, 12 March 1907, *Collected Letters of Jane Morris*, p. 402.

131 Jane Morris to Wilfrid Scawen Blunt, 13 February 1896, ibid., p. 266.

132 Jane Morris to Cormell Price, 6 March 1887, ibid., p. 151.

133 Edward Burne-Jones, quoted Stephen Wildman, *Edward Burne-Jones: Victorian Artist-dreamer*, New York: Metropolitan Museum of Art, 1998, p. 148.

134 Jane Morris to Cormell Price, 6 March 1887, *Collected Letters of Jane Morris*, p. 151.

135 Edward Burne-Jones, quoted Burne-Jones, *Memorials*, vol. 2, p. 65.

136 Edward Burne-Jones, letters to Castellani, quoted Richard Dorment, *Burne-Jones and the Decoration of St Paul's American Church, Rome*, PhD thesis, Columbia University, 1976, p. 275.

Chapter 13: Into the Garden, 1890–1896

1 William Morris to H. Hyndman, reported in *Justice*, 10 October 1896, quoted MacCarthy, *William Morris: A Life*, p. 663.

2 'Art, Craft and Life: A Chat with Mr William Morris', *Daily Chronicle*, 9 October 1893, p. 3, in Pinkney (ed.), *We Met Morris*, p. 73.

3 Sydney Cockerell, quoted MacCarthy, *William Morris: A Life*, p. 630.

4 'The Poet as Printer: An Interview with Mr. William Morris', *Pall Mall Gazette*, 12 November 1891, pp. 1–2, in Pinkney (ed.), *We Met Morris*, p. 54.

5 William Rothenstein, quoted MacCarthy, *William Morris: A Life*, p. 591.

6 Sara A. Tooley, 'A Living Wage for Women', *The Woman's Signal*, 19 April 1894, in Pinkney (ed.), *We Met Morris*, p. 90.

7 Jane Morris to Charles Fairfax Murray, 3 September 1895, *Collected Letters of Jane Morris*, p. 259.

8 'The Poet as Printer: An Interview with Mr. William Morris', in Pinkney (ed.), *We Met Morris*, p. 54.

9 William Morris, quoted Mackail, *Life of William Morris*, vol. 2, p. 227.

10 Jill, Duchess of Hamilton, Penny Hart and John Simmons, *The Gardens of William Morris*, London: Frances Lincoln, 1998, p. 109.

11 William Morris, 'The Prospects of Architecture' (1880), quoted ibid., p. 9.

12 William Morris, 'Making the Best of It' (1879), quoted ibid., p. 13.

13   Ibid., p. 15.

14   May Morris, quoted Hamilton, Hart and Simmons, *Gardens of William Morris*, p. 62.

15   Jane Morris to Wilfrid Scawen Blunt, 8 March 1895, *Collected Letters of Jane Morris*, p. 259.

16   William Morris, 'Hopes and Fears for Art', quoted Hamilton, Hart and Simmons, *Gardens of William Morris*, p. 16.

17   William Morris to Georgiana Burne-Jones, 27 April 1896, Henderson (ed.), *Letters of William Morris to his Family and Friends*, p. 382.

18   Jane Morris to Cormell Price, 30 July 1893, *Collected Letters of Jane Morris*, p. 244.

19   William Morris, 'Making the Best of It', quoted Hamilton, Hart and Simmons, *Gardens of William Morris*, p. 13.

20   Jane Morris to Wilfrid Scawen Blunt, 17 August 1893, *Collected Letters of Jane Morris*, p. 245.

21   Jane Morris to Wilfrid Scawen Blunt, 30 September 1894, ibid., p. 256.

22   May Morris, quoted Hamilton, Hart and Simmons, *Gardens of William Morris*, p. 62.

23   William Morris to Jenny Morris, quoted ibid., p. 60.

24   Ibid., p. 63.

25   William Morris to Philip Webb, 27 April 1896, Henderson (ed.), *Letters of William Morris to his Family and Friends*, p. 381, and William Morris to Jenny Morris, quoted in Hamilton, Hart and Simmons, *Gardens of William Morris*, p. 63.

26   William Morris to Jenny Morris, quoted in Hamilton, Hart and Simmons, *Gardens of William Morris*, p. 60.

27   Jane Morris to Wilfrid Scawen Blunt, 8 March 1895, *Collected Letters of Jane Morris*, p. 259.

28   Jane Morris to Wilfrid Scawen Blunt, 18 February 1895, ibid., p. 257.

29   Jane Morris to Wilfrid Scawen Blunt, 27 February 1892, ibid., p. 228.

30   Jane Morris to Wilfrid Scawen Blunt, 22 November 1892, ibid., p. 237.

31   MacCarthy, *William Morris: A Life*, p. 615.

32   Jane Morris to Wilfrid Scawen Blunt, 22 November 1892, *Collected Letters of Jane Morris*, p. 237.

33 Jane Morris to Wilfrid Scawen Blunt, 28 December 1892, ibid., p. 239.

34 Jane Morris to Wilfrid Scawen Blunt, 11 March 1893, ibid., p. 243.

35 William Morris, *News from Nowhere*, quoted MacCarthy, *William Morris: A Life*, p. 586.

36 William Morris, quoted MacCarthy, ibid., p. 584.

37 William Morris, 'News from Nowhere', *Collected Works*, vol. 16, p. 9.

38 Ibid., pp. 190–1.

39 Ibid., p. 205.

40 Ibid., p. 31.

41 Ibid., p. 12.

42 Ibid., p. 92.

43 Ibid., p. 132.

44 Ibid., p. 101.

45 Ibid., p. 60.

46 William Morris, quoted MacCarthy, *William Morris: A Life*, p. 595.

47 Edward Burne-Jones, quoted MacCarthy, ibid., p. 596.

48 *Honeysuckle* portière, designed by William Morris, 1876, silk on linen, embroidered by Jane and Jenny Morris, in (Parry (ed.), *William Morris*, V&A, 1996, p. 242.

49 William Morris, 'News from Nowhere', *Collected Works*, vol. 16, p. 174.

50 Ibid., p. 14.

51 Ibid., p. 57.

52 Ibid.

53 Wilfrid Scawen Blunt, diary entry, 1889, quoted in Faulkner (ed.), *Jane Morris to Wilfrid Scawen Blunt*, p. 31.

54 William Morris, 'News from Nowhere', *Collected Works*, vol. 16, p. 137.

55 Ibid., p. 202.

56 Ibid.

57 Ibid., p. 208.

58 Ibid., p. 210.

59 William Morris, quoted Quintus Flestrin, 19 November 1892, *Clarion*, in Pinkney (ed.), *We Met Morris*, p. 64.

60 William Morris, quoted by May Morris, *Introductions*, vol. 2, p. 416.

61 May Morris, *Introductions*, vol. 2, p. 415.

62 Ibid., p. 429.

63 Ibid., p. 428.

64 William Morris, quoted, ibid., p. 424.

65 William Lethaby, quoted MacCarthy, *William Morris: A Life*, p. 619.

66 W. R. Lethaby, quoted Linda Parry, in Parry (ed.), *William Morris*, V&A, 1996, p. 332.

67 Jane Morris, quoted MacCarthy, *William Morris: A Life*, p. 592.

68 May Morris, *Introductions*, vol. 2, p. 389.

69 Edward Burne-Jones, quoted MacCarthy, *William Morris: A Life*, p. 656.

70 Burne-Jones, *Memorials*, vol. 2, p. 265.

71 Edward Burne-Jones, quoted by Thomas Rooke, typewritten notes of conversations with Burne-Jones, V&A Museum, 5 December 1895, p. 68.

72 Edward Burne-Jones, quoted Linda Parry, in Parry (ed.), *William Morris*, V&A, 1996, p. 331.

73 William Morris, quoted in *Bookselling* (Christmas 1895), in Pinkney (ed.), *We Met Morris*, pp. 119–20.

74 Ibid., p. 55.

75 William Morris, 16 October 1891, Mackail, *Life of William Morris*, vol. 2, p. 251.

76 William Morris, 'Gossip about an old house on the Upper Thames', *The Quest*, November 1895.

77 Ibid.

78 Edward New, 1895, quoted Parkins, *Jane Morris: The Burden of History*, p. 146.

79 Wilfrid Scawen Blunt, quoted Longford, *Pilgrimage of Passion*, pp. 280–1.

80 Wilfrid Scawen Blunt, quoted MacCarthy, *William Morris: A Life*, p. 628.

81 Marie Spartali Stillman, quoted David B. Elliott, *A Pre-Raphaelite Marriage: The Lives and Works of Marie Spartali Stillman & William James Stillman*, Woodbridge: Antique Collectors' Club, 2006, p. 142.

82 Jane Morris to Wilfrid Scawen Blunt, 23 August 1893, *Collected Letters of Jane Morris*, p. 246.

83 Jane Morris to Wilfrid Scawen Blunt, 26 October 1895, ibid., p. 260.

84 Jane Morris to Wilfrid Scawen Blunt, 20 June 1892, ibid., p. 230.

85 Jane Morris to Wilfrid Scawen Blunt, 22 July 1892, ibid., p. 232.

86 Jane Morris to Wilfrid Scawen Blunt, 25 October 1895, ibid., p. 260.

87 Charles Rowley, quoted Parkins, *Jane Morris: The Burden of History*, p. 145.

88 Jane Morris to Theodore Watts-Dunton, 10 February 1890, *Collected Letters of Jane Morris*, p. 201.

89 Jane Morris to Wilfrid Scawen Blunt, 13 June 1896, ibid., p. 273.

90 Jane Morris to Wilfrid Scawen Blunt, 28 February 1891, ibid., p. 214.

91 Jane Morris to Wilfrid Scawen Blunt, 13 April 1891, ibid., p. 216.

92 Thomas Cobden-Sanderson, March 1891, quoted MacCarthy, *William Morris: A Life*, p. 626.

93 Jane Morris to Wilfrid Scawen Blunt, 16 July 1891, *Collected Letters of Jane Morris*, p. 218.

94 Jane Morris to Wilfrid Scawen Blunt, 15 December 1894, ibid., p. 256.

95 Jane Morris to Wilfrid Scawen Blunt, 12 February 1889, ibid., p. 179.

96 Jane Morris to Wilfrid Scawen Blunt, 11 December 1891, ibid., p. 224.

97 William Morris, quoted Mackail, *Life of William Morris*, vol. 2, p. 307.

98 Georgiana Burne-Jones, quoted Mackail, ibid., p. 317.

99 William Morris, quoted ibid., p. 319.

100 Ibid.

101 Jane Morris to Wilfrid Scawen Blunt, 12 March 1894, *Collected Letters of Jane Morris*, pp. 249–50.

102 Jane Morris to Lucy Faulkner Orrin-Smith, 2 March 1896, ibid., p. 267.

103 Jane Morris to Wilfrid Scawen Blunt, 20 April 1896, ibid., p. 269.

104 MacCarthy, *William Morris: A Life*, p. 658.

105 William Morris to Philip Webb, quoted MacCarthy, ibid., p. 659.

106 Jane Morris to Rosalind Howard, 29 March 1896, ibid., p. 268.

107 Jane Morris to Wilfrid Scawen Blunt, 1 May 1896, ibid., p. 270.

108 William Morris to Georgiana Burne-Jones, 27 April 1896, Henderson (ed.), *Letters of William Morris to his Family and Friends*, p. 382.

109 Edward Burne-Jones, 11 May 1896, quoted Rooke, typewritten notes, V&A, p. 230.

110 Jane Morris to Wilfrid Scawen Blunt, 9 June 1896, *Collected Letters of Jane Morris*, p. 272.

111 Jane Morris to Georgiana Burne-Jones, 14 June 1896, ibid., p. 274.

112 Jane Morris to Wilfrid Scawen Blunt, 19 June 1896, ibid., p. 275.

113 William Morris to Philip Webb, 14 June 1896, Henderson (ed.), *Letters of William Morris to his Family and Friends*, p. 383.

114 Jane Morris to Wilfrid Scawen Blunt, 27 June 1896, *Collected Letters of Jane Morris*, pp. 276–7.

115 Burne-Jones, *Memorials*, vol. 2, p. 278.

116 William Morris, 'The Beauty of Life', lecture (1880), quoted MacCarthy, *William Morris: A Life*, p. 602

117 William Morris to Philip Webb, quoted MacCarthy, ibid., p. 666.

118 William Morris to Philip Webb, 18 August 1896, Henderson (ed.), *Letters of William Morris to his Family and Friends*, p. 385.

119 William Morris to Jenny Morris, 20 August 1896, ibid.

120 Jane Morris to Cormell Price, 5 August 1896, *Collected Letters of Jane Morris*, p. 279.

121 Cormell Price, diary, 6 September 1896, quoted MacCarthy, *William Morris: A Life*, p. 667.

122 Jane Morris to Wilfrid Scawen Blunt, 28 July 1896, *Collected Letters of Jane Morris*, p. 207.

123 Thomas Cobden-Sanderson, 12 September 1896, quoted MacCarthy, *William Morris: A Life*, p. 668.

124 William Morris, 'News from Nowhere', *Collected Works*, vol. 16, p. 206.

Chapter 14: Wanderings, 1896-1914

1   Jane Morris to Sydney Cockerell, 12 March 1900, *Collected Letters of Jane Morris*, p. 339.

2   Jane Morris to Wilfrid Scawen Blunt, 9 May 1897, ibid., p. 292.

3   Jane Morris to Cormell Price, 22 December 1896, ibid., p. 284.

4   Ibid.

5   Wilfrid Scawen Blunt, quoted Longford, *Pilgrimage of Passion*, p. 323.

6   Wilfrid Scawen Blunt, diary entry, 29 November 1896, in Faulkner (ed.), *Jane Morris to Wilfrid Scawen Blunt*, p. 107.

7   Jane Morris to Cormell Price, 22 December 1896, *Collected Letters of Jane Morris*, p. 284.

8   Wilfrid Scawen Blunt, diary entry, 5 October 1896, in Faulkner (ed.), *Jane Morris to Wilfrid Scawen Blunt*, p. 106.

9   Wilfrid Scawen Blunt, quoted MacCarthy, *William Morris: A Life*, p. 670.

10   Mackail, *Life of William Morris*, vol. 2, p. 348.

11   Wilfrid Scawen Blunt, May 1896, quoted MacCarthy, *William Morris: A Life*, p. 661.

12   Mackail, Manuscript notebooks, vol. 1, William Morris Gallery, p. 4.

13   Jane Morris to Sydney Cockerell, 3 October 1898, *Collected Letters of Jane Morris*, p. 318.

14   Ibid.

15   Jane Morris to Wilfrid Scawen Blunt, 2 August 1897, ibid., p. 294.

16   Jane Morris to Sydney Cockerell, 8 August 1897, ibid., p. 295.

17   Jane Morris to Katharine Adams, 23 January 1904, ibid., p. 375.

18   Philip Webb to Revd. Horace Meeres, 9 May 1898, *The Letters of Philip Webb*, vol. 2: 1888–1898, letter 579, n2.

19   Philip Webb to Jane Morris, 30 August 1898, ibid., letter 607.

20   Philip Webb to Jane Morris, 24 June 1899, John Aplin (ed.), *The Letters of Philip Webb*, vol. 3: 1899–1902, London: Routledge, 2015, letter 638.

21   Sydney Cockerell to Jane Morris, 15 May 1903, *The Letters of Philip Webb*, vol. 4: 1903–1914, letter 868n.

22   *Daily Telegraph*, 5 October 1896, quoted MacCarthy, *William Morris: A Life*, p. 672.

23   *The Times*, quoted Paul Greenhalgh, in Parry (ed.), *William Morris*, V&A, 1996, p. 362.

24   *Clarion*, 10 October 1896, quoted MacCarthy, *William Morris: A Life*, p. 672.

25   Mackail, *Life of William Morris*, vol. 2, p. 350.

26   Philip Webb to Sydney Cockerell, 23 February 1899, *The Letters of Philip Webb*, vol. 3, letter 626.

27   Philip Webb to Sydney Cockerell, 24 May 1899, ibid., letter 633.

28   J. W. Mackail to Sydney Cockerell, 22 September 1898, quoted Parkins, *Jane Morris: The Burden of History*, p. 86.

29   Philip Webb to Jane Morris, 24 October 1898, *The Letters of Philip Webb*, vol. 2, letter 612.

30   Philip Webb to Jane Morris, 31 October 1898, ibid., letter 613.

31   Philip Webb to Jane Morris, 17 April 1903, *The Letters of Philip Webb*, vol. 4, letter 867.

32   Ibid.

33   Philip Webb to Jane Morris, 28 January 1899, *The Letters of Philip Webb*, vol. 3, letter 619.

34   May Morris to Anne Cobden-Sanderson, 7 July 1900, quoted *Collected Letters of Jane Morris*, p. 326n.

35   May Morris, *Introductions*, vol. 2, p. 736.

36   Jane Morris to Lady Anne Blunt, 19 September 1897, *Collected Letters of Jane Morris*, p. 299.

37   Jane Morris to Theodore Watts Dunton, 29 July 1897, ibid., p. 294.

38   Jane Morris to Sydney Cockerell, 4 October 1899, ibid., p. 330.

39   Jane Morris to Cormell Price, 15 July 1898, ibid., p. 315.

40   Jane Morris to Wilfrid Scawen Blunt, 3 December 1897, ibid., p. 301.

41   Jane Morris to Sydney Cockerell, 15 March 1898, ibid., p. 309.

42   Edward Burne-Jones, quoted ibid., p. 182n.

43   Jane Morris to Judith Blunt, June 1898, ibid., p. 313.

44   Jane Morris to Cormell Price, 15 July 1898, ibid., p. 315.

45   Philip Webb to Jane Morris, 22 January 1899, *The Letters of Philip Webb*, vol. 3, letter 618.

46   Jane Morris to Sydney Cockerell, 29 July 1913, *Collected Letters of Jane Morris*, p. 463.

47   Jane Morris to Wilfrid Scawen Blunt, 20 December 1904, ibid., p. 383.

48   Burne-Jones, *Memorials*, vol. 2, p. 1.

49   Jane Morris to Wilfrid Scawen Blunt, 20 December 1904, *Collected Letters of Jane Morris*, p. 383.

50   Jane Morris to Wilfrid Scawen Blunt, 3 December 1897, ibid., p. 301.

51   Jane Morris to Wilfrid Scawen Blunt, 23 December 1908, ibid., p. 416.

52 Jane Morris to Sydney Cockerell, 12 March 1900, ibid., p. 338.

53 Jane Morris to Cormell Price, 27 December 1902, ibid., p. 360.

54 Jane Morris to Wilfrid Scawen Blunt, 25 February 1903, ibid., p. 362.

55 Jane Morris to Wilfrid Scawen Blunt, 21 October 1913, ibid., p. 564.

56 Jane Morris to Cormell Price, 29 April 1907, ibid., p. 403.

57 Jane Morris to May Morris, summer 1912, ibid., p. 458.

58 Jane Morris to Sydney Cockerell, 12 May 1898, ibid., p. 311.

59 Jane Morris to Cormell Price, 19 June 1903, ibid., p. 363.

60 Marie Spartali Stillman to Vernon Lee, 19 September 1901, quoted ibid., p. 350n.

61 Richard Le Gallienne, quoted by Oswald Doughty, *A Victorian Romantic: Dante Gabriel Rossetti*, New Haven: Yale University Press, 1949, p. 374.

62 Jane Morris to Wilfrid Scawen Blunt, 17 January 1913, *The Collected Letters of Jane Morris*, p. 459.

63 Jane Morris to unidentified recipient, 1 January 1914, ibid., p. 465.

64 Marie Spartali Stillman to Sydney Cockerell, 28 January 1914, ibid., p. 466n.

65 Obituary, 28 January 1914, *The Times*, quoted ibid., p. 469.

66 Jane Morris to May Morris, 9 March 1912, ibid., p. 451.

Index

The following initials are used for reference in sub-headings throughout the index:

WSB – Wilfrid Scawen Blunt

EBJ – Edward Burne-Jones

GBJ – Georgina 'Georgie' Burne-Jones

JM – Jane Morris

WM – William Morris

DGR - Dante Gabriel Rossetti

ES - Elizabeth Siddall